Explorations
in
Canadian
Economic History
Essays in Honour
of
Irene M. Spry

Explorations in Canadian Economic History.

Essays in Honour of Irene M. Spry

Edited by
Duncan Cameron

University of Ottawa Press
1985

Canadian Cataloguing in Publication Data

Main entry under title:
  Explorations in Canadian economic history: essays in honour of
Irene M. Spry

Bibliography: p.
ISBN 0-7766-3111-X

1. Spry, Irene M. — Addresses, essays, lectures.
2. Canada — Economic conditions — Addresses, essays, lectures.
I. Cameron, Duncan, 1944- II. Spry, Irene M.

HC113.E96 1985   330.971   C85-090095-6

ISBN 0-7766-3111-X

Printed and Bound in Canada

Contents

Acknowledgements

In the various stages of preparation of this book, the editor received valuable assistance from a number of friends and colleagues at the University of Ottawa. Sylvia Van Kirk of the University of Toronto and Susan Mann Trofimenkoff were responsible for initiating the project. Professor John Kuiper, formerly Chair of the Department of Economics, provided wise counsel and support at an early stage of its preparation. Susan Mann Trofimenkoff and Robert Armstrong gave freely of editorial advice and encouragement. The Department of Political Science provided the editor with material support. William Badour, Dean of the Faculty of Social Sciences, was instrumental in seeing that the project became a book. Janet Shorten and Daniel Woolford of the University of Ottawa Press deserve special thanks for the care and attention they devoted to preparing the manuscript for publication.

Introduction

Duncan Cameron
University of Ottawa

The intellectual history of Canadian social science has yet to be written. When it is, many of the themes discussed in this volume will be central to it. In itself, this is a measure of the intellectual breadth of the person whose scholarly life inspired this collection of essays. Political economy, resource development, and Canadian community are the subject headings for these essays presented to Irene M. Spry in honour of her work. Each has to do with Canadian economic history; all touch on aspects of scholarship that motivated her teaching, appear in her publications, and stimulate her communication with other researchers.

If, as one wit would have it, "the modern university is a collection of departments joined together by the central heating system", perhaps it is because few universities benefit from enterprising individuals who, like Irene Spry, are able to ignore institutional barriers and cross disciplinary boundaries, in pursuit of the higher value of scholarly community. Her commitment to clear and rigorous exposition of ideas, her determination to "get it right" without undue heed to established convention, current fads, or prevailing dogma — this is what we treasure in her. She has impressed upon colleagues and students alike that if knowledge in the social sciences is at once relative, approximate, and anything but neutral, this does not imply that concepts can be used without full and complete understanding of their significance, or that evidence does not have to be sifted, checked, and re-checked.

Generous with her time, Irene Spry applies the same criteria to the travail of others as to her own. Her well-honed critical talents are regularly sought out by those who prefer their pride to be stung before publication rather than after. Pity the graduate student and advisor who think that a thesis "good enough to get by" will make it past Irene Spry without additional labour. Woe betide him or her who utters a loose comment over lunch about "monopoly" rent or "public goods". The eyes narrow, her mind leaves the starting blocks, and one hundred intellectual metres later it is again time for one to re-think what was thought to be known.

To understand Irene Spry, and appreciate what knowing her means to colleagues, students, and friends, it is helpful to have some indication of her scholarly ambition. First, her drive is undiminished though her seventy-fifth birthday is history and she is now virtually blind. Second, her intellectual associations, especially at Cambridge

(Pigou, Robertson, and Keynes) and at Toronto (Innis), while influencing her views of what scholarship is about, have not made her into a Keynesian or an Innisian. She simply would not allow that independent thought should be confined within the visions of even the geniuses of our times. Rather she holds, with the stubbornness of the historian on the trail of new evidence, a view that she developed as a young woman, that scholarship is most benefited when individuals think for themselves.

As Gerald Friesen points out in his biographical essay in this volume, it was at the University of Toronto that Irene Spry became a Canadian historian. But it was in fact at Cambridge that, joining together with others in a group that identified themselves, no doubt in fellowship, as the "heretics", she made up her mind as to her scholarly creed. One should be sceptical, work out ideas through exchange with others, rely as little as possible on established authority, and view credulity with amusement, not to say disdain.

Having adopted such an unforgiving stance and demanding attitude, and having spent much of her life in the solitary pursuits of the researcher, Irene Spry might well have become a difficult person. In fact, nothing could be more alien to her nature, which is to be engaging, courteous, sociable and, above all, helpful to those who cross her path.

Her mode of scholarship implies controversy. Rather than avoiding intellectual differences, she seeks them out, believing as she does that it is precisely through the process of debate that intellectuals labour, and that knowledge and understanding flow from argument, conducted with passion if necessary, albeit in pursuit of disinterested accounts of human realities.

Irene Spry has been the "writer looking over our shoulder" for many of us, and the role model for more than one Canadian historian. These collected essays recognize her contribution, carrying on that particular tradition which represents what is best about university life: honouring a colleague of distinction through a publication that celebrates their life work and indeed in some small measure contributes to its advancement.

These essays suggest that Canadian economic history can best be depicted and understood through the use of theoretical insights appropriate to the Canadian context. In the political economy section the reader will find much to justify Irene Spry's interest in the work of H. A. Innis and the controversy engendered by his treatment of the staples economy. Paul Phillips and John Richards assess different aspects of the debates that have arisen as economic historians reflect on the legacy of the Innisian framework.

Phillips argues for the pertinence of staples theory to the study of conflict between commercial and industrial interests during the national policy period. Richards recasts the debate among western populist historians and the founders of the staples tradition in the light of contemporary concerns about Canadian industrial policy.

Ian Parker finds in the insights of Innis' political economy the foundations for his theory of communications. Arthur Ray has undertaken to reconstruct the price structure of the fur trade in order to assess empirically the generalizations of other historians and provide new standards for historical judgement. Mario Seccareccia suggests that Canadian political economy provides a useful framework for understanding British immigration to Canada; one that goes beyond supply-led and demand-led accounts. It is the human dimension of economic history that has always motivated Irene Spry; in the essay which opens this volume R. B. Bryce examines the federal government response to the unemployment crisis of the 1930s.

Speaking in the context of Canadian broadcasting policy, Graham Spry admirably summarized a significant theme in Canadian history when he suggested, ''The choice we have to make is between the state and the United States''. The first two essays in the resource-development section bring different perspectives to bear on the role of the Canadian state in that important domain. Jeanne Laux investigates the policies adopted by Saskatchewan governments with respect to potash development, while Anthony Scott provides an appreciation of the difficulties that water rights create for economic, legal, and political theory. Enhanced technological capacity is often cited as one of the benefits of foreign investment. Robert Armstrong and Alexander Dow assess the evidence concerning technological change in two Canadian industries, asbestos and metal mining. The differences in their conclusions indicate the importance of careful historical investigation and suggest that it is difficult to generalize about the determining role of imported technology in Canadian resource development.

Canadian community, a theme which evokes much of the spirit of early settlement, is also a subject which inspires scholarly investigation of the nature of Canadian society. Cornelius Jaenen shows that relations between the society of New France and Amerindians can be traced and depicted through the practice of gift-giving. Carol Judd looks at the development of mixed-blood communities in Moose Factory and Red River. She finds that social relations, rather than racial or linguistic characteristics, are the significant aspects of the two experiences. John Batts takes us, through the medium of Irene Spry's diary, with the young researcher on her visit to Northern

Canada. Jean McNulty brings the dream of modern technology down to earth in her analysis of satellite broadcasting. Ray Jackson enumerates a series of shifts in thinking about the world which, in economics, have become grouped around the idea of a conserver society.

Taken together, these explorations in Canadian economic history recognize the contribution to Canadian scholarship of Irene Spry, Professor Emeritus of Economics at the University of Ottawa. The readers of these essays may find therein something of the character of the country, and its attraction for the historian. If so, they may find themselves to have been well served. May they also sense what many have drawn from their association with Irene Spry: sheer delight in the presence of intellect at work.

Political
Economy

1.   The Canadian Economy in the 1930s

Unemployment Relief under Bennett and Mackenzie King*

R. B. Bryce

Former Deputy Minister of Finance, Ottawa

The Great Depression of 1929-1939 was deep, worldwide, and persistent. It was particularly severe in North America, where the United States and Canada had enjoyed a high level of prosperity in the late 1920s. For Canada it involved a rapid decline in exports of farm products, notably wheat; of raw materials, such as lumber; and of major manufactured products such as newsprint and automobiles. Prices of farm products and raw materials declined drastically along with the decline in the volume of trade; the prices of manufactured products declined less severely, depending on the circumstances in each industry. Widespread unemployment began to appear in 1930; it became severe during 1931, and was at its worst in 1932 and 1933. The low prices of farm products, and recurrent years of drought in the Prairie Provinces, caused severe hardship for many farmers and their families.

This severe unemployment had serious social effects upon a nation that had no unemployment insurance, and very few and inadequate arrangements to provide assistance to the poor in general, or to particular groups made destitute by unemployment, drought, or the catastrophically low prices for their farm, fishery, or forest products.

This essay gives a brief account of the main relief measures undertaken during the 1930s to deal with these severe social effects of the Depression.

---

* This essay draws upon writing and research by the author in connection with a study of the history of the Department of Finance.

Poverty and Relief in Canada[1]

Even during the prosperous period of the late 1920s, there were many poor people in Canada—the subsistence farmers of Quebec and the Maritimes eking out a bare living with small farms and perhaps some fishing or work in the woods, the unorganized workers in low-wage and seasonal industries, the unskilled drifters who took what work they could get, and a variety of unemployables who were physically or mentally unable to work, including the old, and single mothers with children. Little was done by governments to help any of these groups until the Old Age Pension Act of 1927, under which the Dominion government would share the cost with any province of a $20-a-month pension to those over seventy years of age and in need. This old age pension plan had been taken up by only the four western provinces before 1930, when it commenced in Ontario. In Nova Scotia, Ontario, and the western provinces there had also been provincial programmes of mothers' allowances to help support dependent children when the male parent was unable to do so for various reasons. But for others, the poor in general, who were in need by reason of unemployment or inability to work, it was left to the local municipality or the churches or other charities to provide whatever aid they felt they should or could provide. When times were hard, as was the case in the period of substantial unemployment that followed the post-war economic crisis of 1920, the Dominion and several provincial governments provided funds to municipalities when they were needed. There were few professionally trained social workers and nearly all of them worked for the voluntary charitable organizations in the major cities.

Thus, when the Depression began in 1929 and became serious in 1930 it imposed unemployment, and reduced farm and fishery prices and incomes, on a society that already included many who were poor and vulnerable and for whom there was little organized means of help. The Constitution had assigned the jurisdiction and responsibility for helping the poor to the provincial legislatures, who in turn delegated it to the municipalities, many of whom could not, or would not,

---

1. The following sources were helpful in writing about relief in the 1930s: A. E. Grauer, *Public Assistance and Social Insurance: A Study Prepared for the Royal Commission on Dominion-Provincial Relations*, Appendix 6 (Ottawa, 1939); M. Horn, *The Dirty Thirties: Canadians in the Great Depression* (Canada, 1972); L. C. Marsh, *Health and Unemployment* (England, 1938); L. C. Marsh, *Canadians In and Out of Work* (England, 1940); L. Richter, ed., *Canada's Unemployment Problem* (Toronto, 1939); National Employment Commission, *Final Report* (Ottawa, 1938); Annual Reports of the Dominion Director of Unemployment Relief, 1931-32; Annual Reports of the Dominion Commissioner of Unemployment Relief, 1933-41.

provide relief on any significant scale. Once the severity of the problem became apparent in the mid-1930s, the Dominion government, while disclaiming constitutional responsibility, recognized the emergency and brought in the Dominion Unemployment Relief Act of 1930, which appropriated $20 million to aid the provinces and municipalities, to cope with the situation. The main action under this initial legislation was the provision of work projects for the unemployed, although these were very slow in starting. There were also the beginnings of direct relief, for example, material aid provided for food, fuel, clothing, and shelter for those in need, usually in kind or by vouchers, not cash. In late 1930 and early 1931 only about $20 million was disbursed for all relief purposes by all governments. At this stage most of the unemployed were having to get along as best they could. Dorothy King, director of the Montreal School of Social Work, wrote in 1938:

> In the early days of the depression, the difficulties of securing aid and its frequent inadequacy were responsible for cases of acute suffering and the breakdown of morale. Many of the unemployed sold their homes and other possessions, ran into debt till their credit was exhausted, and endured serious privations before reaching the unemployed aid lists. In many areas no rent was paid and evictions were common; in a still greater number, house-holders could secure no allotment in lieu of rent, with the result that payments on taxes and insurance were impossible and foreclosures on mortgages occurred frequently.[2]

In 1931 the main emphasis in relief programmes continued to be on municipal work projects, but the need for direct unemployment relief increased, and in the West the drought in Saskatchewan and some areas of Alberta led to special Dominion assistance there. The problem of transient unemployed men, women, and even families was being recognized and resented seriously by municipalities who had enough trouble dealing with their own residents. As a result, the provincial and Dominion governments agreed to share equally the whole of the costs of relief for transients. The total expenditures for relief reached $95 million dollars by the 1931-32 fiscal year, and the Dominion had to finance just over one-half of this amount.

By 1932, unemployment had reached massive proportions—twenty-six per cent of the wage earners were unemployed, and this did not include the young, or the wives who had never had a job, nor the destitute farmers and fishermen. Moreover, the widespread nature of the collapse in the international financial system and the banking systems in the United States and central Europe caused many to recognize that there was no early end in sight for the serious situa-

---

2. D. King, "Unemployment Aid (Direct Relief)", in L. Richter, *op. cit.*, p. 106.

Table 1
Number of Persons and Expenditures on Relief

	1932	1933	1934	1935	1936	1937	1938	1939
1. Total on direct relief	833,989	1,227,558	1,135,901	1,162,729	1,148,083	965,907	870,103	808,040
2. Total on drought-area relief	74,667	80,396	156,412	134,179	127,933	—	—	—
3. Total on agric. relief	—	—	—	—	283,252	305,951	312,261	219,882
4. Total on unemployment relief	759,322	1,147,162	979,489	1,027,551	913,351	659,956	557,842	588,158
5. Total on unemployment relief—highest month	1,170,290	1,427,746	1,205,863	1,161,579	1,240,074	879,283	652,690	704,694
6. Total on unemployment relief—lowest month	456,713	920,310	824,553	886,463	707,293	455,839	444,732	488,984
7. Heads of families on unemployment relief—highest month	223,037	267,803	257,503	244,862	257,284	186,292	144,696	155,291
8. Employable persons on unemployment relief	212,610	321,205	274,256	287,947	282,757	187,204	148,289	156,780
9. Wage earners unemployed	639,000	646,000	521,000	483,000	430,000	337,000	407,000	386,000
10. Employable persons on relief as percentage of wage earners unemployed	33.3	49.7	52.6	59.6	65.8	55.6	36.4	40.6

11. Ex post estimates of "persons without jobs and seeking work"—June	741,000	826,000	631,000	625,000	571,000	411,000	522,000	529,000
12. No. with jobs in agric.	1,237,000	1,257,000	1,277,000	1,298,000	1,319,000	1,339,000	1,359,000	1,379,000
13. Heads of families/individual cases on agric. relief	—	—	—	—	—	66,162	69,584	48,339
14. Heads of families/individual cases on agric. relief as percentage of those with jobs in agric.	—	—	—	—	—	4.9	5.1	3.5
15. Total relief expenditures ($ millions)	95	98	158	173	160	165	—	—

Rows 1-6 Figures given are monthly averages. Totals include heads of families, dependants and "individual cases" receiving relief. *The Unemployment and Agricultural Assistance Act, 1940: Report of Dominion Commissioner of Unemployment Relief for the Fiscal Year Ending March 31, 1941* (Ottawa, 1941).

Rows 2-3 After August 1936, the category "drought area" was no longer used in the annual reports of the Dominion Commissioner of Unemployment Relief. Instead, the number of persons receiving relief was divided into "agricultural" and "urban" categories.

Row 4 Total on unemployment relief = (total number on direct relief) − (total number on drought and agricultural relief).

Row 7 Annual reports of the Dominion Commissioner of Unemployment Relief, 1932-39.

Row 8 Figures given are monthly averages. For 1932-36 the number of persons on relief = (total number on relief) − (dependants, farmers, and unemployable persons on relief) as calculated in J. K. Houston, *Dominion Unemployment Relief: An Appreciation of Relief as Related to Economic and Employment Tendencies in Canada* (Ottawa, 1936). For 1937 figure, see S. A. Saunders, "Nature and Extent of Unemployment", *Canada's Unemployment Problem* (Toronto, 1939), p. 36. For 1938-39 figures, the number of persons on relief = number of fully employable persons on urban aid. *The Canada Year Book, 1940*, p. 762.

Row 9 *The Canada Year Book, 1940*, p. 751.

Rows 11-12 Urquhart and Buckley, *Historical Statistics of Canada*, series C47-55, p. 61.

Row 13 *Report of the Dominion Commissioner of Unemployment Relief for the Fiscal Year Ending March 31, 1941*.

Row 15 Expenditure figures are *not* for calendar years; rather, they refer to the fiscal year ending closest to the December of the year given in the table. For example, the 1932 expenditure figure refers to the 1932-33 fiscal year.

Table 2
Number of Persons Receiving Indirect Relief and Total Number Receiving Relief, Direct and Indirect. 1932-1939

	1932	1933	1934	1935	1936	1937	1938	1939
1. Total assisted other than by direct relief—highest month.	73,020	140,452	146,061	118,859	85,607	83,052	100,087	104,985
2. Total assisted other than by direct relief—lowest month.	19,032	64,711	90,290	60,269	17,912	31,368	30,377	42,605
3. Persons employed on municipal relief works (monthly average).	15,506	7,422	20,833	1,909	1,170	694	1,365	4,301
4. Persons employed on provincial relief works (monthly average).	1,948	14,565	36,873	22,181	18,518	11,741	7,146	11,859
5. Persons employed on federal relief works or special projects.	182	188	426	958	525	2,736	1,093	1,055
6. Persons on National Forestry Programme.	—	—	—	—	—	—	—	1,320
7. Single homeless men on camps and farms.	20,237	48,038	38,318	35,724	15,175	1,330	—	—
8. Persons on "Farm Placement" programme.	817	4,999	4,636	4,011	7,612	18,389	14,416	8,598
9. Persons on relief settlements (cumulative total).	2,469	9,668	15,834	18,383	18,350	19,963	27,549	37,382
10. Persons on youth training programme.	—	—	—	—	—	3,558	13,785	7,512
11. Older persons on rehabilitation programme.	—	—	—	—	—	—	40	1,658
12. Total (including dependants) receiving relief, direct and indirect (monthly averages).	875,149	1,312,437	1,252,850	1,245,916	1,209,894	1,024,535	935,495	881,724
13. Total receiving relief, direct and indirect, as percentage of Canadian population.	8.3	12.3	11.7	11.5	11.0	9.3	8.4	7.8

Rows 1-13: Compiled from information in *Report of the Dominion Commissioner of Unemployment for the Fiscal Year Ending March 31, 1941.*
Row 4:   Number employed on provincial relief works includes those employed on Trans-Canada Highway.

tion. While work projects were preferred as the way to provide support for the unemployed, they could not be financed (or properly organized) on the scale necessary to meet the urgent needs of the hundreds of thousands requiring aid. Consequently, at the request of the provincial governments[3] public works were greatly curtailed under the 1932 legislation and there was a decided shift towards direct relief. In this year the Dominion Department of Labour began collecting statistics on the numbers of people receiving aid; these are summarized by years and various categories in Tables 1 and 2. It was also necessary to develop special plans for looking after unemployed homeless men, usually by establishing provincial camps for them in western Canada, and by placing them on farms, with only a few dollars a month in cash for each, or for the farmer for whom he worked.

The Dominion-Provincial Conference of January 1933 was organized primarily to discuss relief, and some progress was made. It was decided that there should be more emphasis on work projects. The Dominion agreed to co-operate with any province that set up its own provincial arrangements to dispense direct aid, as Saskatchewan did, rather than leaving it to the municipalities. The provinces agreed that those provinces in greatest need should get a larger proportion of support from the Dominion. Later in the year drought was more widespread in the West and all three Prairie Provinces got special assistance for the dried-out areas. After July 1933, the Dominion, through the Department of National Defence, took over direct responsibility for looking after the unemployed homeless men in camps. This action had the initial advantage of keeping them off the trains and out of the cities, but eventually the camps became centres of criticism and, ultimately, of political agitation. The meagre twenty cents a day allowed for pocket money (in addition to their accommodation, food, and clothes) was a matter of derision. By this time two programmes were well under way to place the unemployed on farms: one to subsidize single persons as hired help for farmers; and the other for the permanent settlement of poor families on new farms, some of these families being from the drought areas in the West. There were rather less successful ventures in Ontario to support those already sunk in rural poverty and in Quebec to colonize underdeveloped areas with poor urban families.

In 1934 and the first half of 1935 the policies and programmes of the preceding years were continued, but with greater numbers needing aid in the drought areas and very little reduction in those

---

3. Grauer, *op. cit.*, p. 18.

requiring direct relief elsewhere, despite the beginning of some economic recovery and a modest increase in the number of employed wage-earners. It was probable, however, that during those years the number of employable persons on relief was increasing relative to the estimated number of "unemployed wage earners" (as shown in line 10 of Table 1) for reasons which Grauer, in his research report for the Royal Commission on Dominion-Provincial Relations, described as follows:

> The deficiencies and lack of standards in the administration of unemployment aid become more serious for the individual family on relief as the duration of the depression lengthens. The needs of the individual family increase for a variety of reasons, — the wearing out of clothing and household equipment of all sorts, the exhausting of available financial help from friends and relatives, the piling up of dental and medical requirements, etc.[4]

The Trek to Ottawa

The only major political demonstration against the relief system of the Depression occurred in June 1935.[5] It began in some strikes organized by the unrecognized Relief Camp Workers' Union in the British Columbia relief camps in April and May. These resulted in a number of parades, "tag days", and scuffles with the police in Vancouver, where the strikers were endeavouring to raise some money for their cause and to relieve their boredom and frustration. Then they organized an "on-to-Ottawa trek", beginning about one thousand strong, seeking to make their way east on railway freight cars. They were welcomed and fed in some towns, and picked up supporters along their way. In Calgary, local sympathizers had arranged an orderly march across the city and they provided food for the trekkers, who rested a few days on the Exhibition grounds. But the trekkers heard ominous news about police reinforcements being assembled to meet them in Regina, and the militia being alerted. They were halted in Regina by the RCMP under instructions from Ottawa, but they had accommodation there, and enough to eat, and a chance to hold marches and meetings. The government in Ottawa agreed to meet with a delegation of eight trekkers, who proceeded by train to see Bennett and some other ministers. The meeting went very badly:

---

4. *Ibid.*, p. 24.

5. An interesting account of the "On-to-Ottawa" trek can be found in Horn, *op. cit.*, pp. 344-89.

Bennett rejected all their demands (even though R. J. Manion, Minister of Railways, confided to the Prime Minister that several of these demands could be accepted in a general way). Both in the meeting and in his report on it to Parliament, Bennett began by concentrating his response on the Communist affiliations and criminal record of the spokesman for the group, Arthur Evans. The delegation had probably been ill-chosen, aggressive, and not really representative of most of the trekkers. But after their representatives were dismissed in Ottawa as ''an organized effort on the part of the various communist organizations throughout Canada to effect the overthrow of constituted authority in defiance of the laws of the land''[6]—a ludicrous caricature — there was a riot back in Regina on Dominion Day in which the RCMP clashed with some three thousand ''relief-camp deserters'' and sympathizers. There were quite a number of injuries, dozens of ''strikers'' were arrested, and one city policeman was killed. A special train was provided to take the relief camp workers back to British Columbia, and the crowd dispersed. Bennett had won the battle— though he was soon to lose the election.

Bennett's intemperate reaction to the trekkers in mid-1935 was not typical of his general recognition, during 1934 and 1935, of the need both for recovery from the Depression and for reform of the system.

The Bennett ''New Deal''

During 1934, Bennett introduced a number of reforms by legislation. One was a special statutory plan for bankruptcy and relief of debt for farmers—the Farmer's Creditors Arrangement Act, which fell under the jurisdiction of the Department of Finance. A second was the Public Works Construction Act, which Bennett characterized as a recovery rather than a reform measure. It was a special programme of public works to create employment, financed by an expansion of the Dominion note issue—the main source of bank reserves—during the last eight months before the Bank of Canada commenced operations. There were important amendments made to the Canadian Farm Loan Act to enable it to be used more extensively at a time when credit was sorely needed, and also to enable it to be used in the process of renegotiating outstanding mortgages and other loans. Finally, and most ambitiously, there was the Natural Products Marketing Act,

---

6. House of Commons (HC) *Debates*, June 24, 1935.

introduced in the spring of 1934, which gave a Dominion marketing board powers to regulate the marketing of natural products, broadly defined to include farm, fishery, and forestry products, and articles of food and drink derived from such products. It authorized the government to approve marketing schemes organized by a representative number of persons engaged in the production or marketing of specified natural products. The law would also permit the government to control the import or export of designated natural products in order to regulate or enforce marketing strategies for those products.

Bennett was subject to a number of influences during 1934 and the two preceding years which had some effect in causing him to embark on these reforms. The first and most important was the action of President Roosevelt, his various advisers, and the U.S. Congress in originating and implementing their "New Deal" programme, which involved not only new economic doctrines but broad new social and political ideas as well. These American thoughts and actions appealed to many in Canada, politicians and intellectuals alike, and some members of the business community. Bennett learned of the U.S. ideas and legislation chiefly through his brother-in-law, W. D. Herridge, who was the Minister in charge of the Canadian legation in Washington, and who cultivated a range of close contacts with leading personalities in the New Deal circles there. Herridge made repeated suggestions to Bennett in 1933-34 about a variety of subjects, including a trade treaty and the building of a St. Lawrence Seaway, as well as Canadian legislation and programmes similar to those undertaken in the United States. He tried to persuade Bennett to adopt a more active interventionist philosophy with which to confront the Liberals in 1935.

A second, and secondary, influence came from the legal side, with two decisions by the Judicial Committee of the Privy Council on appeal from the Supreme Court of Canada. In these two cases—one concerning jurisdiction over aeronautics and the other, jurisdiction over radio broadcasting—the Judicial Committee ruled in favour of the Dominion Parliament having jurisdiction, mainly by reason of the general power granted Parliament under the "peace, order and good government" clause of section 91 of the BNA Act. These rulings encouraged Bennett and other Canadian lawyers and politicians (but not all) to believe that the Judicial Committee might well approve other legislation that was not clearly within the specified powers of Parliament or the provinces. The Natural Products Marketing Act was one example. Unemployment insurance might be another.

Bennett had favoured legislation of this kind before 1934 and set his private secretary, Rod Finlayson, and others to work on it.[7]

A third and more disturbing influence during 1934 from the actions of H. H. Stevens, the volatile Minister of Trade and Commerce. Early in the year, Stevens delivered a strong speech in Toronto criticizing the department stores and other mass retailers and wholesalers for using their bargaining strength to force down prices and wages in many of the weaker industries from which they bought, while themselves selling at quite profitable prices. Bennett soon after appointed Stevens Chairman of a House of Commons Select Committee on Price Spreads which found much evidence that supported Stevens' case. The enquiry was not finished when Parliament prorogued early in July 1934, and Bennett agreed that it should continue as a Royal Commission, with Stevens as Chairman. Meanwhile, Stevens made another inflammatory speech, attacking specific businesses, to a group of M.P.s. Copies of it reached the press and caused intense controversy and threats of lawsuits. When he was severely criticized in Cabinet by Cahan, a senior minister from Montreal who had close ties with conservative business interests, and it was suggested that he should apologize, Stevens resigned from the Cabinet and as Chairman, but not as a member, of the Commission.

The Commission reported at length to Parliament in April 1935, making a whole list of recommendations relating to commercial and competitive practices, the Combines Investigation Act, the Companies Act, changes in labour laws and their administration, encouragement of trade unions, the establishment of minimum prices for primary products, and many other more specific items. Indeed, it was not clear whether the Commission really favoured competition or not. The principal organization proposed was a "Dominion Trade and Industry Commission" to regulate many of these matters.[8]

Before the Price Spreads Commission had reported, Bennett had captured the initiative from Stevens and emerged as an ardent reformer, with the assistance of Herridge and Finlayson. The Prime Minister made five speeches over the radio early in January 1935. He described how bad things had been during the Depression, the measures that had been taken by the government, and the distinction he saw between recovery measures to increase employment and prices, and reform measures to improve the capitalist system. He

---

7. Horn, *op. cit.*, p. 586.

8. *Ibid.*, p. 511. See also Royal Commission on Price Spreads, *Report*, 1935.

proclaimed himself in favour of reform and against *laissez faire*. He proposed bringing in unemployment insurance and a new contributory old age pension system, and doing "likewise" for health insurance.[9] He would take action on the recommendations of the Price Spreads Commission when they submitted their report, if they made a good case. He proposed to establish an Economic Council of Canada. He ended his final address by speaking about the difference between the *laissez-faire* Liberal party and his own party, which stood for the reform of capitalism.

These flamboyant speeches were the object of much puzzlement and concern both in Ottawa and across the country. Were they a programme for Parliament in its final year or a platform for an early election? This was quickly resolved. Parliament was opened soon after the addresses, and the Throne Speech, which exaggerated the degree of recovery that had been achieved, stated that reform measures would be submitted to that session "as part of a comprehensive plan designed to remedy the social and economic injustices now prevailing".[10]

Substantial reform measures were, in fact, enacted at that session despite Bennett's absence, first due to illness and later because he was in London. Six International Labour Organization Conventions were ratified in order to lay a legal basis for acts to establish minimum wages, a weekly day of rest, and an eight-hour working day. The most important measure was the "Employment and Social Insurance Act", which was to establish a system of unemployment insurance and an Employment and Social Insurance Commission. The Commission was to have only investigatory and advisory powers regarding national health insurance and payment of "assistance" to unemployed persons not qualified for insurance benefits. A second rather sweeping measure was the Dominion Trade and Industry Commission Act, intended to carry out many of the detailed recommendations of the Price Spreads Commission. Initially, at least, the members of the Tariff Board were to serve as commissioners. They were to administer the Combines Investigation Act, and to investigate industries to determine whether or not "wasteful or demoralizing competition"[11] existed. If the Commission found that such competition did exist, it could recommend that the Governor-in-Council

---

9. "The Premier Speaks to the People", pamphlet of Bennett's second radio broadcast, January 4, 1935, R. B. Bennett Papers, PAC, microfilm reel M1401, p. 437387. All further references to the Bennett Papers are those located in the PAC.

10. Speech from the Throne, HC *Debates*, January 17, 1935, p. 17.

11. R. B. Hanson, *ibid.*, June 11, 1935, p. 17.

approve agreements regulating that industry's prices and production. The Commission was given other, less sweeping powers of investigation and reporting. The Companies Act was amended to carry out recommendations of the Price Spreads Commission relating to "watered stock". Several other statutes were amended. Finally, Bennett's government introduced a compromise Wheat Board Act, which was passed with the agreement of the Liberals.

Some reform was accomplished in that session, or appeared to have been accomplished, but Stevens expressed his deep disappointment with the legislation. Mackenzie King, as Leader of the Opposition, did not oppose the reform legislation or even let his followers debate it at length, although he did occasionally question the constitutional status of what was proposed. He encouraged the split between Bennett and Stevens, which he thought would reduce the public impression of Bennett as a reformer. And so it did. Before the session was over Stevens was strongly critical and quit the Conservative party. He sought to form his own Reconstruction Party to fight the election that summer but he was its only member to be elected.

In the election of October 14, 1935, the Liberals gained an overwhelming victory and King was quickly back in office. One of the first actions of the new government was to refer Bennett's "New Deal" measures to the Supreme Court to ascertain whether or not they were *ultra vires*. The Supreme Court's decisions had to be appealed to the Judicial Committee of the Privy Council to get final rulings. These were handed down on January 28, 1937. As many had expected, the Judicial Committee struck down a majority of these reform statutes as *ultra vires*. These included the whole of the Natural Products Marketing Act, and the Employment and Social Insurance Act. These two most important reform measures had also been found *ultra vires* by the Supreme Court of Canada. The three labour acts, intended to implement Conventions of the International Labour Organizations, were also declared *ultra vires*; on them the Supreme Court had been evenly divided. The Dominion Trade and Industry Act, which was largely a response to the Price Spreads Report, was declared *ultra vires* because of its main provision, which authorized the Governor-in-Council to legitimize agreements regulating prices and production where "wasteful or demoralizing competition exists". The rest of that Act was considered within the powers of Parliament but it related chiefly to organization and procedure rather than to substantive powers. On the whole, there was little left of the reform legislation except the Farmer's Creditors Arrangement Act—which was not originally thought of as part of the "New Deal"—and a new section of the Criminal Code penalizing discriminatory or predatory pricing, which probably was of importance in meeting some of the problems identified by Stevens and his Commission. The generally negative decisions of the Judicial Committee were an object of much criticism and expert argument in Canada. Even if the decisions had gone the other way, it would have done little to expedite recovery from the Depression in Canada, although unemployment insurance would have begun several years earlier than it did, and marketing schemes for natural products might have blossomed in the late years of the Depression to the benefit of a minority of farmers, fishermen, and others, at the expense of consumers.

The Slow and Incomplete Recovery, 1936-1939

In his biography of King during the 1930s, Blair Neatby opens his chapter on the Liberal response to the Depression by saying: "In 1936 Mackenzie King would learn that even with a Liberal government in office at Ottawa the depression was still there, shading every aspect of Canadian life in sombre gray."[12] Gray it would remain for the life of that Parliament, until the fall of France in 1940 coloured all with the flaming light of unexpected dangers.

In October 1935, Mackenzie King selected a Cabinet which was both smaller and more capable than the former Bennett Cabinet. It included many strong ministers—among them Ernest Lapointe, Charles Dunning, C. D. Howe, T. A. Crerar, Norman Rogers, and J. L. Ilsley—but they were handicapped at the beginning by a very conservative economic and financial policy in which King, influenced by his easy economic experience of the 1920s, devoutly believed. He selected Dunning, another believer strong enough to carry out a programme of financial restraint, to be Minister of Finance. Both King and Dunning favoured lower tariffs obtained by trade negotiations as the chief instrument of recovery.

In his budget of May 1936 (so different from his complacent optimism of May 1930), Dunning had to begin with these serious qualifications:

> The most welcome feature in the fiscal year which has just closed has been what it indicates of a movement toward recovery. I do not wish to exaggerate the extent of that recovery, for to those who are charged with the responsibilities of government in these hard times the distance yet to go and the problems still to be solved are the features of our economic record which are most impressive—and at the same time most distressing.[13]

---

12. B. Neatby, *William Lyon Mackenzie King: A Political Biography*, vol. 3, *The Prism of Unity* (Toronto, 1976), p. 153.

13. Dunning, HC *Debates*, May 1, 1936, p. 2362.

The Minister found that the government's deficit for the previous year had been $162 million. He announced a new policy of making "an immediate approach to a balanced budget"[14] which would "show that complete equilibrium can be reached within a reasonable time", a policy which he identified as "a doctrine of deflation".[15] He announced new restrictions on expenditures, and increased rates both of income and sales tax. This mis-timed austerity had been worked out only a few months after the appearance of John Maynard Keynes's *General Theory of Employment, Interest and Money*, which was to be the intellectual foundation for a framework of analysis which would show that such a doctrine of deflation, and the measures giving it effect, were quite wrong in the circumstances of 1936.

Relief Reconsidered[16]

In the 1935 election campaign, King did not try to match Bennett's "New Deal" promise of an unemployment insurance programme. He preached financial restraint, arguing that the country could ill afford the expense of a large extension of social services. But despite his reluctance to increase federal expenditures on relief, King was aware that there were many inadequacies in the existing relief system. His selection of Norman Rogers, an intelligent and able political science professor from Queen's, as his Minister of Labour was evidence of the seriousness with which King approached the problem. Rogers very quickly attempted to make some major reforms of the Canadian relief system.

He began his assault on the problem by investigating what was undoubtedly the most criticized of all federal relief programmes, the relief camps organized and run by the Department of National Defence. In November 1935, a committee was appointed to review the relief camp situation and to make recommendations to the Minister of Labour as to how it could be improved.

The Dominion-Provincial Conference of December 1935 provided the first opportunity for the provincial premiers to discuss the problem of the costs of relief with members of the newly elected

---

14. *Ibid.*, p. 2384.

15. *Ibid.*

16. Much of the "Relief Reconsidered" section was drawn from the following sources: Annual reports of the Dominion Director of Unemployment Relief, 1931-32; Annual reports of the Dominion Commissioner of Unemployment Relief, 1933-41; National Employment Commission, *op. cit.*; Grauer, *op. cit.*

federal government. In order to help the provinces through the winter months, the Dominion government agreed to a substantial increase in its grants to the provinces. This increase in funding was, however, only a temporary measure designed to tide the provinces over until the existing relief system was revamped. Under Rogers as Chairman, a Conference Committee on Unemployment and Relief proposed a series of measures to improve the efficiency of the relief system. Among the Committee's recommendations was a nationwide registration and classification of all relief recipients. The Committee also suggested a possible division of the responsibility for providing relief among the various levels of government. The federal government would provide relief to all employable men and women and their dependants; all others in need of relief would be the responsibility of the provincial and/or municipal governments. The most significant recommendation of the Committee was that a national Commission on Employment and Relief should be established. This commission was intended to assist the provinces and municipalities in organizing the nationwide registration of all relief recipients, to establish standards and regulations which the provinces should meet in order to qualify for federal assistance, to supervise the distribution of Dominion grants, and to plan and co-ordinate a consistent programme of public works and employment projects. Altogether, the Committee's recommendations called for a closer supervision of a more uniform relief system. The provincial premiers were anxious to receive the additional funding promised by the Dominion government, and they readily agreed to the establishment of the federal commission. Thus, from December 1935 to March 1936 the provinces received larger grants from the federal government for relief purposes. However, in April 1936, when King and Dunning were shocked at the increase in the federal deficit, they convinced the Cabinet to agree to a cut in federal grants to the provinces.

Early in 1936, the committee reviewing the relief camps made its recommendation to Rogers. On February 26, he announced in the House of Commons that the Dominion government planned to close the camps by the summer. In order to provide alternate employment for those in the camps, the government had made arrangements with the Canadian National and Canadian Pacific Railways to hire an extra ten thousand men to perform maintenance work on the railway tracks. In addition, Rogers hoped that with the co-operation of the provinces it would be possible to extend the farm placement programme to absorb some of the men who were working in the camps, and that others would find employment in forestry conservation and other development projects. The co-ordination of the placement of these men would, he commented, be handled by the National Employment Commission, which had yet to be set up.

In April 1936, an act was passed by Parliament authorizing the establishment of a National Employment Commission. This Commission, chaired by Arthur Purvis, one of the most able Canadian businessmen, was to investigate and make recommendations concerning the country's relief system.[17] In order to do so, the Commission began the first nationwide registration and classification of all relief recipients. The Commission was also granted the authority to control the disbursment of Dominion government expenditures on relief.

While the Commission conducted its study, the Dominion government continued to provide financial and material aid to the provinces for relief purposes. Various agreements were entered into by the Dominion and provincial governments for the construction of numerous public works projects, including the Trans-Canada Highway and provincial highways. The Dominion government also continued to contribute to the relief-settlement programme.

By July 1936, the National Defence relief camps were closed. Many of the men in the camps were offered employment with the Canadian National and Canadian Pacific Railways. Others were placed on farms, in accordance with special agreements made between the Dominion government and the provinces (with the exception of Ontario and Nova Scotia). In order to ensure further employment for the relief camp workers, the Dominion government agreed to pay fifty per cent of the costs of operating forestry and other works undertaken by the provincial governments of British Columbia, Alberta, Manitoba, and New Brunswick, for the specific purpose of employing single persons unsuitable for farm labour.

Because of the acute drought in the Prairie Provinces, special assistance was given to the provincial governments of Alberta, Saskatchewan, and Manitoba in 1936 and 1937. The Dominion government assumed all costs for direct relief in the drought areas of these provinces from September 1, 1936 to August 31, 1937. The Dominion government also allocated funds to pay for the cost of feed and fodder for livestock in these areas.

Saskatchewan was by far the province most seriously affected by drought, which came on top of the disastrously low grain prices of 1931 to 1935. There were five successive years of drought, reach-

---

17. The National Employment Commission consisted of Arthur Purvis (Chairman), Tom Moore (Vice-chairman), W. A. Mackintosh, Alfred Marois, A. N. McLean, Mary Sutherland and E. J. Young.

ing a climax in 1937 when the average yield of wheat per seeded acre in Saskatchewan was about one-sixth of the average yield per acre during the decade 1920-29. In that disastrous year, two-thirds of the farm population of the province were destitute and on relief, and ninety-six per cent of the rural municipalities sought financial assistance from the provincial government; it, in turn, required special assistance on a large scale from the Dominion government. For the whole period from 1930 to 1937, total relief costs in Saskatchewan were 13.3 per cent of total provincial incomes; the average for all provinces was 3.6 per cent. It is remarkable that the province and its people survived without permanent damage.

By July 1937, the National Employment Commission had published an interim report, which included the results of its nation-wide registration of relief recipients. This compilation of all persons receiving relief was used, whenever possible, as the list from which candidates were selected to work on public works projects. The Commission was also instrumental in establishing a training program for unemployed young persons. Following its recommendation, Parliament approved the expenditure of one million dollars for this purpose.

Before the Commission completed its final report, King was informed of its major recommendation. Mary Sutherland, a member of the Commission, forewarned King of the intention of the majority of the commissioners to recommend that the Dominion assume full responsibility for the provision of relief to all unemployed employable persons (in addition to unemployment insurance, to which the government was committed in principle and about which it had proposed to the provinces, in November 1937, a constitutional amendment giving the Dominion exclusive jurisdiction over the subject). King was both alarmed and dismayed by the financial implications of this recommendation. He argued that it was beyond the terms of reference of the Commission (which appears to have been the case) and showed the political naiveté and irresponsibility of the commissioners (which was not the case!). King blamed this on Purvis, who he thought was too much of an insensitive businessman, and on W. A. Mackintosh, another member of the Commission, whom King considered academic and theoretical. The Prime Minister had further harsh words for trade union leader Tom Moore, also of the Commission, who he claimed had "been helped more than anyone else by this government".[18]

The Commission's decision had apparently been the subject of some discussion with Rogers, who defended it when King reported

---

18. National Archives, King's Diary, January 12, 1938, Ottawa, Ontario.

Sutherland's conversation in a meeting of the Cabinet. King's faith in his Minister of Labour was undoubtedly shaken. He insisted that Rogers see Purvis and get the Commission to change its decision. Rogers resisted, although he did talk with Purvis. In due course, Purvis and Mackintosh suggested some changes to their colleagues on the Commission, which persuaded them to hold to their view against that of Sutherland, as expressed in her dissenting memorandum.

In essence, the majority report of the National Employment Commission stated that when the proposed change in the Constitution led to the establishment of a nationally administered system of unemployment insurance and an employment service, it would require "a supplementary system of Unemployment Aid to meet those phases of unemployment need which experience abroad has shown cannot be covered by Unemployment Insurance".[19] The Commission then stated that such a supplementary system would in its opinion be best administered by the Dominion. This further step would require determination by the Royal Commission on Dominion-Provincial Relations of the financial basis upon which such a system should be established, and, in the light of all relevant considerations, of the wisdom of further constitutional and financial changes.

Sutherland alone dissented from these carefully worded conclusions, and her views were strongly commended by the Prime Minister to his colleagues.

But King was not displeased with the final result of the Commission's recommendations. Although the commissioners had refused to abandon their view of the desirability of Dominion government responsibility over the provision of relief, they had backed down to the degree of admitting that because of the financial implications of their recommendation the matter required further study by the Rowell-Sirois Commission. Thus, the determination of whether or not the relief system proposed by the Employment Commission was financially feasible was shunted off to another royal commission. The desperate need for a comprehensive reform of the relief system fell victim to Ottawa's desire for a more general review of Dominion-provincial financial relations.

Dominion contributions for relief purposes in 1938 and 1939 continued much as they had in 1937, although the work of the National Employment Commission had some impact on the allocation of government expenditures and the creation of relief programs. Grants to the provinces continued, and special assistance continued to be

---

19. National Employment Commission, *op. cit.*, p. 28.

provided to the drought areas of Saskatchewan and Alberta. Relief applicants and recipients were registered and classified according to the specifications first established by the Employment Commission. Dominion contributions to the relief-settlement programme and public-works projects were maintained. A Youth Training Act was passed by Parliament to provide for the continuation of the youth training programme, which was expanded in 1938-39. Parliament also appropriated funds in 1938-39 for the rehabilitation of older unemployed persons, as had been recommended in the report of the National Employment Commission. Although far from perfect and despite government reluctance, by the end of the 1930s the Canadian relief system had become more organized and uniform.

The unemployment situation remained serious, as the economic recovery remained quite incomplete, up to the outbreak of war in September 1939, particularly in the field of construction and other capital investment by business. In terms of our current concepts it has been estimated that 11.4 per cent of the total labour force (including the thirty percent still in agriculture) were out of work and seeking jobs. The situation required the continuation of relief measures for the first eighteen months of war. During this period the Constitution was amended to give the Parliament of Canada specific jurisdiction over ''Unemployment Insurance'' (but not over ''aid'' for other employable unemployed persons), and the Unemployment Insurance Act was passed in August 1940. By the time the first benefits under it were payable in 1942 they were hardly needed, as the war had by then brought about practically full employment.

2.   Staples, Surplus, and Exchange

The Commercial-Industrial Question in the National Policy Period

Paul Phillips
University of Manitoba

Introduction

The investigation of Canadian political economy has undergone a renaissance in the last decade or so. This follows a hiatus of a number of years when the Canadian tradition, once so firmly rooted in the staple approach, appeared to have reached its limits in the analysis of the pre-industrial staple trades.[1] Throughout this period, which coincided with the period of hegemony in economics of the neoclassical-Keynesian synthesis, traditional political economy seemed to die in most Canadian universities, maintained only by a small cadre of respected but largely ignored academics, including such people as Irene Spry, Vernon Fowke, Clare Pentland, and Stanley Ryerson.

Despite a common interest in Canadian economic history, however, there was no common theme that bound them together in the way that the staple and Lawrentian approaches had provided the cohesive mastic of the Toronto School of Innis and Creighton. Spry and Fowke continued in the staple tradition, albeit with a different, western perspective. Pentland and Ryerson, on the other hand, were linked by a common interest in the rise of wage labour and of industrial capitalism in central Canada and by a Marxist perspective in their analytic use of class. There was, however, a common interest: the period of transition in Canada from a number of economically disparate colonies to a national economy—the National Policy period

---

1. The classic statement of this position is K.A.H. Buckley, "The Role of Staple Industries in Canadian Development", *Journal of Economic History*, Vol. 18, no. 4 (1958).

(1850-1930)—and the role of the state in that transition. Nevertheless, there was little integration of the two perspectives that could be related back to a common theoretical foundation. Clearly, there was no common concept or theory underlying these approaches that would comprise an internally consistent general model.[2]

One answer to this schizophrenia was to argue that the Innisian staple approach was applicable in Canada only to the middle of the nineteenth century, at which time an industrial model (either the orthodox neoclassical growth variant or the Marxist variant) superseded the staple model as a viable explanation of Canadian economic growth, at least in central Canada. Nevertheless, the staple approach might still be useful in analyzing economic development in the western agricultural regions. This view, however, left many questions unanswered, not least of which were the nature of the Canadian state and the class formations that underlay the emerging nation.

In any case, this compromise was undermined by the debate that followed the publication of Naylor's "The Rise and Fall of the Third Commercial Empire of the St. Lawrence", which re-opened discussion of the nature of the Canadian élite in the National Policy period and, indeed, the nature of the Canadian state in that era.[3] The controversial debate will not be reviewed here. Rather, the purpose is to explore the possibility that the controversy is the same one that bedevilled the seven blind men in their description of the elephant—a problem of different perspectives and limited information. Was the National Policy a scheme of merchants to advance their interests by extending their empire to an internal and captive agricultural frontier? Or was it the agenda of a new industrial élite attempting to extend its market and protect it from external competition? Though the debate has raged, it has lacked a theoretical foundation.

---

2. The study of political economy in Canada lost its pre-eminence to a new breed of economic historians who specialized in quantification and the application of neoclassical economic models to limited questions in Canadian economic history. These "new economic" historians attempted to circumscribe the debate by ignoring it, by eliminating any distinction between commercial and industrial capital and reducing any determination to that between theoretical market prices and real market prices. Though such a distinction may make sense in terms of static economic theory, it does not contribute much to Canadian analysis precisely because it ignores both regional and class elements in analysis. Nevertheless, it gained centre stage at least in part because of the apparent incompatibility in the political economy approach between the staple analysis with its integral regional approach and capital/labour analysis with its integral class approach. While each was compelling in its arguments, there was no unanimity in approach or theoretical formulation.

3. Tom Naylor, "The Rise and Fall of the Third Commercial Empire of the St. Lawrence", in Gary Teeple, ed., *Capitalism and the National Question in Canada* (Toronto: University of Toronto Press, 1972).

Indeed, there is a common theoretical framework which not only makes sense of the competing political-economy interpretations but also sheds more light on the subsequent invasion of American ownership and control of Canadian industry. We must look to a formulation that makes it possible to reconcile the regional interests of commercial capital with the class interest of an emerging industrial capital, and which will also encompass the nature of the economic relations between the western farmer (an independent commodity producer) and the grain merchant, as well as those between the industrial worker and the rising stratum of industrial capitalists.

Theoretical Foundations

The roots of this alternative interpretation lie in a combination of class analysis and dependency analysis. The interpretation differs from the implicit dependency of Innisian staple theory in that it incorporates class as a vital determinant in income distribution, and the role of the state in adjudication between the interests of commercial and industrial capital. It differs from much orthodox Marxist interpretation in its recognition of the importance of merchant capital and of independent commodity production in the incomplete, and regionally uneven, transition to industrialism in Canada in the last half of the nineteenth century and, indeed, well into the twentieth. This neglect of the importance of independent commodity producers as a vital component of the Canadian economic reality is a failing of both Marxist and non-Marxist economists, and gives added weight to Innis' contention that it is necessary for Canadians to develop a unique Canadian political economy. Fundamental concepts in the synthesis suggested here are the theory of surplus and the theory of unequal exchange.

In the capitalist mode of production the worker creates value, but is paid less than the value he creates by virtue of the employer's ownership of the capital utilized. While total surplus value may be considered the difference between the total value created and the subsistence level (however defined) of wages, it is not necessary that the capitalist appropriate the entire surplus. Depending on bargaining power, which in turn may depend on the state of the labour market or the employers' strategic response to class conflict, the employer may share part of the surplus with all or some of his workers. The essential point, however, is that the worker is employed part of the day for himself and part of the day for the capitalist.

For the capitalist to realize profits, however, a second condition must be met: the price obtained from the sale of the production must be sufficient to render to the employer the surplus value, so that capitalist consumption and accumulation may proceed. Class conflict, of course, arises from the dispute over the distribution of surplus and, secondly, over the absolute size of the surplus, since capital wishes to maximize its surplus whereas labour may be content merely to produce a comfortable surplus, by means of limiting the intensity of work.

However, there is also a basis for collaboration between labour and national capital on issues such as the tariff, or untaxed resource exploitation, to the extent that realized surplus is increased either from others in the country (such as independent producers) or from natural resources on which no economic rents are paid (a portion of those saved rents shared with labour).

In the case of merchant capital and the independent commodity producer, however, the situation is very different. The independent commodity producer embodies both labour and capital. Hence the distribution of surplus is immaterial when it can be retained by the producer for consumption and accumulation. It is possible for the independent commodity producers to realize all or part of the surplus if, singly or collectively, they possess sufficient market power to command a selling price that provides a monetary surplus over and above subsistence. The question is merely an application of the familiar realization problem faced by capital but here applied to the petty producer.

On the other hand, merchant capital can appropriate part of the surplus only if it can use its ownership or control of circulating capital to manipulate prices, so that it can buy at a price below value and sell at a price at or above value; that is, to "buy cheap and sell dear". The essence of such a strategy is to monopolize markets so that prices favour the intermediary. The point is that, though merchant capital may not create surplus (except in the function of transportation), it can redistribute surplus through manipulation of the terms of trade or control of the price system.

Thus the essence of the problem in dealing with the accumulation role of commercial capital in relation to the independent commodity producer is the degree to which the commercial capitalist can use monopoly power in the market to reduce the price paid the producer, so that the return to the producer is less than what would otherwise be the "free market" price. Therefore, if the commercial capitalist is able to appropriate the full surplus of the independent commodity producers, the income of the latter will approach that of wage labour. The key element in this appropriation of surplus is the relative market power of commercial capital and the basic producer. If access to commercial capital is easy, and there are no other barriers of access to commercial institutions (that is, if the commercial sector is competitive in the neoclassical sense), there is no mechanism for the intermediary to appropriate surplus, and the difference between the buying and the selling price will approximate the (unproductive) labour cost plus other costs involved in the intermediary function. Whether or not the basic producer accumulates the surplus is another question related to the general problem of capitalist realization, the selling price in the final market reflecting the vagaries of supply and demand, and the terms of trade between goods bought and sold.

Economic rent adds a further complication to the analysis. Rent as such arises because of price and is not a component of cost. It accrues due to a natural or artificial limitation of supply of a natural resource. Because supply is ultimately limited (for any given level of technology), by the bounty of nature, any increase in demand for the resource, or the product of that resource in the case of agricultural land, will cause the market price of that resource to rise and, since other costs (wages, capital, intermediary imputs or, alternatively, variable and constant capital) may be assumed to remain constant, a surplus will initially accrue to the owner of the natural resource. This surplus is defined as rent.

However, it is important to also distinguish between intra-marginal rent and monopoly rent. Intra-marginal rent grows out of the fact that not all naturally occurring resources are of equal quality. As output is increased, bringing into production less and less productive resources, the cost of production rises. This means that the costs of producing a given output of a specific resource will be different for different resource bodies and, at any given price, the most marginal body will accrue no rent at all. It should also be noted that any rent surplus will continue only as long as the resource does not deteriorate or become exhausted, new resource sources are not found, demand and price levels do not fall, and the cost of constant and variable capital does not rise.

However, it is not necessary that the basic producer (whether an independent commodity producer or a resource capitalist) appropriate the entire rent surplus. Intra-marginal rent may be transferred to a middleman if that middleman has sufficient market power to force the original producer to sell to him at a price below the market price. Governments, likewise, can appropriate part of the rent surplus by imposing a royalty, or by such measures as auctioning off mineral rights (or, in the days of the fur trade, trading post rights).

It should also be recognized that wage labour could also share in the rent surplus if it were sufficiently strong and if capital were willing to share it with labour as a strategy to diffuse class conflict and divide the working class. Higher wages would be represented by an upward shift in the cost of production. This would also result in the loss of some marginal production (that is, production where little or no rent accrues) unless what appears historically to have been the case occurs—segmentation of the labour market, providing lower wages for workers in less productive resource areas and sectors. Similarly, resource surplus can be increased, at least for a period, if producers can avoid the real costs of conservation of the resource (for example, reforestation) or pass them on to government; or if much of the fixed infrastructure cost (for example, transportation facilities) is absorbed by government. Again, this surplus may be shared among commercial and industrial capital, labour, and independent commodity producers, depending on the balance of class power.

Monopoly rent is a somewhat different concept. It arises out of limits of supply. In some cases that limit may be an absolute limit of nature (such as the amount of building land available within an urban centre), though more commonly it is associated with artificial restrictions on supply (zoning, quotas, timber-cutting licences, mineral rights, patents), or the exercise of market power, the most recent example being the oil cartel OPEC (the Organization of Petroleum Exporting Countries). Note that monopoly rents can also accrue in the long run *if* the restrictions or the market control are maintained.

It is a central contention of this paper that commercial capital, under certain market conditions or institutions, can appropriate to itself at least part of the economic rent, just as it can appropriate at least part of the surplus value out of production through the mechanism of uneven exchange. This is most notably the case when commercial capital is the intermediary between independent commodity producers, who are fragmented (as a class) and as a consequence lack market power, including access to international markets which are distant from the point of production in both time and space.

Secondly, it will be argued that large-scale industrial capital, in conjunction with financial capital, became vertically integrated into, or out from, resource industries in order to subsume the commercial capital function. This replacement of the market increased the ability of ''monopoly capital'' to appropriate the entire surplus, production surplus and rent, or at least as much of it as its strategy of dealing with class conflict would permit.

Finally, it will be argued that the nature of class and nation in Canada reflects not only the conflict and alliances between industrial capital and labour, but also between commercial capital and the independent commodity producer; between the independent commodity producer and labour; and between industrial and commercial capital.

The Canadian State in the Formative Period

For purposes of comparison, the positions in the debate, between those who argue that Canada's National Policy represents the continuation of the "Commercial Empire of the St. Lawrence" and those who see it as the programme of an emerging industrial capitalism, are stated in somewhat simplistic terms which, while hardly doing justice to the elegance of their exposition, at least have the merit of highlighting the issues. The fundamental contentious issue is whether the National Policy (comprising three pillars, a transcontinental railway, the opening of the agricultural west, and a national system of protective tariffs), and the institutional framework of that policy, Confederation, reflected the rise of industrial capital, or whether the National Policy was the last major initiative of Canadian merchant (or commercial) capital. The primacy of the industrial-capital position, associated with the writings of Ryerson, Pentland, and McDonald, argues that pressure from a rising class of industrial capitalists was behind the move to Confederation and the National Policy, particularly the National Policy tariffs, and including the Caley-Galt tariffs of the 1850s. Pentland and Ryerson are quite willing to concede that commercial capital was also involved, particularly with railway policy. McDonald, following Marx, argues that railways are industrial capital and hence the railway promoters were, by definition, industrial capitalists. This, however, begs the question. The major purpose of the railway promoters is the critical issue, and it is at least arguable that their prime purpose was to engender commerce within the monopoly control of the merchant class.[4]

In sharp juxtaposition is Naylor's argument that the National Policy instruments originated in, and were implemented by, commercial capital, a class originally identified by Creighton as the ruling élite and men of national vision. Furthermore, Naylor argues, the aspirations and methods of commercial capital were in conflict with

---

4. The major references for this position are H. C. Pentland, *Labour and Capital in Canada, 1650-1860* (Toronto: Lorimer, 1981); Stanley Ryerson, *Unequal Union* (Progress Books, 1963); and L. R. MacDonald, "Merchants Against Industry: An Idea and its Origins", *Canadian Historical Review*, September 1975.

the nascent industrial capital class by directing scarce capital into the staple trades rather than into industrial capital formation. The consequence was the supplanting of Canadian industrial capital with American, branch-plant capital, leading to foreign control of Canadian industry.[5]

A number of people who have studied the period are willing to concede that the effect of the National Policy development strategy, and more specifically the National Policy tariffs, was the invasion of American industrial capital, though most would be hostile to Naylor's contention that the National Policy was commercially inspired and that a significant, or numerically strong, Canadian industrial capitalist class did not exist.

Indeed, the argument that the foreign ownership of Canadian manufacturing was the direct, if unintended, result of the protective tariffs has attained the acceptance of canon by orthodox and revisionist economic historians alike. However, the argument is open to question, at least in its simpler form. First, if that were the case, then why was there not a comparable influx of British direct investment before the First World War? Second, while the argument might hold for manufacturing (and even for pulp and paper in Ontario and Quebec, due to provincial government protectionist measures to prevent the export of unprocessed pulp wood), the argument does not apply to American investment in other resource-based, export industries where foreign investment was also manifest. Third, while there was an influx of branch plants immediately after the tariffs were introduced in 1879, the number was relatively small and tended to be in industries where advanced, or new, technology gave the American firm a decided advantage. That is, they were branch plants that replaced imports, not domestic capital.[6]

While this puts a quite different complexion on the orthodox interpretation of the role of the National Policy in fostering foreign ownership, it offers scant support for Naylor's contention that there were two alternative routes to industrial-capital accumulation in Canada—the growth of existing small firms to large size or the arrival of large foreign firms.[7] At that point, these were not real alternatives because control of the new technology, both product technology and mass-production technology, was firmly in the hands of an emerging

---

5. Naylor, *op. cit.*, p. 24. See also his *History of Canadian Business* (Toronto: Lorimer, 1975), Vol. II, p. 97.

6. For a discussion of the nature of early branch plants, see Mira Wilkins, *The Emergence of the Multinational Corporation* (Cambridge, Mass.: Harvard University Press, 1974).

7. Naylor, *History of Canadian Business*, Vol. I, p. 38.

and expanding American big business. Canadian business could not compete because the capital costs of attempting to match the new American products and processes were generally beyond its limited resources.

The evidence is clear that there was a rising chorus of demands by Canadian manufacturers for protection, even from those who had previously given little or no support to protection. In addition, there was strong support from large segments of labour.[8] This suggests that there were one or more new elements in the equation. Two possibilities can be allowed for. One is that the nature of Canadian industrial capital was in the process of changing from artisan-type production (the manufactory) with inherent built-in natural protection provided by transportation costs and local markets, to large-scale factory production with its need (due to much higher capital/labour ratios, the requirement for a disciplined and experienced labour force, and production in expectation of finding a market) for stable regional, if not national, markets. Such markets could not be created without protection, given Canada's proximity to United States sources of competing supply. In Adam Smith's dictum, the division of labour is limited by the extent of the market. The only way to extend or even maintain the market was by protection.

Second, at the same time as this transition from the manufactory to the factory was beginning to take place in Canada, the process was maturing south of the border. The rise of monopoly capitalism was considerably more advanced in the United States. It is perhaps not coincidental that the National Policy tariffs were implemented in the same year as the Standard Oil Trust was formed. Capital formation in the United States had been proceeding at a rapid pace since the Civil War and the limits of the national market were being approached, contributing to problems of realization of surplus, particularly in the depression that followed 1873. The response by capital could be either to extend the market to include Canada, a tactic indicated by Canadian complaints of American competition and of dumping in the Canadian market, or to limit supply, a tactic indicated by the trust movement and, when trusts were made illegal, by the consolidation and merger movements. The imposition of the National Policy effectively curtailed the former but could do nothing about the growth of monopoly capitalism, which by the maintenance of profit levels and restriction of supply growth effectively generated

---

8. Brian Palmer, *A Culture in Conflict* (Montreal: McGill-Queens, 1979), ch. 4; Pentland, *op. cit.*, pp. 164ff.

excess capital—an excess that sooner or later sought alternative
frontiers of investment to counter the general tendency of a fall in
the rate of profit.

There is no debate that one of the intents of the National Policy
for the Canadian political élite was to entice an inflow of American
industrial capital into the country, but it was assumed that, as in the
past, this would be primarily in the form of the immigration of both
entrepreneur and capital. This was a natural assumption in a period
when the manufactory was still the predominant, if declining, business form. Canada's élite did not foresee the rise of international industrial capital; nor could they have been expected to. Yet, the growing
intensity of branch plant formation as consolidations progressed in
America indicates that the *push* effects of developments in the United
States economy were as important as the *pull* of Canadian protection,
if not more so.

One can only speculate about what would have happened if
protection had not been extended in Canada when it was. The
de-industrialization experience of the Maritimes relative to central
Canada between the 1880s and the 1920s suggests what would
probably have been the fate of central Canada *vis-à-vis* the American
industrial region.[9] The growth of the United States capacity to serve
continental markets, and the favourable transportation costs of serving
Canadian markets from American supply bases rather than from a
central Canadian base, would have undoubtedly led to a comparable
de-industrialization of Canada and, by removing the protection of
the east-west movement of goods and staples along Canadian railways,
almost inevitably have resulted in the collapse of the Canadian nation,
at least as a functional economic unit.

Naylor's contention that the 1872 patent legislation had a
significant long-run effect of attracting branch plants would appear
to be at least as sound as the simple tariff argument. Indeed, the patent
is a legal monopoly and a direct control on competition which makes
possible the cornering of specific markets; this legal monopolization
was greatly strengthened by the 1872 legislation. As Naylor notes,
the pattern emerged of a concentration of American participation in the
"high-technology, capital-intensive, rapid-growth industries. . . ."[10]

It is difficult to see in the patent legislation strong support
for the position that commercial capital controlled the Canadian state
in the immediate post-Confederation period. The legislation received

9. T. W. Acheson, "The Maritimes and the National Policy, 1880-1910", *Acadiensis* 1, no. 2.

10. Naylor, *History of Canadian Business*, Vol. II, p. 64.

vigorous support from the voice of national industrial capital, the Canadian Manufacturing Association, not yet the spokesman for American branch plants. At the same time, Canadian wholesalers were integrating backward, an evolution from commercial to industrial capital quite familiar in British and American experience, forming joint ventures with American technology and capital to manufacture in Canada. It is difficult in this process to identify any conflict between the interests of commercial and industrial capital, since the motivation of merchant capital was, at least in part, to guarantee a supply of tradeable goods to compete with American commerce and to control the terms of trade with suppliers.

Thus, instead of asserting the dominance of industrial or commercial capital in the formative years of the Canadian state, it would appear relevant to ask why a Canadian industrial capital class which, despite Naylor, did exist (though it must have been relatively small) attained only a dependent, comprador status. The answer is at the same time both simple and complex. It is simple in the sense that it fits very well the Marxian model of progressive concentration. Bigger, more technically progressive firms simply drive out of business or take over smaller, less advanced firms—and American firms were more advanced and larger than their Canadian counterparts. On the other hand, it is complex when one considers the mechanisms and timing of the stunted industrial development that proceeded through a number of steps.

Capital was scarce in this country, particularly when viewed against the enormous capital demands of the transportation infrastructure, and the scarcity was made more serious by the failure of earlier transportation investment to generate a re-investable surplus. To the extent that the staple trades generated a surplus, the capital was usually retained in the trades or the commercial banks, or, as in the case of the Hudson's Bay Company fur trade or in the square-timber industry, repatriated to Britain. In any case, it is pointless to argue that the merchant class lacked entrepreneurial spirit or blocked the flow of capital to industry, when it is readily apparent that the profits, or expected profits, from the staple trades and the transportation infrastructure were sufficient to attract all of the available surplus, and frequently with government guarantees of repayment. This was particularly true in view of the thinness of the Canadian market for most manufactured goods and the inherent instability in a specialized, natural-resource and agricultural economy. The nineteenth-century decline of the Quebec economy towards subsistence no doubt reinforced the thinness of the market. In those manufacturing industries—particularly agricultural machinery, boots and shoes, textiles, bakery and confectionery, and iron and steel—where a larger, more stable market existed, industrial capitalism did flourish, and remained largely under Canadian control.

Naylor argues that a large part of the blame for the techno-logical inferiority of Canadian manufacturing lay in the government's failure to promote vocational-technical education and research because the education system was "commercially dominated", leading to a concentration on classical education.[11] This would seem to ignore the very fundamental point that, as Pentland has pointed out, in the manufactory labour process, technology was in the hands and heads of the artisans, and the process of communicating this knowledge was contained in and controlled by the apprenticeship system. Public insti-tutions for the propagation of technology are the product of the factory system, the age of scientific management, and the rise of the monopoly or large-scale corporation.

All of this points in a single direction. The failure of Canadian industrial capitalism to dominate Canadian manufacturing, which has led to dependence and regression to comprador status, was due to the *relative* retardation of industrial capitalism in Canada *vis-à-vis* the United States, an example of the law of uneven development. The rise of monopoly capitalism in the United States gave that country both a technological superiority and a source of investable surplus against which Canada could not compete. In this regard, the 1879 tariffs were not too great or too small, but rather too late, a defensive reaction to economic change in the republic to the south. What they did do was to prevent de-industrialization of Canada. But, at the same time, they led progressively to the replacement of immature Canadian industrial capital by more mature American industrial capital, which took the form of the multinational corporation.

How can we integrate into this industrial–merchant class analysis of metropolitan interests the kind of regional perspective that Fowke brings to any discussion of the National Policy? First, Fowke makes little distinction between industrial and commercial capital, using rather a simple dichotomy between farmer and business. Translated into class analysis, this is a conflict between a capitalist class and the class of independent commodity producers. In this view, the dispute over the distribution of income is imbedded in the respec-tive position of farmer and business in the price system. The context is the western grain economy, and the relative monopoly power in the grain market. Second, the conflict over the distribution of surplus

---

11. *Ibid.*, p. 57.

had a regional component originating in the primacy of central Canadian banking and railway institutions. Thus in Fowke's interpretation, the early period of the farmers' movement was primarily aimed at curbing the monopoly power of the grain-handling system and of business generally. The farmers, correctly, identified the tariffs as a necessary condition for Canadian monopoly. However, the similarity of their grievances with those of American farmers suggests that repeal of the tariffs would have served only to shift the locus of market power from Canadian capital to American capital. Fowke implicitly recognized this when he argued that Canadian railways were not the alternative to no railways at all, but rather a more expensive alternative to American railways. The argument can likewise be applied to manufactures. In short, the tariffs protected both Canadian commercial and Canadian industrial capital.

In the later period, roughly after the First World War, the farmers' movement shifted the emphasis of its attack from abolishing monopoly in the grain-handling system to the creation of countervailing monopoly power in the form of the pools, a tactic that proved somewhat more successful after the failure of the farmers' movement to pressure government to maintain the short-lived wartime Wheat Board. The relative success of the pools during the 1920s does appear to have dispersed part of the surplus among the primary producers, contributing to a decline in accumulation in Winnipeg. The role of the government was critical. It was willing to intervene to correct grievances that retarded the rapid economic growth of agriculture, but drew the line at any demand that threatened the central institution of commercial-capital control of the grain trade, the grain exchange, and the so-called open market system of grain marketing.

What does this disparate evidence indicate about the nature of the Canadian state in this formative period? The argument made explicitly by Pentland and implicitly by Fowke is that the National Policy represented a coming together of the interests of commercial and industrial capital so that they "spoke with an undivided voice". This did not bode well for either labour, which had supported industrial capital on the tariff issue, or for the farmer. It is possible to argue that of all classes, the farmers were the hardest hit by the emerging system, in that part of the surplus produced by the independent commodity producers, plus their resource rents, were transferred to central Canada through the terms of trade, and to some extent shared with favoured segments of the labouring class in capital's strategy of diffusing class conflict.

Implications for Interpretation

In the staple literature, little or no distinction is made between a staple trade and a staple industry. Yet this is critical in resolving the seeming contradictions between the staple tradition of Innis and the radical critics working from a class perspective. In a staple *trade* the primary producer, usually an independent commodity producer (or, in the contemporary classification, a "dependent contractor"), deals with commercial capital, which in turn develops a number of monopolizing mechanisms of the price system in order to expropriate through unequal exchange the surplus originating from the labour and capital of the primary producer. Historically, the most common of these mechanisms has perhaps been debt peonage: the use of credit to bind a producer to a merchant or financial institution. The monopoly chartered company was another mechanism. In the case of the grain economy, the more significant were the natural monopoly of the railway (augmented, in the case of the Canadian Pacific Railway, by the monopoly clause), the cartel of the grain companies in concert with the Canadian Pacific Railway (the Northwest Line Elevators Association), and the dependency of the trade on enormous supplies of seasonal credit for moving the product, not to mention longer-term credit for mortgages, to finance elevators and terminals.

Individual farmers, of course, did not have access to large-scale credit and it was only with the organization of the farmers' movement, farmer elevator companies, and the pools that any countervailing power could be mobilized. Some success was achieved, particularly with the creation of the Canadian Wheat Board, in the late 1930s (and the wartime period), and with the maintenance of the Crow's Nest Pass grain rates for three decades after the war (for which, incidentally, Fowke deserves a great deal of credit).

These developments did little, of course, to ameliorate the transfer of surplus to industrial capital through the tariff system, or arrest the decline in relative power of commercial capital in Canada as compared with industrial capital, an issue which was conclusively decided politically in the 1911 federal election. The abolition of the Crow rates in the 1980s is likewise an indicator of the declining political power of grain farmers as the dominant stratum within the independent commodity-producer class, and of the farm movement generally.

In any case, the success of unequal exchange in expropriating the production and rent surplus should be reflected in farm income (and that of fishermen, independent loggers, trappers, etc.) approximating that of wage labour. In fact, this generally appears to have been the case.

The staple *industry*, of course, uses the very different mechanism of wage labour. But it is not always clear that surplus extracted from wage labour will necessarily accrue to the industrial capitalist if the industrial capitalist is in an inferior market position *vis-à-vis* financial or commercial capital exporting the staple product. In the instance of timber and sawn lumber, market power was held by commercial capital and although wage labour was extensively employed, the export of squared timber and sawn lumber ("deals") was referred to as a trade rather than as an industry. In contrast, pulp and paper, mining, energy, modern lumber, and hydro are properly staple industries because of the dominance of industrial capital and the absence of an independent merchant class controlling the market. In fact, the commercial and financial functions of export are largely subsumed (by the industrial organization) through vertical integration within these industries. In short, the market is internalized, and industrial and commercial capital are combined.

It is possible to separate commodity production conceptually into four categories: primary independent commodity production destined for an export trade; secondary independent commodity production destined for the local market (petty production); primary industrial production destined for export; and secondary industrial production for the domestic market. The first two rely on independent commodity producers and petty production, and to a greater or lesser extent, commercial capital; the latter two on wage labour and industrial capital. Class conflict between independent commodity producers and commercial capital finds expression in political demands for state regulation of commerce, financial institutions, and transportation; the organization of marketing and purchasing co-operatives and co-operative financial institutions; public- or producer-controlled marketing boards; demands for "easy money" (that is, easy access to circulating capital); the abolition of tariffs; and measures to eliminate monopoly—in fact, the various programmes regularly associated with populist movements whether of the right or left. Class conflict between labour and industrial capital is expressed in industrial conflict and demands by working-class-based political parties for labour standards and for varying degrees of social ownership of industry.

It is thus easy to see why it is possible to interpret the Canada of circa 1870 and after in two very different ways. From the central Canadian perspective, industrial capital, particularly in manufacturing, was emerging as dominant, while from the western viewpoint, commercial capital retained centre stage, except perhaps in a few centres like Winnipeg, where manufacturing was significant, and in the Alberta and Saskatchewan coal fields and British Columbia's mines and forests. It was precisely these areas in the west where class conflict was historically most manifest. (In the Maritime region it was in the mines of Cape Breton that class conflict was centred.)

Nevertheless, the overwhelming dominance of independent commodity production in the Prairie region gives the impression of classlessness, an impression that has heavily influenced scholars in their interpretation of regional social movements, which have tended to emphasize regional grievances and downplay class grievances.

To some extent, of course, the two grievances coincided historically, the grain trade being in a real sense a continuation of the commercial empire of the St. Lawrence, and leading to both class and regional grievances against commercial capital in central Canada. Despite the rise of the new mineral and energy staples, developed under multinational industrial-capital control, however, the classless image is maintained, and plays an important role in legitimizing demands by provinces such as Alberta to share surplus from natural resource rents with industrial capital rather than with the nation at large.

Conclusion

Paralleling the debate over the class basis of the National Policy has been the debate over the relevance of the staple approach to Canadian economic growth in the period after the mid-nineteenth century. Despite several quantitative studies which are remarkably supportive of the staple approach in the twentieth century,[12] the transition to industrialism in central Canada, beginning in the second half of the nineteenth century, seemed to undermine this approach, and with it the unifying theme of Canadian political economy. Staple theory appeared to lose its usefulness in interpreting the eastern Canadian economy at just the time when it became a powerful tool in understanding western Canadian development.

The resurgence of a Marxist-informed political economy in recent years, by contrast, was useful in interpreting developments in central Canada but of little application to the hinterland regions of the country, particularly in the interpretation of regionalism. The major reason was a preoccupation with industrial capital and wage

---

12. See particularly Richard Caves and Richard Holton, *The Canadian Economy* (Cambridge, Mass.: Harvard University Press, 1961); Kenneth Norrie and Michael Percy, "Westward Shift and Interregional Adjustment; A Preliminary Assessment", Economic Council of Canada, Discussion Paper No. 201, May 1981.

labour, to the virtual exclusion of analysis of the position of independent commodity producers and commercial capital. Dependency theory went some way towards providing a more radical version of the staple approach, but without a clear analysis of the class relations and the mechanisms of surplus appropriation.

What is suggested here is that much of the recent debate over the nature of the Canadian state and the relevance of the staple approach after the mid-nineteenth century is not about substance but about perspective, ignoring (a) the importance of relations between independent commodity producers and commercial capital, and the associated mechanisms and regional implications of surplus appropriation, (b) the ambiguity of the tariff as both a class and regional issue, and a misinterpretation of the relation between the tariff and the invasion of American capital, and (c) the distinction between staple *trades* under the control of commercial capital and staple *industries* under the control of industrial capital.

In the National Policy period, 1850 to 1930, Canada was undergoing the transition from merchant to industrial capitalism, from a dependency on staple trades to a dependency on staple industries; while at the same time, industrial capitalism was undergoing the transition from competitive capitalism to monopoly capitalism, where much of the commercial-capital function was absorbed by industrial capital through the mechanism of vertical integration. Only when this is recognized can one hope to reconcile Kealey's contention that Ontario was undergoing capitalist industrialization by the 1870s with Johnson's statement that Canada only became industrialized with the Second World War.[13] Only when this is recognized can one understand the relationship between the regional analysis of Fowke and Spry and the class analysis of Pentland and Ryerson.

---

13. Gregory S. Kealey, *Toronto Workers Respond to Industrial Capitalism* (Toronto: University of Toronto Press, 1980), ch. 2; Leo Johnson, "The Development of Class in Canada in the Twentieth Century", in Teeple, *op. cit.*, p. 171.

3.   The Staple

Debates

John Richards

Simon Fraser University

Early staple writers, most notably W. A. Mackintosh and V. C. Fowke, while highly critical of many policy decisions included in the National Policy, never doubted that staples could be an effective catalyst for economic growth, that appropriate government intervention in resource markets was necessary, and that their task was to excoriate the foolish and advocate the wise among policy options. Yet since 1960 this approach and its politically interventionist policy conclusions have come under attack.

On the left, the "neo-Innisians" have criticized this pragmatic staple tradition for providing an intellectual rationale for alleged distortions of Canadian public policy: an excessive emphasis upon development based on current comparative advantage in staples and closely linked sectors, at the expense of policy to promote a broad range of secondary manufacturing. On the right, neoclassical economists have criticized the staple tradition on two accounts. Most recently, the critique has become a variant of the "tragedy of the commons", the analysis of inefficiencies of resource exploitation that arise under conditions of collective ownership. Earlier, Chambers and Gordon[1] constructed an ingeniously simple general equilibrium model of the prairie wheat boom. In their initial article they concluded that, even at the height of the wheat boom during the decade 1901-1911, it accounted, at a maximum, for only 8.4 per cent of the observed increase in per capita income over the decade. (They have since revised this figure downward.) Despite profound theoretical differences between the neo-Innisians and Chambers-Gordon, they are both arguing that the pre-1960 staple tradition overemphasized the comparative advantage of the Canadian economy in staples over manufactured goods, and that it has always been feasible to divert

---

1. E. J. Chambers and D. F. Gordon, "Primary Products and Economic Growth: An Empirical Measurement", *Journal of Political Economy* LXXIV, no. 4 (1966), 315-32.

capital and labour from the former to the latter, with little or no sacrifice in the long run of aggregate or per capita income.

Although much of the debate has turned around the Canadian
experience during the half-century following Confederation, the
motivation for these staple debates has ultimately been contemporary
rather than historical issues. From the neo-Innisians come conclusions about the need to foster by political means a domestically owned
manufacturing sector, and the debilitating consequences of continued
Canadian reliance upon income from a succession of staples. From
the Chambers-Gordon position come diametrically opposite conclusions. The relatively high per capita incomes achieved in Canada have
depended not on linkages from staples directed by public policy
towards the domestic manufacturing sector, but on certain industries,
among them manufacturing, wherein Canada has achieved international productivity levels. Rather than state intervention to foster
particular sectors, public policy should espouse freer trade, in order
to remove artificial barriers to the mobility of labour and capital into
those sectors in which Canada is at a comparative advantage, and
out of those in which it is not.

Perhaps neither side in this debate has got it right. It will be
argued here that both the left and right underestimate the potential
for improved economic performance from tough-minded public policy,
particularly on the part of provincial governments, designed to increase
the long-run efficiency of resource exploitation. This essay is an exercise in advocacy rather than a comprehensive review. The staples
approach is examined (Innis and Mackintosh, and the "populists"
Fowke and Buckley) and certain aspects are defended against post-1960
critics.

Presumably the reader is familiar with at least some aspect
of the amorphous staple tradition in Canadian economic, historical,
and political writing. For anyone who has inadvertently stumbled onto
this essay in complete ignorance of it, let us at least define "staple
industries". Following Bertram, they are industries "based on agriculture and extractive resources, not requiring elaborate processing and
finding a large portion of their market in international trade."[2]
Bertram extends the concept of staples to include not only industries
within the traditional bounds of the primary sector, but also "primary
manufacturing". By primary (as opposed to secondary) manufacturing
he refers to activities (such as flour milling) in which the value added

---

2. G. W. Bertram, "Economic Growth in Canadian Industry, 1870-1915: The Staple Model",
reprinted in W. T. Easterbrook and M. H. Watkins, eds., *Approaches to Canadian Economic History*
(Toronto: McClelland & Stewart, 1967), p. 75.

by manufacturing is low relative to the value of the staple input, or highly capital-intensive activities (such as the production of simple petrochemicals) upgrading a staple into some standardized intermediate good. By contrast, secondary manufacturing activities (textiles are the classic example) involve more processing of the primary inputs and usually generate more employment per unit of capital invested. These tend to produce finished goods, and typically depend on domestic markets to a larger degree than does primary manufacturing.

The Founders: Innis and Mackintosh

Beginning with the cod fishery in the sixteenth century and continuing to the present, an obvious positive correlation has existed, for most regions within Canada, between the level of income generated by a succession of dominant staples and the level of total regional income. Within the staple tradition there is a useful distinction to make between opposing theoretical responses to this pervasive relationship.[3] The first, which can be traced to Harold Innis, has been one of economic determinism. Independent variables relevant to an explanation of Canadian economic development (or lack thereof) are associated initially with the European, in later years American, metropolis. Innis' disciples have considered business and government élites within Canada to be acting, to a greater or lesser extent, as colonial agents of an imperial power. Within Canada classes and regions have allegedly prospered only to the extent that they responded to the exigencies of the metropolitan economy. As a corollary, those classes in pursuit of economic strategies independent of, or in competition with, metropolitan interests have been systematically frustrated. The following quotation from Innis provides something of the flavour of the analysis, including the idea that the metropolitan power invariably forced the colony to concentrate economic resources upon staple production. Here it remains implicit, but many recent writers have, as we shall see, been quite explicit in stating that the concentration upon staples has prevented the growth of a more diversified and, for Canada, more desirable economic structure:

---

3. The first to make this distinction were Easterbrook and Watkins in the introduction to the aforementioned excellent collection of articles on Canadian economic history. See W. T. Easterbrook and M. H. Watkins, *op. cit.* Included in this collection is Watkins' article "A Staple Theory of Economic Growth", perhaps the most carefully argued attempt at a synthesis of the Innis and Mackintosh positions.

The economic history of Canada has been dominated by the discrepancy between the centre and the margin of western civilization. Energy has been directed toward the exploitation of staple products and the tendency has been cumulative. The raw material supplied to the mother country stimulated manufactures of the finished product and also of the products which were in demand in the colony. Large-scale production of raw materials was encouraged by improvement of technique of production, of marketing, and of transport as well as by improvement in the manufacture of the finished product. As a consequence, energy in the colony was drawn into the production of the staple commodity both directly and indirectly. Population was involved directly in the production of the staple and indirectly in the production of facilities promoting production. Agriculture, industry, transportation, trade, finance, and governmental activities tend to become subordinate to the production of the staple for a more highly specialized manufacturing community.[4]

If the first response within the staple tradition can be identified as economic determinism, the second can be characterized as a variant of export-led growth theory. Here the presence of staple industries has been concluded to be a necessary, albeit far from sufficient, condition for the economic development of the country. W. A. Mackintosh is to this branch what Innis is to the first. Mackintosh concluded categorically in his first article on the subject in 1923:

> The prime requisite of colonial prosperity is the colonial staple. Other factors connected with the staple industry may turn it to advantage or disadvantage, but the staple in itself is the basis of prosperity.[5]

Sixteen years later, in 1939, in his classic economic history of Canada prepared for the Rowell-Sirois Commission (Royal Commission on Dominion-Provincial Relations), Mackintosh remained equally adamant that "rapid progress in . . . new countries is dependent upon the discovery of cheap supplies of raw materials by the export of which to the markets of the world the new country may purchase the products which it cannot produce economically at that stage of its development."[6] Writing at the end of a decade of economic depression whose most severe impact had been in the agricultural economy of the Prairies, no one could be unambiguously sanguine about the consequences of staple-led growth. (During the

---

4. H. A. Innis, *The Fur Trade in Canada: An Introduction to Canadian Economic History* (1930; revised, Toronto: University of Toronto Press, 1956), p. 385.

5. W. A. Mackintosh, "Economic Factors in Canadian History", *Canadian Historical Review* IV (1923), 14.

6. W. A. Mackintosh, *The Economic Background of Dominion-Provincial Relations*, Appendix III of the *Royal Commission Report on Dominion-Provincial Relations*, edited by J. H. Dales (Toronto: McClelland & Stewart, 1964), p. 13.

agricultural boom of the late 1920s per capita personal income in the prairie region marginally exceeded the national average. In 1928, for example, average Saskatchewan and Canadian per capita personal incomes were $465 and $463 respectively. By 1933, with drought abetting the effects of collapse of international trade, Saskatchewan per capita income was $150; the national average was $318. During the decade 1929-1938 Saskatchewan per capita income was, on average, less than fifty per cent of the national figure, which in turn was at depressed levels.)[7] Admitting that "incomes derived from the export of raw materials are notoriously variable", Mackintosh summarized the central problems of any staple-based development as "those that occur when fluctuating incomes are coupled with the rigid expenditures occasioned by heavy debt charges".[8]

Both branches of the staple tradition agreed that in many instances excessive resources were devoted to the expansion of new staple sectors. But whereas the Innisians tended to perceive the problem as a passive adaptation of the Canadian economy to the import requirements of more industrialized economies, the second branch emphasized the quality of decisions impinging on staple sectors taken by private and public agents *within* Canada. For example, if the wheat boom were interpreted as Canada's adaptation to the growing import requirements for cereals on the part of the United Kingdom, then the fundamental solution to the economic trauma of the Depression presumably lay in a diversification of the Canadian economy away from staples that would simultaneously make the economy more autarkic. Conversely, for Mackintosh, the problem lay not *per se* with economic specialization upon staples, but with the irrational past response to the intrinsic uncertainty of such industries. After the appearance of Keynes's *General Theory*, Mackintosh was quick to realize that his version of the staple tradition could be cast in terms of aggregate demand theory. Where Keynes emphasized the instability of investment, Mackintosh was concerned primarily with the instability of export demand for staples.

It is worth recalling that the immediate political crisis which brought the Rowell-Sirois Commission into being in 1937 was the virtual bankruptcy of many provincial treasuries, most noticeably those of the prairie provinces. The specific causes of the distress of the prairie

---

7. All figures are derived from *National Accounts Income and Expenditure 1926-1956*, 13-502 (Ottawa: Statistics Canada, 1962), Table 29, 65. Figures for 1933 are in 1928 dollars, inflated by the GNE price index.

8. Mackintosh, *Economic Background of Dominion-Provincial Relations*, p. 13.

governments were numerous, but underlying virtually all of them were exaggerated expectations with respect to the wheat boom: over-investment in public goods and ill-advised subsidies to railroad construction based on unrealistic expectations of the rate of settle-ment; massive relief payments, exacerbated by earlier federal and provincial encouragement of settlers to extend the grain belt into arid regions whose mean rainfall could not support cereal crops and which, when a few "dry years" succeeded the "good years", were aban-doned to pasture. Mackintosh obviously should not, nor did he, assign irrationally optimistic expectations to provincial politicians alone. Their federal counterparts and private investors were equally guilty; he elaborates, for example, upon the costly second and third transconti-nental railroads, built primarily upon the expectations of uninterrupted prairie growth held by private developers and federal politicians during the height of the boom in the two decades prior to World War I. Both railroads were bankrupted by the first pause in prairie growth, from 1913 to 1915. Throughout Mackintosh's discussion of the problem of uncertainty and unrealized expectations in Canada's staple sectors in the 1930s (British Columbia and the Maritimes were also dispropor-tionately affected by the collapse of their respective staples sectors) is a tension between, on the one hand, his appreciation of the need for aggressive risk-taking and borrowing of foreign capital in order to develop a new industrial economy and, on the other, the need to improve the quality of future economic planning and of future decisions regarding public and private investment:

> . . . rapid development is further dependent on the ability of a new country to borrow capital abroad and to adopt also technical knowledge and equip-ment developed in older countries. Without such borrowings and adop-tions, progress is inevitably reduced to the slow pace of domestic accumu-lation of savings and the development of local inventions . . . . There is, under these circumstances, a strong and natural inclination on the part of a new country to borrow extensively and thus build up heavy debt charges. Since incomes derived from the export of raw materials are notori-ously variable, the economic difficulties in which new countries so frequently find themselves are those that occur when fluctuating incomes are coupled with the rigid expenditures occasioned by heavy debt charges. When, as is so frequently the case, an attempt has been made to cheapen the cost of borrowing by lending the credit or guarantee of the government or by the government itself making the necessary expenditures for improvements, economic difficulties find their reflection immediately in the financial difficulties of government. Pioneers are by necessity and selection sanguine people. They are prone to take over-optimistic views of the effects of such community investment on future income and to assume that government guarantees may be given at no cost.[9]

---

9. *Ibid.*, pp. 13-14.

The Populists: Fowke and Buckley

The tandem of Vernon Fowke and Kenneth Buckley provided in the
1950s one of the most elaborately sketched portraits of export-led Canadian economic history. It remained within the "old" descriptive
economic history. Fowke provided the literary version, Buckley the
statistical accompaniment. In their explanation of Canadian industrialization in the half-century following Confederation, prairie agriculture provided the leading exogenous sector during the crucial two
decades prior to World War I: between the census years 1901 and
1921 fully forty-five per cent of the absolute Canadian population
increase occurred in the Prairies. Both the prairie and aggregate Canadian economies continued to expand rapidly in the decade of the 1920s,
but by then the wheat economy was absorbing a declining proportion of the labour force and investment. The economy had become
more complex as major manufacturing sectors and new staples such
as pulp, paper, and mining assumed prominence. A secular increase
in European demand for cereals, reflected in increases in real grain
prices after the mid-1890s, coincided with a decline in the elasticity
of supply of American agriculture due to the "end of the frontier".
Fowke and Buckley stressed the extent of linkages from the wheat
economy, and the openness of the prairie economy within a national
economy partially closed by the tariff and transportation policies
grandiloquently labelled by Sir John A. Macdonald as the "National
Policy". The all-Canadian railroad system running north of the Great
Lakes assured, at higher unit costs than a route south of the lakes
through Minneapolis, Chicago, and Detroit, that prairie development
could proceed independently of American political or commercial pressures exercised over transportation. The tariff diverted the linkages
of the wheat economy towards the growing industries located primarily
in central Canada. The backward linkages comprised not only the
obvious, such as farm implements and hardware, but much of the
demand for British Columbia lumber. The most important forward
linkage (considering grain at the country elevator as input to the transportation sector) were railroads, and a derived demand therefrom for
iron and steel. Finally, the relatively labour-intensive technology of
homestead farming (at least relative to previous staples such as the
fur trade) provided for considerable final demand linkages to
consumer-goods industries supplying a range of household effects from
furniture to kitchen appliances.

　　To Fowke and Buckley, the wheat boom was necessary to
Canadian industrialization because it alone provided a sustained high
level of demand necessary for the Canadian manufacturing sector to

"take off". Without wheat Canada would have had a much smaller domestic market and, given serious barriers to any new manufacturing exporter, manufacturers could not easily have substituted export for domestic markets; their level of activity would have been seriously curtailed. Since realization of scale economies and "learning by doing" are important aspects of any nation's industrialization process, the absence of the prairie wheat economy would probably have retarded, and rendered more protracted, Canada's industrial "take-off".

Since their writing in the 1950s, economic historians have documented impressive manufacturing growth in decades after 1860, leading to an earlier dating of Canada's industrial "take-off".[10] This evidence lessens, but does not remove, the significance of the wheat boom. The two decades prior to World War I remain the period of most rapid growth in Canadian real output until the 1950s, and the wheat boom was the catalyst for much of it. (We shall defer discussion of the Chambers-Gordon argument that the wheat boom was a sufficient, but not necessary, catalyst.)

The work of Fowke and Buckley can be seen as an attempt at synthesis of the two branches of the staple tradition. In their empirical work they basically lent support to the Mackintosh branch, although they had theoretical doubts that growth in Canadian regions had been staple-based as early as 1820.[11] Seen as describing a region possessing a comparative advantage in primary industry, the second branch of the staple tradition has always been compatible with the conventional economic analysis of individual agents maximizing some objective function subject to constraints. However Fowke, more than Buckley, was very much a "political economist" for whom events also depended upon the outcome of political bargaining undertaken by collective institutions: classes, political parties, regional alliances, etc. Throughout his academic life, he remained sympathetic to the populist sentiment that unequal political power impinged significantly on government regulation of the economic game to the farmer's detriment:

> The inevitability of competition among agricultural producers and consumers because of the atomistic nature of agricultural production and

10. For a good survey of this evidence see R. Pomfret, *The Economic Development of Canada* (Toronto: Methuen, 1981).

11. Buckley argued the need to explain the growth of particular Canadian regions, as early as 1820, in terms other than staples. His article was useful in emphasizing that staple-led growth theory has its limitations, and is most relevant to "new" regions where a newly arrived labour force faces a favourable labour/"land" ratio. However, his attempt at generalization of export-led growth theory proved vacuous. See K. Buckley, "The Role of Staple Industries in Canada's Economic Development", *Journal of Economic History* XVIII (1958), 439-50.

the resultant multiplicity of agricultural producers has been indicated . . . .
The facility with which the rigours of competition may be avoided by the
other parties in markets where farmers buy and sell has also been indicated. The inequality of the bargaining strength of agricultural producers
as compared with that of the groups to whom farmers sell and from whom
they buy is the inevitable complement of freedom of enterprise which accords
equal tolerance to freedom of combination and freedom of competition.
    One of the most significant features of the national policy has
been a persistent disregard of the competitive inferiority of agriculture within
the price system. The major era of the national policy which ended in 1930
witnessed no serious attempt on the part of government to ameliorate or
even to assess that inferiority.[12]

Such a concern with political power was closer to the Innisian view
of staples, but for Fowke the dynamic of unequal power was internal,
not external, to Canada. In his mind, the accumulation of protectionist and *dirigiste* policies aimed at industrialization, first by the colony
of Canada and after 1867 by the Dominion government, were very
much the product of autonomous indigenous business-political élites.
The passive hinterland adapting to this strategy was not Canada as
a whole, but those toiling in the staple-exporting regions without whom
the strategy was doomed to failure.

The Neo-Innisians

Prior to 1960, the staple tradition seemed to be couched in somewhat
parochial academic accents. Admittedly Mackintosh had realized the
affinity of his version to Keynesian aggregate demand theory, and
Innis was an academic of broad vision, who eclectically integrated
many theoretical perspectives. But it was only after 1960 that those
addressing the staple tradition, both from within and without, did
so in contemporary sophisticated academic languages.

    Those inspired by the first tradition, whom we might label
"neo-Innisians", have been unremittingly critical of the "potential
for growth via primary-commodity exports". An increasingly harsh
assessment of the consequences of staples has become their lowest
common denominator. The neo-Innisians are an eclectic group ranging from *dirigiste* planners writing for the Science Council of Canada[13]

---

12. V. C. Fowke, *The National Policy and the Wheat Economy*, (Toronto: University of Toronto
Press, 1957), p. 290.

13. For a sample of the Science Council perspective see J.N.H. Britton and J. M. Gilmour,
The Weakest Link: A Technological Perspective on Canadian Industrial Underdevelopment, Background
Study 43 (Ottawa: Science Council of Canada, 1978).

to academic economic historians. Despite their differences in style, they share an underlying argument about the risk of structural rigidities associated with staple development.

If, for example, the technology of a staple industry is capital-intensive, if it displays important scale economies, and if the quantity of the newly discovered resource input is large relative to domestic savings of a "new" country, then recourse to imported capital becomes highly probable—especially if rapid growth is a high political priority. Many early writers in the staple tradition were wont to view such a process benevolently, as a means of breaking down the parochial nature of colonial society and of integrating the local into the world economy. However, importing foreign capital may pose serious problems. If the nature of the technology relevant to exploitation of a resource is complex, it is naïve to think that the resource owner—in the Canadian context this has usually been the Crown at either the federal or provincial level—will have, at least at the early stages of development, access to knowledge equal to that of potential foreign investors. It is frequently impossible for the Crown to organize truly competitive markets among potential investors for the rights to exploit such resources. Assuming the resource is expected to yield revenue above that required for "normal" returns to labour and capital, we have the Crown, as resource owner, and one or a few foreign firms, as owners of specialized technology, bargaining over the return to their respective property rights. What are, for one party, resource rents rightfully accruing to the Crown are, for the other party, a legitimate return for technological expertise specific to the firm. Typically, the firm fears technological entropy—the communication over time of its technology to competitive firms and to the host government—and therefore seeks long-run contracts before investing in any fixed plant and equipment. Not infrequently, in Canadian history, the Crown has fared poorly in this bargaining process. Furthermore, many of the linked industries, from research functions to resource processing, may be essentially "footloose", in the sense that unit costs are not substantially affected by the decisions to locate near the resource in the host country or near the market in the home country. In such instances it is reasonable to expect the government of the home country to exert pressure on the owners of capital invested abroad to assure they locate linked investment at home.

The existence of a staple sector, whether owned domestically or by foreigners, may engender a "*rentier* ideology" that has a deleterious effect on the potential of the economy to evolve creatively. If "satisficing" (the definition of goals in terms of minimum constraints to be satisfied and not in terms of maximization) is a relevant description of much actual behaviour, then the host government may do no more than procure sufficient rental income from the staple to "satisfice" public expectations for public goods and the politicians' aspirations for bureaucratic growth. A second scenario, based on the corrupting influence of rents, envisions trade unions within the staple sector erecting barriers to entry into the industry and collecting a portion of the rent via wages higher than those prevailing elsewhere for work of comparable skill. The demonstration effect of the small, relatively well-paid work force in the staple sector may provoke attempts to raise wages elsewhere in the economy. If non-staple workers succeed, they presumably (although not necessarily under certain assumptions about differences by class in expenditure patterns) reduce aggregate domestic demand and employment. Furthermore, workers within the staple sector may seek to maintain traditional wage differentials and thereby generate a wage-push inflationary process that adversely affects the balance of payments, and forces recurrent currency devaluations. A third scenario is concerned with the impact of rental income on the domestic business and financial classes, who may develop risk-averse attitudes and be content to re-invest rents, interest, and profits in staples and immediately linked industries. The presence of a relatively certain return on staple-linked investments diverts capital from other (manufacturing) industries in which a less risk-averse, more aggressive entrepreneurial class might otherwise invest.

The neo-Innisians assert that since Confederation any comparative advantage in staple industries over manufacturing has been specific to particular regions, and does not apply to the aggregate economy. The Mackintosh version of the staple tradition emphasized the successful implantation of staple export sectors as a necessary preliminary to linked manufacturing development—staples as necessary, although not sufficient, for future industrialization. For the neo-Innisians, staples are neither necessary nor sufficient for the creation of a fully developed industrial economy. At best, staple-linked development produces a "dependent" industrialization that has a propensity to excessive foreign control of industrial assets, and in which only those sectors closely linked to the staple sectors flourish. The core of the neo-Innisian preferred alternative for development is the re-investment of domestic savings into a manufacturing sector owned by Canadians as opposed to foreigners. Necessary to the alternative is import substitution. Since many domestic manufacturing industries will, initially at least, be at a cost disadvantage relative to offshore competition, they obviously cannot secure significant export markets, and can only secure the domestic market if favoured by a combination of subsidies, public investment, tariffs, and quotas. Ultimately, the neo-Innisian defence of such state intervention is the infant industry argument, the potential to "learn by doing".

One of the most extreme applications of the critique to Canadian experience with staples is Tom Naylor's revisionist history of Canadian economic development from Confederation to World War I. He begins his critique by posing the staples versus secondary manufacturing distinction:

> Two fundamental structural attributes of the Canadian economy in the period from 1867 to 1914 must be made central to analysis. First, it was a colony, politically and economically. In terms of commercial patterns it was a staple-extracting hinterland oriented toward serving metropolitan markets from which, in turn, it received finished goods. In such a structure, any economic advance in the hinterland accrues to the benefit of the metropole and perpetuates the established division of labour, for relative cheapening of the cost of production of staples lowers the cost of production of the finished product in the metropole. Canada's commercial and financial system grew up geared to the international movement of staples, rather than to abetting secondary processing for domestic markets. It was also the recipient of the largest amount of British investment of any country or colony of the period, excluding the U.S.
>
> Canada's social structure, and therefore the proclivities of its entrepreneurial class, reflected and reinforced its innate colonialism. The political and economic élite were men associated with the staple trades, with the international flow of commodities and of the capital that complemented the commodity movements. They were wholesale dealers and bankers in Montreal in particular, and to a lesser extent in Toronto and Halifax.
>
> A second trait of the economy of the period, in part derivative from the first, was that it had only begun to make the difficult transition from a mercantile-agrarian base to an industrial one. Wealth was accumulated in commercial activities and tended to remain locked up in commerce. Funds for industrial capital formation were in short supply. Commercial capital resisted the transformation into industrial capital except under specific conditions in certain industries, in favour of remaining invested in traditional staple-oriented activities.[14]

Naylor's conclusion is that financial and commercial interests, both indigenous and foreign, twisted capital markets in favour of staples (wheat in particular) and immediately-linked industries (railroads, iron and steel, farm implements), and away from the broad range of secondary manufacturing activities required to reduce Canadian dependence on manufactured imports and to generate a more innovative entrepreneurial élite: "The strength of commercial capitalism in Canada was the result of the British colonial connection, and together

---

14. R. T. Naylor, *The History of Canadian Business 1867-1914*, (Toronto: James Lorimer, 1975), I, pp. 3-4.

they served to lock the Canadian economy into the staple trap.''[15] Although American direct investment has replaced British portfolio investment as Canada's dominant external source of finance, the pattern of over-investment in a succession of staples (pulp and paper, minerals, oil, and gas) at the expense of secondary manufacturing has allegedly been repeated throughout the twentieth century. Because of this bias in favour of staples, Canada has developed, such critics conclude, a "dependent" economy.

It should be noted that the neo-Innisians use the word "dependent" in two senses. The mathematical expression $y = f(x,z)$ means simply that y is a dependent variable whose value depends on the values assumed by the independent variables x and z. Obviously, by positing international trade in staples as an exogenous stimulus for development, *all* versions of the staple tradition imply models in which the level of national or regional income is mathematically dependent upon, among other variables, the level of foreign demand for staples. But "dependent" has another related meaning in ordinary language: "determined or conditioned by another, relying on another for support, subject to another's jurisdiction".[16] In the first sense, Canadian national income has been significantly dependent upon exports to other countries. Has there also been dependence in the second sense? This is a different, more complex question, and one must not, as the neo-Innisians are wont to do, obtain an affirmative answer by sleight of hand, by assuming the question refers to the first meaning. Independence in the first sense is meaningless. In any economic theory, whether it posits a country engaging in extensive international trade or in none, national income will be a dependent variable in a set of implicitly or explicitly defined functions, and income levels will be mathematically dependent upon exogenous variables, such as the supply of natural resources, the costs of transport to major markets, etc.

The first non sequitur in the neo-Innisian position is to affirm dependent industrialization as an inevitable, as opposed to a possible, outcome of staple-led development. Only by denying the significance of the wheat boom can one conclude that Canadian industrial development prior to World War I was seriously distorted. A great deal of manufacturing investment occurred,[17] and the evidence of central Canadian merchant opposition to industrial diversification, where

15. *Ibid.*, II, p. 283.

16. *Webster's New Collegiate Dictionary*, 1977.

17. Bertram, *op. cit.*

profitable, remains dubious.[18] In the case of the mineral resource development in the Canadian Prairies after World War II, the first generation of political and indigenous business leaders responded in a manner to warrant a charge of "dependence". But, as Larry Pratt and the author have argued in *Prairie Capitalism*,[19] the passive *"rentier* ideology" of the first generation has not persisted. The post-1970 regional business and political élites have mustered the requisite political power, technical expertise, and financial independence to bargain effectively with external corporations over the region's future economic development.

The second non sequitur is to infer that the alternative, of indigenously owned manufacturing and import substitution, will be exempt from problems analogous to those attributed to staple-led growth. Despite examples of successful autarkic development, that of the Soviet Union being the most important, the economic literature is replete with case studies to demonstrate the failure of many national development strategies—pursued by governments of the left and right—heavily biased towards secondary manufacturing and economic autarky. A *"rentier* ideology", analogous to that potentially circumscribing staple development, may arise in a manufacturing sector operating behind protective barriers. Both capitalists and workers within such a sector may display an inertia debilitating to the overall economy, while capturing a disproportionate share of investment funds, skilled labour, and entrepreneurship.

In summary, the value of the neo-Innisian contribution has lain not in the blanket condemnation of staple development, but in its pursuit of one of Mackintosh's themes—the social determinants of entrepreneurial decisions. Consider the problem of optimal investment in staple sectors characterized by much uncertainty in supply and/or demand. In repeated instances private and public agents have initially made large fixed-capital investments justifiable only by extrapolating the most optimistic growth rate of a boom. When expectations have not been realized, investment has collapsed for an extended period. Why have such seemingly irrational investment cycles been a prominent feature of staple industries? Mackintosh offered an explanation in terms of social psychology (namely, the passage cited above) that is reminiscent of Keynes.

---

18. L. R. MacDonald, "Merchants Against Industry: An Idea and its Origins", *Canadian Historical Review* LVI, no. 3 (1975), 263-81.

19. J. Richards and L. Pratt, *Prairie Capitalism: Power and Influence in the New West* (Toronto: McClelland & Stewart, 1979).

With a nice touch of irony, Keynes concluded that we form expectations about the future via three techniques:

> 1) We assume that the present is a much more serviceable guide to the future than a candid examination of past experience would show it to have been hitherto . . . . 2) We assume that the existing state of opinion as expressed in prices and the character of existing output is based on a correct summing up of future prospects . . . . 3) Knowing that our own individual judgment is worthless, we endeavor to fall back on the judgment of the rest of the world which is perhaps better informed.[20]

To the extent that individuals adopt such ad hoc techniques they are abdicating responsibility to conduct an independent assessment of the underlying deterministic and stochastic forces at play in the economy.

The Mackintosh tradition was content to leave the analysis at the level of social psychology; the neo-Innisians have, I think correctly, emphasized the deleterious structural impact of foreign investment, particularly direct investment, on the potential of domestic agents to improve their expectations formation and their ability to undertake entrepreneurial decisions. Admittedly, in certain cases, for example the post-Leduc western Canadian petroleum industry, the large foreign investors initially displayed far more sophisticated long-run profit-maximizing strategies than their smaller Canadian-owned competitors. Had such Canadian firms dominated the petroleum industry and provincial regulatory policy, there would probably have been more premature investment and shut-in capacity than did in fact occur. The problem is one of "learning by doing". Reliance on foreign direct-equity capital almost inevitably retards the process whereby domestic private investors and public authorities learn the intricacies of the technology and markets relevant to an industry. *Ceteris paribus*, the greater the technological complexity of the industry, the longer the delay.

Despite attempts by governments as resource owners to organize competitive markets for the alienation of their property rights over resources, such markets frequently degenerate into essentially bilateral negotiations between a few foreign corporations possessing superior technology on the one side, and governments on the other. By the second generation, technical knowledge may become diffused among indigenous business and political leaders, but the presence of foreign-based multinational firms, with their external lines of command and communication, usually retards the process.

---

20. J. M. Keynes, "The General Theory of Employment", *Quarterly Journal of Economics* LI (1937), 214.

The Neoclassical Critique: Chambers-Gordon

Let us turn now to the counterfactual exercise proposed by Chambers-Gordon: "[W]hat would have happened if all the [prairie] land that was brought under cultivation between 1901 and 1911 had been impenetrable rock?"[21] By way of answer, they construct a simple general equilibrium model of the pre–World War I Canadian economy, and then conduct an exercise in comparative statics—contracting the supply of the resource input, land, necessary for wheat production.

Chambers-Gordon represent the economy via three competitive industries: an export staple (wheat), a manufactured good (gadgets) of which Canada is an importer, and a manufactured good (haircuts) which, due to tariffs and/or the natural protection afforded by transport costs, is supplied uniquely by domestic producers. Chambers-Gordon allow for only two factors of production: homogeneous labour, required in all three sectors, and land, the resource input for wheat. Constant returns to scale are assumed for all three sectors. This implies constant average (and marginal) labour productivity in gadgets and haircuts, and declining marginal productivity of labour and land in wheat production. The inclusion in all three production functions of a neoclassical capital good available at a fixed world-rental price leaves unchanged the central Chambers-Gordon results: (1) the wage level is determined by labour productivity in the gadget sector independently of activity in any other sector, and (2) provided all capital is imported, and hence all payments to capital exported, the loss to Canadian residents of a decrease in prairie land is solely the decrease in land rent, which in turn will be proportional to the decrease in land.

Competition implies the equalization of wage rates across sectors as workers migrate to maximize income. In the case of farming, tenant farmers earn the prevailing wage, but the income of homesteaders must be analytically divided into two components: the wage income they could earn in alternative employment; and rent, the residual.

The demand for wheat is assumed, quite reasonably, to be infinitely elastic at the prevailing Liverpool price. A much more dubious assumption is that, over the relevant range, the demand for gadgets is also infinitely elastic at the protected price equal to a fixed world price plus the Canadian tariff. The domestic demand for gadgets is normal—partial derivatives with respect to national income and gadget

---

21. Chambers and Gordon, *op. cit.*, p. 317.

prices being positive and negative respectively. An infinitely elastic supply of imported gadgets at the protected price effectively establishes the protected price as a fixed parameter. This assumption trivializes the problem of generating a market demand for Canadian manufactured goods. It implies the ability to increase domestic gadget production and displace imports without incurring a deterioration of comparative advantage; it implies further that, over the relevant range for the counterfactual exercise, Canada remains a net importer of gadgets. The demand for haircuts is likewise a normal function of national income and the price of haircuts, with appropriately signed partial derivatives. In this sector all supply is domestically produced.

Aggregate labour supply to the Canadian economy is an increasing function of the real wage rate (measured with wheat as *numeraire*). The labour force is fully employed in the three sectors. National income accrues either to the producers of wheat, gadgets, and haircuts or, in the case of tariff revenue from imported gadgets, to government.

Much of the solution flows sequentially from the assumption of an infinitely elastic demand for gadgets and its implication that the domestic gadget price (relative to that for wheat) is a fixed parameter. Now, the gadget price, multiplied by the average productivity of gadget makers, sets the prevailing wage in the economy. Given competition, haircut prices will exactly equal cost. Cost here is the going wage. Thus, knowing average labour productivity in this sector, we can determine haircut prices. With the wage rate and both relative prices set, the real wage and hence aggregate labour supply to the Canadian economy are determined. Note that this model determines a good deal about the economy—relative prices, wage rate, and aggregate employment—without any reference to the staple sector.

In the wheat sector, labour is combined with the available land in a proportion such that, in equilibrium, the productivity of additional homesteaders equals that of gadget makers and barbers. The number of farmers and level of wheat production will vary directly with the quantity of land available, and inversely with the prevailing wage.

The counterfactual exercise of reducing the quantity of available land is a good deal simpler to analyze than the foregoing might suggest. Given the fixed protected gadget price and constant returns to scale in the gadget sector, the prevailing wage cannot vary. Haircut prices will also be unchanged. With no change in either wage rate or relative prices, aggregate labour supply remains unchanged. Equilibrium income must fall, however, and this for two reasons: (1) a decline in rental income from prairie land, and (2) tariff revenue lost as the domestic gadget sector expands to absorb displaced farmers and barbers. Employment of barbers declines somewhat in the face of the decline in national income.

Empirically the only important effect on national income is the decline in rental income. After discounting the effect of increased productivity in the gadget and haircut sectors during the decade 1901-1911, Chambers-Gordon conclude that rent lost due to the counter-factual exercise of transforming the Prairies into impenetrable rock reduced the increase in per capita income by 8.4 per cent at most. That is an upper limit, because it assumes no immigration occurred in the expectation of agricultural rents. Presumably some people did migrate for such reasons, and therefore the actual effect of the wheat boom on the increase in per capita income must have been less than 8.4 per cent.

The two important conclusions from this model are: (1) for a "small country" possessing both a primary export and a manufacturing sector subject to net imports the wage level is a function of manufacturing productivity alone, and is entirely independent of the resource endowment, and (2) ignoring the small tariff-revenue effect, the benefit derived from a natural resource endowment is the rent generated which, empirically, is likely to be small relative to other factors affecting growth of per capita income.

Chambers-Gordon performed a valuable service in establishing a new level of rigour for further contributions to the staple tradition. However, the two central conclusions are the product of a particular set of assumptions and do not hold generally. Although his analytic treatment was flawed, Lewis[22] emphasized perhaps the most serious analytic weakness of the Chambers-Gordon model, namely, its trivialization of the demand-side analysis. The model adopts the "small country" assumption of international trade theory, that Canada faced an infinitely elastic demand at fixed international prices (plus the tariff where relevant) for the commodities it bought and sold. The "small country" assumption is reasonable for wheat, a homogeneous commodity of which many industrial countries of Europe, Britain in particular, had become net importers. Both industrial labour and capital within these countries had an obvious interest in assuring free trade in cereals, and welcomed new sources of supply, such as Australia, Argentina, and Canada. Turning to gadgets, we might reasonably make the small-country assumption so long as Canada remained,

22. F. Lewis, "The Canadian Wheat Boom and Per Capita Income: New Estimates", *Journal of Political Economy* LXXXIII, no. 6 (1975), 1249-57.

under the counterfactual exercise, an importer of gadgets. Even here there is a problem. By assuming a single homogeneous gadget sector Chambers-Gordon ignore the fact that Canada's comparative advantage in the manufacturing of different gadgets must have varied, and therefore the process of substitution of domestically produced for imported gadgets would have required a lowering of factor rewards and/or additional protection were it to have been extensively undertaken.

In the absence of prairie land, however, Canada would probably have become a net exporter of gadgets. Such is more or less implied by the neo-Innisians, had "industrial" capitalists dominated "merchant" capitalists, had Canada not fallen into endless "staple traps", and had it resisted foreign ownership. International markets for manufactured goods are less competitive than those for homogeneous primary commodities. Barriers to new entrants abound, and the export demand for Canadian gadgets should not be presumed to be infinitely elastic at some well-established international gadget price.

With a finite export demand for gadgets the relative prices of finished goods can vary. The hypothetical exercise of reducing available prairie land now results in complex shifts in the supply of, and demand for, labour in the various sectors. In general, the number of farmers declines; some displaced farmers are absorbed into the manufacture of gadgets, but this sector can expand only by a lowering of Canadian gadget prices and the prevailing wage (always measured in terms of the amount of wheat a gadget-maker can purchase). To the extent that gadgets are produced and consumed within Canada, a decline in gadget prices merely redistributes income from Canadian gadget-makers to Canadian consumers; to the extent that gadgets are exported, the benefits of the price decline are shared with the rest of the world. If the importers of Canadian gadgets are poorer than Canadians, which is quite probable, the decline marginally improves international income equality. More realistically, if less altruistically, the benefits of the wheat boom should be restricted to their impact on changes induced in per capita domestic consumption.

The constant relative price before and after the Chambers-Gordon counterfactual exercise generates no price effects. In the more general case, per capita consumption declines for three reasons: (1) as before, lost agricultural rent; (2) a decline in average output per farmer resulting from the wage decline which, in turn, lowers the opportunity cost of homestead labour and induces substitution of labour for land in wheat production (this effect will be more important the larger the elasticity of substitution of labour for land in wheat production); and (3) a negative terms-of-trade effect arising from the decline in the price of Canadian gadget exports relative to that of wheat imports. The central point of all this is that, in a more realistic model, no longer does the gadget sector dictate the wage rate independently of the level of activity in the staple sector.

The significance for policy debates of Chambers-Gordon's two fundamental conclusions—that the wage level depends entirely on productivity in the manufacturing sector and not at all on any resource sector present, and that natural resource rents are, except in a few cases such as oil, empirically insignificant—extends well beyond the arcane inquiry into the significance of the prairie wheat boom prior to World War I. The conclusions have been enthusiastically taken up by, among others, the Economic Council of Canada. In a 1979 Economic Council study on regional income inequalities in Canada, Copithorne concluded that only in exceptional cases have resources mattered:

> . . . we believe it is important to illustrate some of the theory and evidence that cause us to doubt the importance of natural resources in the whole regional disparities picture . . . . As long as the natural resources relative to population theories of regional disparities hold sway, there is an obvious danger that public policy will tend to concentrate on natural resource activity and migration to the exclusion of policies aimed at raising productivity (in non-primary sectors).[23]

Copithorne's theoretical basis is Chambers-Gordon. He insists, "We must take seriously one of the conclusions of this theory, namely, that a region's general wage level is determined in its non-primary trading sectors [namely, gadgets], quite independently of the size and quality of its natural resource endowment."[24] Further, Copithorne states his scepticism of the potential for any Canadian government to realize substantial rents from any resource it owns. Were a government to nationalize a resource industry and attempt to increase rents by a reduction of output and increase in price, the high elasticity of supply by producers beyond the government's jurisdiction would frustrate the exercise. "That is why", he concludes, "nationalization of Canada's potash, nickel and asbestos deposits would likely yield disappointing rent collections."[25]

Copithorne is patently wrong in this conclusion. By nationalization of one-half capacity and by new taxes, the Saskatchewan

---

23. L. Copithorne, *Natural Resources and Regional Disparities* (Ottawa: Economic Council of Canada, 1979), pp. 6-7.

24. *Ibid.*, p. 13.

25. *Ibid.*, p. 46.

government increased, between 1973 and 1978, the level of provincial government rental income from potash by a factor of ten. Under the New Democratic Party, the management of the provincial Crown corporation pursued long-run rent maximization in a more systematic manner than had private firms. Accession to office in 1982 of a Conservative government hostile to public entrepreneurship has unfortunately curtailed the Crown corporation's role. In Manitoba the provincial New Democratic Party is slowly gaining the requisite expertise to significantly increase provincial income from its nickel industry.

The Neoclassical Critique: The Tragedy of the Commons

The "tragedy of the commons" property-rights argument has inspired a second line of neoclassical attack on the tradition of staples-as-catalyst-for-growth. The basic argument here is that, for optimum development of a resource, some private agent must exercise over it the full set of property rights. "Optimum" in this context means management of a resource so as to maximize the sum, appropriately discounted, of the stream of annual net income generated. The essence of private property rights over an asset is the residual right to do with it anything not explicitly prohibited by law. In addition, it entails two rights: *exclusivity*, the right to exclude others from benefits arising from exploitation of the resource, and the corresponding obligation to bear the costs attendant upon development; and *transferability*, the right to buy and sell property in a market. Exclusivity is required if property owners are to internalize all costs and benefits associated with resource exploitation. Only with exclusivity will a resource owner seek to maximize the discounted present value of potential income. Why incur the cost of reforestation, for example, if you cannot exclude others from cutting the trees when mature? Transferability permits those who can make more efficient use of a resource to obtain the property rights to it by outbidding the less efficient.

Arguing in this vein, Southey[26] has elaborated a model in which the open-access nature of homesteading dissipates all prairie agricultural rent. Once off the boat in Montreal, the pre–World War I immigrant faced essentially two options—homesteading out West or gadget-making in central Canada. For nominal sums the Dominion government granted titles to homesteads on a "first-come-first-served"

---

26. C. Southey, "The Staple Thesis, Common Property, and Homesteading", *Canadian Journal of Economics* XI, no. 3 (1978), 547-59.

basis, subject to regulations that the homesteader reside on and break in his land. Labour mobility between the two sectors was large, sufficient to push the agricultural frontier out to the point where the discounted present value of expected net income from homesteading should equal that from working as a gadget-maker. In other words, open access reduces the present value of agricultural rent, that income above the opportunity cost of wage income, to zero. In equilibrium, the expected rental income on a homestead, as a function of time, should be initially negative (due to the remoteness from a railroad terminal among other reasons), but rise to become positive at some future date. Dominion regulations forced land-breaking and farming to occur almost immediately; a homesteader could not hold on to his land awaiting the optimum time, in terms of maximizing the discounted present value of rent, to begin farming. Optimally, the homesteader would "speculate" by waiting until rent on his land became positive. More specifically, the optimum time arises when the present value of rental income lost by delay in farming equals the gain, by delay, in lowering the present value of the cost of breaking the land.

In Southey's terms, land-subsidized railroad construction was just homesteading on a massive scale, in which railroad promoters competed among each other to advance the date of construction and settlement in a given region until all potential rent was dissipated. Gordon, in a commentary on the debate initiated by his original joint article, has suggested that Dominion propaganda designed to spur western settlement may have succeeded, in the short run, in creating inflated expectations which advanced the settlement date of any particular region and may have made actual aggregate rent negative.[27]

Norrie and Percy[28] provide a second good example of this "tragedy of the commons" critique. Like Chambers-Gordon, Norrie and Percy are interested in assessing the impact on per capita income of a boom in a staple sector, after allowing for adjustment in a general equilibrium model. Here the staple is oil and natural gas in contemporary Alberta. The counterfactual determines the effect on a number of summary statistics (such as per capita Alberta Gross Domestic Product [GDP]) arising from a one per cent energy price rise. Under the base case ("classic staple boom"), private agents own the reserves

27. D. F. Gordon, "A Further Note on Export-Led Growth", unpublished (1978).

28. K. H. Norrie and M. B. Percy, "Province-Building and Industrial Structure in a Small Open Economy", paper prepared for the Second John Deutsch Roundtable on Economic Policy, "Economic Adjustment and Public Policy in Canada", Queen's University, Kingston, Ontario, November 1982.

and capture all incremental rent. In the long run, allowing inter-regional migration of labour and capital, their model predicts a per capita Alberta GDP rise of .11 per cent.

Norrie and Percy then consider three options for provincial government interventions: (1) fiscally induced migration—government captures resource rent, taxes capital, and disburses the revenue via a fiscal dividend to all residents, regardless of length of residence; (2) expansion of public-sector output—government captures resource rent, taxes capital, and uses this revenue to finance expansion of public-sector output; (3) same as second option, but government also insulates provincial primary manufacturing sector from energy price rise. Under these options a one per cent energy price rise induces, in the long run, changes in Alberta per capita real GDP ranging from zero to minus .05 per cent. By extracting the incremental rent from private owners of energy reserves, the provincial government obtains the revenue to permit "province-building". By a combination of distortions of factor prices and direct purchase of public-sector output, the government expands, relative to the classic staple boom, the size of the provincial economy. But government intervention, facilitated by collective ownership of oil and gas reserves, introduces a degree of "tragedy of the commons". Under any of the three options for government intervention national income is below that in the classic staple boom.

Why are rent-dissipating strategies pursued? Norrie and Percy offer an explanation in terms of the classic public choice argument, "concentrated benefits, diffuse costs":

> There are probably two basic reasons why these province-building strategies are pursued politically despite the fact that they reduce real incomes below those potentially available. The first is that the owners of immobile factors, particularly urban land, tend to benefit from the extensive growth such strategies generate. It is argued by Richards and Pratt that this group, for example, forms the nucleus of support for such development strategies. As we have argued elsewhere, the distributional consequences of province-building strategies are very similar to those of tariff protection. The benefits are disproportionately captured by a small group, giving them the incentive to lobby for their implementation and maintenance. The costs, in the form of allocative inefficiencies, are too diffuse to elicit much active opposition. Becuse of this, much of the economic rent produced by the western energy boom ends up dissipated through resource inefficiencies and excessive immigration. The second reason is that province-building is a form of economic nationalism and as Johnson argues, the latter often manifests itself as a desire for an indigenous manufacturing activity regardless of cost. Thus the apparent cost of province-building strategies represents the price which residents are willing to pay for the status that they associate with increased industrialization.[29]

29. *Ibid.*, pp. 55-56.

The policy conclusions of the "tragedy of the commons" line of argument are unremittingly conservative: political agents should restrict themselves to working out the intricacies of "privatization"— the definition of a set of transferable private property rights that permit private agents to internalize all costs and benefits arising from their decisions with respect to resource exploitation.

Implicit in the neoclassical critique is the assumption (to which we shall return) that private economic agents base their decisions on "rational expectations" about the future, rational in the sense that they are formed from agents independently utilizing all available information about future outcomes. It follows logically that, if political agents seek to maximize the same objective function as their private counterparts (for example, the expected present value of discounted net income from a resource), if they both have access to the same information about future outcomes, and if they include the same costs and benefits in their respective calculations, then, on average, political agents cannot increase the net income realized relative to that generated by private agents.

Furthermore, political agents face unbalanced lobbying, the result of which is to bias their decisions in such a manner as to lower aggregate net income. This last argument, a cornerstone of public-choice economics, is based on two intuitively appealing ideas: (1) for an interest group to achieve any given level of political influence, the cost of effective political participation/lobbying by that interest group rises with the number of people to be co-ordinated, and (2) the benefits (and costs) of any particular public policy are unequally distributed, typically considerably benefiting a few at the expense of impoverishing many by a small amount each. Provided that per capita benefits exceed the per capita costs of effective lobbying, the group of potential gainers will accept such costs. If the per capita losses of the remainder are less than the per capita costs of effective counter-lobbying, this group will "apathetically" do nothing. If, as is quite likely, the sum of the small per capita losses exceeds the sum of the large per capita benefits, public policy under the influence of lobbying must reduce aggregate income relative to a laissez-faire market outcome.

How should one respond to the "tragedy of the commons" line of attack? To begin, it is churlish to deny that public-choice economics—the general world view into which this line of argument fits—provides an accurate generalization of much that goes on in the sub-optimal world of *realpolitik*. By their disabused conclusions that public policy favours the well-organized interest group at the expense of the rest of us, public-choice economists display, ironically, an affinity with many Marxists. Here one can consider the latter a special case of the former, the difference being that Marxists conclude that owners of capital constitute the only effective lobby. Among both is a suspicion of pluralist democratic political institutions. The one displays an obsessive desire to blame government intervention as the source of all market imperfections; the other, an unbridled faith in the ability and willingness of planners in a revolutionary one-party state to increase the efficiency of an economy and to redistribute its fruits equitably.

Within a society of democratic political institutions and free markets there remains merit in public intervention, up to and including the level of nationalization. The rationale exists on grounds of both distribution and efficiency. First, distribution.

A high level of income equality is a necessary prerequisite to a successful democracy, and conversely democracies provide instruments whereby adversely affected groups can thwart market outcomes that rapidly and significantly redistribute income, especially if the redistribution increases the inequality of overall distribution. One should qualify this by asking, how much equality is a prerequisite? To what extent do democracies in the long run thereby thwart economic efficiency? But if one values democracy, one must be prepared to support many redistributive interventions. No one should be surprised that, to cite an obvious recent example, provincial and federal governments unilaterally violated contracts with resource firms on maximum royalties, redrafted tax laws, and even nationalized resource assets in order to capture for the public sector much of the incremental revenue arising from the early 1970s rise in the price of resources, of oil in particular. The potential income redistribution in favour of shareholders of resource companies would have been, in the absence of new taxes and royalties, too inequitable for a democracy to tolerate. Despite serious imperfections in the political redistributive mechanism, the value of this redistribution has been far greater than the costs of economic inefficiencies it created.

In many instances of Canadian resource development, one firm, or a cartel of firms, possesses the requisite engineering and geological expertise. Were ownership of the resource widely distributed among unco-ordinated individuals, the resource cartel could organize a market for development rights in which, as sole purchaser, it extracted most of the potential rent. Owners of the resource could improve their bargaining power by co-ordinating their actions, making one joint offer to the potential developer. Admittedly imperfectly, Crown ownership of resource-development rights has served that function, transforming the market into an approximation of bilateral monopoly. In bargaining with private developers over resource-rent distribution, the ultimate threat of the Crown as owner of a resource must be to develop it on its own account by means of a Crown corporation. Subject to a number of caveats, it may be desirable for the Crown, as opposed to a private firm, to develop a resource, even if the Crown is less efficient. The caveats are those required to assure the equity gains from public resource development outweigh any efficiency losses. Implicit here is the premise that increased equity of income distribution will be desirable, that the citizens of the resource-owning jurisdiction will be on average poorer than the shareholders of the resource firm, and that the provincial government will distribute resource rent equitably among its citizens. If the government, as resource owner, accepts privatization as the limit of its options, it may well find that whatever the set of private resource rights it devises, it can capture for the provincial citizens only a small part of rent. By ideologically proscribing public entrepreneurship as an option governments must, on balance, lessen their ability to capture rent for redistribution.

Second, efficiency. Surely Mackintosh and Keynes's theories of ''irrational expectations'' remain relevant, particularly in resource industries. Private entrepreneurs and politicians continue to form expectations about future trends in prices and quantities on the basis of group-dynamic processes wherever uncertainty looms large enough to prevent delineation of a transparently optimal strategy.[30] In such contexts, the specification of what constitutes an optimal income-maximizing decision is too complex and costly, and agents resort to group-sanctioned conventions. These conventions range from the ''gut feel'' among farmers about next year's wheat prices to the choices computer modellers make of the year 2000 energy price to include in discounted cash flow exercises.

There is no guarantee that government planners will do better in choice of conventions than their private counterparts. But, in the Canadian context, governments have frequently devoted considerable energy to long-term resource planning. Why restrict the search for better income-maximizing strategies to the private corporate sector? One neoclassical reply is to argue by analogy to evolutionary theory. Superior biological mutants do not need to be consciously aware of their superior adaptability in order to replace inferior members of their species. Similarly, firms with superior planning ability will be

---

30. This discussion derives in part from Simon's ideas on ''bounded rationality''. See, for example, H. A. Simon, ''Rational Decision Making in Business Organizations'', *American Economic Review* XLIX, no. 4 (September 1979), 493-513.

more profitable than those of inferior ability, and will come to dominate their respective industries even if their managers cannot articu-
late in what respect their entrepreneurship is superior. However, in
resource sectors in particular, the required fixed investments are
frequently massive, and to rely on "weeding out" poor entrepreneurs
by market selection takes an unacceptably long period and generates
large external costs borne by those who have made linked investments
in physical and human capital.

"Privatization" is an inelegant neologism referring to government policy intended to increase economic efficiency by defining an
appropriate set of transferable private property rights for assets
currently owned collectively by the state. We need to analyze more
carefully "publicization", an even more inelegant neologism referring to the institutional arrangements conducive to efficient public
intervention.

In conclusion a few ad hoc observations on the theme of
"publicization" are offered:

(1) The costs of gathering all relevant information about the
geology, technology of production, transportation, financing, and
marketing of most resources is high. The smaller the population of
the intervening jurisdiction the larger the per capita cost of financing
information acquisition, and the more likely it is that the government
will scrimp on such costs. Another reason for scrimping is the difficulty
of evaluation of the productivity of additional investment in
information.

(2) The first observation implies that the efficiency of government intervention increases the larger the jurisdiction's population.
An important offsetting factor is that the per capita costs of sub-optimal
public policy are larger the smaller the political jurisdiction. The larger
the per capita stake, the more insistent will citizens be that government pursue income-maximizing resource policy. An implication of
the first and second observations is that the Canadian constitutional
practice, whereby provincial governments undertake most resource
planning, is probably more efficient than one in which public resource
planning either devolved to local government or became centralized
in the national government. The unequal per capita distribution of
resource revenues across provinces leads Canadians into obvious problems of equalization of government resource revenues. Complete
equalization, however, destroys the incentive of larger per capita
benefits as inducement to generate income-maximizing public policy.

(3) If the benefits of income-maximizing resource policy are
transferred to the voter in a transparent manner, he/she will more

directly experience the cost of blatantly sub-optimal policy, and be more likely to oppose it.

(4) If the probability is high that citizens of the resource-owning jurisdiction must migrate beyond it, and if, as will usually be the case, they can only establish their per capita claim to resource income by remaining a resident of the jurisdiction, they will heavily discount potential future resource income. High mobility will tend to bias citizen preferences towards short-run returns, which may well result in sub-optimal policy.

(5) There is no escape from Montesquieu's conclusion, that democracy is the most demanding form of government in that it requires "virtue" from its citizens. A necessary, if far from sufficient, condition for optimal resource policy is that citizens invest in the care and maintenance of "populist" political parties capable of aggregating the general interest in income-maximizing policy, and of resisting the temptations to yield to "vested interests".

4.   Harold Innis

Staples, Communications, and the Economics of Capacity, Overhead Costs, Rigidity, and Bias

Ian Parker
University of Toronto

Innis: just supply and demand.
Robert Mundell[1]

Harold Innis was the greatest economic theorist I ever knew.
Harry Johnson[2]

Our study of overhead cost will be largely a study of unused powers of production.
J. M. Clark[3]

We seem destined in economics to follow the meteorologist in modifying equilibrium analysis and turning to what he has called the polar front theory in which the meeting of economic masses becomes important rather than trade between nations. There are serious weaknesses in the analogy of flowing from high to low pressure areas, and great advantages in discussing pressure groups. The economics of losses is not less significant than the economics of profits.
Harold Innis[4]

With the bias of an economist I may have extended the theory of monopoly to undue limits, but it is a part of the task of the social scientist to test the limits of his tools and to indicate their possibilities, particularly at a period when he is tempted to discard them entirely. Similarly an extension of cyclical theory may seem to have been carried too far but the neglect of the field of communication in studies of cycles warranted a consideration of the extent to which monopolies of knowledge

---

1. Oral communication to author, American Economic Association meetings, Toronto, December 29, 1972.

2. Oral communication to author, Yale University, February 1973.

3. J. M. Clark, *Studies in the Economics of Overhead Costs* (Chicago: University of Chicago Press, 1962), p. 1.

4. Harold Innis, *Essays in Canadian Economic History* (Toronto: University of Toronto Press, 1956), p. 272.

> collapse and extraneous material is lost, to be followed by the prospect of an emphasis on a fresh medium of communication and on a fresh approach.
>
> Harold Innis[5]

At the outset in *Empire and Communications*, Harold Innis noted, regarding the analytical strategy of that work, that "we have been concerned with the use of certain tools that have proved effective in the interpretation of the economic history of Canada and the British Empire."[6] In so remarking, Innis affirmed his belief that there existed an *analytical* continuity between his earlier works in Canadian economic history (the so-called "staples" studies) and his later studies of the role of communications in the historical development of empires in Western civilization. In the passage from the preface to *The Bias of Communication* quoted above, Innis explicitly noted his extensions of the theory of monopoly and of cyclical theory in discussing the analytical foundations of his economic-historical study of communications. In a parallel vein, Robin Neill, in the concluding sentence of his study of Innis, has suggested that "Quite probably some important aspects of the communications studies will continue to be misunderstood by those who have no knowledge of their roots in the nature and problems of price theory."[7]

The purpose of the present essay, in this context and in relation to Innis' one-time student Harry Johnson's judgement, is to consider Innis' later communications studies as contributions to economic or political-economic theory, with particular reference to the role of the cluster of concepts centred on Innis' generalizations of the theory of capacity and overhead costs in his interpretation of the bias of communication in the historical process. The most important work done to date in systematically elucidating and extending Innis' wide-ranging use of the capacity and overhead-cost concepts in relation to *Canadian* economic history is contained in a series of papers by Irene Spry.[8] In a very real sense, this essay represents an

---

5. Harold Innis, *The Bias of Communication* (Toronto: University of Toronto Press, 1964), p. xvii.

6. Harold Innis, *Empire and Communications* (Toronto: University of Toronto Press, 1972), p. 6.

7. Robin Neill, *A New Theory of Value: The Canadian Economics of H. A. Innis* (Toronto: University of Toronto Press, 1972), p. 125.

8. See in particular her "Overhead Costs, Time Problems, and Prices", in H. A. Innis (editor), *Essays in Political Economy in Honour of E. J. Urwick* (Toronto: University of Toronto Press, 1938), pp. 11-26; "Innis, the Fur Trade and Modern Economic Problems", in Carol M. Judd and Arthur J. Ray (editors), *Old Trails and New Directions* (Toronto: University of Toronto Press, 1980); "The Role of Staple Exports in Canada's Economic Development" (mimeo, December 1979); and "Overhead Costs, Rigidities of Productive Capacity and the Price System", in W. H. Melody, L. Salter and P. Heyer (editors), *Culture, Communication and Dependency: The Tradition of H. A. Innis* (Norwood, N.J.: Ablex, 1981), pp. 155-66.

attempt to extend her analysis in relation to Innis' later communications studies. This extension is intended to underline some of the strong elements of theoretical continuity which link Innis' so-called "staples" and so-called "communications" studies; to indicate that Innis' turning from the former to the latter studies involved a longer time period, a more complex range of factors, and less of a radical theoretical disjuncture than might be suggested by some accounts of the shift; and to illustrate the range of Innis' applications of the capacity concept in the communications studies.

From this perspective, it becomes possible to suggest that the distinguishing *theoretical* feature of Innis' *"staples"* studies, as well, is less a concern with the natural and physical characteristics of the principal commodities exported by a staple-producing region, or with media of transport and communication, in themselves—although both factors assume undoubted importance in his theoretical framework—than a focus on the social-ecological preconditions or determinants and implications of qualitatively different types of capacity within social-economic formations or systems; on the overall capacity of systems for expanded reproduction; on system capacities in their qualitative and quantitative aspects as determinants of forms and processes of intra-system and inter-system competition, parasitism, and symbiosis; and on the extent to which contradictions implicit in concentration on certain forms of specialized capacity are associated with rigidities which contain the potential for system change or collapse. Moreover, Mundell's offhand comment that Innis' framework is "just supply and demand" can be seen to have a certain validity, in one sense, given a recognition that the way in which Innis takes the concepts of supply and demand to their *limits* undercuts many of the axiomatic foundations of conventional neoclassical economic theory, and that his generalized conceptions of "supply" and "demand" provide a means of dealing theoretically with the dialectics of historical change in a form which is beyond the capacity of conventional economic theory.

The body of the essay begins with an outline of some of the principal ways in which questions associated with the existence of bounded capacity, "fixed capital", and overhead costs assume importance in economic theory. It next provides a sketch of Innis' use and development of the concepts in the course of his shift from studies in Canadian economic history to the study of empire and communications. It then examines Innis' later writings, in order to illustrate how his use of the generalized "capacity" concept underlies much of his historical analysis and renders it more theoretically integrated than its apparently fragmented and aphoristic mode of presentation might initially suggest. Finally, the paper outlines some of the possible implications of Innis' approach to communications for neoclassical economic theory and for Marxist analysis.

Three inescapable characteristics of human productive activity are that it is a process which occupies time and space, that is, an historical process; that it involves the human transformation of nature; and that what can be produced in a particular time in a particular location is qualitatively and quantitatively bounded, or finite. While extension of the temporal or spatial dimensions of a productive system can relax these qualitative and quantitative bounds on production, it cannot eliminate them. Thus the notion of "capacity", or of temporally and spatially defined bounds or limits on production, is inherent in the notion of production itself.

The "capacity" concept hence finds expression in neoclassical economics in the emphasis on "scarcity" apparent in the Robbinsian definition of economics as the study of human behaviour "as a relationship between ends and *scarce* means which have alternative uses"; and in Marxist political economy, in the focus on "reproduction", and on the preconditions, processes, and barriers, limits or contradictions of system reproduction. In any temporally and spatially bounded productive system or social-economic formation, these qualitative and quantitative upper bounds on the absolute volume of production are imposed by the range, distribution, and magnitude of natural resources or raw materials present in, or available to, the system; by the size and demographic characteristics of the population; by the stock of knowledge and technical ability contained within the system and by its growth or decline and distribution; by the social relations of production, as manifested in forms of co-operation, property rights, and division of labour, and in modes and patterns of distribution and exchange; by the social forms of human fear and desire, as embodied in cultural presuppositions, military, juridical, religious, and related social institutions, and socially prescribed, permitted, and proscribed patterns of material and non-material productive consumption; and by the inherited stock of produced means of production and communication, as augmented by processes of investment or accumulation and reduced by physical depreciation and obsolescence.

Five features of this catalogue of determinants of productive capacity are worth briefly noting. The first is that the notion of "capacity" implicit in the foregoing catalogue is an index of *potential*, or of an *upper* bound on the rate and amount of production. That a given combination of products *could* be produced by a system does not in any way imply that it *would* be produced, even if somehow there were to exist a generally accepted social evaluation of it as uniquely superior to all alternative production programmes, and *a fortiori* if there were not such a common social determination of its relative value. Secondly, these determinants of system productive capacity do not simply affect capacity in isolation from each other; rather, they are themselves dialectically related and mutually or reciprocally determining, in direct and indirect or mediated fashion. The very definition of particular natural phenomena as "resources", for example, is determined by the character and extent of social knowledge and the nature and level of development of the means of production and communication, *inter alia*, while the presence of substantial natural resources of a particular character can in turn exert an influence on the character and pattern of development of the stock of knowledge and of the means of production and communication. A third characteristic of these determinants of system productive capacity, viewed individually, is that not all of them necessarily impose effective limits simultaneously on the level of production: in the language of the mathematical programmer, not all constraints are necessarily continuously binding. This fact implies a fourth feature, in a sense a corollary of the preceding one: all social-economic systems generally operate at consistently less than "capacity" levels, in the sense that they are continuously characterized by what J. M. Clark described as "unused powers of production". Such unused capacity may be associated with waste, inefficiency, or inadequate co-ordination, but it may also constitute the basis of a surplus or reserve permitting security, flexibility, experimentation, innovation, and system transformation. Situations of "full-scale mobilization" of the resources of a system such as occur in wartime provide a partial index of the extent to which measured production can be reorganized and increased by more intensive and extensive utilization of unused powers of production, although there appear to be temporal as well as other limits to such mobilization, as evidenced by the development of shortages, by the emergence of unused capacity in spheres of social-economic activity relatively devalued in relation to wartime priorities, and by the accelerated physical depreciation and cultural exhaustion which often accompany mobilizations of extended duration, in addition to the loss of lives and resources directly attributable to the prosecution of a war.

The final feature of the catalogue which is worth noting is that it is effectively more general, and implies a more general notion of system capacity, than that which underlies much of the economic theory of overhead costs and capacity utilization. That theory was developed initially in relation to capitalist conditions of machine-industrial production, by writers such as Torrens, Senior, and particularly Marx, and subsequently in response to unused-capacity problems of railways, which were also seen to be relevant to a much wider range of productive activities in which "fixed capital" figured prominently, as J. M. Clark noted in his brief historical sketch of the development of the theory.[9] In the theory as it developed, much of economists' attention was therefore focused on the characteristics of fixed capital or means of production which generated situations of unused capacity, on the overhead-cost problems produced by the existence of fixed capital and unused capacity, and on their implications for economic behaviour and the allocative efficiency of the price system. Innis utilized this body of theory—some elements of which are outlined immediately below—but, following hints implicit in the work of J. M. Clark, Thorstein Veblen, and to a lesser extent others, he began from an early stage of his researches to generalize its sphere of application so that it transcended the narrow focus on fixed capital and price-system economics which had initially generated it.

The term "*fixed* capital", with its connotations of permanence and stability, is in some ways misleading—indeed, from certain standpoints, such as that of Marx's conception of the circuit and continual metamorphoses of capital, self-contradictory[10]—unless it is appreciated that what it involves is only a *relative* fixity, a formal continuity which persists *significantly* longer than that of other forms in which capital is invested in the spheres of production and circulation. The relative fixity of fixed capital (in its technical, financial, and organizational aspects) thus places it at one end of a temporal continuum of the forms which capital may assume. The characteristics commonly associated with fixed capital which are most germane to the present essay include its durability, its irreversibility, its indivisibility, its specificity, its role in the determination of productive capacity,

---

9. Clark, *op. cit.*, pp. 5ff.

10. One may conjecture that Marx's relative shift away from the use of the term "fixed capital" and towards a primary focus on the "organic composition of capital" between the *Grundrisse* and *Capital* has to do in part with a recognition of this contradiction, as well as with his desire to focus on the value-relation in the "*constant* capital—*variable* capital" distinction of his theory of capitalist exploitation (which could have generated ambiguity and semantic interference in combination with the "fixed capital—circulating capital" distinction). Nonetheless, the gain in clarity in this respect was purchased at the cost of a certain loss of discriminatory capacity regarding the implications of "fixed capital" subsequently pointed to by the Austrian school (particularly Bohm-Bawerk), rigorously established by Piero Sraffa, in his *Production of Commodities by Means of Commodities* (Cambridge: Cambridge University Press, 1972), and amplified by Joan Robinson, Ian Steedman, and (from a "neo-Austrian" perspective) John Hicks, in his *Capital and Time* (Oxford: Clarendon Press, 1973). Marx's principal references to "fixed capital" in *Capital* itself occur, naturally enough, in the second and third volumes of the work.

and (viewed as a system) its complementarity, heterogeneity, and interdependence.[11]

The *durability* and *irreversibility* of fixed capital assume significance in several ways. Most basically, the irreversible commitment of resources in a world of uncertainty to durable, long-lived means of production involves creating hostages to fortune, insofar as many of the anticipated gains from such investment will not be realized until after a considerable lapse of time, during which time conditions may change, thereby disappointing expectations. This fact (although it is now recognized that the Austrian concept of an "average period of production" is not wholly satisfactory) underlies the grain of truth in the Austrian notion of the greater productivity of "roundabout" methods of production: it is not that all "roundabout" methods are necessarily inherently more "productive", as the cartoonist Rube Goldberg took pains to show; it is rather that if a certain "roundabout" method of production is to be adopted, in the face of such temporally distant expected returns and uncertainty regarding the future, it *must* be more productive than alternative, less "roundabout" methods. The durability of fixed capital is also manifested in the often lengthy "gestation period" between the initial commitment of time, energy, and resources to a project and the realization of any positive net returns from it, which implies some access to sources of finance or surplus resources relative to immediate consumption needs (in debt or equity form) on the part of the investors. Furthermore, the extended inter-temporal complementarity of inputs and outputs in production processes utilizing fixed capital, the fact that at any point in time, for all industries and the economic system as a whole, there exists a complex age-structure of fixed capital of different vintages with differing productive potentials in varying circumstances, the heterogeneity of information and expectations about the future, and the fact that investments, once made, are irreversible and therefore "sunk" or more or less irretrievable, imply major theoretical and practical imputation problems in price-determination, and considerable indeterminacy in market processes of price-adjustment, some of which are considered below.

The *indivisibility* which frequently assumes significance in the accumulation of fixed capital—the classic example being that of a road

---

11. The following discussion (for reasons of space) is quite terse and elliptical. More detailed and systematic accounts of some of the issues raised may be found in W. Arthur Lewis, *Overhead Costs* (London: Unwin, 1970); A. J. Youngson, *Overhead Capital* (Edinburgh: Edinburgh University Press, 1967); Ludwig M. Lachmann, *Capital and Its Structure* (Kansas City: Sheed Andrews and McMeel, 1978); and the references cited in notes 3, 8, 10, 12 and 13.

or rail line between two points—often implies a certain "lumpiness" of investment, or the necessity of accumulating large masses of capital which may exceed the capacities of individual capitalists, particularly as the development of machine industry and technology generate increasing returns to scale and increase the minimum economic scale of competitive operation in an industry. This "lumpiness" may also be associated with a relatively high overhead-to-variable-cost ratio, which can result in declining unit costs for each firm in an industry as output increases. Such an industry cost structure generates strong incentives for *all* firms to expand output towards their limits of productive capacity, thereby intensifying potentially destabilizing competitive pressures within the industry. These consequences of the indivisibility of fixed capital, together with the problems posed by its durability and irreversibility, tend to increase the level of insecurity and uncertainty of individual capitalists, and to necessitate the development of market and non-market forms of control of their environment by capitalist firms. The development of the corporate form of capital, the growth of financial intermediation, the expansion of state economic activity, and the refinement of techniques of market competition and control (as in vertical and horizontal integration, mergers, cartels, collusive agreements, advertising, and lobbying structures) have all been accelerated by the implications for accumulation of these characteristics of fixed capital.

A fourth important characteristic of fixed capital that reinforces the above tendencies is its *specificity*, in several respects. Functionally, particular forms of fixed capital are more or less restricted in the range of commodities they can readily produce—certain machine tools, for example, being reasonably but not infinitely flexible or adaptable to various uses, while Fourdrinier papermaking machines are highly rigid or specialized. Fixed capital is also frequently spatially or locationally highly specific, notably if it depends on, and has been constructed in relation to, natural features of a specific site, given the substantial and sometimes prohibitive costs of moving machinery, buildings, and equipment and the impossibility of moving mineshafts. Finally, fixed capital often implies specific preconditions for its successful utilization in production, both in terms of access to required natural or material inputs with specific qualities and in its presupposition of certain social, legal-political or juridical, cultural, and other institutional forms and processes. The specificity of fixed capital in this sense constitutes an important nexus for the concrete working out of what Marxists refer to as the dialectic between the forces of production and the social relations of production.

Given its specificity, its inter-temporal fixity and the often lengthy gestation periods required to bring it into production, fixed capital also has a fifth characteristic: it is often the effective determinant of the maximal technically feasible or unit cost-minimizing level of production ("capacity production") by an enterprise or industry, particularly in the short run. This technical-economic rigidity is significant not only as a capacity limit or upper bound on production, but also insofar as a shortfall of demand relative to fixed capacity (whether as a result of an unforeseen drop in demand, a foreseen regular fluctuation in demand, or a temporary gap between potential supply and demand caused by construction "ahead of demand" of technically indivisible fixed capital)[12] is associated with unused capacity and overhead-cost pressures of the sort described above.

Finally, internally to a firm, an industry, or an economy, fixed capital is characterized by the complementarity, heterogeneity, and interdependence of its constituent elements.[13] The production of a wide range of diverse commodities by means of commodities within an economic system implies not only the intersectoral flows captured in input-output and backward and forward linkage analyses but also a systematic interdependence among the heterogeneous constituents of the structure of fixed capital of the system. Particularly with the generalization of commodity production or production for exchange, new investment in fixed capital is made with reference to, and is hence dependent on, the capacity of a specific pre-existing stock of fixed capital, so that compatibility or complementarity of such new investment with the existing stock, taken as a whole, tends to become a *desideratum* even in cases of direct competition or substitutability of a new element and a *particular* component of the existing stock. The technical complementarity and the market interdependence of the forms of fixed capital can not only exert a conservative influence on the path of development of the system of fixed capital, but also (with the increased spatial and temporal integration of economic activity associated with the extension of market relations of production, the penetration of the price system, and the development of communication) increase the likelihood that disturbances in one part of the system will be rapidly transmitted throughout the system.

---

12. In addition to I. M. (Biss) Spry, "Overhead Costs, Time Problems", see also Nicholas Georgescu-Roegen, *The Entropy Law and the Economic Process* (Cambridge, Mass.: Harvard University Press, 1971), especially pp. 211-75, and (for the case of regular, repetitive, foreseen changes) Gordon C. Winston, *The Timing of Economic Activities* (Cambridge: Cambridge University Press, 1982).

13. See Ludwig M. Lachmann, *op. cit.* and *Capital, Expectations and the Market Process* (Kansas City: Sheed Andrews and McMeel, 1977), especially pp. 197-213.

The above characteristics of fixed capital underlie a number of the central preoccupations of economic theory. The indivisibility of fixed capital has been associated both with the high overhead-cost to variable-cost ratios and the decreasing-cost conditions of production that can generate destabilizing cut-throat competition, and (in a sense the obverse side of the same coin) with the barriers to entry that promote and maintain concentration and monopoly (including so-called "natural" monopolies). Patterns of centralization and decentralization of power, wealth, and information are not unrelated to the character, relative extent, and imperatives of fixed capital.

Furthermore, the durability of fixed capital in the form of producer goods plays a crucial role in the "acceleration principle" which Innis' teacher, J. M. Clark, emphasized as an important contributing factor to business cycles. "Austrian" and "neo-Austrian" theories of the business cycle as developed by writers like Hayek, Schumpeter, Lachmann, and Hicks have drawn attention to the role of rigidities incidental to the lengthening of the time-structure of capital, "forced savings", and the development of imbalances or shortages of complementary forms of fixed capital in producing cyclical peaks or ceilings and downturns of economic activity. Pressures for the cumulative contraction of commercial and industrial credit that often accompany and intensify cyclical downturns can be traced in part to the requirements of meeting fixed or rigid financial commitments previously undertaken concomitantly with accumulation of fixed capital, in order to avoid bankruptcy. Measures taken by firms individually to reduce the likelihood of bankruptcy can contribute to the increased frequency of bankruptcies for the economic system as a whole. Keynes's "liquidity trap" may be viewed as in part the consequence of a foreshortening of the time-horizon of investors resulting from the increased insecurity and uncertainty of periods of crisis, which induces a reluctance to commit resources to the formation of durable fixed capital.[14] Marx's "realization problem" becomes more acute with an increase in the relative importance of fixed capital, and capitalist crises associated with problems of under-consumption or of disproportionality, accentuated by the importance of fixed capital, can in turn necessitate the downward revaluation of existing fixed capital as part of the process by which the rate of profit is raised sufficiently to enable the pace of accumulation to increase.

---

14. If a "liquidity trap" exists in a particular historical situation, other factors (such as expectations regarding possible future increases or internal relative changes in the interest-rate structure, based on assumptions regarding "normal" levels of interest rates) may also be operative.

In addition to the theory of monopoly and cyclical theory (the two areas explicitly noted by Innis as theoretical bases of his communication studies),[15] fixed capital (in its relation to overhead costs, unused capacity, and rigidities) also raises major theoretical problems for a number of areas of price-system accounting and, more fundamentally, for the notion of the allocative efficiency and "optimality" properties of the price system itself. Tjalling Koopmans and others have shown, in a negative theoretical conclusion with wide-reaching practical ramifications, that if there are indivisibilities of the sort associated with fixed capital in a transport system linking a number of spatially separated trading centres, such that situations of unused capacity emerge (intensified by the lack of a precise correlation between volume, weight, and value of the traded commodities), then general trade equilibrium is indeterminate or unattainable.[16] Sraffa's treatment of fixed capital as a special case of joint products not only plays a significant role in his implicit critique of neoclassical theory but also enforces a reconsideration of the epistemological status of Marx's concept of the "organic composition of capital" and indeed of the labour theory of value.[17] W. A. Lewis, in a careful discussion of "fixed costs", using for his definition of "fixed" the criterion of "inescapability", has argued that for a going concern with the necessity of periodic renewal of constituent elements of its fixed capital, "There is no such quantity as 'the marginal cost' of output; . . . there is a large variety of costs to choose from, depending merely on how far ahead you choose to look . . . ."[18] Innis likewise noted, using the inter-relationship of hydro-electric power, pulp and paper, and department store newspaper-advertising as an example, that "overhead costs have contributed to lack of precision in accounting . . . . In paying for electric light or for groceries one cannot be certain how much is paid for newspapers."[19] The spheres of "social-overhead capital" and "public goods" similarly pose difficulties for narrowly market-focused economic approaches, insofar as "external economies" associated with the provision of services such as defence, transportation, communication, education, and health services cannot be fully appropriated, utilizing the market mechanism alone, by those who

---

15. See note 5 above.

16. Tjalling C. Koopmans, *Scientific Papers of Tjalling C. Koopmans* (New York: Springer-Verlag, 1970), pp. 258-81.

17. Sraffa, *op. cit.*, pp. 43-73, especially pp. 67-68.

18. Lewis, *op. cit.*, p. 12.

19. Innis, *Essays in Canadian Economic History*, p. 267.

provide them, so that (in neoclassical economic terminology) the marginal social net benefit exceeds the marginal private net benefit of providing them.[20] This divergence provides one of the principal neoclassical economic *rationales* for participation by the state in economic activity.

Even more fundamentally, in a discussion which extends the Koopmans conclusion above to the price system itself, Innis noted that actual markets (as distinct from the costless, smoothly functioning markets of neoclassical economic theory) in fact consume resources for their creation and maintenance,[21] and, moreover, consume resources *in the form of fixed capital*, which implies precisely the same pressures of overhead costs and unused capacity *for markets and for the price system itself* as characterize individual firms and industries. The theoretical and practical implications of this aspect of the price system as an economic institution are still more radical than is suggested in the neoclassical economic literature on "incomplete sets of futures markets" and "transactions costs": the problem is not simply that there is a shortage of markets, or that costs of transactions need to be incorporated systematically into an otherwise satisfactory theory; it is rather that even if there were a complete set of markets, and transactions costs were included, the logical impossibility of "rationally" allocating the *overhead* costs of *market*-maintenance to individual market transactions introduces an essentially arbitrary element into the market determination of prices which is incompatible with claims regarding the capacity of the market to generate efficient or "optimal" allocations of resources, and hence regarding the putative *a priori* superiority of the price system or "the market mechanism" relative to alternative modes of resource allocation and distribution.[22]

Two final economic spheres where the overhead-cost and capacity concepts have theoretical ramifications that became important in Innis' analytical development, relate to the notion of political-

---

20. See Youngson, *op. cit.* A pioneering discussion of the issue is contained in Karl Marx, *Grundrisse* (Harmondsworth: Penguin, 1973), pp. 524-33, although Adam Smith's discussion of defence as opposed to opulence in *The Wealth of Nations* (to which Innis referred) also deserves mention.

21. Harold A. Innis, *Political Economy in the Modern State* (Toronto: Ryerson, 1946), p. ix.

22. It will be appreciated, moreover, that this difficulty is not obviated by the Chicago-type suggestion that there is (actually or notionally) a "market for markets", in that if establishment of a market appears sufficiently profitable, in light of the expected demand for its services, it will be established by some profit-maximizing "market-supplier". Even if this were an adequate general characterization of the process of market-*establishment* (and there are reasons for scepticism on this score), the actual *operation* of the market system so established would be subject to the difficulty outlined in the text.

economic *systems* and the problem of historical *change*. Not only is the theory of the price system altered by acknowledgement of the existence and significance of overhead costs, but (as J. M. Clark recognized, in his discussion of "costs of government as overhead outlays")[23] so is the economic theory of the state. In the first place, the costs of required state activity may be regarded as necessary overhead costs, from the standpoint of the reproduction of the political-economic system as a whole.[24] Secondly, with the expansion of state activity the overhead costs and rigidities of individual components of state expenditure and finance systems both necessitate the transformation of government finance and heighten the likelihood of periodic fiscal crises of the state. Innis' observation in 1938 on capitalism and the state ("Where capitalism followed the more rigid channels of surviving commercialism or where it arrived later in a highly centralized state, it was a part of governmental machinery. In Germany, Italy, and Japan and in the British Dominions the state became capital equipment.")[25] is a straightforward metaphoric extension of J. M. Clark's analysis.

Clark also argued that from the standpoint of the economic system as a whole, the costs of reproduction of the working class could be treated as overhead costs, insofar as "there is a minimum of maintenance of the labourer's health and working capacity which must be borne by someone, whether the labourer works or not," and that "If this . . . step is taken, overhead costs are seen to be a universal fact."[26] In this argument, of course, Clark was essentially adopting the "reproduction" perspective of classical political economists such as Marx,[27] or (more precisely) showing how a consistent application of the economics of overhead costs to the sphere of labour led one necessarily to a "reproduction" conception of the economic system.

---

23. Clark, *op. cit.*, especially pp. 451-58.

24. This fact incidentally necessitates attention to the requirements, difficulties and modes of financing these "overhead costs", as reflected in the neoclassical theory of tax incidence, the Marxist emphasis on the fiscal dimensions of class hegemony, and Innis' concern with "imperfect regional competition and political institutions" and "the political implications of unused capacity" (*Essays in Canadian Economic History, passim*, especially pp. 321-26 and 372-82), and with the overhead costs of empire which he discussed in relation to European empires in North America and the ancient empires of the Near East and Europe.

25. Innis, *Essays in Canadian Economic History*, p. 260.

26. Clark, *op. cit.*, pp. 15-16.

27. As noted above, Clark was familiar with Marx's *Capital*, and his *Overhead Costs* contains as a significant substratum an ongoing dialogue with the "socialist critics" of capitalism, in which he demonstrates a not unsympathetic understanding and an acceptance of certain theoretical positions developed by Marx.

Marx himself had viewed as one of his central theoretical contributions the distinction between "labour" and "labour-*power*", which he explicitly termed "*capacity* for labour": what is sold in the "labour" market is not labour, but labour-*power*. This provided Marx both with a *consistent* theory of the basis of capitalist profit and with a means of analyzing the ways in which the contradiction between capital and labour works itself out in practice in the sphere of production.[28] The extension of the theory of overhead costs by Clark to comprehend both the state and labour was significant for Innis' development both in itself, as showing how overhead costs pervaded all spheres of economic systems, and insofar as it suggested the possibility of *further* generalization of the cluster of concepts beyond these spheres which Clark had examined.

With regard to the problem of historical change, a focus on fixed capital, overhead costs, rigidities, and unused capacity promotes a different vision of the process of change than that implicit in the primary neoclassical economic focus on the continual smooth shifting of resources between sectors towards equilibrium positions, through the operation of a costless market system in response to the imperatives of profit- and utility-maximization. Innis' remarks on the need for a "polar front theory" in economic analysis which focused on "the meeting of economic masses" and on "the economics of losses" provide an index of his dissatisfaction with conventional short-term comparative-static equilibrium analysis.[29] They also signal his awareness that the durability, irreversibility, indivisibility, specificity, heterogeneity, and complementarity or interdependence associated with fixed capital imply the necessity of a concept of social-economic change that lays significantly greater weight on rigidities; on patterns and processes of concentration or centralization, and dispersion or decentralization, of political-economic power; on the dialectical relationship between centres and margins of organized force, wealth, and knowledge; and on change itself as being not merely quantitative but also structural or qualitative, and as potentially involving social-economic disjunction, disruption, crises, and violence. Writing of the implications in Canada of concentration on the production of resource-based staples for export to more highly industrialized areas, he suggested: "Each staple in its turn left its stamp, and the shift to new staples invariably produced periods of crises in which adjustments

---

28. Karl Marx, *Capital*: Volume I (Moscow: Progress Publishers, 1965), pp. 173, 508-63, and *passim*.

29. See note 4 above.

in the old structure were painfully made and a new pattern created in relation to a new staple.''[30] He expressed the concept of historical change that emerged in his later studies in related fashion: ''The bias of communication in space or in time involves a sponge theory of the distribution of wealth which assumes violence.''[31]

The role of the economics of capacity, fixed capital, and overhead costs as sketched above in Innis' analysis of *Canadian* history has been clearly documented by Irene Spry and others.[32] Its role in Innis' studies of the political economy of communication, however, has received less attention. In part, this relative neglect may be attributed to the effects of the division of academic labour, insofar as Innis' earlier works have in the main been more carefully studied by economic and other historians, while his later studies have received closer attention from communication and political theorists. Nonetheless, a sharp dichotomization of Innis' work into earlier ''staples'' and later ''communications'' periods conduces to a neglect of several important aspects of his intellectual development. In the first place, as even a cursory inspection of his publications from 1940 to 1952 suffices to demonstrate, it is simply not the case that Innis abandoned the field of Canadian history after 1940, when his principal research focus came to centre increasingly on the political economy of communication (even if one were to exclude from consideration writings emerging from his work on the 1946 Manitoba Royal Commission on Adult Education and the 1949 Royal Commission on Transportation).

Secondly, and more significantly from the standpoint of this essay, many of the characteristic preoccupations and methods of analysis of the ''communications'' studies constitute a significant strand in his earlier works, although their place in most of these studies is less central. Indeed, Innis' very first publication, a brief article in 1918 on ''The Economic Problems of Army Life'', may be viewed, as well, as his first *communications* study. A consideration of the *minutiae* of the daily life of the enlisted soldier, principally those concerned with ''the getting and the spending of an income'', in which Innis remarked that ''the question of spending money is inextricably bound up with the spending of time'', provides the basis for a materialist

---

30. Innis, *Empire and Communications*, pp. 5-6.

31. Innis, *Bias of Communication*, p. 76.

32. In addition to the references cited in note 8, the work of writers like Daniel Drache and Melville Watkins and Neill's *A New Theory of Value* (pp. 51-61) provide interpretations of the theory as embodied in works of Innis such as *Essays in Canadian Economic History*, pp. 62-96, 123-55, 372-82 and *passim*.

interpretation of the production of the culture or "habits" of the
returning soldier:

> Such are the influences which have been at work on the life of every soldier.
> Hampered by the habits which these influences have occasioned he is faced
> with a new task very different from the old work of the army. If he should
> find it difficult at first to accommodate himself to the new task, it behooves
> the world to have patience.[33]

Three elements in this analysis deserve mention: first,
"habits" are conceived of as *produced* and reproduced, through the
expenditure of time and money, in relation to the exigencies of living
or survival; secondly, they are conceived of in relation to the *capacity*
to perform "tasks"; and thirdly, they are conceived of as having a
degree of *rigidity* or inflexibility in the face of changed circumstances
and tasks, insofar as capacity in relation to the performance of certain
tasks is equivalently incapacity in relation to new or different tasks,
and hence altered circumstances generate the necessity for potentially
painful and costly adjustment of capacity. The economics of capacity
in this rudimentary form was thus basic to Innis' materialist understanding of the process of cultural production even before Innis had
taken his first course with J. M. Clark at the University of Chicago.

Innis' debt to Clark's studies in the economics of capacity and
overhead costs has already been suggested. In his articulation and
extension of that theory in relation to the political economy of communications and culture, however, it is probable that Innis was also aided
considerably by his acquaintance with the works of Thorstein Veblen
and Graham Wallas. Innis' relationship to Veblen has been widely
acknowledged, if incompletely analyzed: in particular, Veblen's
influence on Innis' conceptualization of the centre-margin dialectic
and of the effects of transferred technology and institutions, not to
mention on Innis' vocabulary, syntax and style, are familiar to students
of both men. Of at least equal importance in the present context is
Veblen's notion of the role of "habits of thought" in cultural development. At one point, defending his use of emotionally charged everyday words as analytical tools, Veblen argued that "these categories
of popular thought . . . , with all the moral force with which they
are charged, designate the motive force of cultural development, . . ."
and went on to suggest (in a passage quoted by Innis) that "if one
would avoid paralogistic figures of speech in the analysis of institutions, one must resort to words and concepts that express the thoughts

---

33. H. A. Innis, "The Economic Problems of Army Life", *McMaster University Monthly*
(December 1918), pp. 106-109.

of the men whose habits of thought constitute the institutions in question.''[34] Similarly, in a discussion in 1925 of ''Economic Theory in the Calculable Future'', Veblen argued that ''the drift and bias of [the] guiding interest'' of economics would arise from ''those characteristic habits of thought that are induced in the incoming generation of economists'' in the course of their ''habituation'' or training; that current events ''will perforce be apprehended and formulated in terms germane to that scheme of knowledge and belief which has been induced in these economists by their past habituation''; and that the mentality of future economists would have ''only that rate of flexibility and adaptation that is conditioned by the inveterate tenacity of fixed preconceptions; and preconceptions are something in the nature of fixed ideas, and they yield themselves to current changes only tardily and concessively.'' In addition to these remarks, which treat economic theory itself as the output of a process of cultural production in which ''fixed *ideas*'' display analogies to ''fixed *capital*'' in their generation of rigidity and ''bias'', Veblen suggested, in a passage which foreshadows Innis' concern with the implications of monopolies of knowledge, that if the results of new economic research ''are to go into the common stock of knowledge and belief as a substantial contribution they will have to conform to those canons of knowledge and belief that rule the road for the time being.''[35]

Innis' generalization of the theory of capacity and overhead costs beyond the scope of Clark's analysis, on lines implicit in his earliest work and in Veblen, was already well advanced by the time he had completed *The Fur Trade in Canada* in 1930. His arguments regarding cargo imbalances and unused capacity in the fur trade as inhibiting settlement, and concerning the high overhead costs of extended trade routes and military posts as a source of vulnerability in New France, are familiar to students of Canadian history (although they warrant further empirical investigation) and are also reasonably straightforward extensions of the economics of capacity. Less conventional was his application of the theory to the question of the exhaustion of beaver supplies as a result of increased European demand for furs:

---

34. Thorstein Veblen, *Essays in Our Changing Order* (New York: Viking, 1934), pp. 30-31, quoted in Innis, *Essays in Canadian Economic History*, p. 25. The Kantian element evident in Veblen's use of terms such as ''categories'' and ''constitute'' derives from Veblen's study of Kant, which produced the lucid interpretation of Kant's *Critique of Judgment* reprinted in *Changing Order*, pp. 175-93 (especially pp. 180-81 on the reflective judgment and ''the exigencies of our *capacity* of knowing'').

35. Veblen, *op. cit.*, pp. 3-5, 9.

> In the language of the economists, the heavy fixed capital of the beaver
> became a serious handicap with the improved technique of Indian hunting
> methods, incidental to the borrowing of iron from Europeans. Depreciation
> through obsolescence of the beaver's defence equipment was so rapid as
> to involve the immediate and complete destruction of the animal.[36]

Innis applied the capacity framework not only to this natural ecological
system, however, but also to the European colonization of North
America itself, and to the associated difficulty of working out "new
cultural traits suitable to a new environment":

> The process of adaptation is extremely painful in any case but the *main-
> tenance* of cultural traits to which they have been accustomed is of primary
> importance. A sudden change of cultural traits can be made only with great
> difficulty and with the disappearance of many of the peoples concerned.
> *Depreciation* of the social heritage is serious.
>
>   The methods by which the cultural traits of a civilization may
> persist with the least possible *depreciation* involve an appreciable dependence
> on [and "heavy material borrowing from"] the peoples of the homeland.[37]

Innis' interpretation of the process of cultural reproduction
in *The Fur Trade* emphasizes its conservative and rigid aspects, omit-
ting consideration of the factors making for cultural flexibility, and
his use of terms such as "maintenance" and "depreciation" is still
perhaps more static and metaphorical than dialectical and analytical.
Yet his interest in extension of the capacity and overhead-costs
framework to the sphere of cultural production is already apparent.
In an undated letter of the mid-1930s to Irene Spry, he wrote:

> the relation of institutions and culture to the economic way of life is of course
> very important. I think MacIver and others . . . have pretty well blown
> up the cultural lag idea in its crude form but there is something in the study
> of economics at first hand . . . . I am sure that a knowledge of technical
> detail and economic organization is important to an understanding of polit-
> ical and cultural organization and that social scientists fail continually
> through their unwillingness to recognize it and end by "blustering" and
> talking about things which are easy to talk about.[38]

---

36. H. A. Innis, *The Fur Trade in Canada* (Toronto: University of Toronto Press, 1962), p. 5.

37. Innis, *Fur Trade*, p. 383. (Italics added.) Significantly, Innis related his analysis at this
point to Graham Wallas' notion of the "social heritage". In his later work, Innis repeatedly
referred to Wallas' influence on certain central themes of the "communications" studies: he
spoke of *Empire and Communications* (p. 9) as "in a sense . . . an extension of the work of Graham
Wallas and E. J. Urwick"; described his 1948 Stamp Lecture as "a footnote on the work of
Graham Wallas" and his concern with "the problem of efficiency in creative thought" and
"the importance of the oral tradition" (*Changing Concepts of Time* [Toronto: University of Toronto
Press, 1952], p. 78); and wrote in *The Bias of Communication* (p. 191) of "an interest in the
economic history of knowledge in which dependence on the work of Graham Wallas will be
evident."

38. H. A. Innis, undated letter to Irene Biss [Spry]. Photocopy available in the Innis Archives,
Innis College, University of Toronto.

If this passage may be read as constituting an implicit expression of intent to develop an historical-materialist analysis of culture and communication, then Innis' brief but pivotal paper in 1935, "The Role of Intelligence: Some Further Notes", written in response to E. J. Urwick's questioning of the possibility of a social science, may be seen as a set of methodological prolegomena to such an analysis. After providing a catalogue of "sources of bias" which reinforces Urwick's argument "as to the difficulties, if not impossibility, of a social science", Innis suggested, adopting certain of Urwick's metaphors, that there was an alternative to nihilism:

> The innumerable difficulties of the social scientist are paradoxically his only salvation. Since the social scientist cannot be 'scientific' or 'objective' because of the contradiction in terms, he can learn of his numerous *limitations*. The *'sediment of experience'* provides the basis for scientific investigation. The never-ending *shell of life* suggested in the *persistent character of bias* provides possibilities of intensive study of the *limitations* of life and its probable *direction* . . . The *habits or biases* of individuals which permit prediction are reinforced in the *cumulative bias of institutions* and constitute the chief interest of the social scientist.[39]

It is at this point in the development of Innis' thought that the basis for the systematic articulation of the economics of capacity in relation to culture and communications appears to have been established. It is precisely because of the relatively "persistent" and "cumulative" character of "bias", its relative temporal *invariance*, that it can serve as an analytical focus and as an escape from the indeterminacy of the Heraclitean flux. If "bias" as *limitation* and *direction* of life is taken as synonymous with "capacity", then the whole of the economics of capacity and overhead costs becomes available as a means of analyzing the material preconditions of cultural production and institutional reproduction over time and space, and the foundation exists for the analysis of communications and empire and the "economic history of knowledge",[40] and hence for the development of a self-reflexive historical-materialist epistemology.

In his studies from the late 1930s onward, Innis continuously refined and increased the flexibility and range of application of the "capacity-bias" framework. His intensified focus on the epistemological biases and capacity limits of the hegemonic forms of economic theory and social science is apparent in the ironic humour of his 1938

---

39. H. A. Innis, "The Role of Intelligence: Some Further Notes", *Canadian Journal of Economics and Political Science* (1935), pp. 280-87.

40. See note 37.

comment, "A study of the elasticity of demand for autarchies is significant to a study of the elasticity of demand for wheat", his political-
economic application of the overhead-costs framework to the problem
of "imperfect *regional* competition", and his deliberately literalistic
interpretation of Keynes's "liquidity preference" as *auri sacra fames*;
and in the catalogue of social forces inadequately captured by economic
theory which he analyzed in tracing "the economic significance of
cultural factors".[41]

The extension is also apparent in Innis' increasingly sophisticated social-ecological approach to the question of the determinants
and implications of different forms of communication capacity, "efficiency" or bias. The bias of communication of any particular historical
system emerges from the interaction of a complex of mutually and
reciprocally determinative factors (geographical, technological, institutional and cultural) including the forms or categories of language and
thought themselves, insofar as they serve as durable forces of mental
production and constitute potential sources of epistemological bias.
Culture itself is defined in terms of informational economy and
decision-making capacity:

> Culture . . . is designed to train the individual to decide how much
> information he needs and how little he needs, to give him a sense of balance
> and proportion . . . . Culture is concerned with the capacity of the
> individual to appraise problems in terms of space and time and with enabling
> him to take the proper steps at the right time.[42]

In this context, Innis' concepts of "control over space" and
"control over time", or of territorial organization and extent and
temporal continuity, flexibility and duration, can be seen as flexible
and basic indices of capacity enabling the long-period comparative-
historical study of communication in widely divergent cultural and
social-economic formations. Similarly, his concepts of "monopolies
of knowledge" and "monopolies of organized force" provide a heuris-
tic focus in analyzing the determinants of patterns and processes of
centralization and decentralization in terms of the generalized overhead costs of institutional reproduction, the associated elements of
complementarity and rigidity, and the resultant, potentially cumulative
and accumulative development of bias and internal and external
contradiction. The term "bias" itself, like the concept of "capacity",
implies a non-deterministic concern with determination, insofar as

---

41. Innis, *Political Economy in the Modern State* (Toronto: Ryerson, 1946), pp. 83-102, 167-200,
229-35, and *passim*.

42. Innis, *Bias*, p. 85.

it connotes tendency rather than teleology, and permits the acknowledgement of dialectical or reciprocal interaction between the determinants of system reproduction without eliminating the possibility of preponderantly unidirectional determination, and without prejudging the question of which types of capacities, or potentials and limits, will prove decisive in any particular historical context.

Innis' later works impose considerable demands on the capacity of the reader, because of their mode of presentation, their historical range, and their focus on "things which are *not* easy to talk about". The present essay has attempted to suggest that the accessibility and usefulness of these later "communications" works can be increased by a recognition of the degree of theoretical continuity which exists between them and Innis' earlier studies of Canadian economic history. It has further suggested that Innis' extensions of "supply and demand" theory constitute both a major challenge to, and a strategy of escape from, the limitations of neoclassical economic theory in dealing with the problem of historical change, as well as a means of analytically and historically supplementing the Marxist notion of the dialectic between economic base and superstructure. These suggestions rest on the view that Innis' primary accomplishment in his studies of the bias of communication was the development of an historically grounded, dialectical-materialist theoretical framework for the integrated analysis of long-period political, social, and epistemological change, centred on the economics of capacity and overhead costs.

5.   Buying and Selling Hudson's Bay Company Furs in the Eighteenth Century*

Arthur J. Ray
University of British Columbia

In 1931, Harold Innis published *The Fur Trade in Canada*. It immediately became the standard reference work on the subject. In 1979,
William Eccles attacked Harold Innis' work in a "belated review".
He claimed Innis was an economic determinist who had not given
enough weight to political and military factors.[1] Eccles argued that
profit motives ceased to be an important driving force in the French
fur trade after 1700.[2] Rather, he argued, imperial concerns became
paramount. With regard to the issue of French-English rivalries, Eccles
took particular exception to Innis' assertion that the English ultimately
triumphed in New France because of the economic advantages they
derived from more efficient domestic manufacturing and their cheaper
access to the heart of the continent via the Hudson River and Hudson
Bay.[3] He claimed that Innis had no concrete data to show that

---

*The author would like to thank Irene Spry for comments on this paper, and his colleagues
in the economic history seminar at the University of British Columbia for comments on earlier
versions. The author would also like to express appreciation to the Hudson's Bay Company
for permission to consult and quote from its archives. The Social Sciences and Humanities
Research Council of Canada provided funds to help defray research expenses. This support
was greatly appreciated.

1. W. J. Eccles, "A Belated Review of Harold Adams Innis, The Fur Trade in Canada",
Canadian Historical Review LX, no. 4 (1979), 419-41.

2. *Ibid.*, pp. 422-23. Eccles has elaborated this point further in a more recent article. See
W. J. Eccles, "The Fur Trade and Eighteenth-Century Imperialism", *William and Mary Quarterly*
XXXX (1983), 341-62.

3. Eccles, "A Belated Review", pp. 428-34.

English goods were cheaper and better than those of the French.[4] With regard to the northern access to the continent, Eccles says the Hudson's Bay Company men "failed" to move inland and therefore did not exploit their strategic advantage. Citing trading statistics from London and La Rochelle, Eccles indicates that the French were obtaining an increasing share of the North American supply of furs down to the time of the Conquest.[5] This fact led Eccles to speculate: "had the Seven Years' War not intervened, the Hudson's Bay Company might have been driven to the wall by the Canadians."[6]

Eccles' attack on Innis prompted a response by Hugh Grant. He accepted Eccles' assertion that the French fur-trade was not pursued for profit motives after 1700. But he chided Eccles for extreme reductionism and for limiting the realm of economics to the study of profits.[7] According to Grant, Innis' major contribution was placing the study of the fur trade in the larger context of the broader interests of European states.[8] Elaborating, he said, "the economic significance of the fur trade . . . was not to be measured strictly in relation to its volume of trade nor in exclusive concerns with the profit motive as Eccles would have us do; rather what was important was how the fur trade was perceived in a period of mercantilism, and further, how this perception was integrated into actual mercantile policy".[9] Grant believed that Innis was correct in stressing that the success of a nation depended upon its ability to organize trade over an expanded territory. This demanded the capacity to deal with rising overhead costs, slower rates of turnover of capital, and control of increasingly lengthy lines of communication.[10]

The Eccles-Grant debate raises a number of basic questions. Can we fully understand either the English or the French mercantile empires without having a clearer picture of how individuals and companies operated within them? More to the point, we need to know the extent to which the actions of traders and companies were constrained by official government policies and goals. An aspect of this question involves considering whether or not governments played equally active parts in the French and English systems. Neither Eccles

---

4. *Ibid.*, p. 430.

5. *Ibid.*, p. 434.

6. *Ibid.*

7. Hugh M. Grant, "One Step Forward, Two Steps Back: Innis, Eccles, and the Canadian Fur Trade", *Canadian Historical Review* LXII, no. 3 (1981), 305-306.

8. *Ibid.*, p. 306.

9. *Ibid.*, p. 307.

10. *Ibid.*, p. 313.

nor Grant appears to have given much thought to this issue. I believe the failure to do so has led Eccles to mistakenly assume that conclusions he has drawn about the French trade can be applied to that of the English. With regard to the issue of overhead costs, it is necessary to consider how the traders dealt with this growing problem. Finally, Eccles and Grant both cite fur import-export figures to come to determinations about the relative positions of the English and French in the enterprise. However, is this the proper use of available data? The problem is that such data do not tell us whether or not a given company or trader was making or losing money on shipments.

These are very broad questions and cannot be adequately dealt with in their entirety here. Therefore, attention will be directed solely to the Hudson's Bay Company's fur trade during the crucial period of English-French rivalry in the middle of the eighteenth century. Furthermore, the discussion will focus on an aspect of the trade that is not well understood, the buying and selling of furs in Rupert's Land and England. An effort will be made to throw light on some of the above issues and questions by attempting to understand how the Hudson's Bay Company's pricing system allowed it to cope with some of the fundamental economic problems of the eighteenth-century fur trade. Hopefully, the approach will demonstrate the value of taking an economic perspective and analysing available data in a systematic manner, rather than in an impressionistic fashion as has been done in the debate thus far. The insights obtained should also serve to throw some light on the nature of Indian and European economic intercourse, which is another dimension of the problem.

The complex set of trading standards that the Hudson's Bay Company used has been of interest to historians since the late E. E. Rich discussed them at length in an important article published in 1960. At that time, Rich suggested that Indians largely dictated the terms of trade at the Company's posts. As evidence, he noted that official rates of exchange showed remarkable rigidity, given that the Company had to deal in the unsteady markets of Europe. Rich posited that the apparent rigidity was attributable to the alleged Indian notion that trade was primarily a political activity and the terms of trade, therefore, were essentially parts of political agreements. This presumably meant that they were not to be influenced by impersonal market forces. Accepting Rich's conclusion, the economist Abraham Rotstein attempted to account for this seemingly peculiar aspect of the trade in terms of the conceptual frameworks offered by Karl Polanyi.[11]

---

11. E. E. Rich, "Trade Habits and Economic Motivations among the Indians of North America", *Canadian Journal of Economics and Political Science* 28 (1960): 35-53, and A. Rotstein, "Fur Trade and Empire: An Institutional Analysis" (Ph.D. dissertation, University of Toronto, 1967).

Subsequently Ray and Freeman demonstrated that the official standards were, in reality, simply the maximum set of prices that the Hudson's Bay Company would pay for Indian furs. The Company traders always paid less than the standards specified, with the amount of variation being determined by local competitive conditions in Rupert's Land.[12] Thus, Rich was correct in arguing that the Indians influenced the terms of trade at the posts, but he erred in concluding that economic considerations were not important to them.

While the fluctuations in the unofficial rates of exchange, in response to changing local economic conditions at trading posts, have been fully examined, the rigid official standards have yet to be accounted for. Of particular relevance here, the relationship between the official standards and European markets needs to be explored. In the light of the more recent Eccles-Grant debate it would be useful to know whether or not the pricing system in use worked to the Company's advantage at the time it was struggling against French inroads into its trade. Also, it is important to determine to what extent economic circumstances in England served to compensate the Company for French advances.

When the Hudson's Bay Company established its operations in the late seventeenth century, it adopted the *Made Beaver* (hereinafter MB) as the unit of account in Rupert's Land. It was equivalent to the market value of a prime winter beaver pelt. All of the furs and provisions that the Indians brought in to trade were valued in MB according to the rates set forth in the *Comparative Standard*. This standard was determined in London each year by the Governor and Committee (who were equivalent to a modern board of directors). The relative stability of this standard is readily apparent in Table 1. This table covers the period of strong English-French trade rivalry in Rupert's Land.

By examining the Fur Auction Books of the Hudson's Bay Company for the period between 1738 and 1763, it is possible to obtain some idea of the relationship between *Comparative Standard* values of furs in Rupert's Land and their real worth on the London market. To accomplish this it is necessary to begin by determining the prices that were paid for beaver in London, and using them to assign an annual sterling value to the MB. Figure 1 (see page 109) shows the average London price paid for the two major categories of beaver pelts (others included cub, damaged and staged [summer], and cut). Of

---

12. Arthur J. Ray and Donald B. Freeman, *Give Us Good Measure* (Toronto: University of Toronto Press, 1978), pp. 125-97.

Table 1
Comparative Standard of Trade

Commodity	1720 Albany	York	1740 Albany	York	1750 Albany	York
Beaver:	MB		MB		MB	
Parchment	1.	1.	1.	1.	1.	1.
Coat	1.	1.	1.	1.	1.	1.
Wolverine	1.50	2.	1.50	2.	1.50	2.
Wolf	1.	2.	1.	2.	1.	2.
Bear	2.	2.	2.	2.	2.	2.
Grey fox	1.	2.	1.	2.	1.	2.
Deer	.50	.50	1.	1.	.50	1.
Cat [Lynx]	2.	.33	2.	1.	2.	1.
Marten	.25	.33	.33	.33	.33	.33
Fisher	1.	—	1.	.50	1.	.50

Source: Ray and Freeman, 1978, p. 65.

importance, although the Company rated each as equal to one MB, parchment actually fetched a higher price in all but six of the years. Therefore, for the purposes of analysis, the average annual price paid for parchment was used to convert an MB to pounds sterling.

The overall trends in the prices paid for beaver are very important and warrant comment here. According to Rich, the Hudson's Bay Company benefited during the middle of the eighteenth century from a strong domestic fur market that was supported by the rapid growth of the British felt hat industry. In 1725 hat exports netted returns of £137,000; by 1730 they had risen to £153,000; and in 1750 they amounted to £263,000.[13] This industry was centred in London, and the Hudson's Bay Company was therefore assured of a strong local market for its beaver.[14]

---

13. E. E. Rich, *The Hudson's Bay Company*, Vol. 1 (Toronto: McClelland and Stewart, 1960), pp. 530-31.

14. *Ibid.*

Figures 2 through 9 (see pages 110-13) portray the *Comparative Standard* MB value of selected key furs expressed in sterling, and the average price the Company received for them at their auctions. Several important facts are readily apparent. Although the Company kept the ratios of various furs to beaver relatively constant in its *Comparative Standard* between 1740 and 1760 (Table 1), the ratios fluctuated on the London market. The question that thus arises is, did the Company gain or lose as a result? As has already been noted, in most years the Company suffered a relative loss by valuing the two major categories of beaver skins at one MB. Similarly, the *Comparative Standard* MB of wolverine (Figure 3) and deer (Figure 7) did not work to the Company's advantage in most years. In contrast, relative to the London market, in most years the Hudson's Bay Company profited from its pricing structure in the case of red fox (Figure 5), bear (Figure 6), wolf (Figure 4), excepting the eight years between 1746 and 1754, and marten (Figure 8). The results obtained for lynx were mixed. From 1737 to 1746, the *Comparative Standard* undervalued the Indians' lynx pelts (a gain to the Company). But from 1747 to 1762 it overvalued lynx pelts relative to the London market (a loss to the Company).

In an effort to determine the net effect of the pricing structure established in the *Comparative Standard* in relation to the changing London market, the total annual quantity of each category of fur that was traded was determined. These totals were multiplied by the annual *Comparative Standard* price converted to sterling, using the current parchment beaver price. These figures were then subtracted from the aggregate annual value of the sales of each type of fur on the London market. The results are presented in Table 2. Several important facts emerge. Reading down the far right-hand column, which provides a summary of the net results for each year, it is clear that the Company profited from its aggregate-pricing structure in eighteen of the twenty-five years examined. Over the whole period, its relative gain on exchange differences between Rupert's Land and London prices amounted to more than £38,000. With regard to individual commodities, the column summaries reveal that the *Comparative Standard* worked to the Company's overall disadvantage in the instances of coat beaver, wolverine, red fox, grey fox, deer, and lynx. The relative loss on coat beaver was particularly heavy. Gains were realized on wolf, bear, and marten.

The relative gains and losses experienced on wolverine, wolf, bear, red fox, grey fox, deer, and lynx nearly cancel each other out. The importance of marten as a high-profit fur is most striking. Most of the net gain of £38,297.97 consists of the excess gain on marten balanced against losses on coat beaver. It is not surprising, therefore,

Table 2
Gains and Losses on Furs: Exchange Differences Between Rupert's Land and London Prices*

YEAR	PARCHMENT BEAVER	COAT BEAVER	WOLVERINE	WOLF	BEAR	RED FOX	GREY FOX	DEER	LYNX	MARTEN	TOTAL GAIN/LOSS
1737	0.0	-492.367	ND**	ND	ND	ND	ND	ND	ND	ND	-492.344
1738	0.0	-997.733	-70.659	13.051	2.266	47.027	ND	ND	307.945	2951.332	2253.272
1739	0.0	-845.641	-36.992	94.502	55.137	23.693	ND	-15.193	425.712	2677.278	2378.495
1740	0.0	-845.600	-34.647	176.305	78.805	29.009	ND	-48.640	416.372	4000.777	3772.375
1741	0.0	-824.660	-55.525	139.428	35.160	54.714	ND	-111.590	78.809	2895.538	2211.868
1742	0.0	-389.418	-43.693	386.715	84.234	33.246	ND	-169.871	174.253	2303.688	2379.157
1743	0.0	-1826.398	-60.221	948.159	195.333	121.426	ND	-51.088	356.967	2910.784	2594.994
1744	0.0	-1390.787	-91.403	220.042	134.880	139.378	ND	-43.584	400.503	3064.125	2433.166
1745	0.0	-550.523	-75.593	273.591	267.834	85.911	ND	-14.068	331.330	2377.511	2695.995
1746	0.0	-3956.874	-278.559	-70.331	108.933	73.505	ND	-50.688	67.599	1651.377	-2455.031
1747	0.0	-3349.520	-355.107	-279.472	88.731	-14.305	-38.822	-34.825	-121.616	1515.635	-2589.306
1748	0.0	-2529.865	-152.776	-6.681	160.252	51.967	-17.148	-39.063	-38.342	6457.450	3885.795
1749	0.0	-1910.953	-11.886	-154.569	184.103	74.347	-27.829	-31.815	21.724	27.334	-1829.549
1750	0.0	-5635.534	-141.317	-60.912	-40.000	-4.173	ND	-194.844	-588.605	2138.645	-4526.740
1751	0.0	-920.032	-58.345	-177.971	204.337	-78.323	ND	-95.657	-467.145	3247.776	1654.639
1752	0.0	-1394.412	-39.046	-146.794	111.143	-135.256	-61.722	-145.746	-1045.778	4698.687	1841.070
1753	0.0	778.051	82.284	-65.940	35.998	294.470	ND	-73.752	-930.977	4203.647	4323.786
1754	0.0	714.216	84.023	51.497	66.021	100.678	ND	-192.647	-525.880	2246.877	2544.780
1755	0.0	617.039	-74.554	85.494	150.635	43.161	ND	-125.101	-137.724	2992.735	3551.681
1756	0.0	8.457	-87.799	261.132	111.250	-96.858	ND	-30.179	-178.450	1334.954	1322.505
1757	0.0	78.695	ND	ND	ND	ND	ND	ND	ND	ND	78.698
1758	0.0	-12.523	-23.336	475.509	112.744	-76.839	ND	-180.744	-94.633	1471.376	1671.548
1759	0.0	-31.471	-229.649	1917.635	290.292	-546.919	ND	-208.241	-177.727	6578.565	7592.488
1760	0.0	-246.916	ND	ND	ND	ND	ND	ND	ND	ND	-246.918
1761	0.0	-1373.219	-288.916	352.530	244.616	-1363.305	ND	-328.185	-380.428	2921.741	-217.164
1762	0.0	-805.573	-84.394	676.889	151.258	-373.011	ND	-306.331	-150.263	2360.224	1468.795
TOTAL GAIN/LOSS	0.0	-28133.560	-2128.110	5109.810	2833.960	-1518.458	-145.522	-2491.853	-2256.356	67028.057	38297.968

*Sales multiplied by current value of MB at comparative standard gives figures in pounds sterling (£) which, when subtracted from aggregate annual value of sales in London (per fur type), gives result shown.
**ND signifies no data.

that the Company steadfastly refused to yield to Indian pressures to offer them a price on their marten comparable to the .50 MB paid by the French in the James Bay area.[15] Had the Governor and Committee done so, they would have substantially reduced their profit margin.

The fact that the Company continued to rate coat beaver equal to parchment is of considerable interest, given the lower profit margins that it experienced as a consequence. Again, pressure from Indians may be the cause, although concrete documentary evidence is lacking. However, it should be recalled that the Indians were able to wear coat-beaver skins before trading them. Thus, these skins had a use and a trade value, unlike parchment beaver which was of only commercial significance.[16] When a technological change in the felting industry caused the coat-beaver market to temporarily collapse in the late seventeenth century, the Company attempted, without success, to get the Indians to cut back on their trade in these pelts.[17] The Company suggested that its traders burn coat-beaver skins in front of the Indians to show how little it valued these pelts.[18] Recognizing that the Indians would not be able to use their beaver pelts if they shifted their output entirely in favour of parchment beaver, the Hudson's Bay Company sent some sheepskins to its posts to see if the Indians would purchase them as substitute clothing.[19] The Indians did not accept the idea and coat beaver continued to pile up at the Bay-side posts. Thus, it may well be that the failure of the Company to devalue coat beaver in later years was due to Indian resistance to the idea. It was clearly in the Indians' best interest to maintain an equal price.

Table 3 shows the current annual prices of the various types of furs relative to the current price for parchment beaver expressed as a base of 100. It provides an indication of what the MB values of these furs should have been had the Company adjusted its *Comparative Standard* to keep it in line with the price structure of the London market. Particularly noteworthy is the relative value of marten. According to the *Comparative Standard*, marten was valued at .33 MB. In London, it was worth .64 to 1.16 beaver. Table 4 summarizes the

---

15. *Ibid.*, p. 183.

16. Whereas parchment skins were only traded, the Indians could continue to consume beaver meat.

17. Rich, *The Hudson's Bay Company*, p. 161.

18. *Ibid.*, pp. 160-61.

19. *Ibid.*

Table 3
Index of Current Fur Prices Relative to Parchment Beaver*

	1737	1738	1739	1740	1741	1742	1743	1744	1745	1746	1747	1748	1749	1750	1751	1752	1753	1754	1755	1756	1757	1758	1759	1760	1761	1762
Parchment Beaver	100	100	100	100	100	100	100	100	100	100	100	100	100	100	100	100	100	100	100	100	100	100	100	100	100	100
Coat Beaver	83.	82.	87.	83.	86.	85.	80.	76.	81.	63.	63.	75.	58.	50.	74.	82.	114.	113.	113.	100.	103.	100.	100.	92.	78.	88
Scrap Beaver	0.	0.	0.	66.	63.	73.	69.	57.	54.	46.	57.	54.	40.	29.	56.	62.	95.	73.	84.	67.	63.	67.	64.	58.	50.	60
Parchment Beaver D/S**	78.	87.	83.	84.	89.	92.	88.	86.	89.	84.	80.	74.	82.	75.	70.	77.	76.	83.	75.	81.	82.	81.	83.	81.	80.	68
Cub Beaver	105.	104.	98.	98.	104.	101.	106.	93.	102.	96.	89.	102.	99.	82.	85.	93.	107.	97.	99.	66.	95.	100.	104.	99.	100.	94
Cub Beaver Scrap	0.	84.	79.	80.	79.	69.	83.	82.	75.	67.	77.	76.	89.	62.	64.	75.	79.	72.	63.	66.	70.	78.	87.	82.	66.	57
Cut Beaver	0.	0.	58.	76.	66.	0.	0.	61.	0.	59.	56.	66.	52.	53.	0.	61.	78.	59.	75.	63.	73.	76.	76.	68.	58.	59
Marten	0.	110.	110.	105.	105.	109.	116.	92.	101.	68.	56.	116.	56.	67.	75.	72.	78.	72.	108.	63.	0.	103.	95.	68.	64.	74
Marten D/S	0.	80.	75.	65.	54.	75.	67.	47.	61.	37.	48.	66.	0.	35.	39.	48.	87.	55.	92.	92.	0.	48.	50.	0.	39.	46
Wolf	0.	159.	199.	226.	221.	295.	350.	254.	251.	133.	110.	148.	126.	120.	127.	116.	133.	164.	163.	193.	0.	215.	220.	0.	178.	199
Wolf D/S	0.	0.	0.	0.	0.	0.	155.	128.	61.	72.	0.	106.	78.	61.	60.	72.	105.	106.	0.	104.	0.	154.	151.	0.	108.	159
Lynx	0.	240.	316.	338.	180.	225.	272.	246.	247.	165.	126.	137.	153.	101.	103.	89.	94.	121.	121.	107.	0.	112.	131.	0.	110.	140
Wolverine D/S	0.	89.	64.	62.	53.	56.	56.	51.	55.	0.	0.	53.	49.	74.	0.	0.	0.	94.	60.	67.	0.	66.	34.	0.	44.	0
Red Fox	0.	165.	135.	140.	149.	150.	208.	176.	148.	149.	94.	108.	137.	98.	72.	67.	161.	137.	112.	83.	0.	72.	61.	0.	0.	67
Grey Fox	0.	0.	0.	0.	0.	0.	0.	0.	0.	0.	0.	0.	61.	0.	0.	40.	0.	0.	0.	0.	0.	0.	0.	0.	0.	0
Black Bear	0.	203.	248.	278.	239.	301.	398.	334.	471.	292.	252.	297.	282.	179.	322.	260.	231.	274.	301.	279.	0.	366.	292.	0.	467.	258
Bear Cub	0.	0.	0.	0.	0.	0.	0.	0.	0.	0.	0.	0.	0.	0.	0.	139.	73.	0.	103.	117.	0.	132.	115.	0.	223.	0
Otter	0.	124.	94.	102.	93.	147.	237.	186.	198.	125.	115.	135.	133.	105.	147.	128.	151.	118.	130.	42.	0.	97.	129.	0.	188.	192
Otter D/S	0.	0.	0.	0.	0.	0.	0.	0.	0.	0.	68.	78.	0.	46.	74.	0.	67.	0.	55.	42.	0.	0.	120.	0.	158.	151
Mink	0.	72.	39.	0.	34.	48.	51.	45.	62.	59.	35.	66.	42.	24.	36.	46.	65.	54.	58.	41.	5.	26.	34.	0.	50.	60
Muskrat	0.	0.	0.	0.	0.	0.	0.	0.	0.	88.	8.	18.	10.	6.	7.	7.	109.	8.	5.	0.	5.	83.	11.	0.	12.	60
Ermine	0.	0.	0.	0.	24.	0.	0.	0.	0.	0.	0.	0.	0.	0.	0.	0.	0.	0.	0.	0.	0.	0.	0.	0.	0.	0
Squirrel	0.	0.	0.	0.	6.	0.	6.	1.	0.	19.	0.	162.	91.	16.	23.	0.	0.	0.	0.	0.	0.	0.	0.	0.	0.	15
Racoon	0.	45.	36.	0.	37.	48.	57.	37.	84.	25.	18.	43.	32.	22.	4.	29.	42.	39.	60.	57.	0.	62.	71.	0.	65.	61
Deer	0.	0.	0.	0.	0.	0.	0.	0.	0.	52.	25.	45.	37.	22.	15.	0.	0.	0.	0.	0.	0.	0.	0.	0.	0.	0
Deer horns	57.	0.	0.	0.	0.	0.	47.	0.	0.	0.	0.	0.	0.	0.	0.	0.	0.	0.	0.	0.	0.	0.	0.	0.	0.	0
Elk	0.	130.	133.	116.	102.	109.	103.	104.	205.	100.	74.	157.	74.	46.	57.	87.	74.	78.	67.	49.	0.	59.	59.	0.	61.	167
Woodchuck	0.	130.	133.	136.	139.	199.	189.	159.	213.	126.	119.	193.	162.	75.	83.	60.	70.	74.	77.	64.	0.	84.	84.	0.	104.	112

*Current price for parchment beaver is used as base price (equal to 100).

**D/S = Damaged and staged (summer).

Table 4
Index of Relative Price Changes by Fur Type*

	1737	1738	1739	1740	1741	1742	1743	1744	1745	1746	1747	1748	1749	1750	1751	1752	1753	1754	1755	1756	1757	1758	1759	1760	1761	1762
Coat Beaver	100.	108.	111.	105.	106.	100.	100.	115.	96.	106.	118.	103.	101.	141.	170.	180.	199.	203.	219.	200.	222.	204.	214.	235.	168	156
Coat Beaver Scrap	0.	0.	0.	100.	93.	102.	103.	104.	77.	93.	129.	89.	83.	97.	155.	164.	197.	156.	193.	159.	162.	164.	164.	175.	128	126
Parchment Beaver	100.	108.	106.	105.	102.	97.	103.	126.	99.	140.	156.	113.	144.	234.	191.	182.	145.	148.	161.	166.	179.	169.	178.	212.	178	147
Parchment Beaver D/S**	100.	121.	113.	114.	117.	114.	117.	140.	113.	152.	160.	109.	152.	226.	172.	182.	142.	137.	156.	174.	188.	177.	189.	238.	184	129
Cub Beaver	100.	106.	99.	98.	101.	93.	104.	112.	96.	128.	132.	110.	136.	183.	154.	162.	147.	137.	151.	152.	162.	160.	177.	200.	169	131
Cub Beaver Scrap	0.	100.	92.	93.	90.	73.	95.	114.	82.	103.	132.	95.	142.	161.	135.	151.	126.	118.	111.	120.	137.	145.	171.	193.	130	93
Cut Beaver	0.	0.	100.	131.	110.	0.	126.	0.	0.	135.	143.	121.	123.	202.	0.	182.	185.	143.	195.	170.	212.	209.	221.	235.	169	142
Marten	0.	100.	101.	98.	91.	89.	101.	98.	84.	80.	100.	111.	68.	131.	0.	111.	106.	115.	146.	128.	147.	221.	142.	0.	97	92
Marten D/S	0.	100.	92.	79.	63.	84.	80.	69.	70.	60.	87.	87.	0.	95.	122.	101.	92.	94.	115.	90.	0.	95.	103.	0.	81	78
Wolf	0.	100.	122.	138.	131.	166.	210.	186.	144.	108.	99.	97.	105.	162.	107.	101.	112.	141.	152.	185.	0.	212.	227.	0.	184	170
Wolf D/S	0.	0.	0.	0.	0.	0.	0.	101.	0.	63.	0.	75.	70.	89.	72.	82.	95.	99.	134.	90.	0.	163.	168.	0.	119	146
Cat	0.	100.	129.	138.	71.	84.	108.	120.	94.	89.	76.	60.	85.	91.	76.	63.	53.	60.	75.	68.	0.	73.	90.	0.	76	79
Cat D/S	0.	0.	0.	0.	0.	0.	100.	126.	118.	111.	82.	96.	135.	170.	126.	155.	108.	97.	100.	94.	0.	103.	160.	0.	131	148
Wolverine	0.	100.	108.	111.	93.	87.	95.	107.	89.	78.	85.	86.	166.	202.	195.	202.	210.	229.	163.	159.	191.	191.	157.	0.	120	152
Wolverine D/S	0.	100.	70.	68.	56.	56.	60.	67.	56.	0.	0.	63.	73.	182.	0.	0.	0.	145.	101.	116.	118.	118.	100.	0.	0	0
Red Fox	0.	100.	80.	83.	86.	81.	121.	125.	82.	117.	82.	69.	111.	129.	77.	69.	131.	114.	102.	77.	69.	69.	61.	0.	44	56
Grey Fox	0.	0.	0.	0.	0.	0.	0.	0.	100.	100.	100.	111.	83.	0.	0.	0.	0.	0.	0.	0.	0.	0.	0.	0.	0	0
Black Bear	0.	100.	120.	133.	112.	133.	187.	192.	213.	186.	179.	154.	185.	191.	280.	216.	153.	185.	220.	210.	0.	282.	236.	0.	378	173
Bear Cub	0.	0.	0.	0.	0.	0.	0.	0.	0.	0.	0.	0.	100.	0.	0.	153.	64.	0.	99.	116.	0.	134.	123.	0.	237	0
Otter	0.	100.	75.	80.	71.	106.	183.	176.	147.	131.	134.	115.	143.	184.	210.	175.	163.	131.	156.	155.	0.	123.	172.	0.	250	212
Otter D/S	0.	0.	100.	73.	0.	129.	0.	0.	0.	0.	138.	116.	0.	142.	185.	0.	127.	0.	117.	92.	0.	0.	281.	0.	369	292
Mink	0.	100.	0.	0.	86.	114.	129.	139.	150.	200.	132.	182.	146.	139.	168.	207.	229.	196.	229.	164.	7.	107.	146.	0.	218	214
Muskrat	0.	0.	0.	0.	0.	0.	100.	25.	0.	100.	11.	17.	12.	12.	11.	11.	129.	10.	7.	0.	7.	114.	15.	0.	18	71
Ermine	0.	0.	0.	0.	0.	0.	0.	0.	0.	450.	0.	3150.	2250.	750.	0.	0.	0.	0.	0.	0.	0.	0.	0.	0.	0	0
Racoon	0.	100.	0.	100.	100.	100.	154.	123.	50.	92.	73.	127.	123.	19.	0.	0.	0.	0.	99.	0.	0.	0.	0.	0.	0	58
Deer	0.	100.	80.	86.	86.	75.	112.	139.	174.	153.	83.	107.	110.	107.	89.	112.	129.	121.	201.	199.	0.	221.	266.	0.	241	189
Deer Horns	0.	0.	0.	0.	0.	0.	0.	0.	0.	0.	0.	0.	0.	45.	0.	0.	0.	0.	0.	0.	0.	0.	0.	0.	0	0
Elk	0.	100.	88.	75.	75.	75.	76.	94.	145.	100.	82.	127.	76.	77.	77.	114.	76.	82.	77.	58.	0.	71.	74.	0.	77	175
Woodchuck	0.	100.	102.	101.	138.	140.	143.	150.	125.	132.	156.	167.	125.	113.	78.	72.	89.	76.	0.	101.	107.	0.	132.	117		

*The first year in which data are available for each fur is used as the base price (100).
**D/S = Damaged and staged (summer).

relative price changes that took place for each commodity between 1737 and 1762. In each instance the base year (100) is the first year of record.

The net impact that declining fur volumes and price fluctuations had on Company fur revenues is shown in Figure 10 (see page 114). It reveals that over the twenty-four-year period for which there are records, an erratic upward trend in revenue is evident. Thus, we cannot conclude that declining fur volumes were "driving the Company to the wall". The fact that the income from fur sales did not suffer as one might have expected may well explain why the Governor and Committee chose to "sleep by the frozen sea", as critics charged, rather than move inland to meet the French head-on.[20] Such a move might have seemed appropriate to imperialist thinkers, but it would have been a questionable business strategy under the circumstances. Inland expansion would have served to augment overhead costs substantially, without any assurance that there would have been a compensating increase in the flow of furs.

The fact that parchment beaver prices exhibited an erratic upward trend over most of the period is of great importance in another respect. It had a significant impact on the profit margin built into the *Standard of Trade*. This was the official price schedule that the Company used to assign MB values to its trade goods. Table 5 shows the official MB prices of the trade goods that would have been included on a typical Indian shopping list at Fort Albany in 1740, 1750 and 1760. As in the case of the *Comparative Standard*, prices changed very little. However, given that the Company never compensated the Indians for the increased market value of their beaver after 1737, this had the net effect of secretly increasing the real prices Indians were paying for trading goods. The effect of change in parchment beaver prices on the hidden cost of the Indians' "shopping basket" is shown in Table 5. It reveals that the "basket" was nearly two and one-half times as expensive in 1750 as it was in 1740. The situation changed only slightly by 1760. Even with the decline in the value of beaver, the Indians were still paying effectively twice as much for the goods as they had in 1738.

Of importance in this context, Company records indicate that the cost of obtaining goods in England did not increase appreciably between 1740 and 1760 (Table 6). Indeed, the prices of a number of basic staples remained virtually unchanged. These include knives, ice chisels, hatchets, kettles, and firearms. Cloth and blanket prices

---

20. *Ibid.*, pp. 533-35.

Table 5
Fort Albany Trade Goods Prices

Trade Goods	1740		1750		1760	
	MB	Sterling	MB	Sterling	MB	Sterling
Powder (lbs.)	.75	.21	.75	.51	.75	.45
Shot (lb.)	.20	.05	.20	.13	.20	.12
Gun (4 ft.)	12.00	3.36	12.00	8.16	12.00	7.20
Flints (20)	1.00	.28	1.00	.68	1.00	.60
Ice Chisel	.50	.14	.50	.34	.50	.30
Hatchet	.50	.14	.50	.34	.50	.30
Cloth (yd.)	2.00	.56	2.00	1.36	2.00	1.20
Tobacco (lb.)	1.00	.28	1.00	.68	1.00	.60
Brandy (gal.)	4.00	1.12	4.00	2.72	4.00	2.40
Knives	.125	.03	.125	.08	.125	.075
Twine (skein)	1.00	.28	1.00	.68	1.00	.60
Kettles	1.00	.28	1.00	.68	1.00	.60
Total	24.075	6.64	24.075	16.37	24.75	14.45

Parchment beaver prices: 1740 = .28, 1750 = .68, 1760 = .60
Sources: Ray and Freeman, 1978, p. 64, and PAM HBC A 48/1.

showed only slight increments. No important items doubled in value. Thus, as in the case of the *Comparative Standard*, the rigid *Standard of Trade* worked in the Company's favour during this critical period.

The built-in advantage of the official tariffs was extended further by the practice of having the traders at the posts exceed the official tariffs by whatever margin local economic conditions permitted. The gain that they made was called *Overplus*. It was reported every year, and therefore we have a good idea of the portion of the total fur returns that were obtained in this manner. The *Overplus* data also enable us to estimate the average annual markup in Rupert's Land.

Table 6
London Prices for Trading Goods*

Item	1740	1750	1760
Beads (lbs.)	22.5 d.	26 d.	26 d.
Blankets (piece)	3/10	4/- to 4/10	4/1- to 5/-
Brandy (molasses)	2/10	2/4	2/10
Cloth:			
Flannel bays (yd.)	11 d.	11 d.	ND**
Duffel (piece)	3/5	3/12/6	ND
Cotton	11 d. (yd.)	11 d. (ell)	14.5 d. (ell)
Woolens (cloths)	5/2/6 to 5/7/6	6/10	6/15 to 7/2/6
Combs:			
Large ivory (doz.)	6/9	7/-	ND
Small ivory (doz.)	5/9	7/-	ND
Firearms (all)	22/-	22/-	22/-
Flints (gross)	ND	ND	15/-
Hatchets:			
large (ea.)	11.5 d.	11.5 d.	11.5 d.
mid and narrow (ea.)	9.5 d.	9.5 d.	9.5 d.
Ice chisels:			
broad (ea.)	6 d.	6 d.	6 d.
narrow (ea.)	3.5 d.	3.5 d.	3.5 d.
Kettles:			
old sort (lb.)	15.5 d.	15.5 d.	15.5 d.
new	—	16.5 d.	16.5 d.
Shot:			
Bristow (ton)	15/-	14/-	# 1-5 14/6
Bullet (ton)	16/-	15/-	# 6-9 15/6
Goose (ton)	17/6	16/6	16/-
Drop	14/-	13/-	18/6
Knives, large (gross)	30/-	30/-	ND

* Prices in Sterling, d. indicates penny.
**ND signifies no data.
Source: Minute Books, Hudson's Bay Company. PAM HBC A 1/37-41

This is shown in Figure 11 (see page 115). It reveals that the prices
of trade goods were being increased forty to sixty per cent above the
Standard of Trade rates. A concrete example of how the Hudson's Bay
Company profited from this two-tiered pricing system can be obtained
by considering the matter of firearms. Between 1740 and 1760, firearms cost the Company 22/-. At twelve MB, the official price of a
gun in 1740 would have been £3/7/2. Adding an additional forty per

cent to the price to allow for the *Overplus*, guns would have cost the Indians as much as £4/13/11. In 1760, with a sixty per cent advance on the standard (Figure 11), Indians were effectively paying £11/10/4 for their firearms, given the current prices being paid in London for beaver. This was more than ten times the price the Company paid for the guns.

From the foregoing it is clear that there is no evidence to support Eccles' assertion that the Hudson's Bay Company was in trouble due to French successes in the fur trade. In fact, his thesis can be stood on its head. It appears more likely that the French helped satisfy the Indian demand for goods, and at the same time diverted enough furs from the London market to assure the Hudson's Bay Company profitable fur sales. The above analyses also serve to demonstrate that the Hudson's Bay Company's fur trade was a very complex system. It cannot be understood solely in political terms, nor can we use our understanding of the experience of the French in the fur trade to safely interpret the actions of this particular group of English merchants. Finally, the present study underscores the need to systematically examine the actions of participating groups of traders in terms of the economic and political parameters in which they had to operate. In the period under study, imperial concerns dictated that the Hudson's Bay Company adopt an aggressive stance *vis-à-vis* the French. However, business considerations indicated an alternative course. Company pricing schedules, and market conditions in England, more than offset French gains. It was a very profitable period for the Company. It managed to pay an average dividend of eight per cent. In short, it did not make good business sense to move inland. But, the failure to do so made the Company vulnerable to imperialist critics in Parliament, who managed to convene a parliamentary enquiry into its affairs in the 1740s. However, the Hudson's Bay Company was able to turn aside this criticism, and this enabled the Governor and Committee to steer a course dictated by practical business concerns rather than the larger concerns of the Empire. A key consideration was keeping overhead costs to a minimum, which it did very effectively by "sleeping by the frozen sea". It is clear that the Company was not floundering in the face of aggressive French expansion, as a superficial examination of fur exports and imports might suggest.

In closing, it must be stressed that the conclusions drawn here cannot be applied to earlier or later periods of Hudson's Bay Company history. However, the method of analysis can be used to obtain better insights than presently exist. In particular, it is important to determine how the Company's system adjusted to inflationary periods in

England, particularly those associated with wartime conditions. The post-1763 period needs careful examination also, because it differed in some fundamental respects from the period of English-French rivalry. Prior to 1763, the two groups competed in the same fur-supply market, but disposed of their products in different European markets. In later years, the Hudson's Bay Company and the North West Company bought and sold furs in the same markets. It is unclear to what extent, if any, this may have adversely affected the fortunes of the two groups of British traders. Clearly, much more work needs to be done, focusing on the ways in which the Rupert's Land and European markets were linked together and the ways in which these linkages influenced the fortunes of the participating merchants.

Figure 1. Beaver Prices

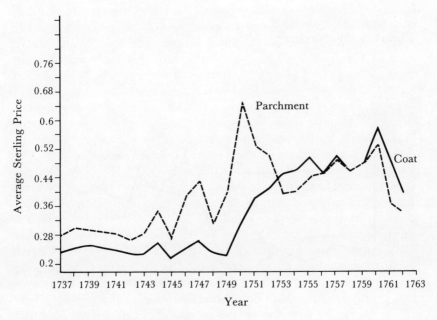

Source: PAM HBC A 48/1

Figure 2. Coat Beaver

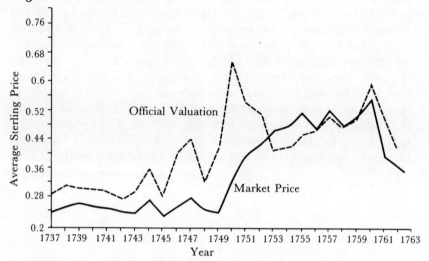

Official Valuation = *Comparative Standard* MB Value x current price of
Parchment Beaver
Market Price = Average sale price of pelt on London Market.
Source: PAM HBC A 48/1

Figure 3. Wolverine

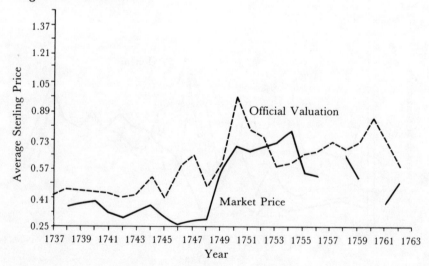

Official Valuation = *Comparative Standard* MB Value x current price of
Parchment Beaver
Market Price = Average sale price of pelt on London Market.
Source: PAM HBC A 48/1

Figure 4. Wolf

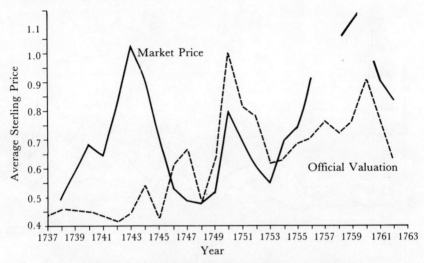

Official Valuation = *Comparative Standard* MB Value x current price of
                        Parchment Beaver
Market Price = Average sale price of pelt on London Market.
Source: PAM HBC A 48/1

Figure 5. Red Fox

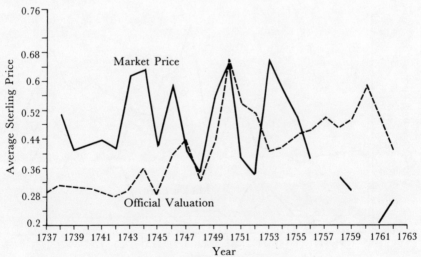

Official Valuation = *Comparative Standard* MB Value x current price of
                        Parchment Beaver
Market Price = Average sale price of pelt on London Market.
Source: PAM HBC A 48/1

Figure 6. Bear

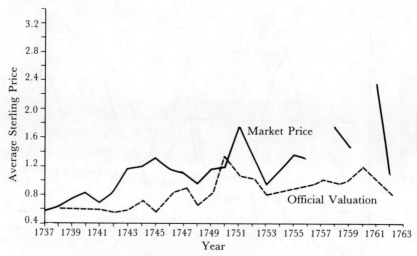

Official Valuation = *Comparative Standard* MB Value x current price of
                    Parchment Beaver
Market Price = Average sale price of pelt on London Market.
Source: PAM HBC A 48/1

Figure 7. Deer

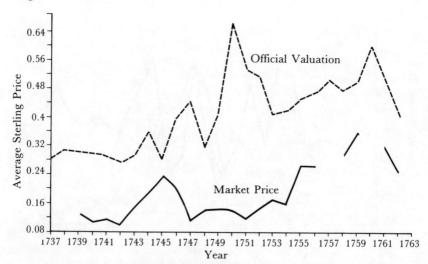

Official Valuation = *Comparative Standard* MB Value x current price of
                    Parchment Beaver
Market Price = Average sale price of pelt on London Market.
Source: PAM HBC A 48/1

Figure 8. Marten

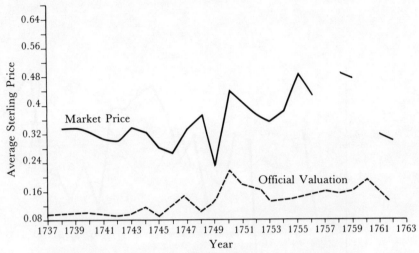

Official Valuation = *Comparative Standard* MB Value x current price of
                    Parchment Beaver
Market Price = Average sale price of pelt on London Market.
Source: PAM HBC A 48/1

Figure 9. Lynx

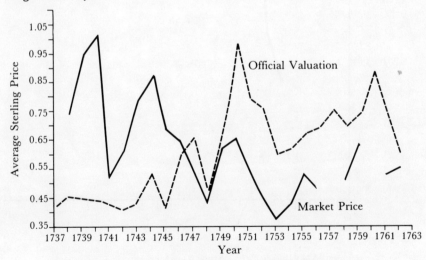

Official Valuation = *Comparative Standard* MB Value x current price of
                    Parchment Beaver
Market Price = Average sale price of pelt on London Market.
Source: PAM HBC A 48/1

Figure 10. Fur Auction Receipts 1736-1762

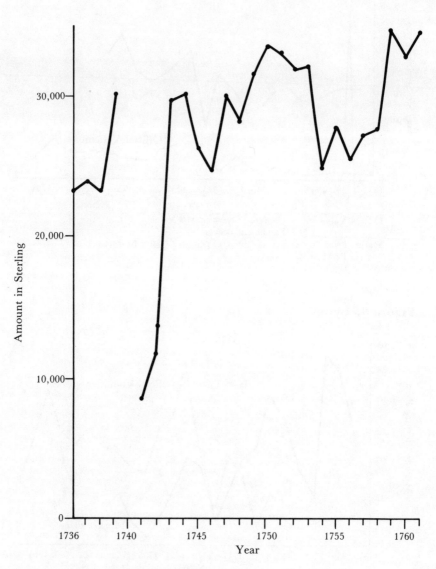

Source: PAM HBC A 48/1

Figure 11. Advance over Official Standards

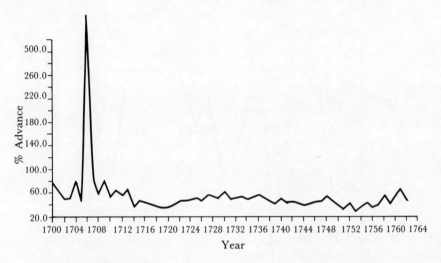

Source: PAM HBC B/d

6. Immigration and Business Cycles

Pauper Migration to Canada, 1815-1874

Mario S. Seccareccia*
University of Ottawa

Introduction

Traditional economics has had a tendency to adopt a monist approach to the understanding of historical phenomena: from its inception, a community of practitioners has sought to apply uniformly the tools of supply and demand to explain market activities. For instance, in the neoclassical vision of the exchange process, labour as a 'commodity' cannot escape this general rule. Conventional wisdom depicts the labour market much as one would a speculative spot market for fresh produce.[1] Given the cyclical movements in demand, individual utility maximizers are assumed to offer their labour services when wages are believed to be relatively high, and to withdraw them when wages are perceived to be unusually low. Actions by participants are thus subjected to the regulatory checks and balances of a competitive process that is all too often emptied of its historical and institutional characteristics.

As old and contemporary debates alike attest, 'the labour market' has been and continues to be the Achilles' heel of mainstream economics. Marx, Veblen, and Keynes, as intellectual heretics, were particularly conscious of the weaknesses of the standard formulations.

*I am particularly grateful to Irene Spry, whose valuable comments and warm support have made this essay possible, and to Duncan Cameron for his expert editorial advice. I also wish to acknowledge the excellent technical assistance of L. J. Koh.

1. The term is borrowed from J. Tobin, who aptly described this as the 'market-for-fresh-produce' view of the labour market. Cf. J. Tobin, "Inflation and Unemployment", *American Economic Review*, Vol. 62, no. 1 (March, 1972), p. 12.

In his *General Theory*, Keynes described the labour market as a sluggish fifth wheel, and he believed it incapable of serving the allocative function prescribed by neoclassical theory. Marx and Veblen preferred to emphasize the social nature of work and the role of institutions in a capitalist economy. While Veblen emphasized the 'ritual' and 'instinctive' character of the labour process, Marx pointed to the underlying social relations regulated by the dominant 'bourgeois' institutions.[2]

The purpose of this essay is to step outside traditional formulations, and through an examination of international migration to Canada, provide some clarifications about the historical development of the Canadian labour market. The immigrant labour market that developed in Canada during the first half of the nineteenth century has been of interest to Canadian economic historians, including H. A. Innis, K. Buckley and H. C. Pentland. This paper argues that pauper migration (and the ensuing labour-surplus economy of the nineteenth century) cannot be understood without a requisite understanding of both the role played by the British state, in disposing of its paupers, and the nature of the timber trade, in providing the only cheap and effective means of transport of the pauper immigrants.

Classical and Neoclassical Theories of Labour Migration

The history of economics teaches us that, as soon as the more subjective 'demand' elements are introduced for the purpose of explaining a specific phenomenon, they have a tendency to dominate the theoretical analysis.[3] This was the case for the theory of value in which 'marginal utility' analysis replaced the classical 'real cost' approach, and this has also been the case for what can be called the theory of 'labour migration'.

To the British classical economists, writing during the first half of the nineteenth century, migration was directly associated with an historically specific phase of capitalist development in agriculture. Whenever the Malthusian pressures of population build-up pushed

---

2. While the ideas of these three great political economists do evoke the vast majority of the heretical literature in this area, one cannot overlook J. E. Cairnes' (1874) well-known criticism of the conventional labour market whereby he further elaborated the Longfield–Mill idea of 'non-competing groups'.

3. The author owes this point to a discussion with J. Henry regarding the Sraffian methodology. For those interested in pursuing this question further, see the special issue of *L'Actualité économique*, Vol. 58, nos. 1-2 (janvier-juin, 1982).

the intensive or extensive margins of cultivation towards levels unable to sustain the minimum subsistence requirements, the state, they argued, should promote emigration. Hence, an increase in the flow of emigrants that is associated with a decrease in the level of real wages, and which, in turn, has been brought about by a decline in labour productivity on the less good arable lands, would be *prima facie* evidence in support of this classical view. J. S. Mill summarized the classical 'supply-led' argument in the following way:

> Besides the importation of corn, there is another resource which can be invoked by the nation whose increasing numbers press hard, not against their capital, but against the productive capacity of their land: I mean Emigration, especially in the form of Colonization. Of this remedy the efficacy as far as it goes is real, since it consists in seeking elsewhere those unoccupied tracts of fertile land, which if they existed at home would enable the demand of an increasing population to be met without any falling off in the productiveness of labour.[4]

Indeed, basing his scheme on these principles of increasing population and diminishing productivity of the poorer grades of the soil, Wakefield was to set up a complete colonization plan for the British colonies. He proposed that the state should extract increasing rents by the sale of British colonial lands and then use these funds to subsidize further migration. In this way, the whole process of colonization would be self-financing.[5] Curiously, many of the proposals of the classical economists, in schemes of the Horton-Wakefield variety,[6] were often used to support the most rigorous forms of state intervention to assist pauper migration.

Towards the end of the last century, the focus of attention shifted dramatically. In reaction to the previous classical supply-led mechanism, neoclassical economists proposed what may be called a

---

4. J. S. Mill, *Principles of Political Economy* (University of Toronto Press, 1965), p. 194.

5. See E. G. Wakefield, *A View of the Art of Colonisation* (London: John W. Parker, 1849), in whose book some of these schemes are referred to. There was, of course, much debate over Wakefield's scheme. For instance, in an article in the *Edinburgh Review*, Vol. 71 (1840), the author refers to Wakefield's proposals in the following way: "To return for a moment to the other favourite doctrine of Mr. Wakefield . . . .—the maxim that, in order to secure the most rapid progress of the best sort of colonization, *the whole proceeds of the land-fund, without exception, should be employed as an immigration-fund*" (p. 542). This and many other articles on emigration during that period are reprinted in *Emigration in the Victorian Age*, ed. by O. MacDonagh (Westmead, England: Gregg International Publishers Ltd., 1973). For an excellent discussion of Malthus' views on both the Horton and Wakefield proposals, see R. N. Gosh, "Malthus on Emigration and Colonization: Letters to Wilmot-Horton", *Economica*, n.s., Vol. 30, no. 117 (February, 1963), pp. 45-62.

6. These proposals are discussed extensively by W. A. Carrothers, *Emigration from the British Isles* (London: P. S. King & Son Ltd., 1929), especially chapters 3 and 5.

'demand-led' model of migratory flows. Since rational individuals were assumed to react primarily to the perceived 'price signals' associated with the alternating degrees of tightness in a labour market, it was a short step to conclude from this that the swings in the growth of labour demand must play the dominant role in the labour-supply decision. To quote Hourwich's classic study on migration:

> The supply of immigrant labor is regulated by free competition, like that of any other commodity. It may sometimes exceed the demand and at other times fall short of it; in the long run, however, supply adjusts itself to demand.
>
> If we compare the totals for industrial cycles, including years of panic, of depression, and of prosperity, we find a remarkable regularity in the ratio of immigration to population. . . . This regularity indicates the character, as well as the volume of immigration.[7]

Given this belief in the allocative function of labour markets, numerous economists, especially in the United States, were to undertake extensive research with the intention of providing empirical support for this demand-led hypothesis.

The most celebrated of these early studies is that of Jerome. Using various indicators of demand conditions, such as the value of merchandise imports and the production of pig iron, he found a close correlation between each of these series and the course of U.S. immigration for the period 1820-1924.[8] Together with D. S. Thomas, he thus dismissed the classical 'push' factors in the United Kingdom and Western Europe as important causes of emigration on the basis of the fact that emigration from the British Isles correlated more closely with the fluctuations in employment and output in the United States than with data series for the United Kingdom.[9]

Jerome's study was followed by the work of Kuznets who, by using the newly constructed U.S. national accounts for the period beginning with 1869, found that the "troughs and peaks in the population rates of growth lag fairly consistently . . . behind those in the

---

7. I. A. Hourwich, *Immigration and Labor* (New York: G. P. Putnam's Sons, 1912), pp. 101-102.

8. Jerome concludes that "whatever may be the basic causes of migration, there is a close relation between the cyclical oscillations of employment and those of immigration and emigration, . . . with considerable reason to believe that this similarity, particularly in the cyclical oscillations, is due to a sensitiveness of migration to employment conditions". H. Jerome, *Migration and Business Cycles* (New York: National Bureau of Economic Research Inc., 1926), p. 243. This was also emphasized by G. Cassel, *The Theory of Social Economy*, Vol. 2 (London: Ernest Benn Ltd., 1932), pp. 573-74.

9. H. Jerome, *op. cit.*, chapter 8. Also see D. S. Thomas, *Social Aspects of the Business Cycle* (New York: E. P. Dutton, 1925), pp. 148-51.

rates of growth of national income."[10] Outside of the more mixed evidence provided by B. Thomas, the single most important post-war study to have supported this demand-led model of migration is the work of Easterlin. In his comprehensive study of the historical patterns of U.S. immigration, Easterlin found that the rate of immigration typically followed with a lag the rate of growth of output, the rate of growth of hourly wages and, to a lesser extent, the movement in the U.S. unemployment rate.[11] Probably more than any other, therefore, this study was to argue that the neoclassical demand-led model (whereby labour supply reacts primarily to the 'price signals' emanating from demand pressures in the host country) provides the most appropriate explanation of the historical facts. Indeed, A. G. Green's well-known and extensive work on Canadian post-war immigration may have been highly influenced by Easterlin's empirical findings and methodology.[12]

Assuming these results to be applicable, especially to the historical statistics of the United States, to what extent would this demand-led model hold true for the historical patterns of nineteenth-century migration to Canada? As will be shown, the available empirical evidence is not strongly supportive of either the demand-led or supply-led hypotheses previously discussed. The statistical findings, however, can possibly be reconciled within the framework of an approach first proposed by Innis, whose explanation relied on the existence of structural 'unused capacity' in the transportation of the dominant staple product of the period for Canada.

The Determinants of the International Flow of Migrant Labour for the Period 1815-1874: Some Empirical Evidence

Trends and cycles in economic activity have long been recognized by economists interested in the dynamics of capitalist development. To Marx, for instance, the ten-year Juglar cycle in investment activity

---

10. S. Kuznets, *National Income: A Summary of Findings* (New York: National Bureau of Economic Research, 1946), p. 66. The link between migration and the Kuznets cycle is also discussed in S. Kuznets, "Long Swings in the Growth of Population and in Related Economic Variables", *Proceedings of the American Philosophical Society*, Vol. 102, no. 1 (February, 1958), pp. 25-52.

11. For a summary of his findings, see R. A. Easterlin, *Population, Labor Force, and Long Swings in Economic Growth* (New York: National Bureau of Economic Research, 1968), pp. 30-36.

12. However, with only a minimum of statistical success, these empirical results are discussed in A. G. Green, *Immigration and the Postwar Canadian Economy* (Toronto: Macmillan Co. of Canada Ltd., 1976), chapter 3.

was connected with what he described as the "total reproduction phase of capital".[13] However, this reproduction phase was itself seen by some as part of an even wider trend pattern recognized by Kondratieff and identified as the 'long cycle'.[14]

During the declining phase of what Schumpeter described as the 'first Kondratieff' wave, the North Atlantic economy of the post-Napoleonic era was fashioned by strong secular tendencies relating to the gradual tapering-off of developments in the British cotton textile and iron industries,[15] and accompanied by a progressive devalorization of primary activities. Depending on the country, this long wave reached its trough between the years 1844 and 1851; and then slowly began its ascending phase, reaching a peak between the years 1870 and 1875.[16]

In the declining phase of the first Kondratieff wave, staple products faced growing world competition, as previously unsettled lands, particularly in North America, were drawn into cultivation.[17] With the aid of preferential treatment from Britain, Canada was in part able to cope with the worsening terms of trade for certain primary products by a steady increase in the export of timber to Great Britain.[18] And even the general erosion of imperial preferences between the years 1842 and 1860 did not spell the end of timber as a leading sector in Canadian economic development. As Innis noted, these negative policy effects on the timber trade during the forties and fifties "were offset in part by lower costs of transportation, incidental to

---

13. Cf. K. Marx, *Grundrisse: Foundations of the Critique of Political Economy* (New York: Vintage Books, 1973, p. 720).

14. Kondratieff affirmed that "long waves arise out of causes which are inherent in the essence of the capitalistic economy." N. D. Kondratieff, "The Long Waves in Economic Life", *Review of Economic Statistics*, Vol. 17, no. 6 (November, 1935), p. 115.

15. See J. A. Schumpeter, *Business Cycles*, Vol. I (New York: McGraw-Hill Book Co. Inc., 1939), pp. 252-302.

16. A precise dating of these 'long cycles', using the wholesale prices series for the four major countries studied, can be found in A. F. Burns and W. C. Mitchell, *Measuring Business Cycles* (New York: National Bureau of Economic Research, 1946), Table 165, p. 432. For a recent work providing evidence using output series, see E. Mandel, *Long Waves of Capitalist Development* (Cambridge University Press, 1980), pp. 2-5. According to Schumpeter, this latter ascending phase of the Kondratieff depended on the fast "railroadization" of Britain and North America. See J. A. Schumpeter, *op. cit.*, pp. 325-51.

17. See, for instance, S. B. Clough, *European Economic History*, second edition (New York: McGraw-Hill, 1968), pp. 330-32.

18. While preferential treatment was also accorded to colonial breadstuffs as of 1825, in 1843 new legislation was enacted and then swept away with the general abrogation of the Corn Laws in 1846. See G. N. Tucker, *The Canadian Commercial Revolution, 1845-1851* (New Haven: Yale University Press, 1936), pp. 88-99.

the completion of the St. Lawrence canals, and by the Reciprocity Treaty of 1854.''[19] Hence, following Innis' staple approach, it can be argued that exports of timber from British North America broadly reflected the general Canadian trends and cycles in economic activity, at least from the end of the Napoleonic era through to the 1850s.[20]

Consistent series on this staple export for the complete peak-to-peak sixty-year Kondratieff cycle (1815-74) are not available for Canada. For instance, the *Appendices to the Journals of the House of Assembly of the Province of Canada* provide only fragmentary data on the export of timber for most of the 1840s. A continuous series on the pine timber shipped from the ports of Lower Canada during the period 1816 to 1842 has been constructed, however, by Aubry. The available series is measured in log pieces.[21] This Aubry series on timber export has then been set against the information on the reference dates and duration of the business cycles for both Great Britain and the United States and, barring a number of isolated years, this series was found to follow very broadly the direction specified by the British and American reference cycles.[22] In the statistical equations to be presented in the table below, this series will be denoted by the symbol X_T.

Due to imperial preferences, the bulk of British imports of timber originated from her North American colonies after 1815 to the 1850s. Indeed, it has been documented that British imports of square timber from the Baltic were to regain their position and exceed the Canadian imports only by 1859.[23] Therefore, a series on British imports of this staple product could be legitimately used as an indicator of Canadian timber exports to the British Isles until the 1850s.

---

19. H. A. Innis, "An Introduction to Canadian Economic Studies" (1937) in H. A. Innis, *Essays in Canadian Economic History* (University of Toronto Press, 1956), p. 161.

20. The importance of foreign trade in explaining Canadian cyclical fluctuations has been shown by most economists studying business-cycle behaviour in Canada. But not all would limit their analysis to the export of one staple product. See, for instance, V. W. Malach, *International Cycles and Canada's Balance of Payments, 1921-33* (University of Toronto Press, 1954).

21. These data were collected and converted under the common denominator by F. Aubry, *Indicators of Economic Growth for Lower Canada, 1760-1850* (Unpublished M.A. thesis, University of Ottawa, 1970), pp. 189-91.

22. The reference dates used are those provided by A. F. Burns and W. C. Mitchell, *op. cit.*, pp. 78-79. While the British reference dates begin with the peak of 1792, unfortunately the American reference dates only begin with the trough of 1834. Hence, while there was some very general agreement with the British reference cycle, only a partial comparison could be made with the American reference dates.

23. W. T. Easterbrook and H. G. J. Aitken, *Canadian Economic History* (Toronto: Macmillan, 1956), p. 201.

Such a series for the period 1821-1857 was published by Jevons, giving the loads of unsawn timber imported by Britain.[24] An alternative statistic, showing the value of timber imports for the years between 1815 and 1829, is published by Mitchell and Deane.[25] These two series will be described by the terms M_J and M_V respectively.

Because of Canadian trade diversification during the upswing of the 'second Kondratieff' wave (from the late 1840s to the early 1870s), it became progressively more equivocal to employ for these latter years a proxy for business conditions based solely on the volume of timber exports. An alternative variable has been proposed to reflect this structural change after 1850. Instead of timber exports, a more general series covering a wider spectrum of commodities might be used to test this hypothesis on the crucial role of demand conditions. The available statistic that could serve this function is the data series on the value of exports from the port of Montreal. Such a series, obtained from the Board of Trade reports for the period 1850-1874, has been published by Hamelin and Roby.[26] More than any other, this variable allows us to test the demand-led hypothesis on international migration. In the estimated equations, the symbol X_V will be used to indicate this variable.

Finally, to the extent that Canadian activities were closely tied to general developments in the British Isles during the period, one may be tempted to use the British movements in the Gross National Product as an approximate indicator of cyclical conditions in the North American colonies. This view would be consistent with the actual facts of the nineteenth century as to the strong dependence of the British North American colonies on imperial demand for colonial goods (primarily their staple products). Deane has constructed such an annual statistical series for the United Kingdom, beginning in 1830, on the basis of prices in 1900. Like the others, this variable, indicated by the term Y_B in the statistical Table, was also regressed against the Canadian immigration data.

In addition to trying to estimate what may be described as essentially demand elements, an attempt was also made in testing for the classical supply factors. The only meaningful statistics that could be found for the period were the Bowley wage series reprinted in

---

24. Cf. W. S. Jevons, *Investigations in Currency and Finance* (London: Macmillan, 1884), p. 30.

25. See B. R. Mitchell and P. Deane, *Abstract of British Historical Statistics* (Cambridge University Press, 1962), p. 289.

26. Cf. J. Hamelin and Y. Roby, *Histoire économique du Québec, 1851-1896* (Montréal: Fides, 1971), Appendix 13, p. 391.

Mitchell and Deane. Indices were available for agricultural workers in England and Wales, in Scotland, and for workers in the British cotton industry, but it was the latter industrial wage index (W_I) which was found to be statistically the most significant in the analysis. Since many of the workers first moved to the British industrial centres, before emigrating to North America, the statistical significance of industrial wages tends to confirm this particular interpretation of the evidence.[27]

Table 1 summarizes the statistical evidence explaining British emigration to the North American colonies. In the first three equations, the dependent variable is the number of British emigrants to Canada. Emigration statistics were used since, prior to 1827, no consistent annual series on immigrant arrivals is available. For instance, Christie provides figures for immigrants arriving at the port of Quebec only for the years 1819-1833.[28] Similar statistics extracted from the *British Parliamentary Papers* have been reproduced by Cowan, but they differ from the Christie series.[29] Indeed, neither the Cowan nor the Christie statistics coincide with the official immigrant returns found in selected issues of the *Appendices to the Journals of the House of Assembly of the Province of Lower Canada* for the period.[30] The only complete annual series indicating the immigrant arrivals at the ports of Quebec and Montreal is supplied by Willcox for the years 1827-1874.[31] Due to the lack of consistent and reliable annual statistics on Canadian

27. Emigrants coming to British North America were by and large unskilled urban labourers. For instance, during the representative year 1857, over 50 per cent of the male emigrants came from the category of unskilled urban labourers rather than agricultural labourers. See *Appendix to the Sixteenth Volume of the Journals of the Legislative Assembly of the Province of Canada* (From February 25 to August 16, 1858), Session 1858 (Toronto: Rollo Campbell Printer), in Appendix No. 41.

28. See R. Christie, *A History of the Late Province of Lower Canada*, Vol. 3 (Montreal: Worthington, 1866, p. 512).

29. Cf. H. I. Cowan, *British Emigration to British North America*, revised edition, (University of Toronto Press, 1928, 1961), p. 289.

30. For instance, this author took a five-year period of emigrant returns (1832-36) given in the *Appendices to the Journals of the House of Assembly of the Province of Lower Canada* (Vols. 42-45 and 47), and compared these with the Cowan statistics. Except in a very general way, these figures were not strictly comparable. In much the same way, most Canadian Almanacs and Yearbooks from 1848 to 1873 give returns for previous years which did not always agree with the Cowan statistics.

31. See W. F. Willcox, ed., *International Migration*, Vol. I (Statistics) (New York: National Bureau of Economic Research Inc., 1929), p. 360.

Table 1
The Statistical Relation Between British Emigration, the Canadian Timber Trade, and Wages for Selected Periods During the Nineteenth Century

Period	1816-42	1815-29	1821-57
Constant Term	75692.50	18532.15	194151.58
	(4.03)	(3.18)	(5.08)
$X_{T_{-1}}$	0.1768	—	—
	(2.61)	—	—
$M_{V_{-1}}$	—	21.26	—
	—	(1.88)	—
$M_{J_{-1}}$	—	—	71.19
	—	—	(5.53)
$W_{I_{-1}}$	-5578.47	-1523.76	-4301.65
	(-3.99)	(-2.65)	(-5.09)
R^2	0.4177	0.2974	0.4949
ϱ	0.72	0.75	0.00
DW	1.97	2.28	2.00

Table 2
The Statistical Relation Between Immigration into Canada, Indicators of Economic Activity, and Wages for Selected Periods During the Nineteenth Century

Period	1850-74	1830-74
Constant Term	-10531.82	27361.75
	(-0.71)	(2.37)
$X_{V_{-1}}$	-0.5024	—
	(-0.75)	—
$Y_{B_{-1}}$	—	92.51
	—	(1.35)
$W_{I_{-1}}$	874.87	-1486.72
	(1.33)	(-1.42)
$\bar{R}^2$	0.00	0.0009
ϱ	0.65	0.45
DW	2.22	2.26

N.B.: The t-ratios are given in parentheses below the estimated coefficients of the lagged variables. Whenever the residuals appeared to be serially correlated, a Hildreth-Lu search procedure was used to improve the efficiency of the estimates. The correlation coefficient adjusted for the degrees of freedom ($\bar{R}^2$), the first-order autocorrelation coefficient (ϱ), and the Durbin-Watson statistic (DW) are reported at the bottom of each estimated relationship.

immigration for the pre-1827 period, the official British annual statistics on emigration to the North American colonies are used for these early years.[32]

These returns probably underestimate the actual number of emigrants travelling to Canada. As long as the trans-Atlantic passage was mainly by sailing vessels, there must have been a great deal of evasion of the restrictions laid down by the British government.[33] It was only with the coming of the steamship lines in the 1850s that evasion, and the overloading of ships, became more difficult.

In spite of these obvious discrepancies, all the statistical series on immigration and emigration fluctuate systematically with one another. Hence, so long as a given statistical series is used consistently, no great problem ought to exist in capturing the degree of correlation between the dependent and independent variables.

The results, displayed in Table 1, show how significant the lagged values (and volume) of the timber trade were in explaining the outflow of migrant labourers from Britain to Canada. This suggests that a rise in Canadian timber exports was generally associated with an increase in the flow of British emigrants (with a one-year lag) to Canada. At the same time, the Table provides some evidence in support of the role of British wages in the decision to emigrate. A decline in wages is shown to be formally associated with an outflow of labourers to British North America. While, in all cases, these variables were found to be statistically significant in explaining the flow of migrant labour (see the t-ratios in parentheses), the overall explanatory power of the model (reflected in the $\bar{R}^2$) is found generally to be somewhat weak.

However, as soon as a more general indicator of economic activity is chosen, the fundamental relationship breaks down. Table 2 provides evidence rejecting both the demand-led and supply-led models of immigration when the total value of Canadian exports and the British GNP data are introduced into the relationship. Applying the standard tests, the coefficients of the variables were all found to be statistically insignificant. From this, one may conclude that a loose empirical relationship exists only when an indicator of timber exports

---

32. These statistics began to be collected under a British Act passed in 1803. This series is found in "Report of Select Committee on Emigration, 1860", *Journals of the Legislative Assembly of the Province of Canada*, Vol. 18, Session 1860 (Quebec: Thompson & Co.), Appendix No. 4, p. 12; it can be found reproduced in *The Year Book and Almanac of Canada for 1872* (Ottawa: James Bailiff and Co.), pp. 162-63; and also partially in W. S. Shepperson, *British Emigration to North America* (Minneapolis: University of Minnesota Press, 1957), pp. 257-59.

33. See B. Thomas, *Migration and Economic Growth* (Cambridge University Press, 1954), p. 38.

(the dominant staple product) is held as argument in the equation. The more general neoclassical demand relationship is not found to conform to the facts for nineteenth-century Canada. Only the more restrictive relationship between international migration and the staple export seems to have some empirical validity. Hence, the object of the next section is to try to show how this seemingly contradictory evidence can be partly reconciled.

A Possible Explanation of the Evidence: Labour Migration as a Joint Product

As Spry and others have emphasized, Innis was keenly aware of the implications that the existence of overhead costs and the associated unused capacity had in explaining both the structural rigidities of the price system and the historical process of Canadian economic development.[34] The effect of the cargo imbalance in the timber trade during the nineteenth century is a striking example of the significance of unused capacity.

Yet, unused capacity may be considered merely a specific form of joint production. According to Marshall, 'joint products' are goods which cannot be easily produced separately and which have a common origin.[35] Since their costs cannot readily be apportioned, the existence of joint products has created innumerable problems for both the classical and neoclassical theories of value. As Mill noted, under joint production, prices do not have a determinate solution.[36] Only the sum of their prices can be derived from their joint unit costs. Hence, there is a certain element of arbitrariness in determining prices under such conditions unless, as Sraffa pointed out, there may exist simultaneously a competing process capable of producing the joint supply in, say, different proportions.[37]

---

34. For instance, as Neill has shown, this followed from Innis' contact with J. M. Clark during his early years at the University of Chicago. See R. Neill, *A New Theory of Value, The Canadian Economics of H. A. Innis* (University of Toronto Press, 1972), chapter 2. The Innis approach has been further developed by I. M. Spry in "Overhead Costs, Time Problems and Prices", *Essays in Political Economy in Honour of E. J. Urwick*, ed. H. A. Innis (University of Toronto Press, 1938), and in "Overhead Costs, Rigidities of Productive Capacity and the Price System", *Culture, Communication, and Dependency, The Tradition of H. A. Innis*, ed. W. H. Melody, L. Salter, and P. Heyer (Norwood, N.J.: Ablex Publishing Corporation, 1981).

35. See A. Marshall, *Principles of Economics*, eighth edition, (London: Macmillan, 1920), p. 388.

36. J. S. Mill, *Principles of Political Economy* (University of Toronto Press, 1965), p. 583.

37. See P. Sraffa, *Production of Commodities by Means of Commodities* (Cambridge University Press, 1960), p. 43. However, since, in the example being discussed, there existed only one method of transportation (the sailing vessel), the Sraffian method may not provide a satisfactory solution to the determination of prices in this case.

This theoretical result is of the utmost importance in understanding the empirical evidence relating to the immigrant trade between Britain and Canada. As stated previously, Canada's timber trade grew primarily out of British imperial needs created by the Napoleonic wars to secure a steady supply of timber. Because of these needs, preferential duties were given for Canadian timber, whose purpose was to guarantee continuity in the trade in colonial timber. In order to induce the timber merchants to build up the tremendous overheads needed for this costly undertaking, the British state set tariffs so as to maintain the higher price which had initially resulted from the interruption of access to the Baltic timber.[38] Consequently, one finds that, even after the end of the Napoleonic wars, the Baltic timber trade was handicapped by the preferential treatment for Canadian timber which lasted until the middle of the nineteenth century. The practical results of the steep rise in the colonial timber trade were the tremendous increase in the amount of sea traffic employed in the transport of this commodity, as well as the existence of strong downward pressures on the price of the passage for an emigrant wishing to travel from, say, Liverpool to the port of Quebec.

Adding to these downward pressures, in 1817, the British Parliament (in support of the shipping and timber interests) modified the transport regulations so as to allow vessels sailing to British North America to carry one passenger for every one and one-half tons, whereas vessels travelling to the United States were restricted to the previous rates of one to five.[39] As a consequence of these changes, the relative cost of the passage to Quebec was cut to about one-half of the passenger rates to New York.[40] This substantial restructuring in the North Atlantic pattern of trade after 1815 thus served to increase and redirect significantly the emigrant traffic to British North America by the 1820s.

The British timber trade with Canada can be envisaged, in this sense, as an indirect transfer of purchasing power from the British consumers to the aspiring emigrants who would ultimately take advantage of the lower cost of transportation. To the extent that the pricing

---

38. W. S. Jevons (*op. cit.*, pp. 146-47) provides a time series of timber prices which shows quite clearly the structural shift in these prices between the year 1800 and the 1840s. There may have been other factors explaining this continued high level of prices, but it would appear that the imperial tariffs were a dominant factor.

39. H. J. M. Johnston, *British Emigration Policy, 1815-1830* (Oxford University Press, 1972), p. 25.

40. *Ibid.*, p. 25. The result of such Draconian measures, according to Johnston, was that, by the 1820s, about 70 per cent of the human cargo had been diverted to the British North American ports.

of timber was governed primarily by the conditions of production and transportation of this staple product from North America, any additional revenue arising from the immigrant passage could be conceived as a sort of 'quasi-rent' accruing to British shipowners involved in this lucrative business. Reflecting on this trade, E. E. Hale noted:

> The importance of this business to shipowners will readily be seen. Ships of large accommodations for freighting, which carry out our bulky raw produce, and bring back the more condensed manufactures of England, have just the room to spare, which is made into accommodations for these passengers. [It has been stated] . . . that the amounts paid for the passage of emigrants go very far towards paying the expense of voyages of ships from America to Europe and back.[41]

The cost of the passage (the price of the joint product of the timber trade) declined sharply during the early period, and this facilitated the rapid development of a North Atlantic triangular movement of human cargo flowing mainly from Britain through Lower Canada and then to the United States.

While the number of pauper immigrants entering the United States from Canada varied in accordance with what Jerome believed to be the general demand conditions in the United States, the flow of immigrants from Britain to Canada fluctuated almost exclusively in relationship to the Canadian timber exports.[42] This is partly supported by the empirical evidence displayed in Table 1 above. Given the fact that the timber trade created the only means of cheap (and indirectly subsidized) transportation to cross the Atlantic, the expected correlation between the export of timber and immigration is confirmed.

---

41. E. E. Hale, *Letters on Irish Emigration* (1852), reprinted in *Immigration: Select Documents and Case Records*, ed. E. Abbott (University of Chicago Press, 1924), pp. 37-38. This quote indicates, therefore, that the emigrant trade did compensate for the high cost of transport, but it did not have a significant impact on the Jevons price series.

42. For instance, during the 1828 peak year, the *Montreal Gazette* (December 13, 1830) reported that one-half of the immigrants proceeded directly to the United States, one-twelfth stayed in Lower Canada and five-twelfths went to Upper Canada. By 1829, instead, one-fifth of the immigrants remained in Lower Canada. This article has been reprinted in *Select Documents in Canadian Economic History, 1783-1885*, ed. H. A. Innis and A.R.M. Lower (University of Toronto Press, 1933). By the trough year, 1832, according to J. Bouchette, and much later according to J. Lowe, one-third of the immigrants settled in Lower Canada, one-third in Upper Canada and one-third went to the United States. See J. Bouchette, *The British Dominions in North America*, Vol. I (London: Longman, 1832), pp. 358-59, and J. Lowe, "Population, Immigration, and Pauperism in the Dominion of Canada", *Canadian Economics* (Montreal: Dawson Brothers Publishers, 1885), p. 217. Although these proportions would be far from exact, the values seem to indicate their high variability. This point is also made by H. I. Cowan in reference to the 1840s. See H. I. Cowan, *British Immigration before Confederation*, No. 22 (Ottawa: Canadian Historical Association, 1968), p. 14.

Yet, the timber trade itself did not always closely reflect the general patterns of economic activity in North America. Frequently, the proportion of those wishing to use Canada as a stepping-stone for eventual emigration to the United States was far in excess of the absorptive capacity of the U.S. economy. During the 1830s and 1840s, there were often large numbers of pauper immigrants stranded in Canada and awaiting better times before moving to the United States. These massive inflows of migrant labourers to Canada were not always connected (as Table 2 shows) with the more general demand conditions here; and these pauper immigrants underwent tremendous hardship and were often maintained in Lower Canada at the public's expense, especially during the winter months.[43]

Immigration and Pauperism: The Nature of Nineteenth-Century Immigrant Labour in Canada

Within the Innis framework, immigration can be considered a by-product of a timber trade that was directly supported through British preference for Canadian timber. Although the question of who bore the cost of this transfer has traditionally been neglected by Canadian economic historians, the reduction of the trans-Atlantic fares was probably significant in attracting a large number of pauper emigrants who would not otherwise have emigrated to British North America. While it would be quite difficult to furnish a reasonable estimate of the magnitude of this subsidy, it did generally increase the attractiveness of human cargo for British vessels on their outbound voyage.

However, British emigration during the first half of the nineteenth century was something substantially more than a method of filling unused capacity in these infamous 'coffin ships' mentioned by Spry. For the British state, emigration became primarily a device for the elimination of over-population arising from the process of industrialization and urbanization. This, however, had not always been the guiding principle. As Johnston has pointed out, it was only in the post-Waterloo era that Britain became aware of the necessity for

---

43. Throughout the 1830s and 1840s, there was a constant complaint in the newspapers of the times of a general glut in the urban labour market, especially in Lower Canada. For instance, in reporting the demands of the rather conservative Montreal Emigrant Society, the *Montreal Gazette* (June 10, 1834) wrote: "Of those who are able to work, scarcely any can obtain employment, and the Committee further stated that there were many more, in other parts of the city, in a similar state of destitution." Also see, for instance, the *Montreal Gazette* (June 30, 1831), the *Quebec Mercury* (July 8, 1842), and *La Minerve* (jeudi, 9 septembre 1847).

an open-door policy on emigration.[44] Prior to 1815, governments still believed in the mercantilist principle that emigration and de-population would weaken the nation-state.

Because of the enclosure movement and the destruction of the rural handicraft trades accompanying the British Industrial Revolution, a large mass of 'surplus' labourers appeared in England. These landless and semi-landless peasants were forced into the overcrowded urban centres to become the paupers to whom Malthus and others referred in their criticism of the relief system laid down by the Poor Laws. The growing unrest in the cities and the increased financial burden that this redundant population placed on the Poor Law system were important factors inducing numerous political economists to favour emigration as either a temporary or permanent remedy for pauperism in Britain. Yet it was not enough for the government to tinker with transport regulations so as to reduce the effective cost of the passage to British North America. For advocates such as R. J. Wilmot-Horton (who was Under-Secretary of State for the Colonies during the years 1822-1828) and E. G. Wakefield (who had enormous influence on Lord Durham), it became clear that the role of the state should be to provide some form of direct assistance to the pauper emigrants.

Except for the indirect spillover effects of the timber trade, it is well known that the large majority of British emigrants during the nineteenth century were unaided in the outward passage to North America. Yet, as will be shown, assisted emigration was both significant and of greater social and economic importance to British North America than the unassisted emigration.

Emigrants travelling to North America can be classified into two main groups: (1) the class of independent capitalist farmers and their 'able-bodied' family members; and (2) the class of landless peasants (or cottiers) and their urban counterparts.[45] The members of the former group who left the United Kingdom were generally unassisted and the majority were attracted to the United States. Comparatively few independent British and Irish farmers settled in the British colonies. According to B. Thomas, two out of every three independent farmers settled in the American republic.[46] On the other

---

44. See H.J.M. Johnston, *op. cit.*, p. 2.

45. See the threefold classification provided by C. G. Otway in his testimony before the Select Committee on Poor Laws (Ireland), *British Parliamentary Papers*, Vol. 15, Part 1 (1849), pp. 53-54; reprinted in *Emigration from Europe, 1815-1914*, ed. C. Erickson (London: Adam & Charles Black, 1976), pp. 36-38.

46. Cf. B. Thomas, *op. cit.*, p. 59.

hand, a large portion of the lower-class labouring groups, such as the landless peasants and the chronically unemployed urban labourers, moved to the North American colonies.[47] It is this latter social group that received assistance either directly from the British Colonial Office, from the parish relief system, or from some landlords who wished to remove the peasants from their estates.[48]

The earliest form of direct assistance after 1815 came from the Colonial Office. The British government favoured the colonizing schemes, such as the Selkirk, the Talbot, and the Rideau settlements, but these were relatively small.[49] It was only by 1818 that the government chose to generalize its policy in order to remove some of the surplus population in the rural and urban areas of Great Britain. This was done by making periodic grants for the emigration of a number of Scottish and Irish cottiers and of technologically displaced workers such as the Scottish weavers.[50] Indeed, the 1820s are dotted with a number of experiments in direct subsidization from the Colonial Office. These attempts have been discussed in detail in the works previously cited by Johnson, Culliton, Cowan, Carrothers, and Johnston.

By the end of the 1820s, this form of direct assistance gave way to a different style of aid under the auspices of the parish relief system. During the years preceding the famous reports of the Select Committees on Emigration in 1826 and 1827, Wilmot-Horton had been very active in proposing that emigration be used as an alternative to payments to the poor (the poor rates). The funds needed to remove pauperism were to be obtained from the parish relief system.[51] Parishes would thus be able to raise money on the poor

---

47. This distinction is made in W. S. Shepperson, "Agrarian Aspects of the Early Victorian Emigration to North America", *Canadian Historical Review*, Vol. 33, no. 3 (September, 1952), p. 257.

48. This is why, in his evidence presented before the Select Committee on Colonization, C. P. Lucas, the Secretary to the Emigrant Information Office, argued: "The people we want to get rid of is the surplus of the towns-people; the people they want in the colonies are country people." *British Parliamentary Papers*, Vol. 10 (1889, p. 71); reprinted in C. Erickson, ed., *op. cit.*, p. 161. This latter group thus includes the "Emmy Grants" that E. Thompson Seton distinguishes from the "Passengers" in his novel *Two Little Savages* (London: Archibald Constable & Co. Ltd., 1904), pp. 104-106.

49. For a survey, see A.R.M. Lower, "Immigration and Settlement in Canada, 1812-1820", *Canadian Historical Review*, Vol. 3, no. 1 (March, 1922), pp. 37-47.

50. Cf. J. T. Culliton, *Assisted Emigration and Land Settlement* (Montreal: McGill University, 1927), pp. 15 and 45.

51. The ideas of Wilmot-Horton and the content of these emigration committees' reports are discussed in, among others, Carrothers, *op. cit.*, pp. 52-59, and Johnston, *op. cit.*, pp. 57-68.

rates to enable those paupers chargeable to the local parish to emigrate. In fact, the struggle in support of this form of state-aided emigration culminated in the Poor Law Amendment Act of 1834 which allowed English parishes to contribute from the poor rates to assist pauper migration.[52]

The number of pauper families assisted under the Poor Laws was far from negligible. Although during 1835 a little less than ten per cent of immigrants reaching the port of Quebec had been financed in this manner, by 1836 close to twenty per cent of the immigrants were state-aided paupers.[53] While this number subsequently declined from its 1836 peak, according to Culliton at least fourteen thousand English paupers had been assisted to emigrate to British North America between 1836 and 1846 alone.[54] This drop in the number assisted during the 1840s (in England) was mainly an act of policy, possibly under the influence of the controversy over Wakefield's plan.[55] But this decline was accompanied by a tremendous rise in the numbers assisted in Ireland and Scotland during the late forties.

Though prior to 1838 in Ireland, and 1851 in Scotland, no direct system of poor relief existed, instead of the English method of direct parish assistance, aid to emigration was made available indirectly by the assistance provided to landlords. For instance, besides the existence of much lower eviction costs, the amendment to the Poor Law Relief Act of 1847 gave power to the parish authorities in Ireland to pay one-half of the cost to a landlord for financing the emigration of a destitute tenant.[56] In Scotland, the Emigration Advances Act of 1851 allowed funds to be set aside for landlords needing to borrow in order to defray the cost of emigration for their tenants.[57] When this massive government aid is added to the large amount of *private*

---

52. See W. A. Carrothers, *op. cit.*, p. 57.

53. See the very interesting data furnished by A. C. Buchanan, "Annual Report from the Agent for Emigration in Canada for 1836", *British Parliamentary Papers, Accounts and Papers*, Vol. 42, Session Jan.-June 1837, pp. 3-28.

54. Cf. J. T. Culliton, *op. cit.*, pp. 46-7; also H. I. Cowan (1961), *op. cit.*, p. 208, and C. Erickson, ed., *op. cit.*, p. 127.

55. See some of the arguments put forward by N. Macdonald, *Canada, 1763-1841: Immigration and Settlement* (London: Longmans, Green & Co., 1939), p. 24.

56. Cf. J. T. Culliton, *op. cit.*, p. 48. According to C. Erickson, ed., *op. cit.*, p. 127, between August 1849 and March 1889, 42,405 paupers had been aided through this form of relief in Ireland.

57. Indeed, according to W. S. Shepperson (1952), *op. cit.*, p. 263, ". . . emigration, as well as draining and ditching, throughout the Highlands made request and received loans for such a clearance of their lands. Consequently, many of the Scottish emigrants sent out during the fifties were indirectly assisted by the government."

assistance provided by the more generous landlords and professional associations (such as those of the weavers) during this period, one is faced with a society that is trying hard to purge itself of pauperism by literally "shovelling out" this destitute class of people onto the shores of its colonies.[58] The rate at which this shovelling took place was not uniquely dependent on either the general demand conditions in the host colonies or the supply conditions of the metropole. These paupers were brought to the North American colonies through the cheap means of transportation available during the period—the unused capacity of the timber vessels on their westbound voyage.

Immigration and Canada's "Labour Surplus" Economy: Some Concluding Remarks

The large-scale dumping of these paupers on the British North American shores laid a heavy burden on the struggling colonies. The health and background skills of these immigrants were often incompatible with the needs of the country. Wherever they landed, the colonies were under the moral obligation to erect hospitals, lazarettes, and pesthouses for the reception of the diseased immigrants. Data for the 1830s shows that nearly twenty per cent of the immigrant arrivals had to be forwarded and 'relieved' by the Montreal Emigrant Society alone.[59]

Not only did these pauper immigrants bring with them disease during years of cholera epidemics (especially during 1832-34 and 1847-49), many of them lingered about in the large cities in a state of total destitution, filling the ranks of the chronically unemployed. The local authorities were particularly critical of the parish-aided immigrants, who often had insufficient means to take them to their specific destinations, say, in Upper Canada. In analysing this phenomenon, Lord Durham was quite quick to identify the problem. He wrote:

> Many of these poor have little or no agricultural knowledge . . . . The consequence is, that after getting into 'the bush', as it is called, they find themselves beset by privations and difficulties which they are not able to contend with . . . . Many resort to the large towns in the Provinces, with their starving families, to eke out by day-labour and begging together a wretched existence whilst others of them (more enterprising) are tempted,

---

58. The term "shovelling out" is used by H.J.M. Johnston to describe the policy of the British state during the period, and it is to be found in the sub-title of Johnston's book.

59. See *Appendix to the XLVth Volume of the Journals of the House of Assembly of the Province of Lower Canada*, Session 1835-36, Appendix W.

by the reputed high wages and more genial climate of the United States, to try their fortunes in that country.[60]

The pauper immigrants' pattern of life in the New World thus followed a very definite sequence. As soon as the crowded emigrant ships began to pour out their quota upon the docks of Quebec and Montreal, the cities became glutted with destitute immigrants looking for work and shelter. Discovering that the immigrant labour market was saturated with cheap labour, many of the pauper immigrants would then try (if and when the opportunity arose) their luck on the land. Lacking the required knowledge, skills and capital, these immigrants either returned to the towns to become chronically unemployed, living on public charity, or, if sufficient funds could be obtained, migrated to the United States where a more secure employment was believed to be found.

This pauper migration thus put enormous strain upon the very limited resources of the colonies. Except for a small, yet regressive, per capita poll tax (which was enacted by the legislature of Lower Canada in 1832 and which lasted between the years 1832-1835 and then again from 1842 until the 1860s), the colonial governments and inhabitants had to defray the bulk of the direct and indirect expenses of maintaining these pauper immigrants—many of whom ultimately emigrated to the United States. For instance, during the normal conditions of the 1830s and 1840s, the tax revenue collected from the immigrants went into paying only approximately one-half of the direct costs of running the quarantine station at Grosse Isle and the emigrant hospitals in Quebec and Montreal.[61]

During the great *déluge* of 1847, however, the public finances became so strained that less than one-eighth of the direct expenses were covered from the collection of the passenger tax. Given the almost total exhaustion of provincial funds and given the public pressure (especially in the larger cities), Lord Elgin wrote a long letter to Lord Grey in August 1847 protesting British emigration policy towards the North American colonies. Since the colonies could not legally control the large-scale pauper migration from the British Isles, he felt that some

---

60. Lord Durham, *Report of the Earl of Durham* (London: Methuen & Co. Ltd., 1902), p. 188. References to the gluts in the urban labour markets with numerous explanations of the definite sequence discussed by Durham can be found in various other sources such as the *Montreal Gazette* of June 30, 1831, June 10, 1834 and June 26, 1834; in a "Letter from Sydenham to a Friend" (November 23, 1840) reprinted in *Select Documents on British Colonial Policy, 1830-1860*, ed. K. N. Bell and W. P. Morrell (Oxford University Press, 1928), p. 220; the *Quebec Mercury*, July 8, 1842; in numerous reports of the immigration agent published in various *Appendices to the Journals of the Legislative Assembly of the Province of Canada*, especially during the 1850s; and in, among others, F. Morehouse, "Canadian Migration in the Forties", *Canadian Historical Review*, Vol. 9, no. 4 (December, 1928), pp. 310-11.

61. Cf. *Appendix to the Ninth Volume of the Journals of the Legislative Assembly of the Province of Canada*, Appendix No. 2, Session 1850, Appendix Y.Y.

financial compensation was due.[62] After a long negotiation, the Imperial government finally agreed in April 1848 to pay solely the direct expenses incurred by the colonial government during the previous year.

This was a far cry from the popular demands urging more control of the flow of immigrants. The reaction of the editors of *La Minerve* well portrays the attitude of the struggling inhabitants of the colonies:

> On peut mettre en question le droit du peuple d'aucun pays de jeter son surplus de population pauvre sur les rives d'un autre pays, lors même que ce dernier serait une colonie et surtout si cette colonie était déjà peuplée et établie. Comme dans l'exercice d'un droit aussi douteux, des milliers d'individus portant avec eux la contagion partout où ils vont, on été jetés sur nos rives cette année, notre conservation exige que notre législature, dans toute l'étendue des pouvoirs qu'elle possède ou qui peuvent lui être accordés pour régler le commerce du St. Laurent, impose pour mettre un frein à ce transport d'individus déjà aux portes de la mort, des restrictions telles qu'elles nous mettent par la suite à l'abri des dangers qu'entraine avec elle une semblable émigration.[63]

In reaction to the popular resentment against the shovelling out of paupers onto the shores of the North American colonies, a law was enacted by the legislature in March 1848 which raised the per capita passenger tax. As with previous laws, this was perceived as a mere cosmetic change which failed to tax those who most gained from this immigrant trade. Instead of on the mercantile interests, the incidence of this tax fell once again on the human cargo.

The large-scale pauper migration to the North American colonies raises a number of issues as to the nature of this labour-surplus economy during the nineteenth century. First, one may wish to know whether the existence of an almost unlimited supply of labour served to weaken or strengthen the economic development of the colonies. From the evidence presented, limited resources of the colonies went to maintaining paupers of whom the healthier and more enterprising merely ended up in the United States. This was a significant financial dead weight, which was not fully compensated for in terms of active participation of these groups in the economic development of the colonies. Therefore, much like today's developing countries, Canada's labour-surplus economy was not necessarily associated with a phase of strong economic growth.

---

62. See G. Tucker, "The Famine Immigration to Canada, 1847", *American Historical Review*, Vol. 36, no. 3 (April, 1931), p. 544.

63. *La Minerve*, jeudi, 19 août 1847.

Secondly, the process of eastern Canadian urban growth became truncated. Because of the presence of a large surplus labour force in the cities, for the local rural inhabitants of Lower Canada urbanization actually meant seeking work in the large industrial centres of New England and the north-central United States. This distinct type of superimposed urban growth seems to have created an uneven ethnic division between the cities and the countryside in Lower Canada; and, in part, it may explain why the emigration of French Canadians to the United States became so significant during this period.[64]

Finally, it has been argued that immigration in Canada was largely dependent upon (a) the degree to which the mercantile interests encouraged this by-product of the timber trade, and (b) the degree to which the British state tried to remove the surplus population. These two relatively independent factors had little relationship with Canadian demand for labour during the first three-quarters of the nineteenth century. Although the direct beneficiaries of the immigrant trade were the shipping interests, the British government did use migration as a safety valve in order to diffuse potential trouble, as during the Irish famine years of the 1840s. However, the third beneficiary, whose net gain must not be underestimated, is the American Republic. Within the North Atlantic triangle, the United States received labourers, many of whom had first been subsidized by the British, and then rehabilitated at Canadian expense.

---

64. Traditionally, Canadian economic historians have not paid much attention to this factor in explaining the patterns of French Canadian emigration during the period. For instance, the study by G. Paquet and W. R. Smith suggests the political unrest in Lower Canada and the crisis of Quebec agriculture as the dominant 'push' factors for the period 1820-1850. See their article "L'émigration des canadiens français vers les États-Unis, 1790-1940: problématique et coups de sonde", *L'Actualité économique*, Vol. 59, no. 3 (September 1983), pp. 440-41.

Resource
Development

7.   Social Democracy
and State Capital

Potash in Saskatchewan[1]

Jeanne Kirk Laux
University of Ottawa

In Canada, there is a long-standing acceptance of a positive role for the state in economic development. From the very outset of statehood, the economic role of government in underwriting investment, securing infrastructure for industry, and framing commercial relations has been sufficiently evident to suggest to historians such as Hugh Aitken that the "distinction between 'the state' and 'private enterprise'" is "artificial" when applied to Canada. For some, the importance of state intervention extends beyond its common function in all capitalist economies—that is, assuring the conditions favourable to private capital accumulation—to the forging of cultural identity. In Hershel Hardin's interpretation, against the centrifugal forces of regionalism and continentalism, state intervention in Canada permitted nation-building on the basis of a "public enterprise culture" distinct from American free-enterprise liberalism.[2]

Historically, the state in Canada (whether imperial British, federal, or provincial) intermittently sought, and more frequently, as in the case of the CNR (Canadian National Railway) or Ontario Hydro, was induced by factions of the bourgeoisie to acquire control of key sectors. Yet only in the post-war period has it become commonplace to see the state substitute itself for private-sector actors and

1. This article represents an extension of research and writing carried out jointly with Maureen Appel Molot, in particular "Multinational Corporations and Economic Nationalism: Conflict over Resource Development in Canada", *World Development* 6 (1978), 837-49, and "The Politics of Nationalization", *Canadian Journal of Political Science* XII, no. 2 (June, 1979), 227-58.

2. Hugh G. Aitken, "Defensive Expansionism: the State and Economic Growth in Canada", in W. T. Easterbrook and M. H. Watkins (eds.), *Approaches to Canadian Economic History* (Toronto: Macmillan, 1956), pp. 183-221; Hershel Hardin, *A Nation Unaware: the Canadian Economic Culture* (Vancouver: J. J. Douglas Ltd, 1974), part II: "The Canadian Public Enterprise Culture", pp. 54-140.

directly assume the role of banker, trader, and producer. Particularly since 1960, an increasing number of federal and provincial state-owned enterprises engage in the production of goods and services for sale in both national and international markets. By 1980, the *Financial Post*'s listing of the top 400 industrial corporations in Canada, ranked by sales, included 23 companies wholly owned by government (8 federal, 15 provincial) and another 8 which had substantial government investment.

When government becomes an investor and producer in profitable and competitive sectors of the economy—as in the case of the potash, petroleum, uranium, aircraft, electronics, or transport industries in Canada—fundamental questions of political economy are raised. We are, after all, witnessing the accumulation of *state capital* once the state itself owns the means of production, engages wage labour, controls the social relations of production, and sells in the marketplace to appropriate the surplus generated. Should we not then expect, or demand, that this transfer of ownership of commercial ventures from private to public hands be used to advance social welfare goals, to move beyond the mere pursuit of profit?

Raising the issue of the *purpose* of public enterprises immediately poses more complex questions of values and of the role of the state in capitalist society. The analysis presented here starts from Irene Spry's premise that there are no economic values as such, only human values, subjectively defined.[3] Thus the objective of economic activity should be to create the material base for the fulfillment of human values, whereas the purpose of a political economy discourse should be to define these collective values and devise the appropriate strategy for their pursuit. Yet in both orthodox Marxist and liberal ideology, despite their very different conceptions of the relative autonomy of the state *vis-à-vis* society, state enterprises must fit into the logic of capital accumulation. Exponents of both ideologies postulate that state enterprises will not operate over time in profitable industries but rather will serve, in the Marxist view, to cheapen the cost of capital for monopolies or, in the liberal view, to salvage essential industries and provide infrastructure for the private sector as a whole. Only within the democratic socialist (or social democratic) ideology are state enterprises seen to be potentially autonomous from the logic of capital accumulation and thus potentially available to serve as instruments for political direction over economic development.

For democratic socialists both in Western Europe and in Canada, despite the erosion of faith in the nationalization of the means of production (an erosion due both to the realities of state socialism

---

3. Personal Interview, Irene Spry, Ottawa, September 1, 1983.

in the East and to the requirements of electoral politics in the West) public enterprises remain a keystone in party programmes. It is argued that state-owned enterprises can advance democratic socialist goals in the mixed-capitalist economy by reducing the total social power of private monopoly capital, by enlarging the scope of economic resources susceptible to political direction, and by creating an opportunity to temper the capital-labour relationship by creating a more humane workplace.

In Britain, for example, Fine's critical review of the nationalized industries (NIs) concluded that:

> We take it for granted that nationalisation of major industries is an essential policy for commanding the economy in a programme for socialism. At the same time, nationalisation has been discredited in the eyes of the labour movement and this is hardly surprising in the light of . . . the capitalist relations under which the NIs have been organised . . . the NIs should form the basis for the planning and control of the economy . . . .[4]

In Canada, too, although social democrats have moved away from seeing public ownership as *the* solution, it remains *one* of the principal means for economic change. ("An NDP government will be prepared to use public enterprise to achieve social control where necessary. . . .")[5] In the resource sector, given the pre-eminence of multinational corporations and their export orientation, the New Democratic Party makes a more forceful case for the need to create public enterprises. ("THEREFORE BE IT RESOLVED that the New Democratic Party commit itself to the central role of public ownership in the development of our primary resource industries.")[6]

In order to explore further the relationship between public enterprise and public welfare, the experience of the CCF-NDP governments in Saskatchewan (the Cooperative Commonwealth Federation was superseded by the New Democratic Party in 1961) offers an excellent historical proving-ground. Here, over a period of nearly forty years since World War II, social democratic parties have sought to use the state to direct economic development, while the exact objectives pursued and the forms of intervention essayed have varied considerably. By reviewing the history of one resource, potash, which ultimately was brought under state control through a series of nationalizations, the hope is to contribute to discussion of the following central question: What are the conditions which favour the promotion of

---

4. B. J. Fine and K. O'Donnell, "The Nationalised Industries", *Socialist Economic Review* (London: Merlin Press, 1981), pp. 277 and 282.

5. New Democratic Party, *1979 Convention Resolutions*, p. 2.

6. New Democratic Party, *1981 Convention Resolutions*.

democratic socialist objectives through the use of state enterprises? A prior question must also be addressed: under what conditions will social democratic governments take control of resource production to accumulate state capital?

In November 1975, the Government of Saskatchewan announced its intent to take control of the potash industry in the province by expropriating if necessary the assets of some of the world's largest multinational corporations. According to the opposition party, commitment to a socialist ideology explains the decision:

> There is one reason and one reason only Mr. Speaker that the government is taking over the potash companies—and that is because they believe in socialism—they believe that the means of production should be controlled by the state . . . .[7]

Yet Premier Allan Blakeney argued, on the contrary, that the nationalization decision stemmed from pragmatism rather than principles:

> The reasons are not any devotion to public enterprise. We simply must have control of production and the rate of return to the public treasury.[8]

In order to understand to what extent ideological considerations structured the policy choice of this social democratic government, some of the irony contained in the two contrasting quotations above must be made explicit. Belief in socialization of the means of production, emphasized by the Liberal opposition, was most clearly articulated under the CCF, which nonetheless oversaw the development of potash in the 1950s by large private foreign corporations! On the other hand, the pragmatic need to assure an acceptable rate of return to government from resource development, which the Premier underscored, did not apparently require takeovers in either the oil or the uranium industries in the 1970s.

Analysis of the provincial state's role in development of the potash industry since the 1940s suggests that despite a consistent formal commitment to public ownership in both CCF and NDP programmes,[9] the translation of formal ideology into political action varies according to four other factors which are listed below in inverse order of the government's ability to control them:

---

7. Ted Malone, ''The Potash Development Act, 1975'', November 27, 1975, mimeograph, p. 12—at the time Malone was the Liberal energy critic.

8. As quoted in the Ottawa *Citizen*, November 14, 1975.

9. The NDP's 1971 electoral programme promised that ''Where feasible, we will reclaim ownership and control of foreign-owned resources.'' The party was returned to power by these elections after seven years in opposition.

(1) Conditions in the world economy relevant to the world potash industry.

(2) Investment and marketing strategies of the international firms engaged in potash production.

(3) Federal-provincial relations, i.e, whether a co-operative or competitive strategy animates Ottawa's economic development policies.

(4) State capabilities, that is, the resources the provincial state is able to mobilize to carry out its policy intent.

Although each of these factors can be identified and assessed "objectively", all play themselves out in a manner which depends upon the participants' subjective perception of the economic and political balance of forces affecting their risks and opportunity costs. By comparing the strategies adopted towards public enterprise by Saskatchewan governments in two time periods (the late 1940s and the 1970s) in terms of the relevance of these four factors, it will be possible to specify the conditions under which state ownership is likely to be used to advance democratic socialist goals.

The announcement of the discovery of commercially viable deposits of potash in Saskatchewan came in 1947. To a province whose economy had been dependent upon one crop, wheat, the discovery of both oil and potash in the 1940s offered an exceptional opportunity for diversification. Potash took on particular importance after the major oil find at Leduc, Alberta, turned companies' attention away from Saskatchewan in 1948. Who should undertake its development—private or public enterprise? John Richards has masterfully summarized the debate over public ownership which took place within the CCF prior to its 1944 electoral victory. In *Prairie Capitalism*, he contends that new personalities, particularly professional civil servants espousing Fabian rather than populist socialism, shifted the CCF as a government away from public ownership towards planning. Despite this shift, and despite the parallel difficulties encountered in managing new Crown-owned ventures in manufacturing, the political will for statism in the resource sector was present—"initially the preponderant opinion within the provincial government was to preserve potash in the public domain."[10]

The CCF government was, however, under no illusion that it possessed either the financial or technological wherewithal to undertake potash development independently. Premier T. C. Douglas turned first to Great Britain, making a personal overture to Sir Stafford

---

10. John Richards and Larry Pratt, *Prairie Capitalism: Power and Influence in the New West* (Toronto: McClelland and Stewart, 1979), p. 137.

Cripps, who gave his tacit support for equity investment and long-term sales contracts provided that Canadian federal government approval could be secured. Richards documents the Saskatchewan Planning Board's attempts to work out a joint venture between the two levels of government and the reasons behind Ottawa's rebuff— essentially perceptions of high risk due to technical uncertainties, high costs, and competition from offshore suppliers. Discouraged by the lack of co-operation from Ottawa and dismayed by the costs and market power of the existing companies, the Planning Board instead invited private companies to develop potash, seeking only to assure a share of the economic rents to be generated. Its 1950 potash regulations set royalty rates while at the same time encouraging investment by means of a three-year grace period for taxes and special depreciation write-off rates thereafter.[11]

Several considerations thus combined in the late 1940s and early 1950s to inhibit a social democratic government intent on developing resources under public ownership from doing so.

(1) In the world economy, consideration must be given to geography (proximity of markets), ownership, and inter-firm relations in order to present an accurate picture of the way in which the world potash market is structured. Geography is a critical factor: "because potash is a relatively high-bulk, low-value commodity, each mining community has a naturally protected market area largely dictated by land transportation costs".[12] At the same time, the degree of state ownership in the world potash industry has tended to distort the market since World War I (when the French government acquired the formerly German-owned mines in Alsace). After World War II, the U.S.S.R. and East Germany became major producers, engaging in state-trading and bilateral balancing of trade with their regional partners (those states now members of the Comecon). The industry was and is oligopolistic. The number of producers world-wide has not exceeded twenty at any time, because the barriers to entry have been high due to the costs—in time, technology, and capital—of shaft-sinking.

(2) Inter-firm co-ordination of marketing was already commonplace. From Western Europe, sales to destinations outside the region were (and are) co-ordinated between national producers.

---

11. *Ibid.*, chapter 8; and Saskatchewan, Department of Mineral Resources, *Potash: Challenge for Development* (1974), p. 24.

12. W. E. Koepke, *Structure, Behaviour and Performance of the World Potash Industry*, Mineral Bulletin MR 139 (Ottawa: Department of Energy, Mines and Resources, 1973), pp. 4-5.

Until 1973, when a European Economic Community (EEC) ruling terminated the practice, prices were set within the West European market by the French and German industries.[13] The proximate market for the new Canadian producer in the 1940s would of course have been the United States, particularly since Canada's virgin prairie lands required very little application of fertilizers. Yet the United States was not only the world's single largest consumer of potash but also its largest producer. A small number of firms operating in the area of Carlsbad, New Mexico, were able (until the late 1950s) to supply virtually all of the American farmer's needs; thus Canadian production would be in competition with that of existing companies.

(3) Recognition of these realities highlighted the state managers' relative lack of capabilities to enter the industry and to secure markets for potash. The Planning Board not only realized the risks involved, in terms of costs and technical skills required to bring a new mine on stream, but also saw that the oligopolistic structure of the industry made it possible for established firms to boycott a new state producer.[14] Indeed, even when the Board turned to indirect regulation of potash development by inviting in private companies, its bargaining power was very limited. The Potash Company of America, for example, was able to push the government into liberalizing the regulations.[15] This retreat is not surprising, since the very invitation to a foreign company to explore and exploit a natural resource is itself an admission by the state that it lacks the basic geological or technical knowledge, the capital, or the marketing expertise to do so itself.

(4) The alternatives open to the provincial state were, however, further restricted by the unco-operative attitude on the part of the federal government in Ottawa. Federal-provincial relations thus intervened between political will and policy implementation by diminishing the provincial state's capabilities: that is, the available resources and thus the bargaining power it could command.

The above considerations expressed themselves in a specific political conjuncture which John Richards has analyzed in terms of class conflict—the pervasive Cold War mentality and the new dominance of business interests in the Liberal party placing the CCF on

---

13. Energy, Mines and Resources Canada, *Potash*, Mineral Bulletin MR 156 (Ottawa, 1976), p. 30; Koepke, *op. cit.*, p. 95, note 76.

14. Richards, *op. cit.*, pp. 138-39.

15. *Ibid.*, pp. 190-93.

the ideological defensive.[16] Lipset's work, however, suggests another way of appreciating political-risk perceptions. Based on interviews at the time, Lipset presents a CCF leadership engaged in a continuous dialectical rapport with *its own social base*—the rural electorate. Public enterprises were seen by the CCF leaders "as one of the best means of increasing the general revenues of the government without raising taxes".[17] The surplus generated would then go for social services. Given its predominantly farm, rather than labour, support, this socialist party could only be on the defensive when partial failures in the new manufacturing enterprises raised criticism. Thus, for Lipset,

> a number of government officials have become wary about engaging in further public enterprises. They fear that government industry operating at a loss will lead to a serious decrease in rural support. The government has therefore modified its original intention of socialising the oil fields, for they are still in the category of a risk investment.[18]

If these are the considerations which induced a social democratic government vociferously committed to public ownership to alter its strategy, how then can it be explained that a more pragmatic NDP leadership devised and successfully implemented a policy of nationalization in the 1970s?

Regardless of party ideology, it can be argued that resource development under the aegis of private enterprise, especially foreign multinational enterprise, will generate government-industry conflict simply because:

> Rents of various kinds are created by the act of production; by almost any concession system prior claims would be established to them, and given any substantial profitability, one party would eventually begin to feel cheated.[19]

Once production is successfully under way, comparative studies of resource development in other jurisdictions make it clear that "the perceived level of risk associated with the enterprise declines precipitately." With this reduced uncertainty, "the bargaining strength

---

16. *Ibid.*, pp. 143-44.

17. Seymour Martin Lipset, *Agrarian Socialism: The Cooperative Commonwealth Federation in Saskatchewan* (Berkeley: University of California Press, 1950), p. 323.

18. *Ibid.*, p. 249.

19. Raymond Mikesell, "Conflict in Foreign Investor–Host Country Relations: a Preliminary Analysis", in Raymond Mikesell (ed.), *Foreign Investment in the Petroleum and Mineral Industries; Case Studies of Investor–Host Country Relations* (Baltimore: Johns Hopkins Press, 1971), p. 54. Irene Spry offers the clearest discussion and definition of "economic rent" in "Rent, Royalties and Taxes", unpublished paper, 1981.

inevitably shifts from the foreigners to the host government.''[20] The conditions of *reduced uncertainty* applied in Saskatchewan in the period 1964-1970 when, after much trial and error, several mines came into commercial production. The second condition, *profitability*, however, applied only as of 1970-1971 when world potash prices began to rise following a four-year decline. Returning to power after a six-year Liberal party interregnum, the NDP government sought to re-apportion rents by introducing new fees in 1972.

The logic of any industry-government conflict over the division of risks and rewards will reach a point beyond which industry refuses to tolerate further reduction of its share. At this point, the dénouement may involve accommodation or—as in the case of potash in Saskatchewan—further escalation of conflict. After an acrimonious battle—including industry's court challenges to provincial legislation, non-payment of fees, withholding of financial statements, and postponement of planned mine expansion despite rising world demand for potash—the NDP government concluded that direct state control of part of the industry was required. Yet that same government retreated from the brink in the case of the petroleum industry and reached accommodation in the case of the uranium industry during the same period. Other multinational corporations operating in the province managed to adjust to state demands for greater participation in resource development.

What then were the new conditions—when we compare the 1970s to the 1940s—which enabled political will to be translated into action as the government bought out the potash interests held by seven international corporations? The outcome of government-industry conflict over potash development appears to hinge on changing conditions in the world economy and in the global potash industry which affected both government's and corporations' perceptions of their relative vulnerability. By the 1970s, the enhanced capability of state managers also made it practicable for government to contemplate and effectuate take-overs of established companies. The resolve to do so was strengthened by the pro-active role of the federal government in seeking to compete with the provinces in order to reap greater benefits—tax revenues—from resource development. To summarize:

(1) Although all host governments were sensitized to the issue of rent-sharing after the oil crisis of 1973 and the apparent effectiveness of the OPEC cartel, the vulnerability of a particular industry

20. Raymond Vernon, "Foreign Enterprises and Development in the Raw Materials Industries", *American Economic Review* 60, no. 2 (May 1970), 124; and Theodore H. Moran, *Multinational Corporations and the Politics of Dependence: Copper In Chile* (Princeton: Princeton University Press, 1974), p. 161.

to government pressures depends, following Raymond Vernon's criteria, on (a) the degree of vertical integration, (b) stability of technology, (c) availability of alternative sources of supply, (d) substitutability, (e) price elasticity, (f) significance and locus of barriers to entry. In the 1970s the potash industry was characterized by insignificant vertical integration, stable and non-proprietary technology, few alternative sources of supply (certainly none of the proximity and quality of the Saskatchewan reserves for American consumers), no substitution, and price inelasticity. Although barriers to entry remained high, these barriers were found *at the production stage*, making take-overs of producing enterprises within the province the least costly mode of entry as compared to creation of a new state-owned mine.

(2) The strategies of the multinational corporations operating mines in Saskatchewan had altered in several significant ways since their start-up of operations during the 1960s. All but one of the fourteen parent companies had Third World experience, and, given the enhanced role of the state in resource development, had come to accept various forms of negotiated joint ventures or joint equity arrangements rather than total control. Most of the companies had diversified their production lines, following the general trend towards risk reduction during the 1960s, so that potash was no longer their major source of earnings.[21]

(3) By the mid-1970s, the provincial state had acquired two capabilities it did not possess in the 1940s—technical knowledge and financial wherewithal. The creation of the Potash Corporation of Saskatchewan, for example, had served the purpose of training specialized geologists and engineers; additional skills were developed in the Potash Management Branch of the Department of Mineral Resources, established to undertake research on the global industry. The provincial government consistently ran budgetary surpluses in the 1970s and had put aside an Energy and Resource Fund amounting to some $400 million.[22]

(4) Acrimonious federal-provincial relations over the issue of revenues from resource development characterized the 1970s. They were not, of course, specific to Saskatchewan—indeed, the provocative decision of the federal government in 1974 to alter tax laws so as to prohibit the deduction of provincial royalties was primarily

---

21. The American-based companies all had to face the fact of depletion of their reserves in New Mexico and of state control over most alternative sources in the Third World. Those companies most reliant on potash earnings did begin exploration in New Brunswick, Manitoba, and Nova Scotia.

22. Moran, *op. cit.*, pp. 166-67; *Globe and Mail*, March 25, 1976.

directed at the Alberta oil industry. Nonetheless, by taking part as an intervener in several court cases challenging potash regulations and taxation, within a general policy effort to restrict any province's ability to garner returns through fiscal measures, the federal government clearly acted as a catalyst, prompting the Saskatchewan government to see direct state control as its only recourse.[23] Several new structural and political realities combined to shape federal-provincial rivalry in the 1970s which had not been present at the time of the abortive joint venture with Ottawa proposed in 1949. The most important were: the build-up of resource-based provincial economies in the 1950s; the drive towards centralizing federalism linked with the accession to power of Pierre Elliott Trudeau in 1968; and, after several decades of Keynesian pump-priming and the accumulation of social responsibilities, federal indebtedness had reached critical proportions by the mid-1970s.

Nationalization of potash mines thus took place under very particular conditions which did not appear conducive to using the new state enterprises to promote social democratic objectives. Having entered the industry primarily for the purpose of achieving a proper share of the resource rents—that is, the level of revenues deemed necessary to meeting existing social policy obligations—the government found itself running a corporation alongside established oligopolists, and indeed in direct competition with them. In the first instance, until 1980, the NDP government's objective was to convince both the private sector and the electorate that it was capable of operating mines for profit by playing according to the ground rules of corporate capitalism. The initial success of the Potash Corporation of Saskatchewan (PCS) can be attributed not only to favourable market conditions, but also to a conservative management strategy. The government chose to retain experienced industry personnel and to avoid changing established industrial relations.[24]

---

23. The tax provision was mildly revised in June 1975, to permit a twenty-five per cent resource allowance deduction. The federal government's intervention was most significant in the cases of the challenge to the province's "reserve tax", found *ultra vires* by the Supreme Court of Canada, and to the Potash Conservation Regulations, deemed by the Supreme Court to interfere with exports, and thus to be beyond the bounds of provincial jurisdiction as well.

24. For further details on the transition strategy, see Jeanne Kirk Laux and Maureen Appel Molot, "The Potash Corporation of Saskatchewan", in Allan Tupper and G. Bruce Doern, *Public Corporations and Public Policy in Canada* (Montreal: Institute for Research on Public Policy, 1981), pp. 189-220. Corporate policy can be deemed synonymous with government policy in this period because of the establishment of the Cabinet Committee on Potash (disbanded in 1978) and because PCS is responsible to its holding company, the Crown Investments Corporation, which includes Cabinet ministers on its Board of Directors.

Once having consolidated a world-scale mineral-producing enterprise, and having achieved a certain acceptance by the private industry, what were the broader public purposes served by the Potash Corporation of Saskatchewan or, conversely, what were the apparent constraints on its use by an NDP government to advance social democratic objectives?

On the one hand, the performance of the Potash Corporation of Saskatchewan appears to confirm Irene Spry's analysis of the difficulty of combining human values and economic entrepreneurship on a large scale in the mixed economy. The basic problem with government *in* business, she argues, becomes its tendency to take on the colours of the private sector. Managerial recruits think in terms of profit—an easy measure for evaluating performance and making planning choices—while unions do not act as a corrective. With their narrow focus on job retention, they become merely the labour side of the business mentality.[25]

Looking at the disposition of surplus earned from potash sales or at capital-labour relations, PCS does not appear to have been an instrument for radical change. PCS made its resource-tax payments like any other company until 1980, when it paid government a $50 million dividend, but the bulk of its earnings were plowed back into expansion. Although a union member sits on the Board of Directors of PCS, one mine remains non-union. The government was more concerned with effecting a smooth transition to state ownership than experimenting with industrial relations. If there has not been any significant change in the social relations of production, the responsibility lies mainly with the unions and the Party. The Steelworkers in particular have never been more than lukewarm about direct participation in decision-making, seeing it as a form of co-optation, while the NDP has no traditional commitment to democracy in the workplace which could offer alternatives to co-optation.

On the other hand, given the realities of dependent development in Canada, especially in the resource sector, the impact of PCS on potash development in the province confirms Irene Spry's conviction that despite their shortcomings, state-owned enterprises must remain central to any democratic socialist strategy. Given the predominance of multinational corporations, whether foreign- or Canadian-owned, government must participate in an industry, if only to identify the rent. Wholly owned state enterprises, rather than partial participation, are required, she argues, for reasons of power—the very

25. Personal Interview, Irene Spry, September 1, 1983.

presence of government companies counterbalances big business both by reducing its lobbying influence (based on its exclusive control of information, capital, and employment in the industry) and by encouraging greater public scrutiny of overall sector development.[26] Indeed, once PCS, through acquisitions and expansion of its mine capacity, reached forty per cent of production, both the market power and the political clout of the remaining companies were eroded. It can certainly be argued that the government's ability to induce companies to give up ongoing court actions and to sign in 1980 a five-year "Potash Resource Payment Agreement"—thus ending years of bitter disputes—was possible due to this shift in power to the state-owned corporation.[27]

Some areas of innovation following nationalization can be identified. Saskatchewan government officials clearly felt that they encouraged state managers to look to a longer time frame for a return on investment than did the private sector. Their objective was not short-term profit maximization, but the long-term stable development of the industry, as the commitment to a ten-year expansion program demonstrated. Procurement policies for PCS—as for any other Crown corporation in the province—promoted local sourcing (Department of Industry and Commerce circulars alert local businesses to purchases planned by government and government-owned companies). Social costs were regarded as necessary capital costs because the government's objectives included creating the conditions for stable development of the potash industry over time. For example, research was initiated to find new techniques of extraction to avoid creation of the salt piles which contributed to soil "leaching" in adjacent agriculture lands, and a Work Environment Board was set up to organize educational and training programmes at the mines, using the resources of the Department of Labour.[28]

Achievement of the objectives sought by the NDP in Saskatchewan—such as stable resource development, secure employment, or research and development—require favourable market conditions. A state-owned enterprise, as compared to a foot-loose private multinational, looks particularly vulnerable—especially without diversified product lines, and when exploiting a resource which does not

26. *Ibid.*

27. The detailed analysis is available in Laux and Molot, "The Potash Corporation", pp. 203-205.

28. Personal Interviews with PCS and government officials, Saskatchewan, 1980. Donald Humphries, "Saskatchewan Potash Corporation unveils $2.5 Billion Expansion", *Globe and Mail*, February 11, 1979, p. B.1.

generate forward linkages. In fact, just as PCS was completing its $2.5 billion expansion programme in 1981, world demand for potash began a slump which was expected to continue to the end of the decade. The fall in prices from $142 to $100 per tonne in the 1981-82 fertilizer year reflected conditions well beyond corporate control: a worldwide recession and consequent reductions in both farm incomes and the budgets of Third World governments, as well as a new U.S. "payment in kind" programme to reduce crop acreage. As a result of these unfavourable conditions, PCS's net income dropped from $141.7 *million* to $607 *thousand* in 1982. Intent on holding employment steady, in December 1981 management announced "no lay-offs", and continued to build up inventory. By March 1982, however, the Crown corporation was obliged to switch miners to refurbishing work while production was curtailed for six months.[29]

The resounding defeat of the NDP in the 1982 provincial election precludes analysis of how this social democratic party might have reacted to continuing adverse market conditions. The Conservative Party's strategy, although a far cry from its election promises to dismantle Crown corporations, signalled an abrupt turnabout. Current production was halted for four months; nearly twelve hundred workers were laid off; expansion plans were cancelled; and a "profits policy" was devised for all commercial Crown corporations, including PCS.[30] This policy in essence amounted to dividend-stripping, and was motivated by Government concern over revenues as Saskatchewan experienced its first budget deficit in twenty years. In 1981, Crown corporations' profits of $115 million had been re-invested after the normal "transfer dividends" to their parent, the Crown Investments Corporation (CIC), were made. In 1982, under the new Conservative government, despite the fact that these same Crown corporations lost $125 million overall, they nonetheless paid the government $42 million in dividends.[31]

The Conservative government's practice thus already appears to reflect the recommendations of its Review Commission, set up to re-assess all government investments. In its report, the Commission had recommended that the CIC be retained but that it "be given as

---

29. PCS *News Release*, March 25, 1981.

30. PCS *News Release*, December 10, 1981, and March 8, 1982; *Maclean's*, May 2, 1983, "State Enterprise and the Tories", p. 39; *Globe and Mail*, July 26, 1981, p. B.1.

31. PCS *News Release*, June 10, 1983; Edward Greenspon, "Crown Dividend Eases Government Deficit", *Financial Post*, May 21, 1983; Richard Cleroux, "Devine Cautious on Undoing Socialism", *Globe and Mail*, April 26, 1983, and *Ibid.*, "Saskatchewan Curbs Provincial Mining Role", p. 5.

its central objective the maximization of dividend payments to the province".[32] Each company under the CIC's direction—such as PCS—must "be clearly profit oriented". In recommending nonetheless that Crown companies pay grants-in-lieu-of-taxes and a guarantee fee on borrowed funds, the Commission sought to "redress the financial imbalance" which supposedly favoured public- over private-sector companies.[33]

Wherever public enterprises must operate in the context of a liberal capitalist system—subject, that is, to both the fluctuations of the market and to the political business cycle, it appears imperative to find ways to protect the gains made for social democratic values if state capital is not to be misappropriated. A first thrust must be to democratize public enterprises so that boards of directors are representative. Giving workers and relevant social groups—such as farmers or communities directly affected by mining—a determinant role in decision-making may help transcend the change of parties in power. Looking beyond any one enterprise, an equally important thrust is to promote what Irene Spry calls "alternative forms of entrepreneurship"—such as worker-operated enterprises and co-operatives —in order to find more solid ground for Canada's future than the current economic discourse mired in the "profit motive", where progressive voices are drowned out by the sound of the clinking horns of the rhinoceroses of big business, business-oriented unions, and bureaucracies—including bureaucracies running such socially unresponsive public enterprises as Ontario Hydro.[34]

---

32. Crown Investments Review Commission, *Report to the Government of Saskatchewan*, December 1982, p. 43.

33. *Ibid.*, p. 45.

34. For a critique of Ontario Hydro's policies and public relations see Bob Rae, "Is Free-Wheeling Hydro Insulated from Reality?", *Globe and Mail*, October 7, 1983, p. 7.

8.   The State and Property

Water Rights in Western Canada

Anthony Scott
University of British Columbia

Introduction[1]

When scholars discuss scenarios for the "reform" of property rights, it is government they see in the role of reformer. One continuous view of Canadian economic history, for example, can easily be pieced together from land-title and property debates stretching from the installation of seigneurial tenure in New France to today's definition of aboriginal rights in western Canada. In each debate, government has been seen as the actor making the reforms.

But the reform scenario could be written without a reformer. As in Greek drama, questions about property rights could be left to the whims of the gods of Mount Olympus. Alternatively, as in an Austrian drama, they could erupt from the "spontaneous" volcanic forces slumbering beneath Mont Pelerin. While few economists express their distinctive views in the form of epic myths, those who do take an interest in property rights and their reform can be violently partisan, and their differences are faintly reminiscent of themes from ancient drama.

For one group of economists, property rights are exogenously defined as titles to things and, like ancient curses and blessings, bestowed on hapless mortals. Even if the rights and their bestowal are not arbitrary, the explanations are beyond orthodox economics. A contractarian cult within this group believes that our property rights

1. Research on the subject of this paper has been contributed by Kathleen Day. The paper also reflects work by earlier colleagues in research on water use and water rights: Richard Campbell, Milan Uzelac, Andrew Thompson, Peter Pearse, Irving Fox, and Robby Jones. Recently, discussions of the rent of hydro-electric sites with Irene Spry and with John Helliwell, Jean-Thomas Bernard, James Johnson, and Ellen Battle have stimulated new interest. Correspondence with Vernon L. Smith has also been a welcome stimulus.

were hammered out around the peace fires, following a Titanic battle between anarchic forces in time immemorially remote.

A second group, in its rejection of this superhuman explanation, adheres to a more mystical approach: the reinterpretation of property rights is like exegesis, with us always. Its working is essentially benign and constructive, so that the system of property rights unfolds in harmony with the unfolding of society. Like such other institutions as representative government, language and money, its shaping is outside the control of any person or group. But property rights are neither arbitrary nor fixed. By a process of selection they evolve to serve society's needs efficiently and naturally. Consequently, with respect to interests in land and natural resources, this second school tends to dismiss the puny attempts of government to create or "reform" property rights. Whatever revision takes place is the response of the whole property system to forces of social change.

In two earlier papers an attempt has been made to describe and order these approaches.[2] The author has suggested to economists that any non-governmental process of revision of property rights must, in our economy, work mostly through the courts. Unsettled conflicts concerning land are resolved by litigation. In the process claimants contribute to the selection of an established list of property interests, accepted by the courts and by dealers in natural resources alike. Because of this acceptance, transaction costs of holding land (under these interests) decline, and as they decline they become ever more standardized.

However, these standardized interests, and the whole system of interests, are not inflexible. An economic shock, such as an exogenous change in consumer tastes or in industrial technology and knowledge, can produce biased or one-sided dissatisfaction with one or more of the accepted legal constraints characteristic of a property system. This dissatisfaction can lead to a bias in the composition of the flow of cases going for litigation before the courts, and a consequent revision of arguments about the meaning of a standard interest. Judgements may eventually respond sympathetically to those new pleadings. By precedent these judgements influence the results of later cases and so lead to a gradual erosion of the offending characteristics. Thus, without government intervention and without politics

---

2. Anthony Scott, "Property Rights and Property Wrongs", *Canadian Journal of Economics* (November, 1983), pp. 555-73; and Anthony Scott and James Johnston, "Property Rights: Developing the Characteristics of Interests in Natural Resources", in Scott, ed., *Progress in Natural Resource Economics* (Oxford, forthcoming 1985), Chapter 13. Extensive bibliographies are provided in these two papers.

the system of rights, and the characteristics of particular rights, are gradually reshaped ''spontaneously''.

This paper investigates the quite different view of the genesis of interests in land and natural resources that attributes to legislatures, Crown, and Parliament the function of designing and reforming property rights. That this view is more pervasive than the ''spontaneous'' theories outlined above is not surprising. Parliament is supreme, and as it often changes laws, why not property rights? Furthermore, most land and resource titles can be traced back to the Crown (that is, to the government) and in many former British countries, at any rate, there is a surviving theory that all real private property is still held by the monarch, conferring on the Crown an ultimate ownership right separate from its power to legislate. In countries of new settlement, such as Canada, government's responsibilities for defining interests in property, especially evident in creating new ways of holding and using natural resources, have been more widely accepted than elsewhere because they have been exercised in the process of disposing of the public domain. It might seem that government's role as resource seller is bound to come to an end. But technological discoveries create new resources; and these are as likely to be in the public domain as outside it. Hence the process of devising packages for transferable parcels of resources has become a long-term government function, made all the more nearly perpetual because final and absolute private control is almost never granted, and because taxes and other carrying charges induce owners to relinquish whatever property has become unprofitable. Thus, ownership of land above exhausted mines, beneath cutover forests, and around abandoned homesteads slips back into the public domain, to be reassembled and sold or leased again.

Government's new property packages are not necessarily of government's own devising. The lease transferring mineral rights to prospectors has been borrowed from private law, conveying a title that a holder can transfer to the extent desired on the general property market. Even government's more inventive tenures such as the tree-farm licence, the pollution right, and the fish-catch quota, though somewhat distrusted in the marketplace as insecure and untested, are modelled on earlier legal forms. The successful government is one that can be seen to be pouring new wine into old property bottles.

But modification is necessary. The old common-law bottles were not designed to deal with modern resource-extraction problems. Indeed, as mentioned above, they were not ''designed'' at all, but evolved by usage: that is, by custom, contract, settlement, litigation and jurisprudence, as bundles of legal characteristics presumably adapted to the technical methods of winning the resources and to the economic structure of the industries dealing in them. Government's modifications of these bundles, and its adjustments of old tenures to new tax, conservation, and citizenship policies have been shaped by governing parties within a complex of social, economic, and financial goals to satisfy shifting groupings of voters.

The purpose of this paper, then, is to investigate government's role by examining the development of interests in a particular natural resource—water. We shall see that there is much reason to adopt the non-government or "spontaneous" view, for there is certainly a vigorous body of common law applicable to water. And we shall see that there is much legislation and administrative water law as well. Is there some sense in which we can say that one is the more basic? For example, can we accept the view that the legislature has simply taken over from the courts the enforcement and definition of standard interests in water law? Some experts act and write as though this were so. Or should we tend to the opposite view, that because of their distributive aspects private property rights are fundamental to our society, so that the role of government has simply been to confirm the slow redefinition of an institution not subject to, but served by, government?

It must be said that this question is not resolved here. At best it is shown that some of the history of water property law suggests that government's role has been modest. If this is correct, then it throws into question much of the vast literature which treats water law as a *policy* question; which investigates the working of the institution in order to suggest amendments to legislation and administrative practice to improve its justice or efficiency. Although the author (with co-authors), has contributed to this literature,[3] one must now ask whether government has ever been in a position to accept the advice of zealous scholars of natural-resource economics.

The System of Interests in Land and Resources

A real property right is best thought of as a bundle of characteristics. This idea is familiar to most of us in connection with interests in rural

---

3. Richard S. Campbell, Peter H. Pearse, Anthony Scott, and Milan Uzelac, "Water Management in Ontario—An Economic Evaluation of Public Policy", *Osgoode Hall Law Journal* 12 (December, 1974), pp. 475-526; and Richard S. Campbell, P. Pearse, and A. Scott, "Water Allocation in British Columbia: An Economic Assessment of Public Policy", *U.B.C. Law Review* 7 (1972), p. 247.

and urban land. For example, most holdings in land are either free-hold or leasehold. Differences between these interests are found in their characteristics or dimensions. Duration is one such characteristic. A freehold tenure is always for an indefinite period (that is, without end), while a leasehold is nearly always for a fixed period. A document conveying an interest in land typically says what parcel of land it covers, how much product the tenant may remove, how many rental payments are to be made annually, and so on. It is the combined effect of such specific characteristics that gives a system of bundles of land rights those more abstract properties sometimes mentioned by theorists of the property system: exclusivity, enforceability, divisibility, and transferability. It differentiates them from other kinds of ownership and from merely contractual relationships.

Forms of land tenure have evolved or developed gradually since the feudal period by changes in the contents of the characteristics bundle. For example, freehold tenure originally called for some amount of military service, work service, or access to forest, waste, and mill incident to the tenure—that is, rights and duties binding on *any* holder of that interest. Modern freehold is descended from this, but its bundle of characteristics is simpler and more general. Furthermore, it is more uniform. It appears that an evolutionary process has selected characteristics for this and other standard interests in land, making each interest simpler, more exclusive, or less costly to defend or transfer.

The process of selection of characteristics of interests in agricultural land has been intensively studied by economic historians and by legal (''constitutional'') historians, for the most part as a side-issue in connection with their work on the enclosure movement and its relationship with rural society, labour migration, farm productivity, and induced technical change. A full bibliography would contain hundreds, if not thousands, of entries, a fair proportion of these concerned with the roles of the courts, legislatures, and Parliament, as the instruments of tenure development.

But much, much less has been done on the question of the development of interests in natural resources other than land; and indeed, little consideration has been given to the division of labour between the judiciary and the legislature in revising or reforming standard interests.

The Market for Changes in Property Interests

How might we envision the process of gradual change in the system of property rights? In concentrating on gradual change it is intended to bypass such important but abrupt events as the forcible introduction of a new system of property rights by outsiders, such as that which may have resulted from the conquest of Saxon England by the Normans (and of the North American Indians by the Europeans); or by internal revolution such as may arise from the enfranchising of women, slaves, and serfs; or from a new egalitarian attitude to the distribution of real wealth and power. Doubtless such major upsets have been important influences on the ways in which land and resources are held and transferred. The purpose here, however, is to explore the problem of a less dramatic process that steadily allows particular standard bundles of rights to adapt to new social and economic forces.

It will be suggested that this evolutionary process is fairly uniform for all types of property interests, regardless of the natural resource over which the interests convey rights and obligations. Though this ''model'' of the process is so general as to be difficult to verify or disprove, there is, nevertheless, something to be said for it. Because it is economic it suggests to the researcher kinds of evidence of individual behaviour or market consequences such as would be commonplace in any model of an economic market. By the same token it enables him/her to classify available information as crucial, or as merely background, and to attempt some discrimination between ''normative'' and ''positive'' economic and legal scholarship on this subject.

The model is *economic* in three senses. First, it presumes that the actors who seek and those who assist in providing changes in the characteristics of standard tenures have the motive of improving the present value of their own production and consumption opportunities. In brief, their behaviour, like that of other people in economic models, is that of profit maximizers in business and of individualistic utilitarians in their private lives. Second, it presumes that actions are the consequences of self-seeking. Thus people participate in political life or go to court out of interest, not disinterest (of course, they may realize that equal benefits may also flow to others who have been free riders on their activities.) Third, much of the public-choice analysis of the provision of public goods applies. In particular, any change in the characteristics of a standard property interest affects equally not only those investing in making the change, but everyone with that interest. Furthermore, with appropriate modifications, much public-choice analysis of the making of constitutional rules may also be applied to the assembling of bundles of property rights. This may not seem important because most public-choice models of constitutional decisions deal mainly with *optimizing* voting rules and sizes of constituencies rather than with actual decisions. However, because constitutional-choice models rely on expected transaction costs to explain marginal adjustments in political institutions, and have already been adapted for analyzing legal liability rules, they are logical candidates for models that explain property interests.

Our economic model is a simple adaptation of a supply-and-demand model. The demand for changes in the definition of standard property interests is considered, then the supply.

Demand for a change in property rights is best seen as individual investment demand, analytically similar to an investor's willingness to pay for an addition to productive assets. For any such lumpy, or long-run, investment the demander can be imagined as deciding on his willingness to pay for it by subtracting its expected cost of acquisition from the expected increase in discounted revenue it makes possible.

An attempt to change the characteristic of a property right can be seen as reducing a limitation or constraint on the firm's future activities. Thus it is similar to investment outlays that will expand capacity, reduce future costs, or lead into new markets. Like them, too, its payoff is subject to discounting for time and risk. And also like them, it is in competition for the investor's capital with alternate ways of achieving an increase in long-run profit.

Shocks such as come from technical change, new resource discoveries, and changes in demand or transportation will cause a shift in a firm's derived demand for attempts to change property rights. This can be observed in two main forms: as demand for government provision of new legislation or for administrative interpretation of a property right; or as demand for private settlements or judicial decisions that will give the firm relief from onerous entitlement characteristics.

Responses to such attempts come either from institutions of government or from negotiations and court proceedings. For brevity, the behaviour of administrators will be assumed here to conform broadly to the preferences of politicians. As for the politicians, they are not specialists on property matters; they are the same actors who participate in all government decisions. They turn their attention to the definition of interests in land or to the disposal of the public domain when voters, interest groups or administrators indicate that new situations call for new policies.

How will a demander exert its derived demand? If we assume it has decided that it would pay to invest in obtaining some change in the property rights that protect or constrain it, its next step will be to compare various private with public investments. The private investments include endeavouring to make new contracts or to renegotiate grants with other resource claimants. As a substitute, the firm can have recourse to litigation in the courts. Under common-law procedures, litigation leads to judgements that in turn become precedents, gradually affecting the interpretation of standard interests in property.

The supply of litigation depends on the available time and alternative earnings of counsel, and also on the provision by government of courts and tribunals. The smaller the supply of these, the higher is the "price" of obtaining property-rights changes through litigation, and the more likely is the demander to have recourse to publicly provided changes.

The supply here will be affected by the cost of political participation and negotiation to obtain changes in property-rights policy. Doubtless, a typical firm will first attempt to obtain help from officers in the government departments concerned with its industry. Failing that, it will invest in direct discussions with individual politicians and with groups and parties. It may also decide to have recourse to explicit voting pressure through advertising, support of parties, and so on. That is, it may attempt either to obtain support from elected politicians or to get new politicians elected who will support its aims.[4]

The remainder of this section illustrates three ways in which government customarily participates in "supply" changes in land and natural resource tenure.

Firstly, **full legislative intervention in making property law** is one course of action for government. The standard English example of this is enclosure: the government, under heavy pressure from a class of landlords, intervened to rearrange holdings, and to change the balance of wealth between that class and those dispossessed. But less extreme instances are with us all the time, for example, in the invention of new tenure such as condominiums and strata-titles, in the imposition of controls over how "waste" is to be treated in lease tenure, in how lease renewals are to be handled, and over what rents may be charged. Land-use zoning is still another type of tenure intervention.

Secondly, **adding to or disposing of the public domain** is another government practice. In Canada the Crown may be considered to act individually, as though it were a personal monarch. In this manifestation, it can acquire land and resources through the

---

4. The above text deals with land-holders' lobbying and litigation. In property matters, of course, third parties can also initiate proceedings that lead to rights revisions.

market, or do so by expropriation, using its full powers to enforce its own bargain.

Even more importantly, it can dispose of the Crown domain independently even of Parliament, by means ranging from full commercial sale of land at whatever price the traffic will bear, to outright concessions, or assisted-and-subsidized settlement on lands reserved for particular groups or uses. These activities were, of course, among the chief preoccupations of Canadian government throughout the nineteenth century. They did not all, by any means, aid existing industries or land users. Land-disposal policies, while no doubt heavily influenced by developers and existing users, were intended also to have macro-effects, such as claiming and holding whole territories in the face of international pressures; affecting relations with railways (and the Hudson's Bay Company); and simply changing the balance of political representation of voters in Parliament itself. With these larger goals in mind, legislators should not be assumed to be passive, or mere puppets of existing groups, in their decisions about the disposal of public resources.

In any case, there are reasons to believe that the statutory decision about the *mode* of alienating parcels of the public domain is ineffective in bringing about permanent change in standard tenures. One historical reason is that officials who administered land disposal often ignored the letter of the law and sold, or gave away, parcels that immediately found their way into the existing systems of land holdings.

Another reason is empirical. The bundles of rights disposed of conformed to, rather than changed, private-sector practice. Most of the former public domain in North America is held and conveyed according to traditional common-law concepts, regardless of the innovations in, or conditions of, original transfer to settlers and grantees. For example, homesteaded land concessions are held and transferred exactly as parcels that were sold. The tenure of both is very similar to that under the procedures and customs in jurisdictions in North America and in England, where original disposals are now overlaid by centuries of common-law modifications.

Thirdly, **provision of enforcement facilities** is expected of government. This power, referred to as "justice" in classical dissertations on the economic role of the state, includes public provision of courts and land registries. Its extent is of course a manifestation of the old theory, inherited from the contractarian and liberal philosophers, that the state exists primarily to protect and facilitate activities based on transactions in private property.

Although government carries out property-related functions in all three ways, it is not politically indifferent as to which route it follows. This is, of course, because most reforms of property rights are bound to antagonize some voters, perhaps explaining why English enclosure acts were introduced with such caution, and why modern licensing schemes for resources have been brought in so hesitantly. From this political point of view, the first of the three powers mentioned above is the most unattractive to politicians. Almost any redefinition of a private property right is bound to hurt someone directly and visibly. The second power, a change in the mode of disposing of resources from the public domain, is the most attractive politically because the gains are obvious, while the losses are diffused among the taxpayers and citizenry. But actions under this power are unlikely to satisfy lobbyists or petitioners. The third power, provision of more courts and machinery, although it too is unlikely to satisfy a pressure group avid for redefinition of existing rights, is easy to use, and has the added attraction that lawyers, counsel and others in the business of land conveyancing will be assisted, and patronage in the form of judicial promotions can be extended (though government may move slowly in instituting labour-saving reforms such as land registries).

Admittedly, these categories and behaviours hardly consti-tute a ''model'' of the process of changing natural-resource tenures. But they do lead to a few expectations that can be examined against what we can learn about the provision of new forms of water rights.

Three Systems of Water Law

The main historical fact about water law in North America is that until 1850 the common-law riparian system was universal.[5] Today, however, it is found only in the eastern, humid provinces and states. In the Alaska–New Mexico band of mountain provinces and states an appropriation system has appeared, although the nineteenth-century displacement of the first system by the second is not complete: riparian rights may still crop up in some jurisdictions as causes for legal action even though all recent water transfers have been of appropriated rights.

---

5. Arthur Maass and Raymond L. Anderson, . . . *and the Desert Shall Rejoice: Conflict, Growth, and Justice in Arid Environments* (Cambridge: MIT Press, 1978), Chapter 6; Arthur Maass and Hiller B. Zobel, ''Anglo-American Water Law: Who Appropriated the Riparian Doctrine?'', *Public Policy*, vol. X (1960), pp. 109-156; Morton J. Horowitz, *The Transformation of American Law 1780-1860* (Cambridge; Harvard University Press, 1977), Chapter 2.

Riparian Rights

To investigate the two systems, it will be necessary to first outline the riparian system as it is found in Ontario. This version is closely linked to the original English system, and relies on the same case law. It is somewhat different from the stylized riparian system referred to in American discussions of water law.[6] Indeed, this account of the common-law system as found in Ontario would be referred to by the western-American expert Frank Trelease as "words from a dead age".[7]

This account is paraphrased shamelessly from the 1974 work of more expert colleagues.[8] Under Ontario law, water is made available to various users through legal arrangements that interweave a common-law warp and a legislative weft. Even this metaphor probably attributes too much importance to statute law, for in Ontario the government has made only small changes to common-law water rights.

English common law concerning property and civil rights became the law of Ontario in 1792, and with it the rule that holders of rights to land bordering a natural stream possess also certain rights to the use and flow of its water. Each such riparian owner has a right to use the water, but this right is subject to similar rights of other riparian owners. Thus, in the words of a 1965 judgement, the "flow" of a stream creates natural rights and liabilities among all the riparian proprietors along its course.

In the eighteenth-century heyday of the riparian system, there was rarely capacity of separate ownership of water for any use. True, there were sole (and public) rights of fishing, and there were public rights of navigation. But neither the fish nor the water could be the subject of separate ownership. The riparian right to enjoy water is one of a number of common-law rights which are incidental to the ownership of land. No separate express grant is necessary when property with riparian rights is transferred. The water right is confined to access and use, and owners are not required to use water in order to preserve riparian rights.

If the riparian owner does divert and capture part of the flow, does the common law limit the volume of water he may take? As interpreted in Ontario, the amount depends on his purpose. "Ordinary use" of water, including amounts that are "reasonably necessary"

---

6. Frank J. Trelease, *Cases and Materials on Water Law*, 3rd edition (St. Paul: West, 1979).

7. *Ibid.*

8. Arthur Maass and Hiller B. Zobel, *op. cit.*, p. 109; Morton J. Horowitz, *op. cit.*, pp. 42-47.

for domestic and livestock needs, may be made by a riparian owner without regard to the effect on other riparian owners. However, the common-law rules that govern "extraordinary" uses are less certain. The volume used must be connected with or incidental to the riparian property, and it must also be "reasonable". For example, the net flows diverted or interrupted by mills or irrigation works must be returned on the watercourse substantially undiminished in volume and unaltered in character.

From such general principles three more specific rules have emerged. First, water diversions away from a stream are not covered by riparian law. Second, in case of scarcity, a system of priorities as between ordinary and extraordinary uses has emerged. While extraordinary riparian users have among themselves equal rights to use water, they must not interfere with a lower riparian owner's right for "ordinary" purposes. Conversely, the flow available for an extraordinary use may be lawfully diminished by ordinary users' withdrawals upstream. Third, the inflexibility of this allocation system was modified by judicial recognition of a "prescriptive" use of water. By means of twenty years of continuous use for some extraordinary purpose a riparian owner can obtain a "prescriptive" right to that flow as against both ordinary and other extraordinary users.

To a purist the apparent opportunity for inconsistency between these three specific rules is upsetting. The first, that no riparian owner may divert water to a non-riparian use, seems to buttress the riparian concept that actual and potential uses along the watercourse are based on some sort of common right to its natural flow. However, equal or common access to natural flow may not be a simple rule: it may be infeasible or costly at certain points along the stream, or in dry seasons. The second rule deals with this by making a distinction among riparian owners or at least among their uses for water (by their nature not all uses being equal). Ontario law distinguishes between "ordinary" and "extraordinary" uses, following an ancient ordering of preferred uses, and is much invoked in neighbouring American riparian-law states, where disputed rights depend on which use is judged the most "reasonable". This departure from the idea of equal access is further limited by the third, or prescriptive-right, rule. Here riparian law is modified to preserve water flows for prior diverters and dam owners in spite of a lowering of volume to which other riparian owners would be entitled under the pure "natural flow" doctrine. In effect, under this third rule a major but ancient stream diversion in time becomes a "natural" feature of the stream, which now has acquired new and different levels and flows available to users on riparian lands. (Ontario has a twenty-year priority rule, but in some riparian-law states a priority of only five or ten years is adequate to give entitlement to more water than can leave the stream in its natural pristine state.)

It is not strictly correct to say that under a system of riparian rights there can be no trade or transfers in water. To a certain extent riparian owners can deal in their respective shares of a natural stream. For example, an extraordinary user can attempt to secure supply by reaching an agreement with upstream riparians to waive their rights to use water for ordinary or other purposes. In order to avoid actions based on the charge that his/her uses were not "reasonable"—that is, for reasons connected with downstream rights to continued return flow—he/she might also negotiate with downstream riparian owners. But such arrangements do not amount to grants of property rights.

A non-riparian owner may obtain water from a riparian owner through a licence or an easement. Here the non-riparian owner acquires a right against only the grantor and his successors. A licence or easement so obtained does not entitle the non-riparian owner to even "ordinary" use vis-à-vis a downstream riparian owner; nor does the licence or easement offer protection against diminished flow caused by an upstream riparian owner's extraordinary or unreasonable use.

Thus, in order to obtain secure rights to flows, a non-riparian owner must overcome the same uncertainties as would a riparian owner. Either must acquire rights from *all* downstream and *all* upstream riparian owners, by purchase of their riparian land, by licence, or perhaps by covenant. Not surprisingly, in places where water was scarcer than in England, men looked for a less costly and more secure régime than this. As Clark and Renard write of the common law of water in Australia, "the rigorous methodology of precedent led to a fear that the rights of downstream riparian owners, even if they suffered no damage, and even if the upstream use was 'reasonable', would be cumulatively built up in common law as an impediment to water diversion and it was a deep, almost hysterical fear of the possible effects of these rules on agricultural development which led to legislative intervention. . . ."[9] That riparian rights, and the systems of rights of fishing and of navigation, have some integrated relevance to several conflicting water uses is a satisfying feature of our common-law inheritance, a feature that has been lost in many constitutional and statutory reforms.

---

9. S. D. Clark and I. A. Renard, "The Riparian Doctrine and Australian Legislation", *Melbourne University Law Review* (1970), p. 479.

For there have been reforms. Few jurisdictions have trusted the unmodified riparian system to provide certainty or security to investors in extraordinary water uses. Ontario, for example, has special legislation to provide water for larger works where security of investment may require security of supply. This legislation prescribes conditions under which water supply, sewage, irrigation, power generation, cooling, flood-control, and amenity uses of the stream can be undertaken and flow, level, or quality of water supplied, free from the threat of legal actions by riparian owners hurt or potentially hurt by the undertakings.

Most of these large-scale uses are governed by a permit system having as its basis the province's general regulatory powers. This means that Ontario does not rely on its extensive proprietary powers (under the riparian system it has owner's rights to waters bordering provincial Crown lands).[10] Without permits, users withdrawing large amounts (more than ten thousand gallons per day) cannot operate. The permits are issued at the discretion of the head of an administrative arm of the government, subject to ministerial and judicial appeal.

On any watercourse, permits are granted on a first-come-first-served basis, subject to the following. First, because high priority is attached to protection of the supplies of "ordinary" users, permits are not issued that would interfere with flows available to them. Second, "extraordinary" users who already hold permits are usually also protected, if they have put their allocation to beneficial use. Beyond this, there is a very flexible setting of priorities among uses, and considerable official discretion is exercised in determining the precedence of one use over another. Permits are issued to the party taking the water, and are not automatically transferable to others.

This account may suggest that the Ontario system of permits leaves much of the riparian system fairly intact. This impression is probably correct so far as small riparian properties and traditional uses are concerned. For these, the newer permit system has merely been an overlay.

For larger industries, however, the permit system may appear to be the source of all water rights. To begin with, a variant of the administered permit system has almost completely supplanted riparian law in matters of water quality and pollution rights. Furthermore, the provincial authorities use the permit system to ration seasonally low stream flow among riparian owners (including municipalities and

---

10. Dale Gibson, "The Constitutional Context of Canadian Water Planning", *Alberta Law Review* 7 (1968-69), pp. 71-92.

large industrial water users). Thus legal questions about the "reasona-
bleness" or "benefit" of competing uses have been replaced by the
multiple criteria of administrative and political procedures. Finally,
permits and other administrative devices are the instrument whereby
relatively large water users obtain "rights" to change a stream's
course, levels, flows, and quality. Riparian rights may still offer some
sort of overall logic to the system, but detailed permits are adminis-
tratively granted, protected and exchanged as instruments of policies unrelated to water issues. So central has the government's role
become that the number of court cases or water disputes that have
reached any court in the twentieth century is extremely small.[11]

Appropriative Rights

The doctrine of riparian rights was seen to have severe disadvantages
when it was transplanted to western North America. Although it was
applied to newly opened settlement areas in the United States in the
years following the Louisiana Purchase, and was generally understood
to be applicable in California in 1849, it was not welcomed.

Two defects were apparent. First, the unmodified riparian
system worked against the making of bargains by which, permanently
or in a dry period, a user could acquire a secure or preferred supply.
Second, it created a presumption that secure water flows and consumption might not be transferred within the water basin or beyond it without unanimous continuing consent from (and probably compensation to) all other riparian owners and potential riparian owners. It
is said by many writers that these two defects would have prevented
miners and ranchers from diverting water, stopped ranchers and riparian owners from making bargains to water stock normally grazed elsewhere and, perhaps worst of all, blocked entrepreneurs from investing in major works to impound, carry, and store water where its use
would pay most. Although a potential diverter could in theory contract
in advance with all other riparian owners to not object to his
diversions—in short, could internalize the stream flows within one
web of covenants—such advance covenants might not bind all later
owners of upstream or downstream lands. To be certain, the would-
be diverter would be forced to buy all lands and so become the sole
owner of the appurtenant rights to stream flows.

The least-cost alternative system required side-stepping riparian rights altogether. This was accomplished by a major property-

---

11. Campbell *et al.*, "Water Management in Ontario", p. 484. See also J. Burchill, "Origins
of Canadian Irrigation Law", *Canadian Historical Review* 29 (1948), pp. 353-61.

rights innovation, the doctrine or theory of prior appropriation.

According to some, it was adapted in the late 1840s from Spanish (civil law) antecedents. Under the Mexican version of these earlier laws, rivers and streams had belonged to the nation. In fact, however, legal access tended to be limited to those who under common law would be considered riparian owners (thus perhaps helping to explain why water law in Quebec and Louisiana, also derived from civil-law origins, does not differ greatly from that in adjoining riparian jurisdictions). The government could make exclusive-use grants on non-navigable streams. But it rarely did so, preferring to let users acquire water rights by prescription, that is, as a result of long-standing use. Such acquired waters could be diverted to non-riparian lands. Although the Mexican system was not a true appropriative-rights system, it did tend to establish the claims of first-comers.

When the western territories were acquired by the United States under a series of treaties and purchases, lands not already disposed of passed (by 1848) to the proprietorship of the federal government. Under common law these lands carried riparian rights to adjoining streams. But the power to make laws concerning land and water under the Constitution had been assigned to such state governments as existed. However, the lands themselves did not become part of a state's public domain, being granted directly by the federal proprietor to individuals, and thus the scope of any state's water law broadened only as the federal domain was alienated.

The states' political scope for innovation by abandoning the riparian system was of course still very broad. In many watersheds there were no riparian land holders (except for the federal government) of the remaining public domain. Therefore, any redistribution of wealth implied by a new mineral or water system would be naturally small and difficult to observe.

Two types of state law warrant consideration: the development of water law, first, in California, and second, in Colorado and Utah.[12]

Some authorities argue that, effectively, California's water property laws emerged "spontaneously", without help from legislature or court. Developed in the mining camps during the 1849 gold rush, their form was presumably influenced by the Mexican law previously recognized, and by the prescriptive right variants of common law then rapidly taking shape in the eastern States. The California

---

12. John Umbeck, *A Theory of Property Rights, with Application to the California Gold Rush* (Ames: Iowa State University Press, 1981).

version was apparently worked out in detail in conjunction with the mining camps' rules for staking placer claims in river-valley workings. The valleys being essentially empty, the mining use was in many places the only one to which rights had to be assigned.

Under this new system, users' rights acquired five new characteristics: (1) instead of being equally available to all riparian owners water was assigned to whomever appropriated it first, (2) a riparian location earned no right until water was used on it, (3) each right was limited to a stated quantity (usually measured in "miner's-inch" units of flow), (4) if a stream's flow fluctuated, a first appropriator's right dominated those of "junior" users, of a later date, and (5) water could be carried beyond riparian land.

Umbeck (writing about the genesis of mineral rights) comments on the water-rights system: "I suspect that in the early 1850s water rights were rationed like land rights—by force."[13] By this he means that each miner's rights were enforced against claim-jumpers and others by the rest of the miners in each camp. This system was later recognized as "customary" by the courts when the new State of California set up its own institutions, and later still it was formed into a statutory system by legislation and by state-court decisions.

As now codified in California, an appropriative water right is acquired easily. The claimant first gives recorded notice that he intends to take or divert from a stream a certain volume of water. If this claim is not found to conflict with an earlier appropriation, the claimant will acquire an appropriate right to the amount actually beneficially used. "Beneficially" is a key word here. Demonstrating "beneficial use" under the appropriate scheme can justify permanent acquisition, by a prior appropriator, of yet more water—perhaps more water than if he/she were to share a stream with other reasonable users under the riparian system.

This procedure raises questions about the constitutional position of water rights. Riparian rights being dominant at the time of the drafting of the United States Constitution, water resources are not mentioned, because water was not a "thing" to which ownership could apply. Any mention of land and its proprietorship was considered automatically to include the water incident to it. (Although rivers and streams were not the subjects of real interests, the rights to navigate and to fish could, as "usufructory" rights, be assigned or deeded to a government or a person.)

On what constitutional basis, then, did the western states assimilate the new water-rights codes? Two theories have been

---

13. *Ibid.*

advanced. One is the "California" theory, that appropriative water rights held by individuals had in effect been granted by the federal government; that government had held them incidentally to its original holding of the public domain. Once these water rights had passed to individuals, it was the function of state law to enforce them and to co-ordinate them with riparian and other rights to use water.

The other theory, identified with Colorado and Utah, is that the federal government relinquished to the states its original rights to waters adjoining all land, private *or* public. Under this "Colorado" doctrine the states acquired a proprietorial power over all waters, which could then be granted on the basis of state law.

California's appropriative system spread to other Pacific Rim jurisdictions, notably British Columbia, Alaska, Australia, and New Zealand: it is known to have been spread to these places, along with mining-claim law, by the highly mobile gold miners of the 1850s. The Colorado theory also spread, not only because its assumption of public ownership fitted the predilections of lawmakers in British colonies, but also because its denial of riparian rights later provided a secure foundation for large investments in diversions and in irrigation schemes, including those in Australia and in the Canadian northwest.

California, having designed and adopted a system suited to the here-today-gone-tomorrow mining industry, did not extinguish riparian rights. It merely confirmed and enforced water appropriations. Under the subsequent agricultural development and industrialization of the new state, new and previously inactive riparian landholders claimed their "ordinary" or "reasonable" share of stream flow, thus confronting the California courts with a fifty-year agenda attempting to reconcile claims under the two systems. These events impressed later jurisdictions, which took strong measures to attempt to eliminate dual systems of water law.

Administered Water Licences

It was not long before appropriative rights came into use in what is now British Columbia as part of the law-making that followed the discovery of gold in 1856. Primarily in response to the need for a civil jurisdiction in the gold fields, a mainland colony was established in 1858. Licensed miners were apparently given title to whatever water was in the neighbourhood, after the "miners' meeting" custom of placer camps in California in New Zealand.[14] These rights were

---

14. F. W. Howay and J. Scholefield, *British Columbia from the Earliest Times to the Present* (Vancouver: S. J. Clark, 1914), vol. 1.

formalized in 1859, in an order that also permitted transfers of water, and indeed the sale of such water, to mineral workings elsewhere. Later orders extending these privileges introduced an essential recording requirement.

Five principles were quickly established.[15] The record requirement implicitly entailed the abandonment of riparian rights, since a water record was needed for even domestic and irrigation uses, and the first recorded title established the preferred right. The record was made appurtenant to the land it served (or to the mineral claim) and referred to a specific water source. It could not be privately reserved or separately transferred. Water rights were ultimately vested in the Crown.

The chief weakness of this ambitious legislation was its failure to provide for accurate registration. The word "record", indeed, did not refer to any actual written roll or list, and the "register" was little more than a recording-fee receipt book. "No track was kept of the records from the same water course and many streams were recorded ten times beyond their available supply."[16] It took until 1916 to establish and test old riparian rights, Indian rights, and riparian rights on former Dominion lands, to reconcile these with recorded water, to identify all as to source, and to link each to the land it was to serve. The newly verified rights were (and are today) known as "licences".

The modern British Columbia licence system has been outlined elsewhere.[17] Under the Water Act the Crown claims the rights to all water flows. Licences are allocated by a controller to applicants in chronological order, in a definite amount, for an indefinite (that is, probably unlimited) term, for specified and "beneficial" uses from a particular point on a particular stream. The Act is easiest to understand when it deals with *flows*. However, it requires that the controller approve licences to construct works that *store*, obstruct or divert streams for power, irrigation, and local supply.

The constitutional basis of the system would now seem to be that the province is the proprietor of all waters in the province (this is also the status of Alberta, Saskatchewan, and Manitoba). Rights

---

15. Robert E. Cail, *Land, Man and the Law: The Disposal of Crown Lands in British Columbia 1891-1913* (Vancouver: UBC Press, 1974), pp. 111-14.

16. *Ibid.*, p. 115.

17. Richard Campbell, Peter Pearse, and Anthony Scott, "Water Allocation in British Columbia", pp. 274-92. See also W. Armstrong, "The B.C. Water Act: The End of Riparian Rights", *U.B.C. Law Review* 1 (1959-63), p. 583.

to water in Ontario, as we have seen, have a different basis: riparian rights to adjoining streams are enjoyed both by the Crown and by private owners, as land holders. That right is not transferable or divisible. However, in British Columbia, a separate identifiable interest in water, in principle tranferable and divisible, has been created by the province. By assuming the underlying ownership of all water flows it has substantially abolished riparian rights, and has created for itself a new real interest, not known to the common law, but not very different from that asserted, say, by Colorado. Moreover, the province has legislatively made provision for a further interest, the water licence, analogous to a leasehold or profit interest, in principle also divisible and transferable.

In brief, under the riparian system as modified by its permit system, Ontario water flows are not subject to dealings in standard units which are negotiable, transferable, and divisible; while it is conceivable that, under British Columbia's Water Act, both freehold and leasehold interests might be traded as standard tenures, shaped and defined not only by government but also by usage and by litigation.

Alberta has an appropriative system of water rights similar to that of British Columbia. The system shows the influences of earlier reforms in jurisdictions where irrigation, seen as a force in land settlements, was the leading water use.[18] Both provinces' systems are derived from the California original. But while British Columbia received its version in the 1850s from miners fresh from the gold fields of the United States and Australia, Alberta's was put in place forty years later, in advance of settlement, under the influence of visionaries, promoters, and railway land companies. Their models were not the California gold workings and camps but the irrigation projects and settlements of Colorado and Australia.

Although the resultant water systems differ among the three prairie provinces, they are similar enough to be treated together. In the late 1870s and 1880s, new arrivals turned to grain growing. Their demand for water flows was small, and the riparian water system was extended from eastern Canada into the prairie territories. Those who found a creek or pond on their land could water stock; those who did not depended on wells. Rainfall and snow were plentiful anyway in the early 1880s, so it was not until the frontier of settlement entered the Palliser Triangle that much thought was given to supplying water. In Alberta and southern Saskatchewan, irrigation was seen by the

---

18. W. A. Mackintosh, *Economic Problems of the Prairie Provinces* (Toronto: Macmillan, 1938).

authorities and land promoters as an exciting improvement over low-value, scattered ranching and grain enterprises, since it called for water use even before land was disposed of. Channels and reservoirs were needed, as well as dense settlement and more infrastructure. All this was unlike mining-ranching water use in appropriative jurisdictions, and it was also unlike the river-bank style of general farming in riparian England and Ontario. Serious agitation for a new water policy by settlers, officials, and railway promoters led to the 1893/1894 Northwest Irrigation Act.

This legislation was derived from two sources: the two neighbouring states of Utah and Wyoming, and Victoria (Australia). Victoria's miners, like those in other Australian regions and in New Zealand, had dealt with gold properties by adapting the California placer-mining law.[19] Their practice was formalized in official enactments between 1851 and 1855. Little is written about water arrangements during this period, but it is usually assumed that, somewhat as in California, miners appropriated and held water-flows in alluvial fields as part of their right to mineral deposits. The subsequent decline of gold mining and the growth of agriculture placed new emphasis on more traditional land settlement near water sources, and on dry farming relying on precipitation and ground water. For these uses the original riparian system sufficed. Thus it was not until nearly 1880 that a prolonged dry period strengthened interest in irrigation works that would distribute not only the reliable flow of large rivers, but also the flood waters of streams of all sizes. The chosen instrument was the Victorian water "Trusts", based on the political doctrine that irrigation farming was a technical prerequisite for Australian social and economic development. This belief was strengthened by accounts, and direct observation, of irrigation in the western American states. Irrigation enthusiasm in Australia led to what seems to have been a "centralizing" tendency in water law. The politician Alfred Deakin and his colleagues, after several visits to western America, declared that riparian rights must go. To obtain large irrigation projects, all water must be under the control of one management, unthreatened by possible litigation from new or old riparian owners. Under such influences, Victoria and the other states by 1885 had vested in the Crown all rights to the use of water, taken steps to abolish the riparian rights of new settlers, and attempted to curtail riparian rights already in existence.

---

19. Sandford D. Clark and Ian A. Renard, "The Riparian Doctrine and Australian Legislation", *Melbourne University Law Review* 7 (1970), pp. 450-75.

Knowing that, in a British common-law environment and under a Parliamentary system, Victoria had managed to keep administrative control (rather than following various American practices where the appropriation system had sometimes led to alienation of water as private property, to the complete exclusion of the state government), the Canadian irrigation enthusiasts evidently felt encouraged to blend the Victoria system with the American systems. Percy comments:

> It is fascinating to note the characteristically different methods which the systems of water law evolved in the western regions of the two countries. In the United States, where settlement tended to precede the arrival of the law, the doctrine of prior appropriation was adopted by bold judicial innovation to meet an obvious and pressing need. In Canada, where the opposite was usually true and orderly settlement was encouraged, the necessary changes were made by legislation after careful study and preparation by a strong government department. However, if legislation had not removed the need to do so, it is just possible that early western Canadian courts might have overcome their normal reluctance to put aside common law doctrine when questions concerning the reception of English law arose, and rejected the riparian doctrine on the ground that it was not reasonably suited to the geographical conditions of the new region.[20]

Percy's opinion perhaps gives insufficient weight to the differences between the land uses for which water was to be provided. Because initially mining and ranching were not capital-intensive, not interdependent, and not closely linked to large dependent communities, conflict or failure of water supply would affect only the operators. Early development of land and water could therefore proceed by bold individual ventures. These in turn would exert a demand for bold judicial innovations in interpreting water rights. Irrigation, however, is capital-demanding and requires day-to-day co-ordination of water-taking by farmers. Many suppliers and secondary activities become dependent on it. Consequently, land must be developed and water captured in *advance* of settlement. It is true that California history does show the courts besieged by developers of such water projects and districts. But the American mountain states and Australia are better precedents: there (as indeed in California in later decades) it was to the legislature and not the courts that the irrigation entrepreneurs turned. So also did the applicants for the Northwest Irrigation Act in the 1890s.

The resulting law is today in many respects like that in British Columbia. Its origin is betrayed by its many provisions about

---

20. David R. Percy, "Water Rights in Alberta", *Alberta Law Review* 15 (1977), p. 146.

setting up, running, financing, and imposing water charges in irrigation districts. Beyond these, the four western provinces' water-right systems all create similar procedures for awarding individual rights to first "appropriators" of Crown water resources, and confer extensive discretionary powers on officers of separate water services. They seem to differ in spirit from the appropriative systems in the neighbouring states in the extent to which Alberta's water users are seen as permittees, enjoying Crown resources on legislative sufferance. While there is considerable variety among the states' legal and constitutional theories, in practice the American user's rights are individual, and their conveyance is a private matter subject less to bureaucracy than to transactions costs and, ultimately, litigation costs.

The extent to which water rights are transferable in the Canadian provinces is the subject of some disagreement among scholars, and more thorough research is probably necessary. Percy, writing about Alberta, concludes that the possibilities for arranging to transfer water under the Act fail to make adequate provision for new and more profitable water uses than the existing licensed uses. The problem is in the rules that licences must be appurtenant to the land or works for which they were issued, and must adhere to the list of statutory priorities.

> . . . If a potential water use emerges, perhaps for industrial purposes, which is of high economic value but lower on the scale of statutory priorities, the Act will not permit a transfer of the licence from the existing uses *even if all the parties concerned are willing to enter into the necessary transactions.*[21]

This suggests that in Alberta the scale of priorities exercises a greater constraint over the controller than in British Columbia. Certainly Campbell *et al.*, eyeing very similar provisions in British Columbia's Water Act, are more optimistic that transfer of water rights may be accomplished through private contract, subject to the approval of the Comptroller. The British Columbia authors do point out that water transfers between locations are difficult if downstream licensees are likely to lose out on the return flows from former uses, for it is the net, rather than the gross amount, that must be transferred.[22] But this is true in Alberta too.

Probably it is Alberta's complicated system of giving priority to large-scale irrigation projects that explains the different conclusions. Alberta's legislation was intended to facilitate community water

---

21. *Ibid.*, p. 164.

22. R. Campbell *et al.*, "Water Allocation in British Columbia", p. 265. See also W. Armstrong, *op. cit.*.

systems. Its farmers were fired with enthusiasm for the new uses that irrigation was expected to bring to western farm lands. Not surprisingly, the water rights they devised make it difficult to transfer water "down" to manufacturing and mineral enterprises.

The Role of Government in Water Rights Reform Reconsidered

To apply the evolutionary "model" suggested in this paper to what has been observed in the domain of water rights, let us first consider supply and demand in California.

So far as demand is concerned, there is no doubt that in 1849 the mining "industry" felt it could gain greatly from a change in the way water was to be held and transferred. The system of riparian rights was too entrenched to change by appeals to the courts or by circumvention—buying off the rights of old or potential future riparian users. In any case the demanders had no political standing, being newcomers, and as it happened they had no legal standing either, as there were no courts. They were faced with a water-demanding technology for an industry that had, in past times in England, been more concerned to rid itself of water than to capture it. And they found themselves presented with legal doctrine that shared water among riparian owners, whereas they were in a dry climate where the technology called for directing flows to selected workings—that is, for allocating water, not sharing it.

So far as we know there was no sector specializing in "supply" at all—water demanders had to provide their own legal reforms. Hence the "spontaneous" mining-camp rejection of the riparian-rights approach and the institution of a first-come–first-served approach. As we have seen, the new rights were different from those appurtenant to riparian land. But the novelty of the principles embodied in them must not be exaggerated. New England "riparian" states were already enforcing prescriptive rights as against the pure riparian system. And some American jurisdictions had already accepted the idea of appropriative *mineral* rights, to which appropriative water rights are obviously related.

Many of the problems of continuous re-allocation of the water were dealt with by the demanders' insistence on "beneficial use". Mines that were paying poorly or abandoned altogether could no longer demonstrate beneficial use, so the water was plainly available for capture: appropriation to another mine. This may be why the appropriative-rights system, so obviously poised on the verge of becoming a system of fully transferable and marketable rights, seems often to have stopped short of that development. Mineral exhaustion made unnecessary a system that would allow miners to sell their access to water.

The miners also provided their own arrangements for disseminating property information, and for enforcing claims to water. To serve the former function, water rights were "recorded" in accepted ways, so that the word "record" itself became the name of the title. To provide enforcement, water diversions were watched by neighbouring miners, unauthorized uses being prevented by social pressure, monitoring, and force. In spite of the frequent migrations of miners to new workings, the social coherence of each mining camp must not be underestimated. All historians of the mining industry refer to it; and even more impressive are politicians' references in their own general accounts of incidents in California, British Columbia, and Australia. Miners were well capable of "spontaneous" action, outside the purview of government.

As we have noted, the supply side of this marketplace was largely empty. California had not institutions in place to prepare courts for litigation of rights, or to legislate new types of interest. The California miners were not much concerned about this, and their attitude, which presumably stemmed from satisfaction with the law and order they provided for themselves, was consistent with their migratory way of life. However, in Utah[23] and Nevada, where more sedentary activities depended on water (irrigation in Utah and lode mining in Nevada), the water users were among those who joined to set up civil or church government and courts.

And, of course, the Californian "anarchy" did not last long. The new civil institutions set to work to clothe the frontier's skeletal water (and mining) law. The legislature set out to enact the water rules in general form. The courts had a more difficult role, for they had to deal with conflicts between the new appropriators and old riparian claimants. The growing population became less interested in the support of mining than in providing water for a variety of more permanent activities, for which riparian law was better suited. Unsuitability was not too important anyway; the mere fact that riparian rights had not been completely extinguished provided welcome loopholes in the new system of appropriative rights.

---

23. Maass and Anderson, *op. cit.*, Chapter 8, "Utah Valley", pp. 325-64.

The appropriation doctrine became a weapon of irrigators and manufacturers, and the riparian doctrine that of speculators and developers. Thus, in 1886, the case of *Lux v. Haggin* epitomized the diverse forces in the water-policy debate. Haggin was a recent upstream appropriator for irrigation, while Lux represented downstream riparian owners with claims based on rights thirty years older. There was an outcry when the courts decided in favour of the riparian owners. The decision was seen as threatening development of non-riparian activity downstream in all river basins, especially when the legislature, as was to be expected, cravenly decided not to strengthen the appropriation doctrine. A milestone in the continuing controversy was a 1928 amendment to the California Constitution. It preserved both riparian rights and appropriative rights, although the powers of riparian owners were modified further by calling for ''reasonable need'' and methods of use as criteria for retention of riparian rights. In such judgements, therefore, the courts and legislature together had supplied a convergence of the two doctrines to reduce their effective dissimilarities.

Let us now examine the market model in British Columbia and Alberta.

On the demand side, the British Columbia miners' initial situation was less desperate than in California. Also, they knew what to ask for: the appropriative rights existing in California and Australia. Governor Douglas did have dealings with irregular miners' groups, who probably stood ready to act if he did not, but (spurred by a fear that in the absence of British institutions the United States government might step in), rules for the allocation of mineral claims and water rights, and for their enforcement, were soon in place. (In any case, the first years of Fraser River mining were characterized as much by too much rain as by too little stream flow.)

On the supply side, there was no institutional vacuum. The rapid creation of a civil administration and its quick adjustment to the mining boom led to the provision of bodies to consider and reinterpret mining and water rights. Douglas' corps of gold commissioners held stipendiary magistrates' powers; and a higher court was soon superimposed. Perhaps as a consequence, legislation on water law remained infrequent until thirty years later, when the government was pressed to make provision for urban, irrigation, power, and lode-mining water uses.

It was relatively easy for the government to provide the demanded characteristics of water law. In the first place, Governor Douglas was for a while a virtual dictator, answerable only to Westminster. He found few conflicting uses of water to contend with mining interests. The Fraser River diggings were in an area of heavy forest and high mountains with few riparian owners and no farmers at all. Surface water and ground water were not lacking, although suitable sites for economical tapping of streams above workings were hard to find. Under such circumstances the water "record" was easily established as the instrument of a non-riparian, appropriative system. It was to be more than thirty years before the province's government or courts had to cope with the birth of new riparian rights on Dominion and provincial lands, and these were more in conflict with each other than with appropriative records or licences.

In Alberta the demand for a decision on water rights came not from disaffected water users or impatient miners but from potential investors, many of them outside the political jurisdiction. Government, a judiciary, and police were already in place. The lands, and therefore the appurtenant waters, belonged to the Crown, so that it was clearly an extension of the land-alienating duties of the state to make decisions about the characteristics of bundles of rights to water use. Furthermore, the population was small. The challenge to lawmakers was mainly to encourage future highly capitalized irrigation investments in new regions without disturbing grain-growing in older regions.

Alberta's task was made even easier by the general acceptance of the idea that water was to be a Crown resource. This, coupled with the fact that irrigation waters were being proposed, rather than used, meant that there were few, if any, serious distributional questions encumbering legislation (except that of the financial subsidy to irrigation). Consequently, the new system of water rights was brought in (by the government in Ottawa) as a relatively painless statutory change from the previous riparian system.

Concluding Observations on Water Rights

The market "model" of water-rights revision can be summarized under six headings. That government has been a major supplier cannot be denied, although abandonment of the riparian rights system occurred outside of existing institutions, and governments copied or adopted what the miners and ranchers had wrought elsewhere. However, the importance of government's role depended on a number of circumstances: (1) how active it already was in supplying new tenures as part of public-domain management and disposal, (2) how much demand was stimulated by increased water scarcity (how valuable water was), (3) whether water management was thought by demanders as well as suppliers to be a matter of special public concern, unlike the use and management of other resources, (4) whether the common-law courts were willing to supply a finding about water rights that had large effects on existing income and wealth distribution, (5) the extent to which politicians were willing to supply water tenure changes that upset voters operating under existing water rights, and (6) whether there was scope for "new entry" into the supplying market in the form of a spontaneous redefinition of water rights based on neither government nor the courts.

(1) Government's role has been highly significant because of the overwhelming problem of disposing of Crown resources. Consider the three areas for government action proposed earlier: (a) intervention in private property law, (b) defining of parcels of public lands for disposal, and (c) provision of courts and tribunals. Under (a), government can be deemed to have consented to demands that water rights should not be automatically granted to riparian owners. Water was to be regarded as a resource disposable in itself. This was an important demand-and-supply decision. But it was somewhat obscured by the difficulties of (b), the manner of disposal of Crown resources. The (a) decision concerned water that was (so far) public rather than private. Hence a (b) decision would have to include a new system of granting water. As we have seen, there were for British Columbia and Alberta readily available models elsewhere. Nevertheless, these had not been used as methods of public-domain disposal. On the contrary, they had been used to regularize rights after water had been privately appropriated from the public domain. The result was that it was to government (not the courts and not "spontaneous" private action) that the role of defining water rights in western Canada was necessarily assigned.

Once this two-part decision is understood, the vagueness of the set of characteristics of western provinces' water rights is better understood. Demanders in our model are now dealing not with private ownership but with the public domain. They are always in danger of legislative initiatives that destroy (or reduce) their water rights. The courts are closed to them. Consequently, further revision of their water rights by the supply-and-demand process, in which demanders choose whether to work through the courts or through legislative and political channels, is scarcely feasible.

(2) It is not to be expected that legislatures will be silent with respect to water rights when they are called upon in every session to make new decisions about other aspects of the public lands. Markets have not (at least not yet) had an opportunity to supplant the administrative channels of ministries for most natural resource sources. Furthermore, the multiple use of portions of rivers and lakes, and of works to impound and divert waters, is not yet an important fact: most waters are developed for one purpose only, and most stream

flows are used in single-purpose establishments. Finally, water access, in British Columbia and Alberta at least, and perhaps also in the most humid parts of Australia, is not yet subject to scarcity. Decisions about water rights therefore do not divide all voting populations as do issues concerning the scarcer types of wealth in the public domain. But where water has already become very scarce and is subject to alternative (conflicting) uses, government is no more free to change the nature of existing water rights than Britain would be to abolish outright (without compensation) its ancient domestic system of rights incident to riparian land. Where water has become scarce a government must, in effect, *buy* water to further its own policies, and it may make laws that facilitate this purpose. But as the value of water increases, it finds that responding to the demands of some users for a redefinition of rights runs into increasing resistance from others who have a vested interest in the opposite definitions.

(3) Leaving aside the definitional questions of economic efficiency in the most rigorous sense, the probable direction of the evolution of "individual" water rights is toward a reduced cost of exclusivity, divisibility and transferability. In this context, the use of water rights to further various planks in a party's political programme is consistent with the fundamental concept of individual rights. At various times water rights become a currency, like money and votes. It seems that even the recent resurgence of interest in the dollar value of water rights can be seen as an aspect of the individualist approach. That aspect has most recently emerged in connection with the value of hydro-electric sites, but it could well have been in connection with irrigation, transportation, or waste-disposal uses of river systems. The writings of Irene Spry, J.-T. Bernard, the Economic Council and the author on such "public" rents as a source of government revenue all depend on an analogy with private ownership and rights to rental incomes. They are therefore consistent with an interest in the reform of *private* or individualist rights to water. In brief, the fact that governments are concerned with managing publicly owned water is not inconsistent with the gradual emergence of a system of private rights.

This proposition assumes more shape when it is contrasted with an explicitly anti-individualist view: that the proper unit for water allocation and planning is the river basin, and that the externalities or leakages through individual use all point to the desirability or inevitability of overall public jurisdiction. This view is not based on the accident or dogma of public ownership of resources. It is related to an emphasis on the hydrologic cycle, the indivisibility of surface drainage, and the interdependence of river-basin water usage and general ecology.

The implications in this approach for government action are fairly obvious: the reform of private rights in water should be in the direction of increasing (or consolidating) the hold of official planners over individual water users. Distributional problems too should yield to this goal: water flows are of public concern (in the sense of their indivisibility rather than their ownership), and both revenue and private-wealth considerations should be seen as subordinate to a generalized public interest.

Thus Dale Gibson, author of an influential paper on the constitutional aspects of water basin management,[24] treats control over water as part of the special agenda of the public sector. The same approach was used earlier by enthusiasts for dedication of available water to irrigation uses. Because this kind of intensive agriculture affects settlement patterns and thus population density and other social characteristics, the government was urged to legislate the abandonment not only of riparian rights but also of small-scale appropriated rights.

The holder of a water licence is not seen as an independent actor, ready to buy and sell water flows like other inputs and outputs in the search for profit or the good life. He/she becomes a dependent of policy, a permittee or concessionaire working on sufferance within a larger water and development plan. It follows that where the licence holder survives, riparian rights and appropriative water rights are changed in order to serve the changing public priorities, and the view that it is a function of government to revise the content of private rights in water and other resources is generally confirmed.

(4) In examining the role of the courts and common-law procedures, the points above have all tended to explain why government's role in defining water rights, especially in Canada, has been a major one. But the underlying basis of the riparian system, and in some jurisdictions of the appropriative system, has not depended for its survival or revision on the government. For example, certain California cases have so modified the "reasonable" use aspects of riparian law that common-law access to water has become increasingly similar to California's own appropriative-rights law. One would not have believed that the courts could, even under an avalanche of cases, be so flexible, or that litigation and precedent can be relied on to transmogrify the riparian system elsewhere. Riparian rights could become the basis of a workable system if compensation payments for actual damages could become the consideration for water transfers. But Clark

24. Dale Gibson, *op. cit.*

and Renard argue that litigation and precedent work the other way. In their view riparian law deals with water conflicts only by creating uncertainty and serious insecurity. Accordingly, they do not expect governments to rest content with court-made revisions of the common law of water use. Are these authors justified in their faith that when the riparian system is creaking government will step in to supplant it? It seems they are unduly optimistic. When the riparian system is under stress, and the value of water access is increasing, government is likely to find itself politically powerless. Consider the example of California, when its courts (disconcertingly) restored certain riparian rights. The state government wished to re-establish the appropriative system by statute. But the redistributive aspects of doing so, once riparian owners' wealth had been confirmed by the courts, prevented it. (If they had done so by paying compensation, the riparian system would have been confirmed.)

It might seem that western Canada's water-rights systems are more flexible, in that they can be changed by revising tenure at the pleasure of the government. Perhaps this is so: the governments of British Columbia and Alberta have in the last few decades shown themselves able to redefine the tenures of users of minerals, oil, gas, and timber in the public domain. But the only aspects of these changes that were explicitly redistributive were the fees or charges involved; and these were clothed as tax increases, rather than as changes in tenure. It could be supposed that, so long as water licences give access to public-domain water, they are less an exclusive, transferable, divisible, enforceable right than even riparian rights, and are more vulnerable to be "flexibly" changed in response to political ends than other interests in real property.

(5) What are the prospects for future change? Water rights characteristics have not been changed frequently. The electoral consequences of the redistribution of scarce rights has prevented the legislature from tampering with them, whether for good or evil. Hence the goal of adapting them to increase their transferability, and so increase the economic efficiency of water use, may be a vain one. Writers like Percy and Campbell, Pearse and Scott, who look forward to a more efficient transferability of water licences, should realize that if revision were that simple the legislature would be just as likely to assign water rights to purposes (such as irrigation in the 1890s) *less* efficient than those which the present framework happens to secure.

(6) Can a new way of holding water appear, outside the legislative and legal systems? It would seem not, short of revolution. The ubiquity of the public domain might once again lead squatters or pre-emptors to design and enforce their own rights systems. We have,

after all, some examples: in the medieval Forest of Dean and the New Forest, and California barely one hundred years ago. The rights thus created were eventually validated by the court, the government, or both, and led, in the west at least, to rights sytems that transcended the policy limits of the public domain. Opportunities to do this occur so rarely that most observers seem to believe that we must look to government for changes in property rights. But few governments are courageous enough to redistribute wealth by redefining existing holders' entitlements to resources already in use. Only the courts have dared.

9. The Quebec Asbestos Industry

Technological Change, 1878–1929*

Robert Armstrong
Canadian Radio-Television
and Telecommunications Commission

The development of asbestos mining in Quebec's Eastern Townships during the late 1870s initiated a trend that would change the face of the region. The quantity of raw fibre shipped from asbestos mines increased from about fifty tons in 1878 to more than three hundred thousand tons by 1929. Asbestos emerged as the province's most valuable mineral product, a position that it retained (except for a period during the Great Depression and World War II) until the 1960s.

The growth of asbestos output occurred in a dynamic North American setting characterized by radical changes in technology affecting mining, milling, transport, and transaction costs. Technological innovations, such as the advent of rail transport, the application of machinery to the processes of mining and milling, the adoption of steam power, and the introduction of hydro-electricity were key ingredients in factor productivity and output growth. Most of the innovations adopted in the Quebec asbestos industry stemmed from mining practices in Great Britain and the United States. However, techniques efficient in other industries and regions were not always suited to the economic environment prevailing in Quebec. The transfer of new technology to the asbestos industry was accomplished selectively in accordance with domestic factor proportions and prices.[1]

---

* This article is the revised version of a chapter drawn from a doctoral thesis directed by Albert Faucher and Jean-Thomas Bernard at the Université Laval. The author wishes as well to acknowledge the helpful comments of George Grantham and Irene Spry.

1. See Robert Armstrong, *Structure and Change: An Economic History of Quebec* (Toronto: Gage Publishing Limited, 1984) for an outline of the Quebec economy during the years 1850-1940. For a general discussion of the technology transfer process, see Nathan Rosenberg, *Perspectives on Technology* (New York: Cambridge University Press, 1976), Part III.

Technological innovation may be defined as any change which permits unit costs to fall when factor prices are constant. Essentially this means that it is possible to achieve more output with the same volume of inputs, or the same output with a smaller volume of inputs. The choice of technique will vary over time with changes in the relative prices of these inputs. The choice of technique will also vary over time with the introduction of new and previously unavailable processes. Technological innovation is therefore governed by both the rate of invention and the rate of diffusion of new techniques.

This paper offers a descriptive account of technological innovation in the Quebec asbestos industry between 1878 and 1929. Factor substitution is shown to have played a role in the diffusion of new techniques in mining and milling during these years. The discussion of technological innovation will encompass changes in the relative prices of various forms of energy: the substitution of hydro-electric power for other sources of energy provided a major stimulus to innovation in asbestos mining and milling in the twentieth century. Furthermore, scale economies also provided an important source of technological innovation in the industry. The size of operations influenced the choice of technique. Much as the individual farmer's decision to adopt mechanical reaping was associated with the decision to expand grain acreage, the decision to mechanize asbestos mining and milling operations was related to growth in the scale of individual mining operations.[2] In the conclusion, it is also suggested that the wage rate prevailing in the asbestos mining regions may have played a role in determining the degree of "outmodedness" of the capital stock in the industry.

Early Mining and Milling Technology

The mining and preparation of raw asbestos for the market can be divided into four stages; each benefited from technological innovation during the period 1878 to 1929. The type of mining practised by the vast majority of asbestos companies was open-pit mining or quarrying, rather than tunnelling as in the coal-mining and many metal-mining industries. The first stage of production therefore involved the stripping and removal of the overburden to permit access to the mineral. This was followed by the breaking of the mineral-

---

2. Cf. Paul A. David, "The Mechanization of Reaping in the Ante-bellum Midwest", in *Technical Choice, Innovation and Economic Growth: Essays on American and British Experience in the Nineteenth Century* (Cambridge: Cambridge University Press, 1975).

bearing rock into pieces suitable for transport. The third stage required the hoisting of the rock to the surface and its transport to the cobbing or milling sheds. Finally, the rock was dried and the veins of asbestos extracted and classified by fibre length prior to shipment.

During the first decade of production, the method of working asbestos quarries was rudimentary. Human labour, aided in some cases by horse power, proved sufficient, given the limited depth and extent of the quarries. The work was accomplished in open pits and the equipment employed did not differ from that used in ordinary building-stone quarries. Initially, a work team removed surface material by pick and shovel or horse-drawn scrapers. Blasting holes, four or five feet deep, were drilled by work teams typically consisting of a worker who held the drill-bit, two, three or four strikers using sledge-hammers, and a water-boy.[3] The miners blasted large blocks of rock down to the floor of the quarry using charges of unstable black powder. The blocks were broken up into smaller pieces by means of "block-holes" created with a small pick and a light hammer, and loaded with small charges of explosive to assist in freeing the asbestos veins. This stage also involved the use of sledge-hammers and hand-cobbing. The initial separation of the asbestos from the waste rock occurred in the quarry; the rock-encrusted mineral was then sent to the dressing sheds and the waste to the dumps. Transport equipment consisted of wheelbarrows, drags, and dumpcarts pulled by horses or oxen. Robert H. Jones, citing L. A. Klein of the American Asbestos Company, suggested that one ton of asbestos produced in this way required the breaking of fifty to one hundred and fifty tons of rock, depending upon the richness of the vein.[4] The surface soil and the refuse rock, which contained large quantities of short fibre, were normally dumped close to the quarry, a practice that later proved costly because it impeded the widening of the pits. Final dressing or cobbing of the mineral took place in nearby sheds staffed by children and young women. The freeing of the long fibres from the remaining bits of rock was done by hand with hammers of various weights and simple hand screens that permitted the classification of the mineral into three grades according to its length. During the first decade of production, both the mining and the cobbing of asbestos constituted highly labour-intensive activities characterized by relatively constant returns to scale.

The arrival of the Quebec Central Railway in the Thetford region provided a crucial stimulus to the take-off of the industry. The

---

3. George W. Smith, *Bell Asbestos Mines Ltd. 1878-1967* (1968), pp. 15-16.

4. Robert H. Jones, *Asbestos and Asbestic: Their Properties, Occurrence and Use* (London: Crosby, Lockwood & Son, 1897), pp. 178-79.

expansion of steam-powered rail transport was the major element in
the transport revolution that led to the break-down of small unin-
tegrated markets during the second half of the nineteenth century.
New information and techniques reached into formerly isolated areas
and integrated them with the emergent continental economy.

The planning of the Quebec Central Railway linking
Sherbrooke and Lévis occurred without prior knowledge of the asbestos
deposits. The Quebec Central had originally been promoted by
businessmen from Sherbrooke and chartered in 1869 under the name
of the ''Sherbrooke, Eastern Townships and Kennebec Railway'' to
connect with the Lévis and Kennebec Railway being constructed from
Lévis.[5] The railroad reached Coleraine in 1876, Thetford in 1879,
and was completed to Valley Junction in 1880. The following year,
the Lévis and Kennebec joined the Quebec Central at Valley Junction,
and the entire line from Sherbrooke to Lévis was opened in June 1881.

The timing of the Quebec Central's arrival in the Thetford
area was fortunate. The railway permitted the rapid transport of
Quebec asbestos to seaports such as Lévis, Montreal, Portland, and
Boston. Asbestos shipments grew slowly at first, from 300 tons in 1879
to 810 tons in 1882. By 1890, however, total fibre shipments had
reached 9,860 tons, and the railway relayed not only mineral output
but information and machinery as well.

The United States provided the largest market for raw asbestos
fibre from Quebec, taking some seventy per cent of all fibre exports
(by value) during the years 1888-1930. The final demand for asbestos
fibre resulted from the demand for the characteristics possessed by
the mineral. Asbestos products had been in use for at least two
thousand years but the industrialization process in the late nineteenth
century stimulated a wide range of new end-uses. The commercial
properties associated with asbestos, such as fire resistance, low conduc-
tivity, tensile strength, durability, immunity from corrosion, acid-
resistance, and weaving qualities acquired a new and growing importance. The industrial employment of steam power, for instance,
required not only reinforced containers, but additional heat and fire
protection as well. The better grades of asbestos fibre were therefore
woven into fire-resistant cloth and textile materials such as steam-
plant packing. The shorter fibres, in combination with other building
materials, were added to roofing compositions, paints, millboard, and
paper.

---

5. 32 Victoria, chapter 57.

The Introduction of Steam Power

As the asbestos industry began to be mechanized in the 1880s, it followed a path already blazed in Great Britain and the United States. In substituting machinery for labour, applying steam power to mining, cobbing and transport, and increasing the use of iron and steel in place of wood, the asbestos industry adopted techniques that were already employed in those countries. In this period technical change involved the transfer of technology from abroad in a virtually unaltered form.

British companies were the leading players in European asbestos mining. The introduction of British capital and management to asbestos mining and milling in Quebec was accompanied by the diffusion of steam power and mechanization. During the second half of the 1880s, British companies began acquiring property rights to Quebec asbestos, and the British-owned asbestos mining operations in Italy simultaneously entered into decline. British companies, with their superior know-how, introduced new mining and milling techniques to the Quebec asbestos industry.

The steam engine offered an alternative to animal and human labour as a source of motive power. It is likely the potential for scale economies influenced the decision to adopt steam. In the five-year period following 1878, total shipments from Quebec mines failed to exceed one thousand tons per annum. But an increase in the relative price of asbestos during the 1880s, together with more information concerning the size of the deposits and the cost reductions associated with steam power, induced several mine owners to expand their operations. Growth in output was rapid in the mid-1880s, and by 1889 the Bell Asbestos Company alone extracted eighteen hundred tons of raw asbestos. Experimentation with steam power and mechanized devices became characteristic of all the larger operations.[6]

Steam power had a revolutionary impact on average labour productivity in asbestos mining. (See Table 1.) Power was first applied to the quarrying of asbestos in 1887 by the Anglo-Canadian Asbestos Company at Black Lake; by 1893, there were forty steam boilers in operation in the industry.[7] During most of the 1880s hand drilling

---

6. Joseph Obalski, *Mines and Minerals of the Province of Quebec 1889-90* (Quebec: Département des Terres de la Couronne, 1889), pp. 100-108.

7. James G. Ross, *Chrysotile Asbestos in Canada* (Ottawa: Department of Mines, 1931), p. 36. Government of Canada, *The Statistical Yearbook of Canada for 1893* (Ottawa: Department of Agriculture, 1894), p. 283.

continued to be used for prospecting and "block-holing" but towards the end of the decade steam or compressed air was introduced. Compressed air was the more popular source of power for drilling because the water introduced into the holes in the process of steam-drilling formed plugs of asbestos that stopped the working of the drills.[8] The first mechanized drills had been introduced to build the Hoosac railroad tunnel in Massachusetts in the late 1860s; asbestos operators apparently adopted the device from American mining practice.[9]

As the industry expanded in the 1880s, and the open pits became deeper, boom derricks worked by horses were put into operation in some mines to lift the mineral and rock out of the excavation.[10] By the end of the decade boom derricks were widely in use. However, boom derricks proved to be efficient only where there was a small amount of rock to be handled, and by 1889 steam-driven cable derricks fuelled by wood and coal had been introduced at the larger mines.[11] During the following decade, the greater reach and carrying power of steam-driven cable derricks (by means of skips or boxes containing up to two tons of rock) resulted in their widespread adoption, as the depth and width of the mines continually expanded.

The first producer to successfully develop a steam-powered milling process was the Scottish Canadian Asbestos Company. In 1886, the company set up shops at Black Lake consisting of a fifty-horsepower engine, a Blake rock breaker, a conveyor belt, a set of Cornish rolls, revolving screens, elevators, shakers, and two large blowers.[12] As it happened, the mines were closed two years later and technological development was interrupted. The Anglo-Canadian Asbestos Company of London, the German-owned American Asbestos Company, the King Brothers, and the Johnson Company also

---

8. Obalski, *op. cit.*, p. 96.

9. H. Barger and S. H. Schurr, *The Mining Industries, 1889-1939: A Study of Output, Employment, and Productivity* (New York: National Bureau of Economic Research Inc., 1944), pp. 119-20.

10. "Boom derricks consist of a mast held by means of guys in a vertical position and a turntable on its own axle, while to the foot of the mast a boom or arm is attached and suspended in a more or less horizontal position by means of ropes stretching from end of mast to end of boom." L. A. Klein, "The Canadian Asbestos Industry", *The Journal of the General Mining Association of the Province of Quebec*, vol. 1 (1891-93), p. 148.

11. "The cable derricks have a mast somewhat similar to the former, but instead of a boom, a cable with a traveller on it, which cable is stretched from top of mast to some point across the pit, allowing by means of the traveller, to hoist from any point of the cable." *Ibid.* The American Asbestos Co., under the management of L. A. Klein, was the first operation to use cable derricks in asbestos mining. Cf. *The Canadian Mining Review* IX (1890), 148.

12. Obalski, *op. cit.*, p. 97, and Klein, *op. cit.*, p. 150.

Table 1

Average Labour Productivity in the Quebec Asbestos Mining Industry, Census Years 1880-1920

Year	Total asbestos output including sand and gravel (tons)	Total number of employees (as reported in the census)	Labour productivity (tons per employee per annum)
1880	380*	142	2.7
1890	9,860**	689	14.3
1900	29,141	823	35.4
1910	125,175	3,193	39.2
1920	190,349	2,694	70.7

* Total exports
** Total shipments

Sources: J. G. Ross, *Chrysotile Asbestos in Canada* (Ottawa: Department of Mines, 1931), Chapter 4. *Annual Report of the Mineral Production of Canada*, 1910-1929 (Ottawa: Department of Mines).

experimented with mechanical crushers and sifters over the next three years. However, these innovations proved unsatisfactory for a number of reasons. Mechanical crushers were insufficiently refined to avoid breaking up the long, most valuable asbestos fibres, and in some cases reducing them to powder. In other cases, the machinery left a considerable amount of rock clinging to the milled material. Buyers were therefore suspicious of all mill grades, whether the mineral consisted of high average quality or not. In the early 1890s, several sales of milled asbestos occurred, but they produced mixed reactions on the part of the manufacturers. For several years customs officials in the United States classified milled asbestos as a manufactured product and levied a twenty-five per cent *ad valorem* duty, thereby discouraging mechanical milling of asbestos for export to the United States.[13]

The mechanization of the asbestos industry in the 1890s was accomplished with the use of steam boilers fired by wood and coal which, in addition to providing steam for running the mill machinery, often supplied power for heating in winter, drying the raw

---

13. *Ibid.*, p. 151.

mineral, pumping rain water out of the pits, running the compressor used for drilling and, where feasible, for hoisting the asbestos-bearing rock and refuse from the pit bottom to the surface.[14] Mill engines ranged in size from fifty to five hundred horsepower, the use of more than one engine being common to prevent total work stoppages in the event of the mechanical breakdown of one engine.[15]

Experiments continued in the search for a machine that would break up the rock without damaging the high-priced long fibre. In 1894 an equipment supplier, W. G. Costigan & Company of Montreal, introduced the first "cyclone".[16] This apparatus broke the rock through impact by whirling it at high velocity against an unyielding surface while maintaining the fibre intact. Cyclone-fiberizing machinery eventually became an essential part of asbestos-milling equipment.

The mechanization of asbestos mining reflected a general trend in North America from selective to non-selective or bulk mining. The decline in the grade of easily attainable ore, the accompanying rise in the costs of extraction, and the partial integration of quarrying with ore dressing accelerated this tendency. The United Asbestos and Bell Asbestos companies opened mechanized milling operations in 1894, and the following year shipments of mill fibre became a permanent feature of the industry.[17]

In the Thetford–Black Lake area, the refuse dumps by the side of the mines eventually began to hamper operations. A group of experts from the American Institute of Mining Engineers who visited the region in October of 1889 commented on the poor planning and management of the dumping grounds and the quality of fine short fibre lying in the dumps. B.T.A. Bell observed in 1891, "even in the newest portion of these dumps veins of asbestos ranging from half to three-quarters of an inch can be frequently seen, all of which should repay extraction if suitable machinery were employed."[18] The mineral potential in the dumps provided an additional incentive to search for mechanical means of separating the

---

14. Joseph Obalski, "Asbestos in Canada", *The Mineral Industry During 1904*, vol. XIII (New York, 1905), p. 21.

15. *Ibid.*, p. 75.

16. J. T. Donald, "The Present Status of the Canadian Asbestos Industry", *The Engineering and Mining Journal* (Sept. 19, 1894), p. 296.

17. *The Canadian Mining Review* XIV (1895), 218, and Fritz Cirkel, *Asbestos: Its Occurrence, Exploitation and Uses* (Ottawa: Department of the Interior, Mines Branch, 1905) p. 49.

18. B.T.A. Bell, "The Canadian Asbestos Industry," *The Canadian Mining Manual*, vol. 1 (1890-91), p. 26.

mineral from the accompanying rock. It also underlined the importance of mining-operations design, and information about the geological structure and chemical nature of the mineral deposits prior to exploitation.

One of the commercial by-products of the substitution of machinery for labour in the 1890s was the discovery of "asbestic", a residue from the milling of asbestos rock containing very low percentages of short fibre. Asbestic contributed to the development of a fireproof compound for roofing and the plastering of walls and ceilings. Jones attributes its discovery to Théodore Boas, a St. Hyacinthe entrepreneur who renewed interest in the Jeffrey mine near Danville and initiated the formation of the Danville Asbestos and Slate Company in November, 1894. Shipments of asbestic from the Danville area began about 1896 and the new product immediately revalued the immense refuse dumps which had proved to be a costly burden in the past.[19]

Two other innovations introduced during the 1880s involved dynamite, and the use of rail locomotives for haulage and dumping at the mine site. Dynamite, in place of black powder, made it possible to break fibre-bearing rock with more assurance and safety, although hand-drilling continued until World War I. The growing scale of mining operations allowed for steam-powered locomotives to transport raw fibre on the site of mining operations. George Smith, manager of the Bell Asbestos Mines, introduced small on-site rail locomotives in 1895. The first steam locomotive was constructed using two cylinders from an old hoisting engine, in connection with gearing machinery and forty-two-inch-gauge metal rails. This type of locomotive gradually replaced the dumping cars hauled by men, horses, or stationary steam power, though dumping cars were still employed in the smaller mines in 1910.[20] Various improvements in transport equipment appeared during the years following 1895. According to a descendant of George Smith, "While the narrow-gauge system sufficed for the transportation of ore to the mill, and mine waste and strippings to the dumps, it became evident in 1906 that significant savings could be made by bringing a standard-gauge siding

---

19. The development of asbestic completely revalued the asbestos deposit associated with the Jeffrey mine and prompted the formation of the Asbestos and Asbestic Company in 1897. In addition to doubling the existing plan and buildings, the new company constructed a feeder line from the mine to the Grand Trunk main line at Danville. Jones, *op. cit.*, p. 173, and Asbestos and Asbestic Company Limited, *Report and Statement of Accounts*, for the period ended March 31, 1898.

20. Fritz Cirkel, *Asbestos: Its Occurrence, Exploitation and Uses*, second edition (Ottawa: Department of the Interior, Mines Branch, 1910), p. 115.

from the Quebec Central Railway to the mill yard so that bagged fibre could be loaded out directly into rail cars."[21] The introduction of rails on the mine site in 1895 also permitted the introduction of a railway-type steam shovel at the Bell mine. This shovel, purchased from the Quebec Central Railway, was employed in the removal of soil and overburden as the pits expanded.[22] However, it did not prove suitable for use in the mine pit itself owing to the rough nature of the pit bed, and the fact that loading required hand-sorting and classification.

The Diffusion of Hydro-Electric Power

The coming of the electrical age at the end of the nineteenth century exercised a profound influence on the asbestos industry in Quebec by uniting two of the province's most valuable resources. Dales identifies the birth of the modern electrical age with the beginning of operations by the Niagara Falls Power Company in the summer of 1895.[23] But already asbestos producers had been informed of hydro-electricity's potential as a source of cheap motive power.[24] By 1897, the Asbestos and Asbestic Company was using electricity to light its new five-storey building near Danville.[25] On the whole, however, the arrival of electrical power in the asbestos area was greeted with scepticism by mine operators until its long-run cost advantages became clear. The rising relative prices of wood and coal, as well as uncertainty concerning their delivery, are the primary explanations for technological change involving hydro-electricity prior to World War I. Cirkel's analysis is as follows:

> Wood as fuel was getting scarce, while the supply of coal was becoming unsatisfactory; indeed, it was no unusual occurrence, that a mine had to suspend operations during the winter, entirely owing to the lack of the

---

21. Smith, *op. cit.*, p. 52.

22. The railway-type steam shovel had been known to American mining since the first workings on the Mesabi range in 1892. Barger and Schurr, *op. cit.*, p. 137.

23. John H. Dales, *Hydroelectricity and Industrial Development in Quebec 1898-1940* (Cambridge, Mass.: Harvard University Press, 1957), p. 13.

24. Cf. J. W. Kirkland (Thomson-Houston International Electrical Co., Boston), "Recent Developments in Electrical Mining Apparatus", and H. W. Leonard (Edison General Electric Co., New York), "The Electrical Transmission and Conversion of Energy for Mining Operations", *The Journal of the General Mining Association of the Province of Quebec*, vol. 1 (1891-93), pp. 38-59.

25. The company was obliged, however, to abandon its plans to power the mill with hydro-electricity in order to meet its production schedule. Jones, *op. cit.*, p. 183.

commodity. The prohibitive cost of coal fuel; the long haul of the latter from Pennsylvania; the blockages on the railways in the winter; as well as the annoyances through coal miners strikes, render the use of coal almost prohibitive.

He continues:

> Owing to the flexibility and facility of the application of the electric current to large as well as to small machinery, it lends itself pre-eminently to all the motive wants in mining work. Electrical apparatus are generally less bulky and less costly than power machines which use a different form of energy. They, therefore, do not require expensive foundations, but can be set up, almost anywhere, within easy reach of the mechanical appliances which they drive. Moreover, the efficiency of electrical machinery is high, so that the energy is used to better advantage.[26]

Low-cost hydro-electricity became available to the Thetford area on a large scale during the early years of the twentieth century. In 1904, the Compagnie Hydraulique St-François opened a power station on the St. Francis River near Disraeli, approximately eight miles from Black Lake, together with a transmission line to the asbestos district. About this time the Shawinigan Water and Power Company extended its operations to the asbestos mining area by way of submarine cable from Trois-Rivières.[27]

Advances in the science of electricity, when combined with the immense waterpower resources of the province of Quebec, opened up innumerable areas of application in asbestos mining and milling. By 1905, most asbestos mills were already using electricity generated in dynamos for lighting, and occasionally to drive small machines. The first company to use hydro-electricity for motive power was the American Asbestos Company, in a new mill completed in 1904. During the first decade of the twentieth century, however, nearly all of the mills in operation had been built prior to 1900 and their layout favoured steam power. The available electric motors did not perform consistently and many losses occurred when on-site hydro-electric power transmission was attempted. Thus the fifteen-by-thirty-inch rock crusher and the two double-shell rotary dryers installed by Bell Asbestos in 1905 did not embody electrical technology. They were

---

26. Cirkel, *op cit.* (1910), p. 148-49.

27. The asbestos market did not grow rapidly and therefore became relatively less important to the Shawinigan Company in later years, but it was a major outlet for power before World War I. Dales, *op. cit.*, pp. 60-61. The St. Francis Company, initially a small operation of 2000 h.p., was purchased by the Shawinigan Company in 1924. Dales, *ibid.*, p. 76, Smith, *op. cit.*, pp. 34-35, and Cirkel, *op. cit.* (1910), p. 149.

powered by steam from tubular boilers fuelled by buckwheat anthracite and slab-wood from a local sawmill. Steam-generated electrical power was employed for the purpose of lighting only.[28]

Table 2

Price Indices of Electricity, Coal and Wood in Quebec, 1900–1913 (1900 = 100)

Year	Electric light in Quebec	Bituminous coal at Montreal	Anthracite coal at Montreal	Pine lumber, all grades, at Ottawa
1900	100.0	100.0	100.0	100.0
1901	100.0	113.8	105.0	100.0
1902	100.0	114.4	114.7	100.0
1903	100.0	116.7	119.0	103.0
1904	100.0	114.4	116.4	106.1
1905	100.0	107.0	115.7	112.1
1906	97.3	104.6	114.9	130.3
1907	96.5	111.5	115.5	124.3
1908	95.8	120.1	115.5	124.3
1909	95.4	117.2	113.9	124.3
1910	84.2	115.1	115.9	124.3
1911	83.5	114.9	119.3	121.2
1912	78.8	114.8	129.3	124.3
1913	77.5	114.8	137.0	130.0

Sources: Government of Canada, *Report of the Board of Inquiry into the Cost of Living*, vol. II (Ottawa: Government Printing Bureau, 1915), p. 318. Government of Canada, *Wholesale Prices, Canada, 1913* (Ottawa: Government Printing Bureau, 1914).

Over the next few years, however, the comparative cost advantage of hydro-electric power (see Table 2) persuaded producers to switch to electricity as a motive power for percussion drills, hoisting engines, dryers, and many other mill devices.[29] By 1909, the cost of hydro-electrical power per horsepower-year was about $25 as opposed to between $35 and $47 for steam plants; the primary difference was a greater loss in the transmission of steam power as compared to electrical power in a suitably designed plant.[30] By 1910, electrical power was predominant. The number of electrically powered devices listed in an article based on fire inspectors' reports in the Thetford district,

---

28. Obalski, *op. cit.*, p. 23, and Smith, *op. cit.*, pp. 30-31.

29. W. J. Woolsey, "Notes on Recent Developments in Asbestos Mining in Quebec", *The Journal of the Canadian Mining Institute*, vol. XIII (1910), p. 411.

30. Cirkel, *loc. cit.*

for example, is striking.[31] But electrical power was not employed to the exclusion of all other energy sources. In 1913, the Superintendent of Mines for Quebec reported that electrical power existed side-by-side with steam power at mine sites as large as those of Bell Asbestos, and that other firms, such as the Johnson Company, continued to employ steam power exclusively. According to Théodore Denis:

> The contention is that although electrical power at the rate at which it is delivered would be cheaper for continuous operations, as there sometimes occur long interruptions in the work owing to various causes, such as shortage of labour, sluggishness in the asbestos market, unfavourable weather to work in the asbestos pits, etc., it is more profitable to install a steam plant and produce steam power.[32]

This would account for continued use of steam power by the smaller producers until 1916. In that year the power companies began supplying power on a metred basis instead of by fixed contract in predetermined amounts. This pricing innovation permitted the temporary shutdown of electrical equipment without paying power costs and further stimulated the diffusion of electrical technology.

One of the major problems facing asbestos buyers in the nineteenth century was the unpredictability of the quality of fibre delivered. In the absence of standardized categories, buyers were obliged to rely heavily on the producer's reputation. About 1906, an important innovation was introduced in the form of a new grading device imported from Europe. The device consisted of a shaker-box machine designed by an Austrian buyer of asbestos fibre. This electrically powered instrument consisted of a series of trays, arranged vertically, each successively lower tray containing a smaller screen. In operation, the screens were mechanically shaken, asbestos fibres filtering down from one tray to another according to their length. The introduction of the shaker-box machine permitted the development of an informal grading system, though industry-wide agreement did not occur until 1930, when the Quebec government established a committee to standardize all grading and testing. The shaker-box machine reduced uncertainties surrounding the classification and delivery of raw asbestos and induced producers to seek improved fibre-quality control.

31. "Fire Protection at the Plants of the Amalgamated Asbestos Corporation", *The Canadian Mining Journal*, vol. 31 (1910), pp. 727-78.

32. Theo C. Denis, "Asbestos Mining in Quebec", *The Canadian Mining Journal*, vol. 34 (1913), p. 612.

By the first decade of the twentieth century the best-practice method of rock breaking consisted either of crushing (jaw crushers, gyrators, and rolls) or breaking by impact (machines of the cyclone type). But hand-cobbing was still widely used because of the coarseness of the available machinery and the low cost of unskilled labour. Ezra Ryder reported in 1909, "with the low cost of labour now obtaining, of $1.75 per 10-hour shift, and the high value of the crude, it is profitable to handle large quantities of rock with a view to picking out the good fibres, which if sent direct to the mill, would depreciate in value as a marketable product."[33] The low relative price of labour referred to by Ryder and others is difficult to document, but some evidence may be obtained by comparing wage rates paid by mining operations at locations in three Canadian provinces. (See Table 3.) Lower relative wages in Quebec may have caused the capital stock in the asbestos industry to adjust relatively slowly to new methods, and thereby lowered average labour productivity. Older, more labour-intensive techniques remained viable as long as average variable costs remained below price.

Table 3

Wage Rates per 10-Hour Day for Surface Labour in Canadian Metal Mines, 1903–1913 (current dollars)

Year	Quebec Eustic District	Ontario		British Columbia	
		Sudbury District	Cobalt District	Rossland District	Coastal District*
1903	1.20	n.a.	1.50	2.50	3.00
1904	1.25	n.a.	1.50	2.50	3.00
1905	1.25	1.50	1.50	2.75	3.00
1906	1.35	1.50	2.25	3.00	3.00
1907	1.50	1.75	2.25	3.00	3.00
1908	1.50	1.75	2.25	3.00	3.00
1909	1.50	1.75	2.25	3.00	3.00
1910	1.50	1.75	2.25	3.00	3.00
1911	1.50	2.00	2.25	3.00	3.00
1912	1.50	2.00	2.25	3.00	3.00
1913	1.50	2.03	2.50	3.00	3.00

* The data for this district refer to a 9-hour work day.

Source: Government of Canada, *Report of the Board of Inquiry into the Cost of Living*, vol. II (Ottawa: Government Printing Bureau, 1915), pp. 476-77.

33. Ezra B. Ryder, "Notes on the King Bros' Asbestos Mine, Thetford, Quebec", *The Journal of the Canadian Mining Institute*, vol. XII (1909), p. 625.

In 1910 Edward Torrey introduced a new type of cyclone at the Asbestos and Asbestic Company, designed to reduce mechanical breakdown and lessen damage to the fibre product.[34] The labour-saving Torrey cyclone permitted the treatment of certain "crude" fibres by machine without reducing their market value. The invention of this device appears to have occurred in response to the rising relative price of crude fibre.[35] The net returns from using the Torrey cyclone outweighed the advantages of employing labour to perform the same task and it became an essential part of asbestos-milling technology.

The Torrey cyclone constituted one of the new original inventions generated by the asbestos industry itself. Most of the new machinery applied to asbestos mining and milling after 1887 was borrowed from mining industries abroad. An industry observer commented in 1906, "the only pieces of apparatus peculiar to asbestos mills are beaters or fiberizers, suction elevators and collectors; all other drying, crushing, grinding, and screening machines are of the well-known standard types."[36] Little original innovation seemed to be taking place in the industry. Instead, well developed machinery was imported from the United States and adapted to local production.

Electrification of the industry continued during and after World War I. Bell Asbestos discarded its steam boilers for electric power in 1916 as a result of the availability of power on the metre system.[37] Similarly, at the King mine, the Asbestos Corporation of Canada replaced its steam locomotives with Canadian General Electric locomotives of the trolley type, both for the rock yard and the dump.[38] This innovation eliminated the uncertainty surrounding the supply of wintertime coal imported by rail from the United States, and thereby lowered average operating costs.

The new cable-derrick equipment installed at the King mine in 1916 provided several new features related to hoisting capacity and speed. All four cableway units ran on wheels and rails so that each

34. Edward Torrey, "The Breaking of Asbestos-Bearing Rock", *The Journal of the Canadian Mining Institute*, vol. XIV (1915), pp. 138-47.

35. See Ross, *op. cit.*, Chap. 4, Table III.

36. *The Mineral Industry: Its Statistics, Technology and Trade During 1905*, vol. XIV (New York, 1906), p. 35.

37. "New Plant at Asbestos Mine", *The Canadian Mining Journal*, vol. 37 (1916), p. 459, and Smith, *op. cit.*, p. 37.

38. W. A. RuKeyser, "Asbestos Mining and Milling in Quebec", *The Engineering and Mining Journal* 113, no. 16 (1922), 671.

derrick could easily be moved from one location to another.[39] Steam and electric cranes were subsequently installed at the Bell mine and by the Black Lake Asbestos and Chrome Company at Black Lake.[40]

The full-revolving steam shovel (in place of the earlier limited-arc shovel) was introduced to North American mining in the years between 1915 and 1920.[41] This shovel, designed for rock loading, did not prove very efficient until taken off the railway track and mounted on caterpillar tracks after the war. The Asbestos and Asbestic Company began using steam shovels in its pits at Danville in 1916, and within two years they had completely replaced the old cable derricks.[42] However, steam or electric shovels initially proved inefficient in the Thetford and Black Lake areas because of the unevenness of the pit floors and the fragile nature of the high-priced long fibres.[43] Not until 1925 did Bell Asbestos install a caterpillar-mounted steam shovel in one of its pits at Thetford.[44]

Although, by 1915, the war had begun to have a positive effect on the demand for asbestos products, the rate of installation of new equipment diminished. Investment funds were available, but the shortage of labour for construction projects and delays in the delivery of equipment slowed the rate of diffusion of new techniques and labour-productivity growth as long as the war lasted.[45] (See Table 4.)

Economies of Scale

During and after World War I, the armaments and defence industries provided a new source of demand for raw asbestos fibre. But the most important source of post-war demand proved to be the motor vehicle industry. The introduction of more powerful engines and higher speeds required better braking and gearing systems. Woven asbestos brake-band linings and clutch facings emerged as the most prominent asbestos products among many; the motor vehicle industry became the single most important user of asbestos products

---

39. "New Plant at Asbestos Mine", *op. cit.*.

40. RuKeyser, *op. cit.*, p. 670.

41. Barger and Schurr, *op. cit.*, p. 139.

42. "New Plant at Asbestos Mine", *op. cit.*

43. RuKeyser, *op. cit.*

44. Smith, *op. cit.*, p. 22

45. "Asbestos Corporation in 1917", *The Canadian Mining Journal*, vol. 39 (1918), p. 87.

Table 4

Labour Productivity in the Canadian Asbestos Mining Industry, 1910–1929

Year	Total Asbestos Output Including Sand and Gravel (tons)	Number of Mine and Mill Employees (yearly average calculated on a monthly basis)	Labour Productivity (tons per man-year)	Labour Productivity (five-year average)
1910	125,175	3693	33.9	
1911	126,491	2707	46.7	
1912	128,211	2955	43.4	41.1
1913	157,359	2951	53.3	
1914	128,611	2992	43.0	
1915	141,988	2394	59.3	
1916	169,620	2821	60.1	
1917	160,028	3114	51.4	56.5
1918	160,316	3074	52.2	
1919	211,709	3567	59.4	
1920	190,349	3572	53.3	
1921	123,377	2570	48.0	
1922	158,023	2418	65.4	78.0
1923	236,659	3021	78.3	
1924	226,469	2472	91.6	
1925	281,718	2462	114.3	
1926	315,876	2656	118.9	
1927	289,989	2835	102.3	107.5
1928	297,306	3023	98.4	
1929	330,180	3194	103.4	

Sources: J. G. Ross, *Chrysotile Asbestos in Canada* (Ottawa: Department of Mines, 1931), Chapter 4. *Annual Report of the Mineral Production of Canada*, 1910–1929 (Ottawa: Department of Mines).

manufactured in the United States. Steady growth in the demand for raw asbestos fibre offered new opportunities for cost-reducing innovations related to scale economies in mining and milling.

In the early years of the twentieth century, the major technological innovation in milling practices involved the application of electrical power, the development of cyclone grinders, less costly means of drying rock, and more reliable methods for grading. After 1914 these new techniques continued to evolve, as well as new developments such as the installation of giant dry storage bins of up to twenty-five-thousand-ton capacity, better fiberizers, fans, and collectors for the partial elimination of dust from the surrounding atmosphere, "jumbos" (a modification of the ordinary pulverizer), and increasingly large rock crushers.[46] Development was complicated and varied, but no longer as revolutionary as in the pre-war years. Changes occurred, not only in the types of machinery and equipment employed, but in plant construction and lay-out as well. Thus, after the war, buildings of steel and brick began to replace the older buildings of wood-frame construction. Better planning resulted in the mills being constructed further from the quarries, at additional haulage expense but with an eye to long-run expansion. Economies of scale became increasingly important and the new technology differed from the old in capacity rather than in technique. Most of the post-war innovations in mining and milling required substantial capital investment which only the largest producers could finance. Scale economies induced the consolidation of production units and the disappearance of labour-intensive operations.

The necessity of large-scale production, the need for product standardization, and the beginnings of trade unionism among asbestos workers stimulated some co-operation among producers and therefore reduced secrecy. Prior to 1909, "it was seldom that the operating heads of the asbestos mines were technically trained for mining asbestos, or in fact, even skilled in other mining operations. It was natural, then, that there would not be a wide dissemination of knowledge about asbestos mining and milling or a stimulus to an interchange of ideas and technical data."[47] The formation of the Amalgamated Asbestos Corporation in 1909, and the disruption of the industry during the war, resulted in the exchange of more information among asbestos producers. But inadequate information exchange remained characteristic of the industry up to the Great Depression. Ross observed in 1927, "Once a method has proved successful in one locaton, it is often copied in another where a more economical system would suggest itself to an engineer or experienced operator from another field."[48] Mining methods were reproduced at different pits by the same company for want of better information. Little information of importance was exchanged among companies. As one analyst commented:

> In contra-distinction to most mining districts of the world, there has been little exchange of information among the asbestos operators of Quebec.

---

46. The fifty-six ton crusher constructed at the Jenckes plant of the Canadian Ingersoll-Rand Co. Ltd. for the Asbestos Corp. of Canada Ltd. in 1919 was one of the largest in Canada at the time. *The Canadian Mining Journal*, vol. 40 (1919), p. 818.

47. RuKeyser, *op. cit.*, p. 617.

48. James G. Ross, "Asbestos Mining and Milling", *The Transactions of the Canadian Institute of Mining and Metallurgy and of the Mining Society of Nova Scotia*, vol. XXX (1927), p. 442.

Flow sheets have been evolved in each individual mill; cost data on operating results have been upheld with the utmost secrecy. Admission to many mines is extremely difficult to obtain and most mills refuse absolutely to receive visitors. Operators have in the past shown little desire to co-operate technically with one another—in fact, a spirit of jealousy has made any attempt at co-operation ineffective.[49]

The post-war economic recession had a serious impact on the levels of asbestos prices and output. Of the fourteen companies active in Quebec in 1923, only the Asbestos Corporation of Canada Limited and the Johnson Company reported profits in Canada. By means of transfer pricing, the three vertically integrated mining companies (Bell, Canadian Johns-Manville, and Quebec Asbestos) declared their profits in the United States and avoided their share of taxes on net revenues.[50] These same companies were the largest, the most attuned to new mining and milling techniques, and the most able to realize economies of scale. Their profit margins and their access to financing made them less vulnerable to the low asbestos prices of the early 1920s. The co-existence of low-cost and high-cost producers gave rise to problems of economic efficiency.

When cost functions and/or market shares vary from firm to firm within an oligopolistic industry, conflicts arise which, unless resolved through formal collusive agreements, interfere with the maximization of collective monopoly profits. And if left unresolved, these conflicts may trigger myopic, aggressive behaviour which drives the industry far from the joint-profit-maximizing solution of its price-output problem.[51]

In any such conflict, the lower-cost producers obviously have an advantage over their rivals. As a result there is a tendency for oligopolistic industries to move toward the maximization of collective profits approximating the pricing behaviour associated with pure monopoly.[52] All of the high-cost Canadian operations, except the Johnson Company, finally combined to form the Asbestos Corporation Limited, in December 1925. The Asbestos Corporation then secured

---

49. RuKeyser, *op. cit.*

50. "Asbestos Industry may be Saved by Form of Government Control", *The Financial Times* (March 28, 1924), pp. 1, 16. "Asbestos Mines Ask Government Aid in Problems", *The Financial Post*, October 24, 1924, p. 17.

51. F. M. Scherer, *Industrial Market Structure and Economic Performance* (Chicago: Rand McNally, 1970), p. 140.

52. *Ibid.*, p. 157.

a contract with the three American-owned producers to handle all surplus output not shipped to their parent companies.[53]

The formation of the Asbestos Corporation did not stimulate a higher rate of labour-productivity growth after 1925. (See Table 4.) On the contrary, noted Ross:

> With the present tendency toward centralized control, there is an even more marked disposition on the part of the operating companies to withhold information which may be of use to possible competitors. An air of secrecy has always surrounded asbestos milling operations, and it is not even considered good form for the superintendent of one plant to study the mill of a fellow superintendent working for the same company.[54]

By the year 1929, a wide spectrum of techniques characterized technology in the Quebec asbestos industry. According to Ross:

> Any generalization as to the comparative cost of quarrying and treatment per ton of asbestos recovered would be of little value, being dependent on the nature of the rock, the percentage of fibre contained therein, the kind of plant employed, and the skill of the management.
>
> In the Broughton district, where the rock is loaded by steam shovel, and practically all of it is milled, costs are low. Based on an extraction of from 8 to 12 per cent of fibre, the actual operating cost varies from $10 to $154 per ton of fibre.
>
> In the Thetford and Black Lake quarries, where the rock is sorted by hand and shovelled into boxes which in turn are raised by cranes or cableway hoists, the operating costs vary from $20 to $60 per ton of fibre. Lower costs may be obtained where steam or electric shovel loading or glory-hole mining methods are employed.[55]

Conclusion

What are the general lessons which can be drawn from the history of technological innovation in the asbestos industry? Three main forces appear to have shaped the diffusion of new technology. One was the

---

53. The history of this agreement is related in Elizabeth W. Gillies, "The Asbestos Industry since 1929: With Special Reference to Canada" (Unpublished M.A. Thesis, McGill University, 1941), pp. 28-30.

54. Ross, "Asbestos Mining and Milling", *loc. cit.* And on the same page, "While the bibliography on asbestos is extensive, published information on present |1927| practice in mining and milling from a technical standpoint may be said to be non-existent. A Department of Mines Memoir by Fritz Cirkel, first published in 1905 and revised in 1910, but now out of print, is still regarded as a standard hand-book on the industry."

55. Ross, *Chrysotile Asbestos in Canada, op. cit.*, p. 57.

flow of new ideas or technical knowledge which altered the range of feasible techniques. Another was the continuing change in relative factor prices which altered the terms of choice between different technical possibilities. Perhaps the single most important force favouring technical change in the asbestos industry was the presence of scale economies.

The flow of new ideas was manifest in the initial mechanization of various mining and milling processes using steam power. Technical advances developed in Great Britain were adopted in more or less unaltered form. They permitted unit costs to fall even when factor prices were constant. At the beginning of the twentieth century a new series of changes was introduced in connection with the inflow of American investment and the diffusion of new technology involving hydro-electricity. Technological change in the production of a new energy source made hydro-electricity relatively cheaper than fuels such as wood and coal. Technological innovation in the asbestos industry during the twentieth century involved both a substitution of hydro-electric power for other sources of energy, and a substitution of capital for labour.[56] The relative prices of labour and capital were influenced by the apparent cheapening of machinery relative to wages, resulting from technical progress in the capital-goods industries in the United States.[57] This induced substitution of capital for labour even when wages and the rental rates of machinery were relatively constant. Part of the increase in aggregate labour productivity in asbestos mining in the twentieth century may therefore be explained by labour-saving biases in the technological advances of the American mining industry.[58]

Finally, scale economies offered such advantages as lower unit financing, production and marketing costs, and lower input prices. There was a general trend towards larger minimum size for optimal plants in the American manufacturing industry during the first half of the twentieth century. S. S. Sands found that average physical output per plant increased between 1904 and 1947 by about three per cent per year in forty-six industries for which comparable data

---

56. H. J. Habakkuk describes a similar phenomenon in the Massachusetts cotton-textile industry during the mid-nineteenth century, *op. cit.*, p. 33.

57. Cf. Rosenberg, *op. cit.*, p. 165.

58. According to Ross, "Other than the suction systems and the cyclone, three varieties of which have been designed in the Quebec district, all units in any asbestos mill are such as are used in other dry milling metallurgy." *Chrysotile Asbestos in Canada*, *op. cit.*, p. 40.

were available.[59] This same kind of technical change was also taking place in the asbestos-mining industry. The large American mining companies were able to mine and deliver asbestos fibre at lower average cost per unit than the smaller Canadian operations. Cost differences arising from scale economies were sufficient to permit the sale of excess production at lower prices than the small producers could afford.

Why did not all producers adopt at least the minimum optimal scale? The size of operations at each location was partly determined by the size and richness of the deposit itself. The economically workable deposits in Quebec were relatively few, and their acquisition permitted a small number of companies to reap scarcity rents. In the non-renewable resource field, the early bird gets the worm. Furthermore, the divergence between average and best-practice labour productivity was a reflection of economy-wide factor prices. Outmoded mining equipment earned economic rents as long as operating costs per unit of output were below price. Since wages and salaries were the most important component of operating costs (accounting for about fifty per cent of total variable costs) the price of labour was an element in determining the degree of "outmodedness" of the industry's capital stock.[60] As Salter has said, "When real investment is cheap relative to labour, standards of obsolescence are high and the capital stock is up-to-date; when real investment is dear, rapid adjustment is uneconomic and the capital stock consists largely of outmoded equipment."[61] The price of labour should not have affected the various asbestos mining companies operating in Quebec in a substantially different way. But combined with variations in the size and richness of the deposits, geographical location and accessibility, the abilities of management, barriers to the diffusion of technological information, and the economies of large scale production, low-wage labour may have accentuated the gulf between recent investors in the latest best-practice techniques and the "tail" of low-productivity mining operators.

59. Saul S. Sands, "Changes in Scale of Production in United States Manufacturing Industry, 1904-1947", *Review of Economics and Statistics* (November 1961), pp. 365-68.

60. Government of Canada, *Annual Reports of the Mineral Production of Canada* (Ottawa: Dominion Bureau of Statistics, 1921-29).

61. Salter, *op. cit.*, p. 69.

10.   Prometheus in Canada

The Expansion of Metal Mining, 1900-1950*

Alexander Dow
University of Stirling

Introduction

Innovation occurs when invention becomes commercial technology, embedded into capital equipment by entrepreneurial foresight and workman's skill. Such innovation is an ingredient vital to the success of modern industry. From time to time doubts have been voiced about Canadians' ability to innovate. For example, in J. J. Brown's *Ideas in Exile*, the notion is strongly put that Canada's innovational experience has been a record of failure, despite evidence of considerable inventiveness. He asserts:

> While it is true that Canadian financial institutions, because of their conservative bias, trap potential risk capital and render it useless, the problem goes much deeper than mere reform of finance. The problem of invention and technology in Canada is basically a psychological rather than a financial problem. Our whole attitude toward innovation, not only in science and industry, but in government and social life, is that of the pre-adolescent who hates anything new. What we Canadians have to do in a word is grow up. Because of our racial and religious prejudices, both French and English, and our peasant forbears, we tend to be terrified little men, clutching frantically at what we have and afraid to take any risk whatsoever even for large rewards.[1]

Likewise, in less explicit form, a hesitant view towards Canadian innovation has been evident elsewhere. Mel Watkins' interpretation of Innis' staple theory, while scrupulous in pointing to the importance of supply-side linkages, rather tilted subsequent thinking

* The research on which this contribution is based has been financially supported by the Social Sciences and Humanities Research Council (SSHRC), Ottawa.

1. J. J. Brown, *Ideas in Exile* (Toronto: McClelland and Stewart, 1967).

towards the importance of demand and of other external influences on Canadian development.[2] In the modern staples approach demand considerations dominate the dynamic of economic growth, even though the detail of its form and effect are moderated by the mode of production of the particular staple.[3]

For example, in the determination of the developmental impact of a natural resource-based export activity the linkages are identified as of prime importance.[4] Also, the distribution of economic rents, and resulting income distribution, are seen to crucially affect the political economy of any staple. Both linkages and economic rents are concepts focusing on the outcome of an economic activity *given a market*. No attention is directed to the question of how a market is gained. Of course one way to sell goods is to produce more cheaply and reliably as a result of successful innovation. In the twentieth century a role must be accorded to such successful enterprise if Canadian development is to be fully explained. To do so is not to reject, but rather to strengthen, the staples tradition in Canadian economic thought.

Essentially this paper takes as its point of departure the need to examine the supply of the staple, not simply to describe its impact on the economy, but to explain the nature and pace of its expansion. In a maturing economy domestic entrepreneurs do more than accept passively a pattern of market opportunity determined elsewhere. Domestic economic initiatives arise.

The provision of capital, entrepreneurship, and technical change are the sources of progress in a modern industrial economy. In another paper elsewhere the attempt was made to show that for base-metal mining (in the period 1918-1955) the main source of development capital was internal to the industry in Canada, being largely ploughed-back profits and economic rents.[5] Entrepreneurship

---

2. M. H. Watkins, "A Staple Theory of Economic Growth", *Canadian Journal of Economics and Political Science* XXIX, no. 2 (May 1963). M. H. Watkins, "The Staple Theory Revisited", *Journal of Canadian Studies* 12, no. 5 (Winter 1977).

3. Others have detected this bias and have considered supply forces independently. See R. E. Ankli, "The Growth of the Canadian Economy, 1896-1920", *Explorations in Economic History*, Vol. 17 (1980), pp. 251-74. Outside Canada the demand-oriented version of the staples approach has assumed the form of a caricature. See, for example, J. D. Gould, *Economic Growth in History* (London: Methuen, 1972), p. 104.

4. Linkages denote the impact of an economic activity elsewhere in an economy. The term was introduced in A. O. Hirschman, *The Strategy of Economic Development* (New Haven: Yale University Press, 1958). Later, M. H. Watkins made the concept central to his exposition of the staples approach as an export-led growth model.

5. A. C. Dow, "Finance and Foreign Control in Canadian Base Metal Mining, 1918-55", *Economic History Review* (February 1984).

too was on occasion Canadian, though many American entrepreneurs stimulated the industry's development. Here it will be argued that substantial technological progress, achieved in Canada, aided the Canadian metal-mining industry to secure profitable foreign markets. Specifically, it is incorrect to view American mining technology as having been taken "off the shelf" and applied to Canadian ore bodies. This view misunderstands the nature of the technology involved.

As a prelude to the main theme, the growth and regional expansion of metal mining from 1900 to 1950 will be outlined. First, the distinction should be drawn between mining in general, which includes coal and structural materials such as stone, and metal mining, which includes only the precious and base metals. Prime among these over the first half of the twentieth century were gold, silver, nickel, copper, lead, and zinc.

After the spectacular but brief gold rush to the Klondike in 1896 had produced large profits, the centre of the Canadian gold-mining industry shifted to Ontario. In the decade before World War I, gold production was established at Larder Lake, Porcupine Lake, and Kirkland Lake in Ontario, and later, production began in the Red Lake district. In the late 1920s gold production expanded in Quebec with the development of the Noranda enterprise at Rouyn.

Much of Canada's gold and silver was found in conjunction with base metal ores. The Noranda operation was based on gold-copper ores. Likewise, in British Columbia the mines of the Rossland area supplied gold and copper for the first two decades of the century. The prairie provinces of Manitoba and Saskatchewan became significant gold producers in the 1930s as a result of the Hudson Bay Mining and Smelting investment in the copper-zinc-gold ores of Flin Flon, though a few specifically gold-producing mines made a contribution as well. In Sudbury, Ontario, the immense nickel-copper operations of International Nickel produced also a profitable by-product of gold, of inadequate value in itself to justify its mining and refining.

These ores offered a challenge to the industry to discover the cheapest and most effective ways of separating and collecting the valuable ingredients in the crushed ores hoisted from the mines. Metallurgy was the discipline which evolved, in Canada as elsewhere, to deal with this task.

Silver in Canada is most closely associated with the Cobalt area of Ontario, where in 1903 a railway construction crew unearthed a silver deposit. This find was particularly important to metal-mining in Canada in permitting, due to the technology required, easy access to small producers who were, in some cases, able to build up fortunes which went subsequently to finance the gold developments in Ontario and Quebec. However, the production of silver from base metal mines, mostly in British Columbia, exceeded by 1930 the production of silver from Cobalt. As time passed the tendency for most silver to be mined as a by-product became more marked.

Nickel, copper, lead, and zinc grew in output to serve military markets and the "new industrialism" of the 1920s. Two world wars and the era of the automobile, electricity, and consumer durables produced a spectacular increase in the use of these metals. From small levels of output in 1900, copper output in Canada grew (in terms of physical units) 28-fold by 1950. Over the same period nickel output expanded 35-fold. Sudbury, and the International Nickel Company (INCO), prospered mightily on sales of copper and nickel. Lead output expanded from a more developed base some five-fold from 1900 to 1950. Zinc grew 26-fold over the shorter span of 1916 to 1950, ensuring the prosperity of the Consolidated Mining and Smelting Company (COMINCO) in British Columbia.[6]

Ontario and British Columbia remained the leading metal-mining provinces over the first half of the twentieth century, though their relative importance did decline somewhat as Quebec and the prairie provinces expanded output from the late 1920s onwards. In the Maritimes metals production was very small throughout the half-century.[7]

During the Depression years gold was the saviour of the Canadian metal-mining industry. For a time more than half the value of metals mined came from gold sales. Thereafter, the proportion fell to a more normal ratio of one-third by 1950.

Innovations in Metallurgy

Two path-breaking innovations affected the world metal-mining industry in the first half of the twentieth century. These advances in metallurgy were electrolytic refining and selective flotation. In addition, a variety of less important improvements in technology became incorporated into mining and metallurgical methods, many as a result of on-the-job modifications. The result of innovation was to turn into valuable materials what would otherwise have been useless rock and

---

6. The data came from a source in which the zinc figures are only consistent from 1916. The source is Dominion Bureau of Statistics (DBS), *Canadian Mineral Statistics, 1886-1956*, Reference Paper No. 68 (Ottawa, 1957).

7. Newfoundland is missing from this review, not having data in the Canadian mining records till joining the Confederation.

to lower the extraction costs of metals already commercially viable under existing technologies.

The Consolidated Mining and Smelting Company of British Columbia contributed to the development of both electrolytic refining and selective flotation. *In this case entrepreneurial vision and innovative capacity are seen at work in a Canadian setting.* The Company's experience runs counter to the perception of those who see a lack of innovation in Canada's economic history.

The Canadian Pacific Railway Company (CPR) built the southerly Crows Nest Pass rail route through the Rockies in 1898. To acquire a local railway charter held by an American mine promoter, the CPR bought as a package several mines in south-eastern British Columbia and a smelter at Trail. So the CPR was drawn almost by chance into the business of mining.

The Consolidated Mining and Smelting Company of Canada was incorporated in 1906 as a CPR subsidiary. The Trail metallurgical works had by then separate facilities to smelt copper-gold ores and lead ores. Also, a lead refinery using the electrolytic method had begun operations in 1902, based on a process patented by A. G. Betts and bought by the CPR. The *Winnipeg Free Press* reported: "In going through the refinery you are among scenes of initiative and originality. The process was actually developed there from the infantine stage of a laboratory experiment."[8]

The point illustrated here (as well as being an innovative first) is that to acquire a patent to a metallurgical process is not to obtain an off-the-shelf recipe which can be implemented readily. Every ore tends to be different in its composition. Simply altering the mix of ores going into a metallurgical process requires modifications. A method used on a certain type of ore, such as lead-zinc, to separate out its metal components, will work in another location with a different ore, of the same type, only after much further experimentation. In the field of metallurgy even buying a patent does not preclude the need to innovate.

The electrolytic refining method is at the end of the chain of exploration and development, ore extraction, milling, smelting, and refining, which makes up the mining industry. After refining, the metal is of high purity and is fabricated by the metal-using industries, or, in the case of gold, stored away in vaults. In the electrolytic method, an anode of the desired metal is cast in a furnace, and suspended in a suitable solution, through which an electric current is passed to the

---

8. Winnipeg Free Press, June 6, 1907.

cathode, on which the pure metal is deposited. Thus the process is an electro-chemical one requiring large quantities of electricity. An important variable is the chemical mix used in the solution, though voltage strengths and voltage drops can also be important.

The acquisition by Consolidated Mining and Smelting in 1910 of the Sullivan mine, which contained a rich lead-zinc ore, once again illustrates vividly that electrolytic refining was not an "off-the-shelf" technology. At once research began to adapt the Betts method to the separation problem. Not until 1916, under the pressures of wartime demand, and after receiving considerable encouragement from the Shell Committee in Ottawa (later known as the Imperial Munitions Board), did an electrolytic zinc-separation process go into commercial production.[9]

Selwyn G. Blaylock, later to become Chairman of the Company, was Assistant General Manager in 1917. He commented as follows, discussing the approach made to the Company by the Shell Committee, interested in receiving adequate zinc supplies for the war effort:

> We had been experimenting on the extraction of zinc in complex ores for two or three years before that. Unfortunately the men who had been doing the experimenting had enlisted and gone to the front. We started experimenting once again and then took on contracts with the Imperial Board to make zinc.[10]

Explicitly referring to Anaconda, the big mining corporation based in Butte, Montana, and normally credited with technological leadership in this era, Blaylock says:

> I may say that when we started the plant we knew very little about the process. Anaconda was very much in the same state. I was down there when they started. We were making about 1000 lbs. a day and they were working along similar lines in Anaconda.[11]

No technological package was available to either Consolidated Mining and Smelting or to Anaconda at this time. Metallurgists based in Trail and in Butte worked along similar lines to create a product to supply the high wartime demand. Given the encouragement of the Canadian state (including financial support) through the Shell

---

9. See Stephen Watson, "The Establishment of Lead, Zinc, Copper and Nickel Refining in Canada: the Role of Government and the Economic Impact of Refining", Centre for the Study of Regulated Industries, McGill University (April 1981).

10. *Nelson News*, May 21, 1917. These men who enlisted may be presumed to have been mainly Canadian.

11. *Ibid.*

Committee, the Trail effort was independently successful, though aided by "friendly exchanges" with Anaconda.[12]

However, useful as the refinery for zinc was in the context of the World War, the electrolytic method proved too expensive to be commercially viable on its own for any but the richest ores from the mine. The successful adoption of the supplementary technology of selective flotation made the Sullivan Mine the engine for Consolidated Mining and Smelting's great commercial success during the 1920s. The 1921 Annual Report first noted that due to "improved processes" production costs were falling faster than metal prices.

The dating of this episode is important in that by one of the industry's own chroniclers the development has been credited elsewhere. C. S. Parsons, writing in the *Canadian Mining Journal* in 1939, credited the Sullivan selective-flotation process to a patent granted in Butte to G. G. Griswold and G. E. Sherridan.[13]

The selective-flotation process, it must be appreciated, is a milling (or separating) technique at the start of the metallurgical chain of milling, smelting, and refining. The input is a liquid slurry in which the ore, taken from the mine, and having been crushed into small particles, is suspended. Important variables to the success of the separation of the desired metal from the other components of the ore are the chemical constituents of the liquid slurry and the size of the particles suspended in it.

The separation takes place by introducing air, either directly or by agitation, into the tank containing the liquid. The result looks like palpitating black porridge. The object is to make particles which are rich in one mineral or another hydrophobic, so that they adhere to the air bubbles which are swept off the surface of the tank. The scientific principle is that "whatever the bodily composition of a substance it will tend to adhere to an air bubble if its surface is not wetted by water".[14] Bubbles with the sought metal clinging to them slip over the sides and are collected, leaving particles which are rich in the desired mineral to form a slag used for feeding the furnaces of the smelter.

This was the technology which transformed the complex lead-zinc ore of the Sullivan Mine into a valuable asset. R. W. Diamond,

---

12. W. M. Archibald *et al.*, "The Development of the Sullivan Mine and Processes for the Treatment of its Ores", *Transactions* of the (Canadian) Institute of Mining and Metallurgy, Vol. XXVII (1924).

13. C. S. Parsons, "Sixty Years of Development in Ore Dressing", *Canadian Mining Journal* (October 1939), p. 705.

14. J. R. Boldt and P. Queneau, *The Winning of Nickel* (Toronto: Longmans, 1967), p. 199.

the man in charge of the research, later claimed that the problem the Sullivan ore presented to a flotation approach was as follows:

> I should remind you that froth flotation as known in America in 1917 consisted of separating all sulphide minerals from all non-sulphide gangue minerals. This was usually, if not always, accomplished in an acid circuit. The problem presented by the Sullivan ore was not one of ordinary froth flotation as then known but one of *selective flotation*. Specifically the problem was to separate this complex ore into three sulphide products: (a) a lead concentrate, (b) a zinc concentrate, (c) an iron concentrate (or tailing) —with each of these three products containing as high a percentage of the respective lead, zinc and iron minerals in the original ore as possible. There was no such separation being made anywhere in the world at that time.[15]

What distinguished the Sullivan ore from ore at Broken Hill in Australia, where a selective-flotation method was initiated in 1912, was the relatively high content of iron sulphide in the Sullivan ore. This feature, along with the intimately associated nature of the minerals in the ore, made the Sullivan separation problem unique, though susceptible to attack by use of principles derived from experience at Broken Hill, Butte, and elsewhere.

The commercial value of the method rose to the extent that it could achieve two outcomes. The first was a concentrate rich in ore of the desired minerals (i.e., zinc) but low in the others (i.e., lead and iron). The second was the degree to which the minerals in the ore were collected rather than escaping with the waste (or tailing). A rich concentrate with a good recovery rate lowered in an important way the cost of smelting and refining.

Such cost reductions were urgently needed. As a result of Russia's exit from the war after the Revolution the Allies found themselves holding excess stocks of zinc. Buying from Cominco was halted. Prices began to decline markedly. In the House of Commons in Ottawa a limited bounty, which had been suspended for the duration of the war, was authorized prematurely to compensate Cominco.[16] However, in February 1917, R. W. Diamond, then a young Canadian metallurgist who had worked for Anaconda, was hired by S. G. Blaylock to undertake flotation experiments on the Sullivan ore. He headed a team that managed to solve the problem

---

15. R. W. Diamond, "A Detailed Account of the Development of the Treatment by Flotation of the Ore of the Sullivan Mine, Kimberley, B.C., 1917-23", unpublished account prepared for the files of the Consolidated Mining and Smelting Company of Canada (1961). Province of B.C. Provincial Archives, North West Collection (Call No. NW 669.028 D537), p. 4.

16. Canada, Debates of the House of Commons, 1918, Vol. II (May 20), pp. 2310-12; (May 23), pp. 2498-2504.

over four years. Looking back after his career was over, R. W. Diamond dated commercial separation of Sullivan ore by selective flotation from August 1920, though continuous improvement was effected in the technique throughout the 1920s and early 1930s.[17] Not until February 1923 did Cominco acquire licence rights to the Griswold and Sherridan patent, which involved adding cyanide as a reagent to the separation slurry in order to decrease the zinc content of the lead concentrate.[18]

In short, the Consolidated Mining and Smelting Company, and its pre-charter constituents, were innovative from 1898 onwards. World technology at the stage of inventions was used for experimentation on particular metallurgical problems with success. Commercial operations were built on these advances. Financial success resulted.

Often innovation does not take the form of dramatic breakthroughs but rather of minor advances arising from the need to surmount a particular problem. Canada seems to have been as adept in this area as Britain, Germany, or the United States where mining and metallurgical expertise was most widespread. One example will show what is involved.

Noranda was incorporated in Ontario in 1922 and smelter production of the Quebec ore began in December 1927. The first revenues came in 1928. The Rouyn ore body was a mixture of copper and gold. As gold prices soared during the Depression Noranda flourished.

One stage in the treatment of the Rouyn ores was roasting, a technique commonly required with Canadian ores to eliminate sulphur.[19] The original specifications of the smelter included four "wedge-type" roasters to supply each furnace. However, it was found possible for each reverberatory furnace to smelt one thousand tons of feed each day, the output capacity of each roaster being only one hundred and fifty tons per day. A roaster was designed with a number of hearths, each of which had two air-cooled "rabble arms", which

---

17. R. W. Diamond, *op. cit.*, p. 24. See also Dominion of Canada, Department of Mines, *Canada: Geology, Mines and Metallurgical Industries.* Handbook prepared for Second (Triennial) Empire Mining and Metallurgical Congress (1927), pp. 174-75. A report in the *Globe* (April 13, 1922) observed that Consolidated Mining and Smelting had just issued the first schedule of prices for zinc in custom ores in the history of Canadian mining. See also the *Nelson Daily News* (April 12, 1922).

18. The U.S. Patent No. 1427235 (August 29, 1922) was licensed to Consolidated Mining and Smelting in February, 1923. Consolidated were the first licensee. See R. W. Diamond, *ibid.*, p. 26.

19. The details which follow rely on W. B. Boggs and J. N. Anderson, "The Noranda Smelter", *Transactions* of the (Canadian) Institute of Mining and Metallurgy (1930), pp. 1-44.

by rotating agitated the material being roasted. By speeding up the number of revolutions of each rabble arm in the hearths, it was discovered, output of the roaster was increased to two hundred and fifty tons per day.

Now roaster output at one thousand tons per day per furnace matched furnace requirements. The difficulty was that, due to the increased speed of rotation, frequent breakdowns were experienced of the rabble arms and of the "lute rings" which formed a seal between the hearths and the rotating column. The solution was found in replacing iron rabble-blades and lute rings by alloy versions. The number of breakdowns fell considerably.

The increased speed of roasting had created another problem. Each hearth was connected to the next within the roaster. The more rapid speeds were associated with a greater air inflow and faster flow through the connected hearths. As a result, in the second hearth of each roaster, fine particles began to stick to and accumulate on the bottom. The rabble arms were impeded in these hearths.

The solution here was a ploughing device attached to each rabble arm in the affected hearths. The device was designed by the general roaster foreman and the shift foreman.

The example illustrates how problems have solutions which create further problems. In these circumstances, in Canada or elsewhere, on-the-job skill is responsible for much innovation, minor in itself, which in aggregate can be of great importance.

To restate our argument may now be useful. It is that no shortage of innovative capacity seems to have existed in Canadian mining, either for major innovation or for day-to-day modification and improvement. Of course, a balanced picture is needed.

On occasion technological know-how was acquired from the United States. Thus, when Noranda decided to build a refinery in Montreal, Canadian Copper Refiners Ltd. was created, a company owned jointly by Noranda, the British Metal Corporation of London, England, and the Nichols Copper Company of New York. The plant was built by Nichols Copper and operated by that company under contract.

At other times expertise was acquired through the labour market. The Noranda smelter was built under the direction of A. R. Wheeler, a consulting metallurgist who had been manager of the smelters of Anaconda, the large Butte-based U.S. copper corporation. Wheeler's experience included smelter design in Africa for Union Minière de Haut Katanga.

The appropriate assessment seems to be that throughout the mining areas of the world corporations were able to draw on a scientific knowledge base and a mobile pool of engineers and metallurgists educated in the appropriate scientific principles. Innovation, on a major or minor scale, was related to problems encountered with respect to specific processes in particular situations. Canada seems to have had the knowledge base, the capital, and the entrepreneurial enthusiasm necessary for success in securing this sort of technological advance.

Finally, a case from a later date will be described to show that Canadian innovative ability did not drain away over the years. Sherritt Gordon Mines incorporated in 1927 with an Ontario charter in order to develop deposits of copper-zinc in northern Manitoba. These deposits were exhausting by the end of World War II, so a plan was initiated to mine a nickel-copper deposit discovered at Lynn Lake on the Manitoba-Saskatchewan boundary. Previously concentrates of copper had been shipped for smelting, using rail links, to the nearby works of Hudson Bay Mining and Smelting at Flin Flon. To develop the nickel deposit Sherritt Gordon had to acquire a full metallurgical capacity for the first time.

To investigate the problem of refining Lynn Lake ore Sherritt Gordon Mines employed Professor Frank Forward of the University of British Columbia.[20] This move was initiated by Eldon Brown, an engineer who had been mine superintendent at Sherridon, the company's copper-zinc mine site developed in the 1930s. Frank Forward's proposal after a year of laboratory work was to use a hydrometallurgical technique, ammonia leaching, to recover the nickel, copper, and traces of cobalt from the Lynn Lake ore. As a refining method ammonia leaching was quite new, and so commercially untested.

The research effort now launched was centred on Sherritt-Gordon's own metallurgy department which, however, canvassed widely for knowledge and help. The Chemical Construction Company of New York had a hydrogen-precipitation technique which was useful to the metallurgical process proposed. A pilot plant was established in Ottawa under the auspices of the Mines Branch of the Department of Mines and Technical Surveys.[21] When insufficient financing was available in Canada, Newmont Mines of the United States stepped in to provide funds, in the end acquiring Sherritt Gordon as a subsidiary.

---

20. Robert H. Ramsey, *Men and Mines of Newmont: a Fifty Year History* (1973), p. 188.

21. A. Ignatieff, *A Canadian Research Heritage: 75 Years of Federal Government Research in Minerals, Metals and Fuels* (Ottawa: Supply and Services Canada, 1981).

In opening the nickel refinery at Fort Saskatchewan in Alberta, in 1954, Sherritt Gordon initiated the first commercial attempt to employ hydrometallurgy for extracting nickel from sulphide ores.[22] The technology has proved popular, being especially suited to relatively small volumes, and having the advantage of eliminating air pollution by sulphur dioxide. Over the next two decades refineries of this sort were built in Finland, Australia, South Africa, and the Philippines. In a technical paper the technology was described as follows:

> In the field of pressure hydrometallurgy one deals with the science and technology of hydrometallurgical reactions conducted above the normal boiling point of water and/or above atmospheric pressure. When hydrometallurgical reactions under pressure are carried out for leaching under oxidizing conditions, compressed air or oxygen is used to dissolve metals such as nickel, cobalt, copper and zinc from their ores or concentrates. Pressure reactions are also carried out under reducing conditions with hydrogen gas to precipitate metals such as nickel, cobalt and copper as pure metallic powders from metal salt solutions.[23]

The Fort Saskatchewan site in Alberta was chosen because of the availability of natural gas. As well as acting as fuel the methane component of the gas was converted on-site to ammonia, the basic leaching agent employed in the process. The by-product of ammonia sulphate was later used to develop a large fertilizer production.

What then were the components of this successful entrepreneurial innovation? The original insight was that of Professor Forward of the University of British Columbia. Research advice was obtained from the Mines Branch in Ottawa and from the Chemical Construction Company of New York. Financing came mainly from the United States via Newmont Mines and even, by means of pre-payment for nickel ordered, from the United States government. Furthermore, E. Brown offered some interesting remarks in 1955:

> There is one point that I would like to mention in connection with the development of this leaching process and that is the great contribution made to it by New Canadian engineers and scientists. The bulk of our research staff as distinct from our operating staff was made up of these men and their ingenuity in solving problems as they arose was one of the major factors in the rapid development of the process. At one time our research and technical staff at Ottawa included representatives of twenty-two different nationalities.[24]

22. H. Veltman and D. R. Weir, "Sherritt Gordon's Pressure Leaching Technology—its Industrial Application", Sherritt Gordon Mines, Fort Saskatchewan.

23. V. N. Mackiw and H. Veltman, "Recent Advances in Sherritt's Pressure Hydrometallurgy Technology," paper presented at the American Mining Congress held at Las Vegas, Nevada (October, 1982), pp. 4-5.

24. E. L. Brown, "The Sherritt Gordon Lynn Lake Project—Notes on Discovery and Financing", *Canadian Mining and Metallurgical Bulletin* (June, 1955), pp. 3-4.

So the innovation must be seen as Canadian in inspiration, but assisted profoundly by immigrant skills and American entrepreneurship. Whatever is to be made of this mix, no evidence exists here for inadequate Canadian innovative capacity.

Prices and Markets

Though similar in the mining and metallurgical methods used to obtain them, and though often found in the same ore body, the markets for precious metals and base metals were quite separate, and responded to different forces.[25] Thus they will be considered in turn, starting with the more important (in economic terms), base metals.

To separate demand forces from supply forces in explaining the growth of any product is notoriously difficult. However, it will be contended that, as far as the base metals are concerned, supply-side factors were of more importance than demand-side factors in determining expansion in Canada.

The argument can be supported in an *a priori* way as well as by adducing evidence. The price elasticity of demand for Canadian base metals, a measure of responsiveness of demand to changing prices, is unlikely to have remained precisely the same over the years. However, the inference is reasonable that, for Canadian base metals, the price elasticity of demand in any period was high for each metal. Price elasticity of demand depends mainly on the possibilities for substitution by buyers. In the "new industrialism", based on electricity, automobiles, and consumer durables, Canadian base metals had to compete with other products, such as bauxite, and with base metals from Australia, Mexico, and the United States. If indeed most Canadian producers faced price-elastic demand curves, and if Canadian innovation brought new supplies "on stream" at competitive prices and sold them successfully in the United States and in Europe, then emphasis on supply seems plausible. New technologies and the innovation and improvement of existing methods lowered costs, transforming into metals what would otherwise have been waste rock.

Yet this picture for base-metal expansion requires qualification. The demand forces at work can be summarized under two headings, consumer demand and military demand.

---

25. For a more detailed description see A. C. Dow, *The Canadian Base Metal Mining Industry (non-ferrous) and its Impact on Economic Development in Canada*, unpublished Ph.D. thesis (University of Manitoba, 1980), pp. 67-113.

Consumer Demand

Base-metals demand expanded in unison with the growth of the new consumer society evident in America from the 1920s. This source of demand for base-metals provided for a steady increase in output, interrupted only by the rocketing demands of nations at war (or fearing war) for strategic raw materials, and by those breakdowns in consumer demand which characterize the capitalist economy.

The goods demanded by newly affluent consumers were automobiles, radios, and electrical equipment of all kinds. Lead was required for batteries. Nickel was used in steel alloys to give hardness and protection against corrosion. Copper wire was the conductor through which the expanding currents of electricity flowed in transmission lines and countless electrical machines. The main use of zinc remained that of galvanizing, to give iron and steel products a corrosion-resistant coating. In various forms this product also came to be used in the building trades, and automobiles used some galvanized zinc metal as well as zinc die-cast components.

The automobile and electrical power were the dominant technological forces driving the new consumerism of North America between the 1920s and the 1950s. The steady increase in demand for Canadian base metals can be traced to this social transformation. Rising incomes, especially in the United States, raised demand somewhat, but Canadian production benefited in particular because of the cost-saving innovations which had occurred.[26]

Military Demand

On three occasions in the first half of the twentieth century military demand caused base-metal production to expand rapidly. These were prior to and during World War I, prior to and in the early stages of World War II, and (in the early 1950s) during the Korean War and subsequently with the advent of the cold war.

Nickel was the war material *par excellence*. Suitable in its steel alloys for armour plating due to its extreme hardness, it clad the battle-fleets of the First World War and protected the tanks of the Second World War. As the military use of aircraft expanded, so did its armour-plating role in the air.

Copper, lead, and zinc also had strategic uses. Lead and bullets come naturally to mind as illustrative, but copper and zinc

---

26. In market terms, had not the supply curves shifted to the right in slack times, or under wartime pressures, then demand curves, even though drifting upwards, might not, in some instances, have intersected Canadian supply curves.

too, in the many electrical and automotive components which contribute to modern warfare, experienced strong military demands.

What then of the contention that the industry's expansion was supply-led rather than demand-led? The qualification this argument requires is to specify that it is consumer demand rather than military demand to which this conclusion applies. Prices before and during World War I, and in the late 1940s and early 1950s, reflected the pressures of military demand; and there can be no doubt that only price controls during World War II prevented prices exhibiting the same signals of a demand upsurge as are evident from 1914 to 1917.

Yet military demand has been erratic. The long-run expansion of base metal mining depended between the wars on the new consumer uses of the metals. The periods 1922-1929, 1932-1937, and to some extent, 1946-1950, saw this groundswell of demand with semi-permanent characteristics. The technological innovations, led by electrolytic refining and selective flotation, permitted output to expand greatly in Canada without increasing costs, indeed while decreasing costs, and they are to be mainly credited with the seizure by Canadian base-metal producers of many new market outlets as the new affluent society emerged.

The empirical picture is consistent with this viewpoint. The price index for Non-Ferrous Metals and their Products in Canada is compared to the General Wholesale Price Index in Figure 1. Only in wartime was the sympathy of the two indices destroyed. Before and during the First World War non-ferrous metals enjoyed a positive price deviation above the wholesale price index which persisted till 1920. The reverse situation arose in the Second World War when for six years controls kept non-ferrous metals at a practically constant price while other items in the wholesale price index moved ahead.[27] Despite rapid post-war price increases in the metals group this differential was not eliminated till 1952.

The absence of any pronounced deviations of non-ferrous metal prices above the all-items index is evidence that demand pressures were not the main force propelling growth in the industry between the wars. Likewise, the lack of rapid price increases, except for 1945-1950, supports an interpretation that reduces demand to a secondary role in the industry's expansion. Demand was adequate with proper cultivation. Only after World War II did a demand-induced boom introduce, with growing military demands, a considerable industry expansion in the 1950s.

---

27. As exports of metals to the United States expanded towards the end of the war the price fixity of the index is an illusion in any event. Such exports were at market prices.

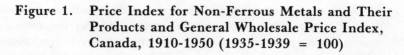

Figure 1. Price Index for Non-Ferrous Metals and Their Products and General Wholesale Price Index, Canada, 1910-1950 (1935-1939 = 100)

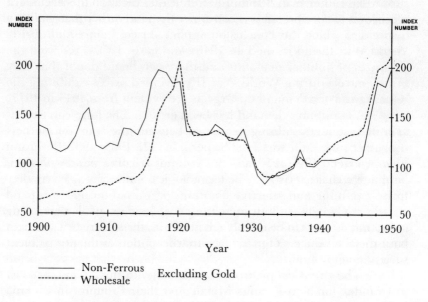

What of the precious metals? As a form of money, the price of gold was a manipulated one over much of the period. However, the price rose in the 1930s, bringing prosperity to the gold producers in the Canadian mining industry. Sometimes, as with Noranda, producers with both precious and base metals in their ores gained a valuable flexibility. However, many lode gold mines came on stream in response to the price incentives of the 1930s, and as a result of government encouragement in the early 1940s—an expansion that led to hard times in the gold-producing sector when costs rose after World War II. Subsidy was initiated by the government in Ottawa in 1948 with the Emergency Gold Mining Assistance Act.

Of course, technological advance made an impact on the production of the precious metals. Both gold and silver were commonly recovered from the slimes at the end of electrolytically refining the base metals. The cyanide process of gold recovery contributed greatly to the recovery of gold from ore in which the precious metal is very finely distributed. (Coarser ores were treated by mechanical methods in which the gold settles out because of a higher specific gravity.)

However, the impression is strong that unlike base metals, demand-and-supply forces operated for both gold and silver with equal weight during most of the period, sometimes with drama, as in the Klondike experience, but more often thereafter through a technical decision to add a precious-metal recovery procedure to a base-metal processing plant. Of course, a demand-led gold expansion can be detected in the 1930s and early 1940s.

Conclusion

The conviction exists in Canada that innovation has not been successfully pursued. In a widely read book H. Hardin was forthright on this perceived failure. He said: "As far as creating new technology, and new industry based on new technology, Canadian private enterprise has been a monumental failure."[28]

Less explicit has been the concentration of writers in the academic staples tradition on foreign demand and domestic linkages, and their subsequent neglect of the role of domestic entrepreneurship and innovation in Canada's development. In what has gone before I have challenged the opinions of those who depict a Canadian failure of innovation, and have tried to repair what amounts to an error of omission in the staples tradition. The case of the metal-mining industry shows Canadian entrepreneurship and innovation without which the industry would not, most likely, have succeeded as it did.

A much more plausible hypothesis to explain Canadian innovation, certainly in metal mining, is that it falls into the category of "necessity, the mother of invention". Financial success in later years often depended upon discovering a commercial process without which the company would have been hard-put to initiate or to continue production. The experience of Consolidated Mining and Smelting and of Sherritt Gordon Mines both attest to innovative capacity unleashed in such circumstances in order to secure the future of the company.

The response of the Canadian companies in the mining industry was not purely a private enterprise one. From the beginning of the century Dominion and provincial governments took a close interest in the mining industry, often helping expansion by giving bounties on exports, by building roads, or by providing subsidized rail links.

---

28. H. Hardin, *A Nation Unaware: The Canadian Economic Culture* (Vancouver: J. J. Douglas, 1974), p. 102.

With respect to innovation, the Mines Branch in Ottawa was moved from department to department in bureaucratic rearrangements, but provided an increasingly sophisticated laboratory to which companies could refer metallurgical problems. In the provinces, funds were directed towards the mining-engineering and metallurgical-research facilities which developed in the universities and colleges in parallel with the expansion of metal mining across the nation.

Skilled manpower was obtained from the graduates of Canadian universities (still privately funded), from Canadians trained in the United States, and from immigrants from the United States and Europe. The free labour market which existed throughout the North American mining industry precluded the possibility of a skilled-labour bottleneck to growth. Of course, many immigrants were "Canadians" in law and in spirit after a few years of working in Canada. Such an ability to attract the talented from elsewhere has been one of the developmental strengths of comparatively young nations. In itself, reliance on immigrants for some innovative functions does not seem to amount, for a country like Canada, to technological dependence.

Overall the market data suggest that growing demand, though a stimulus, was not the sole driving force behind industry expansion. Faced by severe commercial problems, companies used technological innovation to survive, and later to prosper. For Canadian base-metal mining at least, the dynamic of growth seems to have been as much a supply-stimulated phenomenon as a reaction to demand opportunities which were too good to miss.

Canadian
Community

11.   The Role of Presents in French-Amerindian Trade

Cornelius J. Jaenen
University of Ottawa

Gift exchange and the giving of presents have been universal practice since time immemorial. Europeans who came into contact with Amerindian cultures were well acquainted with such formal presentations in both the diplomatic context and the commercial context. The Amerindians, for their part, had their own long-established practices which were observed *de rigueur* and not as mere formalities. In the contact experience of the French with various Amerindian bands and tribes in the far-flung territory claimed as New France, these presents took on a special character and significance superseding the qualities ascribed to them in both native and intruding cultures.

Presents, in anthropological terms, have been seen primarily as "something given in the expectation of reciprocation". The circumstances in which they are offered—for example, to appease revenge, as tribute, as peace pledges—indicate the involvement of a degree of compulsion or obligation which is not necessarily economic but which may very often be social and moral.[1] Gifts in European societies were often perceived as spontaneous and voluntary offerings, although it can be argued that diplomatic gifts (particularly as offered since the time of Charlemagne, who delighted his peers with gifts of polar bears and white falcons from America) involved a measure of compulsion and social obligation. Karl Polanyi has identified three modes of such exchanges: the reciprocal mode which presumes an obligatory gift exchange; the redistributive mode which is obligatory to a specific area; and market exchange, which is part of purchase and sale with reference to a value (price) system.[2] By giving gifts,

---

1. Marcel Maus, *The Gift: Forms and Functions of Exchange in Archaic Societies* (New York, 1967), pp. 1, 71.

2. David L. Stilts, ed., *International Encyclopedia of the Social Sciences* (New York, 1968), Vol. V, p. 239.

people and groups create, alter, or maintain relationships among themselves. Amerindian gift exchanges, which were already well established and ritualized at first European contact, were never disinterested actions. Purpose underlay every present because something was expected in return, whether in attitude or action.

The importance of gift-giving in Amerindian societies probably has been under-estimated. On the Pacific Coast, for example, the potlatch (said to derive from the verb "to give") grew out of the institution of slavery. The goods acquired through the labour or services of slaves were distributed by the owner at a ceremony which marked his status and social prestige. It was, in a sense, a demonstration of the principle that "it is more blessed to give than to receive". But the potlatch also involved some obligations because by tradition the recipients of largesse were expected to return in a reciprocal ceremony double the amount they had received, or else shamefully admit their inferiority and incapacity. The potlatch represented a very real financial investment capable of reaping substantial returns in time. Similarly, it seems to us, all Amerindian gift-giving involved obligations. The French, by being drawn into utilizing the distribution of presents, both personal and state, to promote their objectives, found themselves increasingly entangled in a web of complex obligations.

Jacob's classic study of the subject makes the useful observation that both the French and the British adopted the Amerindian custom of identifying presents with "words".[3] Each *parole* was embodied in a present. These "words" could offer a petition, light a council fire, cover the dead, console the mourners, dry away tears, etc., in the metaphorical language so dear to the various tribes. The French were quick to observe that in North America, gifts were offered at the naming of a child, at marriage, at death, in condolence, in compensation for injury or murder, for healing, for declaring war, for negotiating peace terms, as tribute, as tokens of friendship and esteem, and so forth. In the framework of their own elaborate rules of etiquette, precedence, and protocol, the French saw that rank, authority, and prestige in the New World were dependent in some measure on the ability to offer gifts, and that generosity was the trait most admired by the Amerindians. The early Jesuit missionaries observed that "these people never speak without making presents", and that "presents speak more clearly than lips."[4] By the end of the

---

3. Wilbur R. Jacobs, *Wilderness Politics and Indian Gifts* (Lincoln, 1966), pp. 13-17.

4. Reuben G. Thwaites, ed., *The Jesuit Relations and Allied Documents* (Cleveland, 1896-1901), Vol. XXV, p. 269; Vol. XXVI, p. 83.

French régime an entire native vocabulary had been adopted to indicate "acceptable" gifts for various individuals, circumstances and seasons. *Aouapon*, for example, denoted the full "uniform" given a native warrior in the French alliance—blanket, shirt, mittens, shoes and breeches—while *apichimon* denoted his winter equipment which included in addition a bearskin, snowshoes, tumpline, and heavy mitts.[5] Women, particularly those among the Iroquois who wielded great influence over the warriors and councillors, were given scarlet hose, calicoes, ribbons and brightly coloured gartering, silver rings, awls for boring leather, needles, hoes, and brass kettles. Children were given shirt material and sometimes toys. Status and precedence were observed in that common warriors received cheap stroud cloth and ordinary guns whereas war captains received duffle cloth and special rifles. Chieftains were given complete ornate uniforms. The Iroquois seem to have received more valuable presents than did other tribes. Nor were the French slow to recognize the significance of wampum "collars" and their value as historical records. A Universal History informed metropolitan readers that

> . . . for example, if it is a question of negotiating with a Nation hitherto an enemy, or if one wishes to communicate some matter to an ally, one will send off as many Collars as one has matters to discuss.[6]

Obviously, presents had taken on great importance in the relationship between European intruders and native inhabitants.

Under what circumstances, and with what motives in mind, did the French present gifts to Amerindians, and in what circumstances, and with what motives, did Amerindians expect or exact such presents? The question is framed to underscore the fact that Amerindians were just as active and dynamic participants in these transactions as were the French. At the time of initial contact, the various tribes and bands may merely have reacted to French initiative and overture, but later intercourse does not support a thesis of French initiative and dynamism as opposed to Amerindian passivity and reaction. The gift-giving ceremonies were the ritualized expression of reciprocal initiatives. General Montcalm had to conclude in 1757 that it was essential for him to remain in Montreal for "ceremonies quite as tiresome as they are useful", when approximately one thousand Amerindian warriors would be given food, clothing, and ammunition to

---

5. *Rapport de l'Archiviste de la Province de Québec, 1923-24* (Québec, 1924), « Mémoires sur l'état de la Nouvelle-France », 1757, p. 66.

6. *Histoire générale des cérémonies, moeurs, et coutumes religieuses de tous les peuples du monde* (Paris, 1741), Vol. VII, p. 111. We have translated all quotations into English to facilitate the reading of the paper.

maintain their martial spirit.[7] The Court instructed Governor Vaudreuil in 1707 that in treating with the Iroquois and other aggressive nations he was to observe with care "to do nothing except with the dignity and decorum which befits you and without betraying to them any signs of fear."[8]

In the competition generated by both the fur trade and the French-British imperial wars the various tribes, whether hostile or allied, were able to negotiate from positions of strength. Presents became almost a form of bribery, with the Amerindians driving up the price in times of strenuous competition or ominous threat. The Micmacs, for example, threatened to turn to the English if the French did not guarantee that their gifts would become *présents ordinaires* distributed annually. The tribesmen refused to comply with any authoritarian demands; they had to be convinced, not commanded. Little wonder that Governor St. Ovide was warned not to be "too demanding" in his negotiations because the Micmacs had to be "attached to the French interest". It was a sentiment which ran throughout the official correspondence and which indicated a cognizance of native initiative.[9]

Nevertheless, it was important to conceal such sentiments as much as possible in order to prevent the natives from becoming too overbearing. In the sixteenth and early seventeenth centuries a number of Amerindians had been taken to France to be educated and put on public display. Some went on what amounted virtually to diplomatic missions. However, by the eighteenth century, casual and unauthorized visits of native chieftains were discouraged by the French Court. In 1740, for example, the unauthorized visit to Versailles of the Micmac Denis d'Esdain and his interpreter drew an official reprimand onto the head of the sea captain who had given them passage. It was deemed necessary, nevertheless, to present the Micmac visitor with a bolt of red cloth, some gold braid and gold fringe, beads, and ribbons of assorted colours, while at the same time the missionary Jean-Louis Le Loutre was instructed "to impress on this *sauvage* the value of the King's presents and to inform him that His Majesty would have treated him better had he crossed over to France with properly authorized people."[10]

---

7. *P.A.C.*, MG1, Series F3, Vol. 15, pt. I, Montcalm to Minister, July 11, 1757, p. 53.

8. *P.A.C.*, MG1, Series B, Vol. 29 (1), Minister to Vaudreuil, June 30, 1707, p. 151.

9. *A.C.*, Série F3, Vol. 50, Pontchartrain to St. Ovide, April 10, 1713, fol. 4; *Arch. Acadiennes*, Séries 1, pp. 5-13, Mémoire sur le Canada, 1711.

10. *A.C.*, Series B, Vol. 76, Maurepas to Guillot, May 2, 1741, fol. 83v; *ibid.*, Series C¹¹V, Vol. 23, Du Quesnel to Maurepas, October 19, 1741, fol. 74-74v.

Gift-giving was associated principally with ceremonial greetings and festive occasions on first contact. Champlain had noted the importance of presents, while his successor Montmagny adopted the custom in 1648 of offering presents to consolidate and seal agreements and compacts, noting as he did so that "what passes for a word and a present at public meetings must be of some considerable value."[11] The missionaries quickly adopted the practice in their efforts to penetrate into the native lodges with their evangelical message. Gifts were offered on special religious festivals. Father Millet went so far as to sing aloud and alone while preparing a feast for his hearers, having, as he recounted, "a fine large porcelain collar in the middle of the cabin", maps and pictures, and at the feet of a statue of Jesus "all the symbols of the superstitions and dissoluteness of these countries." Then he made the expected "harangue" accompanied "with the ordinary presents".[12] On the other hand, Father Du Poisson, upon embarking on his mission to the Arkansas in 1727, avoided ceremonial occasions as much as possible because of the expense these entailed. He confided to a co-religionist:

> . . . . some of the chiefs spoke to me again on the subject of receiving the calumet: I amused them as I had done hitherto, for it is a considerable expense to receive their Calumet. In the beginning, when it was necessary to manage them, the directors of the grants of M. Laws, and the Commanders who received their Calumet, made them great presents, and these Indians have supposed that I was going to revive the old custom. But even were I able to do so, I should act with exceeding caution, because there might be danger that at last they would not hear me speak of religion except for motives of interest since moreover we know from experience that the more one gives to the Indian, the less probability there is of his being contented, and that gratitude is a virtue of which he has not the least idea.[13]

The engineer Louis Franquet indicated that on visits to the reserves Europeans were expected to offer appropriate gifts. To the Sault St. Louis "domiciled" tribesmen he offered "two bottles of brandy which they poured around to all and drank to my health", then he gave "a roll of tobacco" which elicited from the "orator" a long harangue explaining that although there was a great dearth of this commodity in the country this gift was regarded "as manna which would bring them back to life." He noted admiringly that "the

---

11. Thwaites, *Jesuit Relations*, Vol. XXXII, p. 187.

12. *Ibid.*, Vol. LIII, p. 269.

13. W. I. Kip, ed., *The Early Jesuit Missions in North America* (New York, 1846), Du Poisson to Patouillet, 1727, pp. 258-59.

custom among the natives is to divide the presents even among the smaller children" so that the parents benefited from the portions which the very young could not use.[14] Likewise, the abbé Picquet described in detail the return of his exploratory party to Fort Frontenac (July 19, 1751) and the ceremonies which marked that occasion. Canoes lined up in equal numbers on each side of the harbour, three flags were raised, and gun salutes were fired before the gift exchanges took place.[15]

Sometimes the ceremonial observances led to disputes over precedence and matters of a similar order, in America as in Europe. When De Céleron arranged a parley with Iroquois villagers in the Ohio valley a heated exchange took place over the location of the council, the natives insisting it should take place in the "cabin designated for Council meetings" and the French commandant holding out for the principle that "it is up to the children to come to hear the father's word at the place where he lights his fire."[16] The French succeeded in establishing the fact that on this occasion they were the hosts, and so the consultation and presentations proceeded without further difficulties.

The observances associated with these assemblies often included the calumet ceremony, a ritual which might involve singing and dancing as well as smoking sacred tobacco, and which has come down in popular literature and parlance as "smoking the peace pipe". Father Du Poisson's experience with the Arkansas, to which reference has already been made, illustrates the obligations that befell the honoured visitor or guest. The Arkansas, their bodies painted in gaudy colours and adorned with the tails of wild cats and tinkling bells, asked the missionary to come "sing the calumet", but he declined because, as he said, "I was not at all like the French chiefs who command warriors, and who came with plunder to make them presents." They insisted, so two days later he agreed to participate "without design", that is, without the obligation to offer any gifts. He was importuned a third time by some young people who wanted to "dance the calumet" for him, so he consented and offered the dancers some maize cooked in a huge borrowed kettle.[17]

Pierre Liette described "singing the calumet" as a ritual meant to indicate honour and respect as well as peaceful preoccupations.

---

14. *P.A.C.*, MG18, K5, Papiers Franquet, Vol. II, Voyage de Québec, 1752, p. 49; *Voyages et Mémoires sur le Canada* (Québec, 1889), p. 36.

15. *P.A.C.*, MG1, Series C[11]E, Vol. 13, Journal of abbé Picquet, July 13, 1751, pp. 253-54.

16. *P.A.C.*, MG1, Series C[11]E, Vol. 13, Relation of Father de Bonnecamp, 1749, p. 316.

17. Kip, *op. cit.*, p. 258.

When honouring an individual they sent forerunners to announce their intention, then sang his praises all night "and afterwards they give gifts according to the ability of each one and in accordance with the honour deserved by the one to whom they sing the calumet and the esteem in which they hold him."[18] Nicolas Perrot said that in addition to honouring a leader it was a pledge of alliance and support:

> When the calumet is presented and sung to him, obedience is due to him from the people of the tribe. The calumet constrains and pledges those who have sung it to follow to war the man in whose honour it has been sung. . . .[19]

The singing of the calumet, or ceremonial smoking of the long-stemmed pipe, in honour of the Governor-General, *Onontio*, at Montreal or Quebec should be interpreted in the same manner. All councils or assemblies, it was reported to Versailles, "invariably terminated with a distribution of presents" to the chiefs, taking into account "the number who have attended the assembly, the importance of the business for which the meeting was called, and the greater or lesser consideration the Village with which one has entered into negotiations merits."[20] This was popularly referred to as "speaking with the hand" or "making words".

As has already been intimated, presents were given also to avoid revenge being taken on a clan, or even an entire village, for a murder or accidental death. Nicolas Perrot observed that "all the old men come together, make up among themselves a considerable present, and send it by deputies, in order to come to an agreement regarding means to arrest vengeance. . . ." If this failed, in order to protect the village "they induce the relatives, by dint of presents, to deliver the guilty man to his comrades, who break his head and then cut it off to send to the dead man's relatives."[21] This native justice went beyond punishment of the guilty party to incorporate a principle of compensation to the victim or his relatives. The Hurons presented Champlain with gifts in 1633 to compensate for the murder of the *truchement* Étienne Brûlé. Champlain not only thanked them and absolved them of all blame, calling Brûlé a renegade and traitor

---

18. Milton M. Quaife, ed., *The Western Country in the 17th Century: The Memoirs of Antoine Lamothe Cadillac and Pierre Liette* (Chicago, 1947), p. 165.

19. Emma H. Blair, ed., *The Indian Tribes of the Upper Mississippi Valley and Region of the Great Lakes* (Cleveland, 1911), p. 185.

20. *P.A.C.*, MG17, A 7-1, Vol. 4, No. 38, « Mémoire en forme d'observation sur les postes », pp. 3020-21.

21. Blair, *op. cit.*, p. 141.

worthy of an ignoble end, but he also seized the initiative to bind them more firmly to the French cause by reciprocating with presents. The *Mercure François* reported:

> Continuing his discourse, he made them the present of kettles, axes, swords, knives, metal arrowheads and other sundries, telling them that in return he was offering them these presents to preserve them always in our friendship, to incite them to come to visit us and to testify to the goodwill we bore them, and that as an earnest of our friendship there were six Frenchmen who wished to go to their country, among others three Jesuit Fathers. . . .[22]

This was not an isolated incident. A smallpox epidemic swept New France in 1717 and among its victims claimed three of six Fox hostages (including chief Pémoussa) being held at Montreal. As word spread to the Upper Country and the reopening of the Fox War seemed probable, de Louvigny thought it wise to go up to Michilimackinac with one of the surviving hostages, a chief who had lost one eye to the ravages of smallpox, to reassure the Fox delegation, to offer presents "to cover the dead hostages" and so induce the tribe to come down to Montreal to ratify the terms of peace.[23]

When an Amerindian notable died at the hospital in Quebec it was always thought necessary to bury him with proper honours and to "display the presents on the grave of the deceased" in order "to lament the dead and to cover his body." Sister Duplessis de Ste-Hélène listed the kinds of presents which were appropriate to such an occasion and to such a ranking individual: "a few red and blue blankets, a few guns, a few pointed knives, a few twists of tobacco." As each one presented his gift he explained its significance: "one will be to dry away the tears, another to wash away the blood shed, another to renew courage, another to calm the spirits or to unite the hearts, and so on for the others."[24]

The adoption of native expressions is remarkable. The death of the missionary Father Rasle so disturbed the Abenakis that Louis XV was induced to send fifteen blankets and forty pounds of tobacco to four of their villages "to cover their grief" at the loss of their spiritual and military advisor. Father de la Chasse, who saw to the distribution of the presents, used the native terminology of "covering" Father Rasle, not burying him.[25]

---

22. *Dix-neufviesme Tome du Mercure Françoiz, ou Suitte de l'histoire de nostre temps* (Paris, 1636), p. 851.

23. F. Emile Audet, *Les Premiers Établissements Français au Pays des Illinois* (Paris, 1938), pp. 83-84.

24. *P.A.C.*, MG3, Series T, Carton 77, Sr. Duplessis de Ste-Hélène to Mme Hecquert, October 17, 1723, pp. 32-33.

25. J. P. Baxter, *The Pioneers of New France in New England* (Albany, 1894), King to Vaudreuil & Chazel, May 15, 1724, p. 272.

Presents were offered also in the context of the fur trade. In fact, the gift-giving ceremonies were an essential prelude to barter. Both parties presented some valuable or spectacular gifts to create an atmosphere of generosity and goodwill. The chief was often given a complete suit of clothes. Alcohol, if given at this time, was carefully rationed in order to avoid abuses, although some unscrupulous traders were not above attempting to defraud their clients and partners by intoxicating them. Bacqueville de la Potherie's description of the ritual at a northern post may be taken as an account of a typical bartering session in the Upper Country. He said that "the Chief of a Nation enters the Fort with one or two of his most distinguished Natives. The person who is in command first offers them a gift consisting of a pipe and some tobacco." There followed an exchange of salutations and good wishes, they smoked together, and then the chief went out to tell his trading party how he had been received. Upon re-entering the fort he presented the commandant with a few choice pelts.[26] There was some haggling over the quality of the goods to be traded, each side boasting of the high quality of its products and diplomatically pointing out the defects in the other's goods. The Amerindians were skilful bargainers who knew precisely what quality they could demand and what quantity constituted a reasonable exchange for their furs in a competitive situation. The commandant then presented pipes and tobacco for all the trading captains and the actual bartering took place outside the fort. There was much haggling between individual members of the trading parties. Not infrequently the Amerindians threatened to go to the English, pointing out the deficiencies or poor quality of certain French items and denouncing any attempt to give them short measure. Once the furs had all been traded a feast was made, with the Europeans providing a huge kettle of peas and corn flavoured with prunes and molasses. The ceremonial smoking of the calumet was again observed, followed by frenzied dancing and the distribution of more tobacco, and sometimes of brandy. The Amerindian trading captains redistributed what they had received in the preliminary gift-giving ceremonies among all the members of their trading party. This principle of equality was so strictly observed that sometimes the chief or leading trading captain was left with nothing of his suit of clothes except the hat, a symbol of his office.

The French never dominated the fur-trading territories and bands. They were forced to bribe, plead, and cajole support from the

---

26. Bacqueville de la Potherie, *Histoire de l'Amérique septentrionale* (Paris, 1722), Vol. I, pp. 179-80.

natives who controlled the trade. A monopoly proclaimed in France still had to be enforced in the colony. Thus it was the French befriended the Montagnais to control the Saguenay trade, and the Hurons to control the Upper Country trade, but they were frustrated by Iroquois enmity in their attempt to gain control of the Hudson river trade. The most effective way to exercise influence was through the giving of presents, an approach which became standardized and institutionalized as the annual distribution of the King's presents. These annual ceremonies were held first at the Montreal trade fair, then at Mobile for Louisiana, at Michilimackinac for the Upper Country, at Port Royal and later on Cape Breton for the Acadian region, and finally at Lévis in the closing years of the French régime.

A couple of incidents will suffice to illustrate the importance of presents in the fur trade. Le Sueur, working in the interests of Governor Frontenac among others, tried to convince the Sioux to settle in permanent villages, take up agriculture and give up hunting beaver (which brought them into conflict with the Cree and Assiniboines, whom the French were attempting to wean away from the Hudson Bay trade) to take up trapping other animals for the French trade. The account of these negotiations concluded:

> . . . and as it is the Indian custom to accompany their words with a present proportioned to the affair treated of, he gave them fifty pounds of powder, and as many of balls, six guns, ten hatchets, twelve fathoms of tobacco, and a steel calumet.[27]

La Vérendrye, three decades later, found it impossible to winter successfully with the Mandans and pursue his search for the Western Sea because of the loss of his presents, stolen by an Assiniboine, and other reverses.[28] The role of presents was so crucial that post commanders and others to whom the trade was farmed out had a guarantee inserted in their contracts. A typical stipulation ran as follows:

> If His Majesty is obliged to make some extraordinary expenditures in the said post of the Miamis, whether on occasion of war or of the shifting of some Indian village, the farmer shall be required to furnish the comman-

---

27. J. G. Shea, ed., *Early Voyages Up and Down the Mississippi* (Albany, 1861), "Voyage up the Mississippi in 1699-1700 by Mr. Le Sueur", p. 109; *A.S.Q.*, Lettres R, No. 50, Bergier to Laval, March 13, 1702; Thwaites, *Jesuit Relations*, Vol. LXVI, Gravier to Lamberville, March 25, 1702, pp. 32-34.

28. Pierre Margry, ed., *Découvertes et Établissements des Français dans l'Ouest et dans le Sud de l'Amérique septentrionale, 1614-1754* (Paris, 1888), Vol. VI, La Vérendrye to Minister, October 31, 1744, pp. 590-91.

dant with the goods necessary to make the proper presents. For these goods the farmer shall be paid by the King at 30 per cent above the original cost.[29]

Such stipulations left no doubt about the frequency and importance of the giving of presents.

Presents came to be offered most frequently in the military context. The Governor gave present for present, speech for speech, when he wanted to win allies. The most spectacular such occasion may have been the signing of peace with the Iroquois and the renewal of alliances with the interior tribes at Montreal in August 1701. The observances, held in a spacious temporary hall erected on a large plain outside the walls of Montreal, included (in addition to the usual harangues, gift exchanges, gargantuan feast, and calumet ceremonies) the singing of a *Te Deum*, the firing of musketry and cannon, ceremonial entries and retreats, and evening fireworks and a *feu de joie*.[30] The fact that France was at war with England required the continued pacification of both friend and foe, even after the accords signed in 1701. Versailles was asked to clarify its policy in the Governor's dispatches of the following year:

> Numerous natives came to Quebec upon news of the war between the English and ourselves, some to assure us of their strict neutrality and others to take up our part. M. de Callières had presents given them to bind them to our interests. I greatly apprehend, Monseigneur, that these natives will involve us in great expenses. I beg you to prescribe whether I must restrict myself to the fund you have set up for that purpose. The sojourn they make at Quebec costs so much that M. de Champigny (the Intendant) has advised me to have prepared a kind of redoubt which adjoins the palace garden to lodge and feed them there. That would cost the King half as much. . . .[31]

Presents were becoming confused with war expenditures and with wages for services rendered the troops. The distinction was never clear in the *état du roy* and probably was even less clear in the minds of the native beneficiaries. Their claim to generous presents was not only legitimized but had become somewhat institutionalized as French-British rivalry became more intense in North America.

---

29. T. C. Pease, ed., *Collections of the Illinois State Historical Library* (Springfield, 1940), "Agreement for trade at a Miami post", April 10, 1747, Vol. XXIX, p. 29. Translation corrected by author.

30. E. B. O'Callaghan, ed., *Documents relating to the Colonial History of the State of New York* (Albany, 1885), Vol. IX, pp. 718-24; Victor Morin, *Les Médailles décernées aux Indiens* (Ottawa, 1916), pp. 72-74.

31. *P.A.C.*, MG1, Series C[11]A, Vol. 20, Beauharnois to Minister, November 11, 1702, pp. 110-11.

Although the Iroquois had desired the cessation of their long-standing hostilities with the French (1609-1701), it also became apparent that the French required Iroquois neutrality for the success of their various North American enterprises. The Intendant confided in 1709 that although it seemed unlikely the Five Nations would again attack the French settlements, it remained essential "to deal very tactfully with these nations and give them presents from time to time" because renewed hostilities would cause the French "great expenses, hinder the cultivation of the land, and daily threaten the inhabitants of the island of Montreal and those who go off to war with torture at the hands of these people."[32] Presents were a means of purchasing the neutrality of potential enemies.

They were just as important in keeping traditional allies content—such as the Micmacs of the Acadian region. These friendly bands had had to move farther inland and adopt a more dispersed settlement pattern as a result of intensified warfare. They came to rely more and more on presents and on the booty acquired through acts of piracy against the English. Their missionary, who had virtually acquired the role of a *shaman* among them, was reminded in 1711 that "the distribution of supplies and ammunition be made with restraint so these last until the end of the winter when you will receive more substantial assistance." Provisions were received not just as presents from the King but as necessary relief supplies to ward off famine which was, at least in part, a consequence of Micmac attachment to the French cause. The abbé Gaulin reported that in spite of the presents the English gave them, the Micmacs remained well disposed to the French; nevertheless, "as there is no more powder left in the country without which the natives cannot survive" he feared the outcome of the ensuing winter.[33]

Similarly, when the New Englanders put more pressure on the Abenakis in the 1720s, the northern tribes turned to the French for support, and they were rewarded with "the yearly presents sent by the King of France."[34] The royal officials at Quebec felt that "it is presents alone that have attached them to us" and that unfortunately "they would have become much more useful had it been possible to subdue them little by little" so they could have become "good citizens"

---

32. *P.A.C.*, MG1, Series C¹¹G, Vol. 4, Raudot the younger to Minister, November 1, 1709, p. 229.

33. *Archives Acadiennes*, Series 1.5-15, Minister to Gaulin, March 30, 1711; Series 1.5-13, Gaulin to Council of Marine, October 1, 1712.

34. W. E. Daugherty, *Maritime Indian Treaties in Historical Perspective* (Ottawa, 1981), p. 25; *P.A.C.*, MG11, A17, Armstrong to Newcastle, 1726, p. 65.

and Christians.[35] As it turned out, they became as firmly attached to their missionaries and the French cause as the Micmacs.

In the late 1740s, a series of minor "revolts" among the allied tribes of the Great Lakes region forced the French to increase the amount of presents and supplies. For a few years a steady procession of Nipissing, Ottawa, Huron, Sauk, Fox, Potawatomi, Winnebago, and Illinois chiefs were entertained by French officers at Montreal. They always returned with arms, brandy, tobacco, and clothing. One officer stationed at Detroit warned that the Upper Country tribes had to be assured of receiving presents regularly; nevertheless, it was equally important that "the persons who head it up manage the presents which the King will offer them in such a way that there not be too many for this would discourage the hunt."[36] In 1754 Governor Duquesne reprimanded an officer in the Ohio valley for having sold essential supplies rather than having offered them as presents, an action which "rendered vile the King's dignity."[37] Abuses had to be avoided. Macarty, on the other hand, took measures to keep the tribes well satisfied, and informed Quebec that "as feeding the Indian costs considerably, it would be well to prepare a refuge for them where they could be furnished with provisions from the warehouse."[38] The situation was becoming quite tense as English presents were finding their way up-country in increasing quantity: "one sees only the most magnificent gold, silver and scarlet braid" reported one commandant, who had only "the most common goods" to offer as counter-presents.[39]

During the Seven Years' War the situation became even more critical and presents were proportionately more important. The residents of Ft. Beauséjour, for example, told the Minister of the Marine that the Micmacs there were in immediate need of flour and other supplies because they had abandoned their homes "to attach themselves to the French".[40] In the St. Lawrence Valley the problem was

---

35. Isabelle Perrault, « On Débarque en Nouvelle-France », *Recherches Amérindiennes au Québec* XI, no. 2 (1981), Beauharnois & Hocquart to Minister, 1730, p. 106.

36. *Rapport de l'archiviste de la Province de Québec, 1926-1927* (Québec, 1927), Journal of Chaussegros de Léry's campaign of 1749, p. 337.

37. Fernand Grenier, ed., *Papiers Contrecoeur et autres documents* (Québec, 1952), Duquesne to Contrecoeur, January 27, 1754, p. 95.

38. Pease, *Collections*, Vol. XXIX, Macarty & Buchet to Vaudreuil, January 15, 1752, p. 428.

39. Grenier, *Papiers Contrecoeur*, La Chauvignerie to Saint-Pierre, February 10, 1754, p. 100.

40. *P.A.C.*, MG18, F12, Pichon Papers, Vol. I, No. 25, Habitants of Fort Beauséjour to Rouillé, 1753, p. 184.

equally pressing by 1757. As one officer wrote, available foodstuffs had been requisitioned in all the seigneuries, hoarders and profiteers were taking advantage of the situation, numerous prisoners of war were a drain on supplies, and the Amerindians were especially burdensome because "they consume an infinite amount of goods as those who are at war have supplies issued for their old people, their wives and children."[41] Montcalm was quite agreeable to sending an officer with 80,000 pounds of supplies and a dozen blacksmiths and armourers, at the King's expense, to the villages of the Iroquois and Loups to keep them from accepting tantalizing offers made by New York and Pennsylvania agents.[42] Presents had become an important item in the imperial contest. The striking of special medals to honour loyal chieftains, first undertaken in the early seventeenth century to promote missions and the fur trade, was now used to arouse and sustain enthusiasm for France's military operations.[43]

The prominent role ascribed to presents raises the question whether the French developed a clearly enunciated policy on the matter. It would seem that the giving of presents, as practised by individual traders and missionaries and official exploratory and military expeditions, was kept within the framework of Amerindian ceremonial exchanges in the seventeenth century. However, by 1701, if not earlier, presents were given in the Upper Country in return for acquiescence in the stationing of French garrisons and the flow of furs to the St. Lawrence Valley. By this time many *coureurs-de-bois* were taking brandy into the hinterland. Also, a few French had started trading with the English as far distant as Carolina. These "disorders" and irregularities required prompt action by the authorities. Accordingly, Governor and Intendant tried to impress on Versailles the urgency of the situation, the need to continue making generous gifts in spite of metropolitan directives to curtail expenditures:

> We will do our best to diminish, as much as possible, the presents we will be obliged to make to the Natives, but we cannot dispense in the present situation with giving them considerable presents, as we have had the honour to inform you before. The natives give no gifts after we give them some. In fact, when we give them something, it is ordinarily when they are ready to leave and when they have finished their bartering, nothing being left of their peltries. The Chevalier de Callières has forbidden the officers who command at Ft. Frontenac and at Detroit to accept any.[44]

41. Charles Coste, ed., *Aventures militaires au XVIIIᵉ siècle d'après les Mémoires de Jean-Baptiste d'Aleyrac* (Paris, 1935), p. 50.

42. H. R. Casgrain, ed., *Lettres de M. de Bourlamaque au Chevalier de Lévis* (Québec, 1891), Montcalm to Bourlamaque, April 10, 1758, pp. 227-28.

43. Morin, *op. cit.*, pp. 11-21.

44. Margry, *Découvertes*, Vol. V, Callières & Champigny to Minister, October 5, 1701, p. 360.

Royal presents were supposed to be a regular annual token of the King's interest in native welfare.

Versailles was anxious that they not become too great a drain on colonial expenditures and not be regarded by the Amerindians as payments for their co-operation—tribute, which in fact they were becoming. The royal response to the colonial Governor acknowledged that the King "finds it good to continue to offer to these natives the presents which the Intendant and he esteem necessary to maintain them in obedience and to draw them little by little to a knowledge and worship of the true God." The key statement setting out policy ran as follows:

> His Majesty is pleased to have them observe with regard to these presents that they must be given without profusion and with a great knowledge of the needs of these Natives, in order that they look upon them as relief for their needs coming from His Majesty's goodness and charity and not as a means of continuing their disorders, nor as the price of our friendship.[45]

The royal instructions to Governor and Intendant repeated the same sentiments in 1703, saying explicitly that "there is always the inconvenience in this kind of presents that the natives regard them as necessary recompense on which they can count."[46]

The problem of increasing costs plagued successive royal officials. Beauharnois told the Minister of the Marine in 1703 that the budget for presents was "so great and so unpredictable" that it was impossible to keep it within the limits stipulated in the *état du roy*, the statement of royal allocation of funds most closely resembling a budget under the *Ancien Régime*.[47] Four years later, Louis XIV ordered a gradual attrition of this expenditure, leaving it to the colonial officials to devise a means of cutting back and eventually dispensing completely with presents. The orders read:

> His Majesty would be very pleased if the giving of presents to the Natives could be dispensed with because it creates an immense expenditure which it is necessary to avoid; besides, it renders them lazy and causes them to regard presents as things which are due them if we give them ordinarily. If, as you pretend, it is impossible to dispense with continuing to give them in order to retain these Natives in the French interest, they must be reduced, little by little, until such time as they can be cut off entirely, and to that end you must direct your attention.[48]

---

45. *P.A.C.*, MG1, Series B, Vol. 23-1, King to Callières, 1702, p. 137.

46. *P.A.C.*, MG1, Series B, Vol. 23 (3), King's memo to Callières & Beauharnois, May 30, 1703, pp. 73-74.

47. *P.A.C.*, MG1, Series C^{11}A, Vol. 21, Beauharnois to Minister, November 16, 1703, p. 172.

48. *Nouvelle-France. Documents historiques* (Québec, 1893), Vol. I, King to Vaudreuil, June 30, 1707, p. 52.

But the presents were never reduced, because the colony was caught up in international warfare, as has been stated.

Moreover, the Crown became aware of an abuse in the distribution of presents. In 1709, those in charge of giving out the King's presents were prohibited from keeping the gifts which the Amerindians sometimes presented in return. The interpreters were also guilty of this practice. Instead, to reduce the colonial expenditures, such gifts made by Amerindians were to be credited to the King's account. Governor Vaudreuil, in particular, was held accountable. The Minister of the Marine sent the following instructions:

> I am informed that the natives who come to Montreal complain about the presents that are demanded of them under your orders, and as I am informed that this has a bad effect and often leaves these Natives unable to buy the merchandise they require and their complaints have reached even His Majesty: His Majesty has ordered me to forbid you to exact any gifts, nor to accept any even if they wished to offer some out of goodwill, because of the inconveniences that this entails, especially on the part of interpreters and other people who are in charge of your interests in this matter. You must prohibit this practice in the future.[49]

Royal officials were expected to profit from their offices, there being no clear distinction as yet between personal and public affairs; nevertheless such perquisites of office must never injure public welfare. The Intendant Raudot responded to the Minister's communication with the observation that many of the military officers in the country seemed to profit from their commands. For example, Joncaire, the interpreter among the Iroquois, received 400 *livres* salary plus another 300 *livres* for his expenses, and he probably made as much again from presents from the natives; but, as Raudot said, "it is a matter difficult to ascertain if true or not."[50]

In 1716, after the Treaty of Utrecht (1713) and the death of Louis XIV, Governor Vaudreuil asked for 30,000 *livres* worth of presents annually to cement the native alliances. French powder and ball were specifically identified as being in great demand because the Amerindians deemed it far superior in quality to what the English offered.[51] The Council of Marine held the line at 22,000 *livres*, or the maximum amount that had been allocated for presents during the

---

49. *P.A.C.*, MG1, Series B, Vol. 30 (2), Minister to Vaudreuil, July 6, 1709, pp. 359-60; *ibid.*, Minister to Raudot, July 6, 1709, p. 319.

50. *P.A.C.*, MG1, Series C¹¹G, Vol. 4, Raudot the younger to Minister, November 1, 1709, pp. 201-202.

51. *P.A.C.*, MG1, Series C¹¹A, Vol. 36, Memorandum of Vaudreuil to Duke of Orleans, February 1716, pp. 118-19.

late war.[52] Vaudreuil did obtain a special allocation of 2,000 *livres* for the Micmacs whose territory was now largely under British sovereignty. In 1723, an additional 2,000 *livres* was allocated to the hard-pressed Abenakis, who resented English encroachments on their lands, and the following year the amount was doubled when most of them decided to remove to Canada, where reserves were set aside for them. In 1728, the allocation was camouflaged somewhat, since it was now a present made to all Abenakis, by taking the 4,000 *livres* from the income of the Royal Domain in Canada "under the name of the Jesuits".[53] By 1724 the giving of presents had become regularized in the Acadian region and each year the Governor at Louisbourg went to Port Toulouse and Port La Joye to give the Micmacs the King's present. The annual allocation in 1725 was 2,950 *livres* and it rose each year until it reached 3,179 *livres* in 1730, and even more dramatically until it reached 5,581 *livres* in 1735.[54] This amount did not include other expenditures such as the stipend paid to missionaries and the wages of interpreters and smiths. Nor did it include bounties and redemption of prisoners of war.

In the face of a deteriorating situation in the Upper Country, the annual presents allocated to Canada were also increased in time, rather than diminished as ordered by the Crown. The ordinary allowance had been fixed at 22,000 *livres* annually but the average annual presents between 1736 and 1739 amounted to 25,400 *livres*, and rose to an annual average of 59,500 *livres* for the period 1741 to 1744.[55]

In 1739, the Ministry of the Marine revived Louis XIV's policy of cutting back on presents. The Intendant Hocquart tried to make the necessary reductions but he was faced with angry reactions from Governor Beauharnois and the military establishment in the colony. The large contingents of western tribesmen who came to confer with the Governor each year (and whose services were useful in the wars waged against hostile tribes in the lower Mississippi region) expected their presents, as usual, and they were not pleased when they learned that even the benefits accorded to interpreters and black-

52. *P.A.C.*, MG1, Series C[11]A, Vol. 37, Deliberations of Council of Marine, February 3, 1717, pp. 82-91.

53. Thomas M. Charland, *Les Abénakis d'Odanak* (Montréal, 1964), pp. 63-66.

54. *P.A.C.*, MG1, Series D[2]D, Carton No. 1, Expenses of Isle Royale, 1724-1745.

55. J. Dale Standen, "Politics, Patronage, and the Imperial Interest: Charles de Beauharnais's Disputes with Gilles Hocquart", *Canadian Historical Review* LX, no. 1 (March, 1979), 26.

smiths in the Upper Country were to be curtailed.[56] In the end, austerity was not imposed. Instead, costs and prices rose dramatically after fighting between Britain and France resumed in 1744, and shipments of goods (which did not always reach the North American colony) were augmented especially "on the King's account to satisfy the need for presents which His Majesty made to the Natives in recompense for the services rendered during the war", as one merchant wrote a decade later.[57]

In 1749, the royal policy was again explained to Governor La Jonquière in the following terms:

> The greater part of the nations are accustomed to send in the spring of each year some deputies to Montreal to receive the presents of munitions and merchandise which is destined for them and the distribution of which is regulated by the Governor and Lieutenant-General, who goes to this town in the month of May to see to this distribution and to the negotiation of the affairs concerning these nations.[58]

The distribution of presents was associated with a renegotiation of the alliances. There were also gift-giving ceremonies in the hinterland—at Michilimackinac, Detroit, and Kaskaskia—which added to the expenditures. In 1751 the commandant in the Illinois country was informed of the colonial practice which he should observe:

> The presents of the natives of the Illinois country were fixed at the time of Mr. de Bienville at 3000 [*livres*] French prices which should make six thousand livres in the Illinois country. Mr. de Macarty will always conform to this regulation in the distribution he will undertake of trade goods which will be sent him for that post, of which he will have a choice on everything.[59]

The fact that commanding officers could profit from the distribution of presents was considered a legitimate perquisite of office. Governor Duquesne explained to an officer in the Ohio country that among the remunerations he could accept "without hurting your propriety or your conscience" was "all that the Natives will give you when you

56. *P.A.C.*, MG1, Series C[11]A, Vol. 71, Beauharnois to Maurepas, November 5, 1739, fol. 84-84v; Vol. 73, Hocquart to Maurepas, November 5, 1739, fol. 84-84v; Vol. 73, Hocquart to Maurepas, October 31, 1740, fol. 335; Vol. 76, Hocquart to Maurepas, October 30, 1741, fol. 57.

57. Anonymous, *Réflections sommaires sur le Commerce qui s'est fait en Canada* (Québec, 1840), p. 2. Pamphlet written shortly after 1763.

58. *P.A.C.*, MG1, G1, La Jonquière Papers, King to La Jonquière, April 30, 1749, p. 11.

59. Huntingdon Library, Vaudreuil Papers, LO 325, Vaudreuil to Macarty, August 8, 1751, p. 16.

distribute the presents the King gives them to consolidate our establishment in the Ohio."[60] It would appear that the royal officials at Quebec were just as interested in keeping Canadian officers in the *Troupes de la Marine* contented as they were in conciliating the Amerindians.

Early in their contact with Amerindian traders and warriors the French were drawn into the native gift-giving complex. Presents to the Amerindians were given on ceremonial occasions but came quickly to be essential components of commercial and military negotiations. The ceremonial aspects, together with their symbolic character, continued to be an important feature of the rituals by which French and Amerindians expressed their mutual relationship. French culture attached great importance to etiquette, precedence, and protocol, so that there was an immediate receptivity and appreciation of North American formalities and practices in this domain. There seems to have been a genuine enjoyment on the part of certain pompous Governors of the protracted ceremonies and harangues of condolence, watering the roots of peace, burying the hatchet, or covering the dead. Some military officers found the formalities somewhat tedious, to be sure. But all were agreed they were indispensable to the maintenance of good relations with the tribes and bands.

Presents involved more than diplomatic courtesies. They became the essential element in the maintenance of good relations, whether in trade, mission work, exploration, or military affairs. Gift-giving was an obligation from which the Europeans could not excuse themselves with impunity. In Amerindian societies the giving of presents had imposed obligations on the recipients, but in the cross-cultural exchange it was the French as donors who also found themselves obliged to continue a practice which became more costly in proportion to their perceived dependency on the native population.

What were the consequences of the alacrity with which the French adopted the practice of gift-giving in North America? Undoubtedly, it bound many bands and tribes to the French cause. But the alliances seemed to require regular reaffirmation, so that if presents were the cement that bound European and Amerindian it may be said, to continue the imagery, that the cement needed frequent restoration. The English, during the same period, were never as successful as the French in winning over and holding the natives to their cause, although they too assumed the burden of giving annual presents.

---

60. Grenier, *Papers Contrecoeur*, Duquesne to Contrecoeur, January 27, 1754, p. 94.

The price exacted on the French treasury was deemed to be
too high, yet in spite of official instructions from the opening decade
of the eighteenth century onwards to gradually reduce the amount
spent on presents until they were completely eliminated, the allocations kept rising. At the end of the War of the Spanish Succession
the *présents ordinaires* were fixed at 22,000 *livres* for Canada and
2,000 *livres* for the Micmacs at Isle Royale. Thirty years later the
expenditures for presents had risen to over 55,000 *livres* in Canada
and over 5,500 *livres* at Isle Royale, not including payments for services rendered, extraordinary military expenditures (such as in the
Chickasaw campaigns), payments to interpreters and skilled work-
men, or stipends to missionaries who acted as diplomatic agents.

It is also possible that the giving of presents had the long-term
effect of acculturating to some degree the Amerindians because they
came to depend more and more on European goods such as arms,
hardware, textiles, clothes, and jewellery. Gunsmiths, blacksmiths,
and locksmiths became important to native villagers. Some tribesmen may even have become lazy as a result of an excessive inflow
of presents. On the other hand, it can be argued, using the case of
the Micmacs after the Treaty of Utrecht, that increased French
presents, while making them dependent, also stimulated their pride
because they saw the French as paying tribute for resources used and
compensation for resources lost. Presents were almost a retainer fee
for future services from the tribes of the Upper Country of Canada.

Finally, it is an incontrovertible fact that the French had also
come into a relationship of dependency. The success of their trade,
their missions and their military presence in the Interior depended
on the consent, favour, and support of the various tribes. Indeed,
their survival and security were tied to a continuing amicable relationship nourished on a regular basis by an increasing amount of
presents. The Crown ordered a curtailment of the expenditures on
presents, as we have stated; nevertheless the economic and politico-
military situation was such that expenditures rose steadily. The tribes
remained loyal to the French cause, by and large, but the price paid
for this attachment was high. Even after the fall of Quebec (1759)
and Montreal (1760) the tribes were willing to contemplate supporting a returning French force of the Great Onontio (Louis XV), who
was said to be temporarily "weak on his legs". It was not surprising,
therefore, that the British should have assumed the burden of annual
presents as the price to be paid for conciliating the Amerindians to
the realities of the Conquest.

12. Moose Factory was not Red River

A Comparison of Mixed-Blood Experiences

Carol M. Judd

Heritage Enterprises, Ottawa

For the past several years students of the fur trade have expressed differing opinions about what to call the people of mixed ancestry who were the children and grandchildren of fur traders and Indian or biracial women.[1] Acknowledging that these people, even within the often-studied community of Red River, did not form a single homogeneous group, scholars have also disagreed over what distinguished or separated them.

Frits Pannekoek has argued that the "Country-born" (children of English-speaking fathers and native mothers) and Métis (children of fur-trade fathers and Indian or biracial mothers who were brought up in francophone society) were deeply divided by long-standing sectarian and racial conflicts. Sylvia Van Kirk has said that ethnic differences, divergent ambitions, and different levels of group consciousness separated the two groups. I have argued elsewhere that biracial groups differed in employment opportunities—and thus status

---

1. Jennifer S. H. Brown, "Linguistic Solitudes and Changing Social Categories", in Carol M. Judd and Arthur J. Ray, eds., *Old Trails and New Directions: Papers of the Third North American Fur Trade Conference* (University of Toronto Press, 1980), pp. 147-59; John E. Foster, "The Country-born in the Red River Settlement: 1820-1850" (Doctoral dissertation, University of Alberta, 1972), opened the discussion by calling the English-speaking biracial group "country-born", a term that has not gained wide usage. Sylvia Van Kirk, for example, refers to the same group as British-Indian people, or mixed-bloods. See her "What if Mama is an Indian?: the Cultural Ambivalence of the Alexander Ross Family", in John E. Foster, ed., *The Developing West: Essays on Canadian History in Honour of Lewis H. Thomas* (University of Alberta Press, 1983), pp. 123-36. While acknowledging that the word mixed-blood is biologically incorrect, Irene M. Spry uses that term to describe the "Anglophone Rupert's Landers of hybrid Indian and White ancestry" in a paper, "The Mixed-Bloods and Métis of Rupert's Land before 1870", in *The New Peoples: Being and Becoming Métis in North America*, ed. Jacqueline Peterson and Jennifer Brown (Winnipeg: University of Manitoba Press, forthcoming). The use of the word mixed-blood, as in this essay, is thus becoming increasingly popular in describing this group.

Table 1
Characteristics of Biracial Groups at Red River and Moose Factory

Biracial Group	Language	Occupational Choices	Geographic Mobility	Number	Access to Gov't	Temporal Span	Religion	Group Consciousness	Activism	Social Status	Fathers
Red River											
Métis	French Cree Bungee (English)	Buffalo hunting Farming Tripping Carting Fishing Free trade HBC	Great	Perhaps 2500 by 1850	Limited access	60 years	Catholic	High "New Nation"	High (1816, 1870, 1885 plus numerous strikes etc.)	Low	French Canadian, (Scots, Orcadian) servants
Mixed-Blood (Progeny of servants)	English Cree Bungee Gaelic (French)	Buffalo hunting Fishing Farming Free trade Tripping Carting HBC	Great	Perhaps 2500 by 1850	Limited access	50 years	Anglican, Wesleyan	Unknown (probably somewhat less than Métis)	(Unknown— probably moderate to high— numerous strikes)	Low	Orcadian, English, Norwegian (French) servants, traders
Mixed-Blood (Progeny of Officers)	English Cree Bungee (French)	HBC Entrepreneur Farming	Great	Unknown (probably less than 300)	Improved access after c. 1840	50 years	Anglican, Presbyterian	Low to high	High (vocal)	Moderate (some high)	Scottish, Orcadian, English Officers
Moose Factory											
Mixed-Blood (Progeny of servants)	English Cree	HBC Goose Hunters Trappers	None	Perhaps 300 by 1890	None	250 years	Anglican	Low to none	Low to none	Low	Orcadian, English, Scottish, Norwegian Servants

All observations based on data as indicated in essay.

in the community—according to the career levels of their fathers within the hierarchical Hudson's Bay Company. Those who did not aspire to their fathers' positions within the Hudson's Bay Company were sometimes content with menial positions or they chose a native lifestyle. Irene Spry identified two divisions, socio-economic status and lifestyle (hunters and plains traders versus farmers and landlords.)[2] Recently, however, historian Arthur Ray has asked us to look past the blinkers of Red River and its environs and past the sons and daughters of the officer class of fur traders to understand the historical roots of present-day Indian, mixed-blood, and white interaction.[3] He has asked researchers not only to look beyond the present philosophical parameters of biracial studies, but to bring to the task a present-mindedness that does not currently exist.

This essay responds to Ray's appeal. It focuses on the socio-economic conditions, opportunities and behaviour of the mixed-bloods (the mixed-blood "experience") at the Hudson's Bay Company post, Moose Factory, and compares them to those of the much-studied Métis and mixed-bloods of Red River.[4] Rather than enabling a better understanding of the roots of present-day interaction, however, this analysis leads to a quite different conclusion. (See Table 1.)

Moose Factory is situated on an island in the Moose River, about eleven miles from the southern shore of James Bay. Although sharing with Kingston the distinction of being the oldest settlement in Ontario, during the entire period under study Moose Factory looked to London, England, as its metropolis and was to a very large extent cut off both physically and culturally from Canada. Hemmed in by the Canadian Shield to the south and a sea to the north that was frozen

---

2. Frits Pannekoek, "The Rev. Griffiths Owen Corbett and the Red River Civil War of 1869-70", *Canadian Historical Review* LVII, no. 2 (June 1976), 133-49; Sylvia Van Kirk, *op. cit.*; Carol M. Judd, "Native Labour and Social Stratification in the Hudson's Bay Northern Department, 1770-1870", *Review of Canadian Sociology and Anthropology* XVII, no. 4 (Autumn 1980), 304-14; Spry, *op. cit.*

3. Arthur J. Ray, "Reflections on Fur Trade Social History and Métis History in Canada", *American Indian Culture and Research Journal*, VI, no. 2 (1982), Special Métis Issue, 104.

4. This essay is based largely on papers I have previously presented and/or published (but attempts to knit them together to form a new set of conclusions), notably: "Employment Opportunities for Mixed Bloods in the Hudson's Bay Company to 1870", paper presented to the American Historical Association, San Francisco, 1978; "Native Labour and Social Stratification", cited above; "Mixed Bloods of Moose Factory, 1730-1981: A Socio-Economic Study", *American Indian Culture and Research Journal* VI, no. 2 (1982), Special Métis Issue; "Race, Sex and Social Status: Native People of Moose Factory, 1730-1980", paper presented to the Ottawa Historical Society, January 1980; "An Uncommon Heritage: A Brief Social History of Moose Factory", in *Moose Factory Island Heritage Survey*, Amisk Heritage Planning and Research, 1981, for Ontario Ministry of Culture and Recreation; and (Carol M. Livermore) *Lower Fort Garry, the Fur Trade and the Colony of Red River*, Parks Canada, Manuscript Report Series, No. 202, 1976.

for half of the year, Moose Factory was geographically isolated and commanded only a restricted hinterland. In addition, opposition fur traders who penetrated from the south to the height of land that delineated the James Bay watershed did little, for much of the period under study, to change the post's isolation and limited sphere of influence.

Moose Factory was build on a relatively fertile island in an area almost totally made up of muskeg. Certainly the physical environment at Moose was much different from the Red River environment. No buffalo roamed within range of the settlement. No farms sprang up around the post. In fact, Moose Factory had no independent settlement. Only fur traders and their families lived there. At Moose Factory there were just two lifestyle choices: live as a fur trader or live as an Indian. There was no middle road, except perhaps that chosen by the small "homeguard" band of fur-trade provisioners—many if not all of whom had fur-trade roots and were hence mixed-blood—based at Moose.

Moose Factory was nevertheless a critically important fur trade post. For almost two centuries it was the port of entry and administrative centre for the Hudson's Bay Company's operations in the James Bay region. After the mid-eighteenth century it supplied fresh vegetables, beef, butter, lumber, and boats to other James Bay posts, and it was considered an important frontier or "buffer" post, preventing the penetration of opposition fur traders to the richer fur-trade areas to the north. Indeed, in terms of its overall significance, Moose Factory was probably the second most important Hudson's Bay Company fur-trade post. Only York Factory was more important to the Hudson's Bay Company's fur-trade operations.

Moose Factory's mixed-blood community had its origins in the group of natives that came from Albany when it first re-opened in 1730[5] to provide that fur-trade post with geese, fish, and game. These natives, whom the traders called the "home" or "homeguard" Indians, set up their tents on the island and lived symbiotically with the post, providing it with "country provisions" and pelts and receiving from it European goods and foodstuffs. In winter when they left the island to trap furs they left their elderly and infirm behind. During times when their own sources of food failed, the homeguard turned to the post for sustenance and only under the most unusual circumstances were their requests ever denied. When the Hudson's Bay

---

5. Carol M. Judd, "Housing the Homeguard at Moose Factory 1730-1982", *The Canadian Journal of Native Studies* III, no. 1 (1983), 23-37; "Sakie, Esquawenoe, and the Foundation of a Dual-Native Tradition at Moose Factory" (U.B.C. Press, 1984).

Company began opening inland posts in the 1770s to meet their Canadian competitors on their own ground, the Company's manpower needs increased. Natives of the fur-trade regions, both Indians and mixed-bloods (homeguard), began to be employed as tripmen (voyageurs). By the turn of the nineteenth century the Hudson's Bay Company was employing mixed-bloods of Moose Factory as inland travellers, farm workers, tradesmen, and in at least one case, to take charge of an inland post.[6] Many of these men worked on a seasonal basis, but others were hired under contracts of three to five years, similar to those held by European servants.

The mixed-blood employees became ever more integral to the Company's labour force, and by 1809 they were considered so valuable that a school teacher was sent out to provide them with the education necessary for becoming Company administrators. In truth, however, only a few children of officers were able to get enough formal education to keep the Company's accounts.[7]

In 1821, the years of heavy competition with the North West Company came to an end with the amalgamation of the two Companies. The new régime brought significant administrative changes to the Hudson's Bay Company. The old North West Company had been built on a nucleus of Scottish officers (called bourgeois) while the transport labour force was almost invariably French Canadians and Iroquois. The North West Company was therefore composed of two main ranks of employees who were separated by race, culture and native tongue. The Hudson's Bay Company, while tending to hire English or Scottish officers and Orcadian (men from the Orkney Islands north of Scotland) or native servants, had been less rigid. Servants could cross the line between servant and administrator, though, in truth, not many mixed-blood employees did so.[8]

Under the new régime a wide gulf developed between servant and officer which was hardly ever bridged. Thus, with the exception of a few sons of prominent officers, mixed-bloods everywhere were forced to occupy the lower rungs of the Company hierarchy. Nevertheless, their services became increasingly important to the Hudson's Bay Company, which seemed to suffer chronic shortages of non-native labour.[9]

---

6. John Jr., mixed-blood son of John Thomas, factor at Moose, 1782-1813. Judd, "Uncommon Heritage", p. 224.

7. *Ibid.*, p. 245.

8. Jennifer S. H. Brown, *Strangers in Blood: Fur Trade Company Families in Indian Country* (U.B.C. Press, 1980), Chapter 2.

9. Carol M. Judd, "Mixed Bands of Many Nations: 1821-70", in Carol M. Judd and Arthur J. Ray, eds., *op. cit.*

At Moose Factory, while the proportion of mixed-blood employees generally increased, their per-capita share of total salaries paid out between 1822 and 1850 fell substantially.[10] This occurred because the jobs made available to mixed-bloods by 1850 were at the lowest end of the economic scale—largely apprentices and boatmen. At Moose Factory, then, a marked loss of economic opportunity occurred in the first generation after the coalition of 1821, and mixed-blood men lost whatever access they had previously enjoyed to higher-paying and more prestigious positions within the Hudson's Bay Company.[11] By the early part of the twentieth century, however, some mixed-bloods were again occupying positions as skilled tradesmen.[12]

What characteristics identified the mixed-blood community at Moose Factory? They were employed by the Hudson's Bay Company, as workers on the farm that produced beef, milk, and potatoes; as workers on the inland or coastal boats; as wood workers—constructing boats or buildings, chopping firewood, or cutting down trees; or, indirectly, as homeguard provisioners, usually as goose hunters or fishermen. Their only other option was to live in the upland area in Moose Factory's hinterland like Indians, by trapping or by provisioning upland posts. They could not become independent farmers, even if they wanted to, because most of the James Bay lowland was muskeg and therefore unsuited to agriculture. For this reason there was no independent settlement near the post, such as existed at Red River.

They were also few in number. Even by 1890 the total population amounted to only four hundred and fifty in summer and one hundred and fifty in winter.[13] The summer population included upland Indians who camped on the island hoping to work on the farm or the boats, and to fish to supplement their income from furs. It included also the mixed-blood population who worked seasonally for the Company, as well as regular Company employees. In winter both the uplanders and the homeguard left the island to tend their trap lines. Only direct employees of the Company (and the aged and infirm) remained behind at the post. Thus, Moose Factory mixed-bloods were

---

10. In 1822, 23.8 per cent of all employees in the Moose district were mixed-bloods. They earned 20.4 per cent of all salaries. In 1850 mixed-bloods, constituting 35 per cent of the labour force, earned 23 per cent of total wages. Judd, "Mixed Bloods", p. 76.

11. *Ibid.*, pp. 76-78.

12. Ray, *op. cit.*, p. 104.

13. HBC Archives, D.26/16 1890, p. 15, E. B. Borron's Report.

few in number and existed in isolated conditions with little opportunity for vertical mobility. They had a long tradition in the small geographical region (dating from 1730, when Albany homeguards were brought in to provide country produce for the Hudson's Bay Company men who were rebuilding the abandoned post), and they had few occupational choices. For their first one hundred and fifty years they had practically nowhere else to go.

That isolation only began to end in 1873, when the officer in charge of Moose Factory recorded, "The high wages now given to lumberers, miners etc. on the frontier make our men dissatisfied and we are consequently losing more men this season than I had expected."[14] At that time the cutting edge of settlement was some two hundred miles distant, across nearly impassable shield country. Despite James Clouston's alarm, few workers actually left Moose Factory. But the isolation was threatened, if not broken, and the Company watched nervously as civilization slowly encroached on the James Bay hinterland. In 1886, a railway line to James Bay was rumoured to be in the works and the chief officer at Moose Factory noted, "This road would utterly destroy the trade of the Bay, so let us hope that its completion is far off. The nearness of the CPR is detrimental enough."[15] In a few more years, independent fur traders were within reach of Moose and the officer in charge noted, "The tendency of sons of Servants here at present, if the Company do not employ them, is to hang about the opposition and assist them."[16] The Company tried desperately to preserve Moose Factory's isolation and keep the natives away from the railwaymen, miners, and lumbermen who willingly paid much higher prices for their furs than the Hudson's Bay Company. Perhaps the Company's tactics were successful, because the gradual opening up of Northern Ontario to settlement had little real impact on the tiny community on James Bay.[17]

There were, however, a few instances of labour unrest among workers and traders at Moose which may have stemmed from the proximity of the frontier of development. For example, in 1886, the boatmen, apparently hearing of high wages being paid for workers

14. HBCA, A.11/47, Moose Factory Correspondence Outward, James Clouston to W. Armit, Moose Factory, February 25, 1873.

15. HBCA, A.11/47, James Cotter, Moose, February 22, 1887.

16. HBCA, D.20/61, J. Fortescue to Joseph Wrigley, Commissioner, Winnipeg, July 10, 1890, p. 79.

17. HBCA, D.20/66, J. Fortescue to Wrigley, May 18, 1891.

on the CPR line now within ten arduous days' travel of Moose, threatened to strike for more pay. James Cotter yielded in part to their demands. However, he refused the demands of the workers who wanted more pay for bringing in the hay. Despite the threats, work went ahead without any actual stoppage.[18] In 1885, the annual ship bound for London laden with furs had gone aground and eventually burned to the water line. Indians took furs from the wreck and attempted to re-sell them to Cotter. He refused to buy them. As a consequence, in that same summer of 1886, some industrious Indians trekked off to the railway line. According to Joseph Fortescue, who took charge of Moose after Cotter retired, "Their eyes were thus opened to the fact that much higher prices would be paid them along the line of railway than they could get at Moose . . . and great discontent arose among the Indians respecting the price of furs." According to Fortescue, Cotter raised the price of furs and lowered the cost of goods, a fatal mistake which provoked "the failure of Moose as a fairly profitable trading post, in fact the comparative ruin of the Southern Department."[19]

Fortescue's account was highly exaggerated. The truth was that the workers and Indians at Moose were in general incredibly docile and passive. They accepted their fate with little resistance. According to an observer from Toronto in 1890, Magistrate E. B. Borron, children at Moose Factory grew up with only the most perfunctory education, which meant they had little chance of earning a livelihood in the outside world and were doomed to remain at Moose where their prospects were "too sad to be contemplated . . . with other than feelings of deepest solicitude."[20] How accurate was this analysis? One would think that mining, lumbering, and railroad construction did not require an advanced education. Another hypothesis must be proposed. Joseph Fortescue said the men were "unwilling to leave their families even for a day or two."[21] Elsewhere he said, "There is a great unwillingness among native families to separate, they try to hang together even though starvation threatens them."[22] Furthermore, the Company actively tried to keep the natives away from the railway lines, "even at the risk of a [financial] loss."[23]

---

18. HBCA, B.135/e/24, Moose Report 1886, James Cotter to J. Wrigley, August 1, 1886.

19. HBCA, B.135/e/29, p. 23, Moose Report 1891, Joseph Fortescue to S. K. Parson, July 18, 1891.

20. HBCA, D.26/16 1980, p. 46, Borron's Report.

21. HBCA, D.20/58, J. Fortescue to J. Wrigley, Moose Factory, February 1, 1890.

22. HBCA, D.20/61, p. 79f, Fortescue to Wrigley, Moose, July 1, 1890.

23. HBCA. D.20/66, Fortescue to Wrigley, May 18, 1891.

It is quite possible that Borron simply repeated what the officers of the Hudson's Bay Company may have told him, as they likely tried to convince the natives, that there was no place for them in the outside world. The combination of the advice of the Company and strong family bonds may well have tipped the balance to keep the natives away from the frontier.

At Moose Factory there was no community of retired servants or officers gaining an independent livelihood as farmers or traders. At Moose Factory there was no civil government. The Hudson's Bay Company had control of both government and wealth. Here, even the missions were under the sway of the Company. Indeed, until treaty payments were made to status Indians in 1905 there was no cash in circulation. Even after that date, most of the money paid at treaty time usually took only a day or two to reach the Hudson's Bay Company's coffers. Those who dealt with the Hudson's Bay Company, either buying, selling, or earning wages, did so entirely on a basis of credit and debit in the Company's accounts and not by cash transactions.[24]

For more than one hundred and fifty years the only immigration to James Bay was controlled by way of Company ships from London, and Moose Factory was more British than Canadian. Although for much of this time limited communication with Montreal took place, and a few officers from Moose retired to eastern Canada, rivers flowing through the shield (the only means of overland transport) were not avenues for immigration—with the exception of a handful of missionaries—and no French-Canadian Métis are known to have lived at Moose Factory.

Christian missions were late coming to Moose Factory. Wesleyans first arrived in 1840 and remained for seven years. In 1851, a representative of the Church Missionary Society (CMS) took over the empty Wesleyan church and mission residence. Although the Roman Catholic Church would have liked to set up a permanent mission at Moose, Sir George Simpson, the Company's overseas governor, allowed them to use only a seasonal chapel to minister to the Roman Catholic upland Indians who worked on the inland boats.[25] Roman Catholicism therefore gained barely a foothold at Moose. Simpson kept the Roman Catholic Church at bay, he said,

24. HBCA, B.135/a/190, July 26, 1913, for one example; also personal communication Bill Anderson, Albany, July, 1980.

25. Carol M. Judd, "The Changing Faces of Moose Factory", in *Moose Factory Community Heritage Survey*, Amisk Heritage Planning and Research, Ontario Ministry of Culture and Recreation 1981, pp. 91-94.

because their presence would "lead to a conflict of different systems of religion, the effect of which would be injurious to the cause of Christianity and anything but beneficial to the native population."[26] In any case the entire population of the island became devout Anglicans (CMS). Today many of the Indians are Roman Catholics, while the mixed-blood community remains almost entirely Anglican.

Two other important characteristics of the mixed-blood population at Moose Factory need to be identified. The first has already been mentioned in passing—their amazing docility. Despite having few opportunities to "get ahead", despite having no say in their own government, and despite being trapped in a society totally dominated by the only employer in the area, the native people of Moose Factory seldom offered any resistance to their fate. When the outside world first moved a little closer to their community, there were some understandable stirrings and rumblings. Forty years previously, in 1847, when the zealous Wesleyan missionary Reverend George Barnley tried to convince the boatmen that they should not travel on Sundays, and preached collective action against their employer to bring about a change of policy, he provoked some response, but even the threat of hell was not enough to lead them to strike.[27] Thus the Moose Factory mixed-bloods represented little threat to the peaceful and profitable operation of the Company.

Normally, life went on according to a well-established and well-ordered routine, actuated by the needs of the fur trade and moving to the rhythm of the seasons. It would appear from the historical record—more from what it doesn't say than what it says—that the mixed-blood population at Moose Factory quietly accepted their way of life. It had been established for many generations. The closing down in the nineteenth century of opportunities to rise in the employment scale, so apparent in the historical record, happened slowly, perhaps slowly enough to be barely noticed by the participants. Today the oldest residents of Moose Factory look back on the fur-trade period without a visible trace of bitterness or discontent.[28] In fact, at Moose the fur-trade period is remembered nostalgically as a time of proud self-sufficiency, when people formed part of a larger society and worked

---

26. HBCA, D.4/70, Simpson to Robert Miles, December 30, 1848, p. 148.

27. Carol M. Judd, "Staff House Report", prepared for Ontario Heritage Foundation, 1979, ch. 7, pp. 4-6. See also HBCA, B.135/a/151, May 29, 1847; D.4/68, Simpson Outward, 1846, p. 189, Simpson to George Barnley, Red River Settlement, September 14, 1846; D.5/49, p. 550, Robert Miles to Simpson, May 12, 1847.

28. Carol M. Judd, "Through Their Own Eyes: Glimpses of the Past at Moose Factory, Ontario", in *Moose Factory Community Heritage Survey II*, 1982.

together for the common good. Life was simple, there was little or no money, but there was somehow a purpose, a meaning to the struggle for survival. With the construction in 1931 of the Temiskaming and Northern Ontario railway (which had its terminus at Moosonee on the mainland, about three miles from Moose Factory), Moose Factory had ready access to the outside world. Suddenly, goods and people could be imported with ease, and local industry seemed to be no longer necessary. Self-sufficiency became a thing of the past and Moose Factory was drawn into the vortex of modern life. Yet the arrival of a modern economy based largely on tourism brought few new opportunities to the mixed-blood natives. Even now most of the "non-status Indian" community benefits only marginally from the tourist trade and the Hudson's Bay Company has become just another store.

Economically, most of the mixed-bloods at Moose are still in a subordinate position to the white population who comprise the doctors, clerics, teachers, and most of the major entrepreneurs in the region. Children are taught almost exclusively by whites and their fathers work for whites. The Anglican church is still the major focal point of the mixed-blood community. Although a few of the more educated and aggressive mixed-bloods at Moose are beginning to gain access to government and managerial positions, in other important social ways the community as a whole still functions very much within the centuries-old fur-trade social tradition at Moose, and the native people generally still suffer from economic and social marginalization. All but a few still act, at least superficially, in a deferential manner towards whites, both the local residents and visitors.[29] Arthur Ray suggests that this behaviour is a holdover from the "paternalistic mercantile capital system of the fur trade", which he says was swept away in Red River after 1870 but has lingered in the North until the present.[30] Before attempting to analyse why this may have happened, one more unusual characteristic of the mixed-bloods of Moose Factory should be discussed.

This is the lack of evidence that they had any sense of separate identity. At Moose Factory the only immigration was a slow trickle of officers and servants brought in from Britain on the annual ship (even this virtually ceased by the late 1880s),[31] or transferred from

---

29. Personal observation, Summer 1979, 1980, 1981; also Ray, *op. cit.*, p. 104.

30. Ray, *op. cit.*, p. 105.

31. HBCA, A.11/47, Cotter to Armit, February 15, 1886, which may account for the fact that mixed-bloods began to occupy positions as skilled tradesmen by the early twentieth century (see p. 6, footnoted statement 12).

some other part of the North. By 1900, however, communication with Canada was beginning to open up—owing to reports that James Bay was rich in minerals—and "prospectors, railwaymen and other travellers" were reported to be "coming in increasing numbers into the country every year".[32] Even so, only a few actually came. These new arrivals do not seem to have been drawn into the mainstream at Moose, but simply passed through as visitors and observers. The mixed-blood community, therefore, remained a reasonably homogeneous group. Furthermore, except for a handful of unmarried Scots and Orcadian officers and servants and the upland Indians who visited the post, everyone at Moose was of mixed ancestry. They simply did not need to have a strong sense of separateness or nationhood.

This lack of a sense of separate identity has recently been described by historian John Long. In an essay about Thomas Vincent, a mixed-blood missionary for the CMS, born at Moose Factory and educated for the Church at Red River, Long says "Vincent's missionary correspondence reveals no feeling of solidarity with any Métis 'cause'". Vincent claimed to be neither Indian nor European. The closest Long could come to a statement of Vincent's perceived identity was a declaration to a friend, "I was free born, and I think I have the right to exercise my privilege as well as the best Englishman that ever lived."[33] Even the Church, Long argues, had a "caste" theory that set upper limits on the career potential of native men.

Today, older mixed-bloods at Moose Factory do not seem to have a strong sense of racial identity other than being neither Indian nor white, although younger people are beginning to become involved with OMNSIA (Ontario Métis and Non-status Indian Association) and are showing signs of developing a sense of "nationhood".[34]

Why was this sense of identity so slow to appear and so imperfectly developed at Moose? Why were the mixed-bloods so docile and accepting of their fate? In both of these important matters they are very different from the much-studied Red River Métis and most English-speaking mixed-bloods, though perhaps they shared more with the narrow élite group Van Kirk has called the "British-Indians".[35]

---

32. HBCA, A.12/FT, James Bay District, 1901-1915, November 4, 1901.

33. John S. Long, "Archdeacon Thomas Vincent of Moosonee and the Handicap of 'Metis' Racial Status", *Canadian Journal of Native Studies* III, No. 1 (1983), 110-11, citing GSA, CMS, Vincent to Chapman, September 16, 1859, A-98.

34. Personal observation summer 1979, 1980, 1981; also personal communication Mrs. Rubina McLeod, Moose Factory.

35. Van Kirk, *op. cit.*

At Red River there were essentially three more-or-less distinguishable groups of mixed bloods: Métis; native children of high-ranking Hudson's Bay Company officers; and native offspring of English-speaking Hudson's Bay Company servants.[36] Although one must be careful to avoid over-generalization, the Métis groups were frequently buffalo hunters, while the mixed-blood sons of servants seem to have inclined also towards farming. Both groups were engaged as tripmen, and later in carting both for the Hudson's Bay Company and independently. For the sons and daughters of the moneyed élite at Red River, who were educated and chose to follow the career pattern of their fathers, rather than the freer but less secure heritage of their mothers' side, it was difficult to obtain the lifestyle to which they aspired.

The two groups who were children of servants shared a similar low social status but were to some extent distinguishable by language and religious differences, while the élite group shared with many of their lower-status cousins a common religion and language. The gulf between them socially, however, made them widely different. Two of the groups have been quite fully observed—the buffalo-hunting Métis, and the children of the élite. Both groups made a lasting impression on the history of their region. We know somewhat less about the English-speaking children of servants.

The Red River Métis are well known for their proud sense of being a new nation, with a well-developed sense of corporate consciousness[37] based on their rights as natives to the soil and the buffalo hunt.[38] To a large extent descendants of the old North West Company employees, they never seemed to be in awe of the Hudson's Bay Company, and were therefore considered to be hard to manage.[39] Alexander Ross wrote of this group, "so strong is their love for the uncertain pursuit of buffalo-hunting, that when the season arrives, they sacrifice every other consideration in order to indulge

---

36. Judd, "Native Labour", see especially model, p. 309.

37. W. L. Morton, ed., *Alexander Begg's Red River Journal and Other Papers Relative to the Red River Resistance of 1869-70*, Champlain Society, 1956, p. 17.

38. John E. Foster, "Origins of Mixed Bloods in the Canadian West", p. 72.

39. Margaret McLeod and W. L. Morton, *Cuthbert Grant of Grantown*, pp. 87-88. HBCA, D.4/87, fo. 8-9f., George Simpson, 1824: "it is necessary to watch and manage them (Metis) with great care, otherwise they may become the most formidable enemy to which the Settlement is exposed".

in this savage habit. Wedded to it from their infancy, they find no pleasure in anything else.''[40]

The children of the élite were set apart from the other two groups by their ''ambition, affluence, education, and social status''.[41] This group was ''frustrated and restless'',[42] and most were ''living on the wreck of their father's fortunes''.[43] Within the Company's service, one officer-father complained, ''halfbreeds as they are called has [sic] no chance there nor are they respected whatever their abilities may be.''[44] Many were thus forced to seek their fortunes outside the Hudson's Bay Company. This group was among those that Irene Spry described in her recent essay, ''The 'Private Adventurers' of Rupert's Land''. These people, too, based their careers on the fur trade and buffalo hunt, but acted as entrepreneurs, as private traders (at first in co-operation with and later in opposition to the Hudson's Bay Company). Some of these men were successful. ''Those who achieved wealth, status, and influence'', Spry concluded, ''had done so on the basis of their own ambition, courage, initiative, energy, and shrewd intelligence and also of their prowess in the chase, on the trail and in boat brigades, and their intimate knowledge of the peoples of the plains.''[45]

Because these men shared the ambitions of the ruling British élite and sought to be enculturated by it (aided by the efforts of their fathers), they felt considerable pressure to deny their maternal Indian heritage. Yet at the same time their claim to rights as natives of the

---

40. Alexander Ross, *The Red River Settlement* (London: Smith, Elder & Co., 1856; reprinted Edmonton: Hurtig, 1972), p. 260. Actually Ross identified three ''classes'' of halfbreed: huntsmen, fishermen at the lakes, and the ''vagrant savages'' who followed the hunters and fishermen. To Ross, these were sub-classes. The community-at-large was divided into the ''European and agricultural party'' and the ''native or aboriginal party''. The above sub-groups, of course, all belonged to the latter party. Ross and his friends belonged to the former agricultural party.

41. Spry, p. 21, ''The Mixed-Bloods and Métis of Rupert's Land before 1870''.

42. *Ibid.*, p. 18.

43. Foster ''The Country-born''.

44. Glenbow—Alberta Institute, Sutherland papers, James to John Sutherland, Red River Colony, August 10, 1840.

45. Spry, ''The 'Private Adventurers' of Ruperts Land'', in Foster, ed., *The Developing West*, p. 62. Although a small clutch of independent traders was licensed by the HBC soon after the coalition in 1821, private trade was soon considered a threat to the monopoly and the Company attempted to quash the group. The ensuing struggle was not simply a dispute over the Company's claim to a monopoly of the fur trade. In Spry's words: ''The traders of Rupert's Land challenged the Company's domination of business activity in the territory, the necessity of Company approval for virtually any business venture, and the limits set on any attempt to explore economic opportunities other than those offered or at least authorized by the Company''. This was the significance of the Sayer trial in 1849.

soil was based on their maternal descent. Sylvia Van Kirk has argued that this pressure led to "irreconcilable conflicts" and resulted, at least in the case of James Ross, in a lack of "the Métis sense of cultural identity based on an acceptance of their dual racial heritage."[46] Van Kirk believes that the Riel resistance of 1869-70 polarized Red River into whites and Métis. "British-Indian leaders such as James Ross", she observed, "were essentially paralyzed by their own ambivalence" and that was their "particular tragedy".[47] Others avoided this ambivalence by completing their enculturation and succeeding within the Company's hierarchy, but most of the children of the élite seem to have managed to avoid the paralysis by striking a balance between their dual heritages. This group was generally successful outside the hierarchy of the Hudson's Bay Company, where their native ancestry was viewed more favourably.

The third group, the English-speaking children of servants, has been less studied: they are less accessible for study, appearing as a mere shadow in the historical record and generally not set apart from any other group having mixed ancestry.[48] Nevertheless, a few conclusions can be made about this group with some certainty. While many of them engaged in the buffalo hunt, they tended also to be farmers, often with only mediocre success.[49] Many were employed in some capacity by the Hudson's Bay Company, as contracted servants and as seasonal workers.[50] Most of these sons of servants probably had little formal education and would not in any case have been considered officer material. But they were not generally happy with the employment they were offered and desertions and mutinies became ever more common.[51] One can only speculate on the causes of the unrest, but a likely explanation is that the policy of allowing these mixed-bloods access only to the lowest levels of servant employment caused frustration. More than likely they were aware of the views

---

46. Van Kirk, *op. cit.*, p. 126.

47. *Ibid.*, p. 134.

48. My own earlier work has tended to consider the British-Indian servant class together with the French-Canadian–Indian servants of the HBC, although recognizing there were differences. See Judd, "Mixed Bands", "Native Labour".

49. The only moderate success in farming may well have been due to the demands of the hunt often keeping them from their farms for long periods of time, especially during the early growing season.

50. In 1832, about twenty per cent of contracted servants were mixed-bloods and by 1850 about half of all servants were from Rupert's Land. This does not include the seasonal labourers (notably tripmen and carters). Judd, "Native Labour", p. 311.

51. *Ibid.*

of their race held by Sir George Simpson and realized they would
never be considered on their merits, but rather through the opaque
prejudice of the Company's overseas governor:

> The half breed population is by far the most extended about the Settle-
> ment and appear to require great good management otherwise they will
> become in my opinion dangerous to its peace . . . they are not the class
> of people that would be desirable [as employees] on any terms as they are
> indolent and unsteady merely fit for voyaging.[52]

Since Red River had a rigid social structure based on a hierarchy
of occupational status,[53] these mixed-bloods had little hope of entering the mainstream of society, yet they were exposed to it daily.
Certainly this would have compounded their frustration at holding
low-paying, low-status jobs.

All people of mixed ancestry shared some common characteristics. When combined they could be a large and powerful group;
by 1850 they numbered about five thousand people.[54] They lived in
a fertile area, could own land and engage in farming, or they could
roam the plains in the semi-annual buffalo hunt. Many did both. After
1849, they were able openly to become free traders. (Indeed, many
had been traders before that.) Red River had a system of civil government, to which they had at least limited recourse. They lived in a
new, evolving society, a polyglot community of many heritages
scattered across a wide geographical area.

The dwindling of the buffalo herds forced the peoples of the
Prairies to forge a new place in the emerging order. After 1870, and
with Ontario immigrants flooding in, most of them were absorbed
into the new system or thrown out onto the Prairies to form satellite
communities. Some were able to make the extraordinary adjustment
necessary but many were not.[55] Before any further conclusions can
be drawn about the fate of the mixed-blood peoples of the Prairies
after the rebellions a great deal more research needs to be done on
the post-1885 period.[56] The prairie, and in particular the Red River
mixed-bloods, can be studied only over a period of less than one
hundred years, while those at the post of Moose Factory can be traced
for two hundred and fifty years.

---

52. HBCA, D.4/87, Simpson's Official Reports, 1824, p. 8.

53. Foster, "The Country-born", p. 39.

54. *Ibid.*, p. 12.

55. Spry, "Private Adventurers", p. 61.

56. This gap in Métis historiography has been noted by Dennis Madill in his excellent *Select Annotated Bibliography on Metis History and Claims*, Treaties and Historical Research Centre, Indian and Northern Affairs, 1983, pp. 22-23.

There were many social, economic, and environmental differences between the mixed-blood communities of Moose Factory and Red River. The chief difference was that at Moose Factory there was only one group of mixed-bloods, while at Red River three groups have been identified.

Resemblances between the two communities include languages, religion, social status, in many cases the ethnicity of their fathers, and their similar occupational opportunities within the Hudson's Bay Company. There the similarities end. The lifestyle choices open to the Moose Factory mixed-bloods were far more limited. Though historian Alvin Gluek has said of the Red River settlers that they were "complacent simply because there was little or no opportunity to be otherwise",[57] in truth his statement applies far more accurately to Moose Factory than to Red River.

Moose Factory's geography limited choices: no buffalo hunt, no private farms, no accessible outside community to provide an outlet for private commerce. The history of Moose Factory's mixed-blood population was also quite different from that of Red River: it began a century earlier, there was little population growth and severely limited and controlled immigration, there was one religion, the mixed-blood people at Moose Factory were the homeguard who evolved into the basis of the Company's local labour force, and there was no civil government at Moose Factory. If the biracial groups at Red River had limited choices the mixed-blood inhabitants of Moose Factory had almost no choices.

These geographical and historical realities certainly contributed to the very different mixed-blood "experience" at Moose Factory and may also have contributed to the vast collective behaviour differences between the mixed-bloods of Red River and Moose Factory.

The mixed-bloods at Moose Factory were far more docile and malleable than the biracial groups at Red River. At the same time the mixed-bloods at Moose Factory failed to develop a group consciousness. Like the élite mixed-bloods of Red River, these people tended to cite their European progenitors rather than their Indian heritage when discussing their ethnic roots. At the same time they did not spurn their Indian ancestry—even today many still make moccasins and enjoy traditional fare such as smoked goose. Their sense of group identity seems to have been focused on the omnipresent Hudson's Bay

---

57. Alvin Gluek Jr., *Minnesota and the Manifest Destiny of the Canadian Northwest*, 1965, as quoted in G. Williams, *Simpson's Letters to London*, p. xxi.

Company that fed, housed, and employed them. This was their sociological point of reference, rather than their race or the values and
expectations of their fathers.

At Moose Factory there was no violent upheaval, no evidence
of psychological paralysis based on conflicts over biracial allegiances,
no "identity crisis".[58] Theirs was simply a traditional fur-trade
society actuated by fur-trade values and points of reference. Today,
the echo of the traditional fur-trade society still lingers at Moose in
the deference many mixed-bloods still, at least superficially, pay to
whites in their community, and the reciprocal paternalism they are
accorded. Perhaps this anachronism, which Arthur Ray labels a vestige
of the fur trade,[59] is explained by the continued relative isolation of
Moose Factory. Though joined with southern Ontario by rail and
air, Moose Factory and Moosonee together are the metropolis for
communities around James Bay, to which they are linked by cultural
ties as well as air and water transport.

How does this situation compare with that of biracial groups
at Winnipeg—modern-day Red River—today? A self-consciously
mixed-blood or Métis community here is harder to isolate, comprising
as it does a small group within a major city. Perhaps here the half-
jesting comment of Antoine Lussier, a Métis academic, that there
were no more Métis—a Métis with money was white and a broke
Métis was an Indian[60]—should be considered more for its insight
than its humour.

Students of mixed-blood history have to begin to think not
in terms of *"the Métis"* or *"the mixed-blood"*. There is no such social
identity. Just as the term "the Indian" denies the diverse heritages
of such groups as Nootka, Iroquois, Chippewyan and Swampy Cree,
so too, the term *the Métis* denies the diverse cultural heritages of the
blended ethnicities the label represents. Instead of looking for similarities or universals perhaps we should begin to recognize and celebrate
the differences, which will be clearly known only when regional histo-
ries from across the country and contemporary sociological studies
reveal the rich tapestry of many diverse Métis and mixed-blood
experiences.

---

58. Van Kirk, *op. cit.*

59. Ray, *op. cit.*

60. Antoine Lussier, CHA Conference, Saskatoon, 1979.

13. "Down North" in 1935

A Diary of Irene M. Spry (née Biss)

John Stuart Batts
University of Ottawa

I

Several centuries have passed since that Renaissance sage, Francis Bacon, urged all young travellers to cultivate the habit of keeping a diary, and his advice has been urged subsequently by many, so one should not be surprised by the number of Canadian manuscript diaries that have been kept over the years, not only by explorers but also by visitors both eminent and unremarkable.[1] Bacon's essay specified the kinds of interests that might be noted as gentlemen personally observed the particularities of countries, cities, customs, etcetera. Latterly, more utilitarian concerns have dominated the diarists' motives, whether in the logs required by the Company to be kept at a Hudson's Bay Company (HBC) fur-trading post, in the field notes of lonely nineteenth-century surveyors, or in the crucial record of daily weather and seasonal activity jotted down by pioneer farmers as each year of settlement passed. In all such writings, there is seldom a diary which is wholly devoid of interest, be the writer unlettered or unleisured. On the other hand, many are undeniably rich in information; one may think here, for example, of the Palliser expedition diaries, edited by Irene Spry.

When, therefore, a diary kept by my distinguished colleague who is the honoured subject of this collection of essays, was encountered in a remote archive, more than personal curiosity was piqued. Amidst a wealth of then-uncatalogued manuscripts in the Prince of Wales Northern Heritage Centre, Yellowknife, N.W.T., I was shown a diary of her first-hand encounter with life in the Northwest.[2] Since

1. *The Essays or Counsels, Civil and Moral, of Francis, Lo[rd] Verulam* (London, 1625; Rpt. Menston, Yorkshire, England: The Scholar Press, 1971), p. 101.

2. Prince of Wales Northern Heritage Centre, Yellowknife, N.W.T.: MS.157. I should like to acknowledge here the assistance given me by Dr. Edwin Welch, F.S.A., Territorial Archivist.

much of her scholarly work has involved the study of manuscript documents, her own diary, "Down North: 1935", should have a special interest for a wide audience.

The manuscript of that summer tour has more than one hundred near-quarto-sized pages, with a variable number of entries on the unlined sheets. The journalizing is not daily but periodic and some entries have obviously been written up some days later. Furthermore, the ink is faint in places and legibility not easy. The lines kept are sufficiently varied so that at no point does the diary take on the character of technical notes, which were, I understand, kept separately. The result is that while the professed subject of the journey was a study of hydro-electric power and alternative sources of energy in the Northwest and the Yukon, the diary remains very much a book about people, and, to a lesser extent, places.

The unusual itinerary for a young lady fresh from university took the diarist to the 1930s equivalent of the Canadian frontier of the last century, the opening up of the Northwest to large-scale commercial exploitation of natural resources. It also brought a glimpse of the timeless struggle for existence which must always have characterized life in the North. Indeed, many of the remoter communities must have seemed like exciting interstices of Canada ancient and modern. The major adventure was to visit isolated mining developments such as those in the region of Cameron Bay on Great Bear Lake and in the valley of the Yukon River. The mode of travel must have spiced the sense of challenge, for the diarist travelled not on the wings of fancy but on the less-than-fanciful novelty of the era— aeroplanes fitted with pontoons—then revolutionizing life in the North. The journey, however, began with that equally innovative transport mode of the previous century, the train; several days were spent trundling from Toronto to Winnipeg, hours and hours of "spruce, muskeg, & rock". Once in Manitoba, she travelled north to The Pas, Dauphin, and Flin Flon, to lesser-known communities at Cranberry Portage and Island Falls, and then via Saskatoon and Prince Albert to Edmonton, arriving on June 25, 1935. Here the northern loop began that was to take her during the succeeding four weeks to Fort McMurray, Fort Smith, Resolution, Rae, Cameron Bay, the geologist's camp that was to become Yellowknife, Fort Simpson, Aklavik, Rampart House, Dawson, Whitehorse, Skagway, and Vancouver.

II

With so much to see and do, it is easy to see why the diary has a built-in narrative frame based on her movements. The myriad impressions, reflections, sketches, and digressions give substance and colour. Distance and time are in turn compacted or expanded, as the diarist wills. Thus the train journey from Toronto to Winnipeg is dismissed in six lines, and the first three pages are devoted to a pot-pourri of items about the Manitoba capital. There she found memories of the strike "still bitter" [f.1]; but the municipal political strife seemed to be remote from the rest of the province, and she noted considerable talk and hopes of mining in the God's Lake and other districts, fuelled by aerial prospecting. Elsewhere she detected enthusiasm for "back-to-the-land rehabilitation". [f.3] Physically, the city had some charming parks and buildings, but there seems to be some regret at the large houses then being pulled down, victims of owners who found the taxes unbearable. The lament was that Winnipeg was paying all the taxes for the province. On visiting the university [Manitoba], she found the President, Sidney Smith, "very genial", despite his institution's financial difficulties.

From Winnipeg the diarist went on the first of many trips to power plants and mines, to Pine Falls. Then it was on to Flin Flon and Island Falls: "Indians all over: papooses, girls in slacks & lipsticks, & old timers" [f.6]—one of whom had staked all the country around Flin Flon in 1915. Indians are, of course, a primary colour in any Canadian diarist's palette over the past three hundred years. A more idiosyncratic sensibility is displayed by the diarist's persistent awareness of flowers and trees: "Trees get more plentiful & country begins to break and roll near Dauphin. Marvellous flowers, esp. lilac at Dauphin."[f.6] Then the train rolled on to the Cranberry Portage: "Mêlée at station: whole town there & everyone struggling to get to hotel first."[f.7] It was here that the diarist first registered her sense (reminiscent of D.H. Lawrence) of the physical oppressiveness of tawdry northern settlements: "Town incredibly ramshackle looking: buildings all sorts of shapes & sizes: street [word illegible] stones & dust. Full of lounging men and dogs . . . . Houses all v. temporary look: paper-covered frame & asbestos. Straggle about ill defined streets & seem almost to mix with mill etc."[ff.7-8] Little wonder the local employer had been troubled by strikes and that one of the perceptive residents opined that the company had not done enough to keep people happy. This diarist is especially concerned with the human element in all of the mining towns she visits; and despite the physical oppressiveness, she was impressed by the hospitality lavished on the rare visitor. "Bridge seems to be *the* diversion. Women wear dinner dresses, men shirt sleeves. Americans dominant on staff. Apart from bridge & drinking & boating on Lake [there] seem to be no diversions . . . ." [f.9] The absence of books and music, however, did not go unremarked.

The next excursion was to Island Falls, undertaken by train followed by motor boat, a canoe trip and some portaging. This was found to be a cheerful community: sports were "plentiful" and the school had musical talent. Less happily, on an Arrow Airways flight back, the diarist felt airsick, a sensation that was to be repeated during the tour.

A rail journey to Prince Albert and then Saskatoon brought the young traveller back to relative civilization. Saskatoon's broad streets and handsome buildings gave it a prosperous air. Likewise, the university pleased the eye: "beautiful site on high cliff over river".[f.15] Politically the air was abuzz with notions of Social Credit: "Liberals well hated. C.C.F. considered rather woolly & lacking in good personnel. Heard a good deal about Social Credit, but by no means general acceptance. C.C.F. seems to have entity here as contrasted with Manitoba."[f.15]

Edmonton was the next brief stop on the itinerary. On June 25 the diarist took a train north for the waterways of northern Alberta and was evidently irritated by its slowness. At each stop "men throng the stations, weather-beaten, rugged & overalled. The average station has two or three elevators . . . two or three gasoline stores . . . a general store or two, . . . several houses and a beautifully kept church and school."[f.18] The topography is noted with fine detail where enthusiasms are concerned; north of Bon Accord "a fair growth of trees, mostly poplar & Manitoba maple but with some willow, a few odd well grown spruce, or strips of scraggy, unhappy-looking spruce bush. Here and there, in sandy places, jack pine appear."[f.19] The passengers were found to be equally "variegated" en route to Fort McMurray.

At McMurray the diarist stayed at a hotel; it did not take long before she was apprised by Mrs. O'Coffey of all the difficulties of keeping staff, by Corporal G. ("strangely vacuous face & manner, but said to be good man") of the Mounties' tasks, and by Dr. Lewis of the local "breeds". Here was the first extended opportunity for the diarist to meet some Indians; the interpreter went to "rustle some up" and soon enough came—"one chief & string of men: hand-shaking. Then some women & children, more men at intervals . . . . Interval for grievances to be aired."[f.26] The treaty Indians complained to Lewis of poor medical service, of lack of a school, about rations, etc. "Indians seemed cheerful, good humoured & ready to laugh at themselves as well as at others. A fair and amicable meeting."[f.28] The views of a number of traders and local inhabitants are also recorded. One evening there, the diarist attended a "tea-dance", and writes in a manner that recalls E. M. Forster's India:

"Whites, merry, ribald, & mocking Indians, took possession. Indian tom-tommers wail & tom-tom rhythmically. Only two Indians danced, curious rhythmic jerk—reminiscent of 'Charleston'. Laurie much disgusted: came away fairly early when started to rain . . . . Indians said to be 'just children' (Green), Bill Jacko says they are shiftless & lazy wasters: no use.''[f.30] Whilst staying at McMurray, the diarist made a visit to the Athabasca River to examine rock salt deposits and the tar water, but it occupies less prose than the tour of the Roman Catholic and Anglican missions. The former was found to be especially primitive—the house was full of mosquitoes, and geared for religious teaching only. The priest in charge, from Boston, thought aeroplanes had been very bad for Indians, and white people were "demoralising". Obviously he was not one to attend tea-dances. The Anglican, supported by the Church Missionary Society, Mr. [?] Blackaller, was much interested in sociological study and had no hesitation about attending dances.

The next part of the journey was by air towards Cameron Bay on the eastern shore of Great Bear Lake. There were many stops for refuelling, delivering mail and supplies, and hence chances to meet some of the inhabitants meantime. One such was the stop at Fitzgerald on the Slave River, where the HBC manager took the diarist to meet his wife, Mrs. McDermot: "a perfectly charming old lady with white hair parted in the middle, a demure black frock & white apron, parchment skin and a sweet smile. Page Rembrandt. She was one of those serene, self-contained people. The house was clean and empty. A nice cat which apparently lives in danger of huskies and freezing. Mrs. McD. came from Fort McPherson—the first white child to be born there.''[ff.35-36] Departure for Fort Smith was delayed briefly by a storm, but soon the plane was refuelling again at the then capital of the Northwest Territories, where an official party of ladies "looked as though they had stepped off a 1924 city street—high heels, furs, etc.''[f.37]

Next came Resolution, a widely spread settlement on the shores of Great Slave Lake: "mission—handsome church school & convent at extreme east & police barracks at the other end. Full of treaty Indians, tents, & dogs.''[f.37] Here there was enough time to visit the usual round of establishments in northern communities, the HBC post, the Mounties, the missions.

A little later, on the other side of the Lake, there was an opportunity to visit the Burwash Prospect, where a "nameless gentleman became somewhat gallant: showed me pet raven—still [?]at fluttering stage—called 'Angus' . . . . Offers of tea rejected.''[f.40]

At Rae the diarist was met by the HBC factor; at Winnipeg she had received from the Fur Trade Commissioner of the Company a letter of introduction to all post managers, asking them to accord hospitality and assistance. This arrangement was extremely valuable. Next was a stop at Hottah Lake, site of a pitchblende camp: "Mosquitoes devilish. Mass of purple-red flowers like Indian paint brush."[f.45] Over White Eagle Falls the pilot obligingly circled for the diarist's closer inspection of the site, but by early afternoon the plane landed at Cameron Bay.

At this point the diary intersperses the accounts of activities with long entries about northern people and local institutions, the radio station, the Police barracks, the HBC, the café, etc. Whilst at Cameron Bay, there were excursions to the B.E.A.R. mine, the Consolidated Mining and Smelting Company's property, the Eldorado site where "uranium stains [were] remarkable in test pits"[f.71] and El Bonanza. More diverting were the moments of social distraction. One of these was a swim at 66 degrees north: "water very cold but not as cold as Morraine Lake."[f.67] Another was an "evening party" for Raoul B., who had been previously and intriguingly described in the diary in these terms: "suave man about town, drinks prodigiously, never drunk, always lady's man, best dancer I've met. Said to be in town all the time."[f.57] Yet of that evening's entertainment the diarist is laconic: "Home-brewed beer: Sergeant [Baker, RCMP] grand impersonator. Otherwise perhaps best unrecorded, but good fun if a little wearing. Slept late next morning."[f.74]

On Saturday, July 6, the diarist flew back to Resolution, via Hottah Lake and Hardisty Lake, Rae, and Yellowknife, picking up more opinions from passengers and officials, and encountering the quaint and the bizarre. At Rae, where the plane party lunched: "place a tumult of Indians and howling dogs. Chief Murphy resplendent in red striped pants. (Later told he wears a huge medallion, having recently come into treaty)."[f.86] Most of the entries at Resolution deal with the views of Mounties and HBC men on a panoply of northern topics.

One of the legendary pioneers of northern aviation, "Wop" May, was her pilot on the hop north to Fort Simpson: "flying just above the water as far as Big Island—hopping one little island . . . . Saw Providence from the air: high by then."[f.101] Simpson appeared "flourishing" and active. Several boats were at anchor including the *Distributor*, from the mouth of the Mackenzie, the *Pelly Lake*, waiting to go up the Liard River, and a scow carrying the Father-General, the Bishop, and party to down-river missions. In this brief sojourn at the confluence of the Liard and the Mackenzie Rivers the diarist stayed with the wife of the radio-station operator, but saw something of local life by attending both the Anglican confirmation service for three local girls—"parson spoke in Slavey, Bishop in English; mass of old ladies and little boys to see it"[f.103]—and later a dance on board the *Distributor*.

Like George Back a century before her, this diarist was impressed by the grandeur of the Mackenzie Mountains below Fort Simpson. The valley continued to fascinate as the morning wore on. At noon the aircraft landed at Wrigley to refuel and exchange mailbags. Before reaching Fort Norman, however, *mal de l'air* had taken its toll of all the passengers except the Mother Superior of the Grey Nuns. Nevertheless, the plane had to make another brief stop at Norman Wells during the afternoon; take-off there was difficult because of the numbers of floating logs. En route for Fort Good Hope, the rugged terrain again took the eye: ". . . ridged to sharp escarpments of sedimentary & apparently fairly soft rock: looked like a series of teeth."[f.104] Crossing the line of the Arctic Circle, she noted the land flattening out to the northwest, and by the time Arctic Red River was reached the beginning of the delta was seen from the air. The long day's flight ended at Aklavik at 10:00 p.m.: "still, shiny night. Mosquitoes Abominable."[f.105]

Next day the diarist visited the local schools and the hospital. The Roman Catholic mission operated a school for seventy children, mostly boarders; the rooms and arrangements are described in detail—for example, the wood-burning furnaces and the Delco-plant electric light system. The Anglican mission school was for day pupils only; but its hospital was also found half-empty, awaiting a summer influx of patients.

Francis Bacon, in his *Essays* (1625), had also recommended that the Renaissance traveller should "not stay long in one city or town", and this was certainly the manner of the diarist's progress.[3] From Aklavik she flew southwest next day (July 13) over the Ogilvie Mountains to Fort Yukon, Alaska. The trip was scenic: snow-capped mountain ranges, meandering rivers, and a dense bush fire that turned the sun into a "mere red ball".[f.107] Having arrived in Alaska, the diarist notes that on refuelling the aircraft in the absence of pumps, the gasoline—"said to be cheaper"[f.107]—was poured in from cans. The entries made here show the range of concerns that enliven the writing. During the brief stay there were visits to the mission hospital, orphanage, and two schools, one for Indians and one for whites:

---

3. "Of Travel", *The Essays*, p. 101.

"teach ordinary city stuff: irrelevant. New inspector: hope to get a change to more sense!"[f.108] The mission house was more attractive and earned the Angela Brazil-like label "ripping", not least because the hymnals were in a native tongue and the altar-cloth was of native-fashioned moose-hide adorned with beads. At the hospital, she met a man who had served the area for twenty-five years, Dr. Burke, well able to relate the medical problems of the inhabitants within a 350- to 400-mile radius. Hence it is noted that malnutrition was a common problem, plus some tuberculosis, and "gallstones common especially among women".[f.108] The town was then in the midst of a measles outbreak, thought to have been transmitted from Dawson City.

Dawson was to be the next port of call as the diarist boarded the stern-wheel steamer *Yukon* and moved slowly up-river. This was a chance to describe a river from a new perspective: "hub-bub of torrents. Flats to just above Circle. Then marvellous craggy scenery: sharply-broken mountains right to river's edge & blue mountains beyond. Bare rocks: spruce creeping up crevices. Sedimentary layers v. plain . . . . Dogs sing to ship's whistle."[f.110] There was a stop at Forty Mile, and a little later near Fort Reliance, ten miles below Dawson, an eagle was spotted, but this page (dealing with July 14-17) is the last one of the manuscript diary in the Yellowknife archive. Perhaps the days were becoming too hectic, or perhaps the diarist was flagging; it is just as likely that the last page or two of the loosely pinned booklet became detached and lost.

The journey continued and is described, in retrospect, elsewhere.[4] Dawson was visited; she tried her hand at panning for gold, and observed the more energy-intensive efforts at placer-mining and dredging. At Whitehorse, terminus of the White Pass & Yukon Railway, she took the narrow-gauge train to Skagway to connect with a boat sailing down the inner passage to Vancouver. Amongst the letters awaiting her there was an apologetic one from Consolidated Mining & Smelting Company stating that they would not be responsible for her visit because they had no means of ensuring comfort for a lady!

III

Travel diaries, with their serial entries of ephemeral impressions, are infamous for their unreadable, guide-bookish style and repeated

---

4. While this chapter was in preparation, Dr. Spry kindly loaned me a copy of her typescript article for the journal *Musk-Ox*, "A Journey 'Down North' to Great Bear Lake and the Yukon in 1935".

mannerisms.[5] No one is likely to be more embarrassed by inordinate praise than Dr. Spry, so that while one cannot claim that her unpublished diary is the best "unknown" specimen of its kind, one can affirm that it is eminently readable. The following comments of assessment, however, may be construed as implicit praise on the grounds that it is substantial enough to warrant the task. The felicitous features include its often lively description of places and of people, and the sheer range of issues which are culled from the daily round.

This diary, private and unpretentious as it is, comes to life because it is more than simply a litany of locations. Cities, towns, villages are frequently described in cameo fashion, whereby a series of highly selective features are juxtaposed in such a way as to suggest the sense of place. Some examples of this kind of writing have already been quoted above but here are further illustrations. Consider this style of diarist's short-hand: "Prince Albert [Saskatchewan] 10 a.m. Good looking town with broad streets (only main ones paved) and substantial buildings. Fine City Hall at top of hill with avenue of ornamental lights leading up to it. Nice park on river bank: R. v. full & rapid. Little red H.B.C. store with some pleasant wampum moccasins."[f.14] The effect is impressionistic and personal, like a snap taken with an old box camera. Not that everything seen was viewed with approbation: "Winnipeg *looked* prosperous", but behind the boom buildings and "marvellous shrubs, especially the lilacs", the diarist noted insanitary houses; likewise, the University of Manitoba aroused mixed feelings: "University good site 5 miles out of city, but v. ugly buildings—red brick surmounted by Chinese pagoda."[f.3] The last phrase there reads like D. H. Lawrence condemning industrial Tevershall in *Lady Chatterley's Lover*, and makes the diarist's point well by its specificity.

Elsewhere in the diary the prose cameos attempt to capture verbally the terrain, new landscapes, and aerial views. The better ones temper the objectivity of the social scientist with a distinctive personal turn of phrase. While flying over northern Alberta, she tersely noted:

> From air hills looked densely wooded; clearing in valley where salt works: oil sands inland from it: water black: river so muddy that trees made black shadow on it: edges very clear-cut: steep limestone banks . . . . (Clear beautiful morning.) Survey lines every here to there & rivers flowing into main stream. Fort MacKay, white house or two. One or two other settlements— one probably the Hay camp. No sign of any buffalo in the Wood Buffalo Park. Should be visible at S. end if at all. Birch Mts. quite formidable to W. Trees still plentiful, but country flattens out & marsh supervenes as approach Chipewyan. Whole S. coast of L. Athabasca flooded out: water courses apparent from lines of shrubs along banks.[ff.32-33]

---

5. Arthur Ponsonby, *British Diarists* (London: Ernest Benn, 1930), p. 27.

The reader is impressed by the scrutiny given to the passing scene below; just the occasional word, such as "formidable", reminds one that the observer is a young woman on a rather daring expedition to gather information in a predominantly male environment. Over Great Slave Lake the diarist jotted down the aircraft's path to the mouth of the Yellowknife River: "Followed shore across delta & mouth of Taltson R. along archipelago of islands: country suddenly rugged again after mud flat of delta. Still very flat, but red rock: innumerable islands, some bare, some growing spruce, but multitudinous, big ones nearest inland, dwindling down to minute clusters around open water."[f.39] Just occasionally do such entries become slightly more personal. One such vignette is the description of a pleasing cloud formation: "Marvellous clouds during day's flight: square blocked base . . . . nearing Rae, wisps of haze on G. Slave Lake: due to ice melting: block of ice still on shore."[f.41] Yet even here the need to rationalize suggests the expression of a scientist on the ground rather than the effusion of a romantic in the air. Even striking sunsets, where noticed, get a brusque treatment: "Fine sunset at Lac La Biche, but drowned out in a rainstorm."[f.22]

A similar diagnosis may be made of the descriptions of some of the mines visited: dispassionate, specific comments for the most part, with the occasional personal detail or telling phrase included. On Tuesday, July 2, the diarist made a trip to the Eldorado site on Great Bear Lake: "Oil tanks, log buildings, & new ones of rubberoid slats . . . . Most of the buildings on shore, but office & rec' hall on hill behind. Finger of tents inhabited by people who want to live alone . . . . Flowers v. fine. Uranium stains remarkable in test pits . . . . Gardens being grown. A slightly dishevelled look about the place. Price of wood $20 a cord."[f.71] The image of the "finger" of tents for the less-social workers has its own felicity.

More important than the diarist's interest in place is the recording of people. This journal presents a gallery of northern folk, most met in person but others only mentioned because of their local reputation or infamy. Their variety of qualities may vie with Chaucer's collection of motley Canterbury pilgrims, even if the latter's skill of presentation is not present. The diary kept "down north" is at its best while above the 60th parallel and is the repository of remarks and stories about many dozens of characters, officials, and Indians. It seems likely that the impressionable diarist, aware that the "white" history of the area was almost all still within reach, made a special point about jotting down her own findings as well as hearsay stories about all those she suspected might have made, or would in the future make some contribution, however minor, to the North. Perhaps inevitably her judgement erred on the side of inclusiveness. Thus, some of the prose reads like informal "potted biogs" of the legion of the now lost. Almost fifty years later one is not wholly gripped by the complaints of mine managers about incompetent prospectors who, rarely stirring from their cabins during the season, were only too happy to live on their grub stake; nor individually do the various non-native complaints against Indians who abuse dogs or who haggle over fur prices make for exciting reading. Yet cumulatively one does get the outline of a perennial human pattern.

Cameron Bay gave the diarist the fullest range of personalities to record. Here one could meet 280-pound "Yukon Jess", who was reputed to have "paid by the lb." to be flown in some months before, and now made a living by taking in laundry, it was said, and by boot-legging; she is described as a "square black substance moving heavily but cheerfully along."[f.48] Then again, there was the young Swedish girl who had run away from home and had suffered from more than uncommon bad luck: her "brother died in motor smash just after father had died on returning from her graduation."[f.48] She herself was currently recovering from a smash, had been abandoned by her geologist boy-friend—he had gone off to South America—and was most recently, in the words of the diarist, "commonly held to be 'Chuck' McLeod's girl." This case had obviously exercised the wagging tongues.

There is always entertainment in reading of excesses, exag-gerations, and eccentricities, but not all the locals were tinged by such bizarreness. The medical officer of health and his nurse wife are described thus:

> [He] . . . seems a trifle bushed. Very ugly hair straight on end: tanned & wrinkled. She a little distrait but both very nice . . . . Live v. irregular hours—never seem to get to bed or get up. Complained that it was fun to begin with. Spirit of the North really existed when they first came in. No longer now. Don't know anyone & never go out . . . . Common reports suggest that a number of people have little confidence in him as medico. Is said to be brusque & alienating.[f.50]

At moments like this the diary's charm is attenuated. Yet at Cameron Bay the roll-call includes a curious collection of temporary locals: Frank Cousineau ("ex-Yukon gambler"[f.54]); Pete Mahoney ("cadaverous English engineman"[f.56]); etc. The text bristles with such contem-porary caricatures.

Like many of the best diarists, this young woman also has an ear for the unconventional and the scandalous, the story and the joke. Boswell himself might have appreciated this sample entry: "Traveller remarked Fr. & Scotch half-breeds. 'Why no English?'— 'Why, mon, the squaws must draw the line somewhere'!"[f.82]

IV

Proverbially, "He that travels far knoweth much." Bacon puts it more precisely: "Travel in the younger sort, is a part of education; in the elder, a part of experience."[6] Yet Bacon also saw the need to register one's impressions—"Let diaries, therefore be brought in use."[7] This particular manuscript of an extensive tour in the Northwest may have been conventional in conception but this chapter will attest further that it is certainly spry in execution.

---

6. "Of Travel", *The Essays*, p. 100.

7. "Of Travel", *The Essays*, p. 101.

14. Satellite Broadcasting in Northern Canada

Jean McNulty

York University

The image often created by politicians, other government spokesmen, or journalists about communications satellites in the North is that of drawing northerners into the mainstream of Canadian society. This warm image of communication among people—wherever they may live in Canada—is reinforced by actions such as calling the Canadian satellites "Anik", the Inuit word for "brother". It is also endorsed by video or print pictures we have probably all seen of Inuit or native Indian individuals using telephones, short-wave radios, or broadcasting studios to transmit electronic messages, in their own language, over vast distances. In 1979, the Clyne Committee said that the satellite system in Canada "is one of the most potent instruments available for the social and cultural benefit of the many thousands, if not millions, of Canadians who are at present, in relation to those who live in more heavily populated areas, deprived."[1] Ah, we may say to ourselves, it is true then that modern communications technologies can improve the social contact among people throughout this land and reduce the isolation of those who live in the North.

What lies behind this image of social benefit is the subject of the following paper. My basic argument is that, despite the rhetoric (whether sincerely believed or carelessly advanced) of federal policy-makers and others that communications satellites can be socially beneficial to the North, the experience has been that such an expensive technology serves best the interests and needs of a few large corporations and institutions—including the federal government itself. The specific use of satellites which I will examine will be their use for the extension of broadcasting services in northern Canada.[2]

---

1. Minister of Communications, Consultative Committee on the Implications of Telecommunications for Canadian Sovereignty (Clyne Committee), *Telecommunications and Canada* (Ottawa: Minister of Supply and Services Canada, 1979), p. 54.

2. Due to space limitations, I cannot discuss the use (experimental or otherwise) of satellites to enhance the delivery of health care, education and other social services to northern residents—although this is a related and equally fascinating topic.

Northern Canada

Northern Canada, or simply "the North", has many possible definitions—geographic, social, political, climatic, economic and so on; and it is not my intention to try to draw a rigid line between northern and southern Canada which satisfies all possible definitions. As a geographic region of Canada, the North is usually taken to mean the two Territories, plus the northern quarter or so of the western provinces, most of the land area of Ontario and Quebec on or near Hudson Bay, all of Labrador, and parts of northern Newfoundland.

In social terms, the North is most strongly identified as the region where the indigenous peoples predominate, or provide a significant proportion of the society. Population figures for such a region are difficult to find because census data is gathered on a provincial or territorial basis. It is known from the 1981 census that, in a total Canadian population of about 24.3 million, there were 45,741 people in the Northwest Territories and 23,153 in the Yukon. Together the two Territories cover an area of about 3.77 million square kilometres, which is more than a third of Canada's land mass.

The Inuit population in all of Canada is estimated to number 22,700, while people of native Indian descent (i.e., status and non-status Indians as well as Métis) number 600,000 to about 1.1 million.[3] There are estimated to be about 16,000 Inuit and 19,450 Indians (status and non-status) in the Territories. In the Eastern Arctic, the Inuit are the largest population group, whereas, in the Western Arctic, non-native people are now in the majority. In the Yukon, non-native people outnumber native Indians by about four to one.

Languages create special difficulties in providing services for native people as a group in Canada. The Indians have about thirty distinct languages or dialects which are spoken today; about ten of these are in use in the Yukon and Northwest Territories. Most Inuit use one of the two main variants of the Inuktitut language, one in the Eastern Arctic and one in the Western Arctic. Many native people, whether they live in the North or in the rest of Canada, speak some English (a relatively small number speak French), but the degree of fluency in the "official languages" is often very limited. In general,

---

3. See, for example, CRTC, Committee on Extension of Service to Northern and Remote Communities (Therrien Committee), *The 1980s: A Decade of Diversity—Broadcasting, Satellites, and Pay-TV* (Ottawa: Minister of Supply and Services Canada, 1980), pp. 22-24. Also, see Raymond Breton, Jeffrey G. Rietz, and Victor Valentine, *Cultural Boundaries and the Cohesion of Canada* (Montreal: Institute for Research on Public Policy, 1980), pp. 79-80.

young people are more likely to speak English than are the older people.

The northern region is so vast and so sparsely populated that to think of its having an economy of its own is to exaggerate its cohesion. However, certain economic characteristics are found in common across this wide expanse: principally an underdeveloped infrastructure of transportation links, financial and trading institutions and communications networks, along with a heavy dependence on resource extraction and export as a means of creating economic growth. In the Territories north of 60°, which are administered by the federal government, an additional economic factor is simply the overwhelming presence of the many federal government departments, agencies, and corporations, and their personnel. In essence, northern Canada is a region of economic hinterland which is dependent on metropolitan areas in southern Canada or outside Canada for its economic life. The metropolis-hinterland relationships of various regions of Canada have been observed and discussed for many years, of course, by Harold Innis and his followers, in their studies of the staple products of Canada. It would be fair to say that northern Canada is the region most dependent economically on external decisions, and its people are the least able to set their own priorities and goals upon the economic actions taken in their vicinity by corporations and government institutions.

The pressures from outside the North towards certain kinds of economic activity have been evident for centuries, most typically in the fur trade and its influences on the life-style of the aboriginal people. Thus, southern Canadian or foreign pressures for economic development of the North (or perhaps more correctly in the North) are not new. The current attention given to the economic value of natural gas and oil reserves in the Far North, and the ways and means of moving these resources to the south (Canada or the U.S.), is simply the most recent of a series of outside efforts to extract wealth from northern Canada. The economic benefits of such development for large corporations, and for the highly paid workers they send in to do the physical work, are easily seen. However, the benefits (economic or otherwise) for people living permanently in the North are less apparent. As such developments have taken place in specific locations, there have been concerns expressed, especially by native leaders, about the high social costs incurred by the local people—costs which cannot necessarily be compensated for by money or jobs (usually short-term and lower-paid anyway). Probably the clearest statement of this current confrontation between the high-powered economic and technical arguments for resource development and the socio-cultural arguments against it can be found in the report and recommendations of the Berger Inquiry into the Mackenzie Valley Pipeline.[4]

The North, especially the Far North, has another significance for southern Canada besides the possibility of new sources of wealth. The proximity of the Canadian Arctic to the Soviet Union makes it a military concern not only to Canada but also (perhaps more so) to the United States. Complete Canadian sovereignty over the area containing the Arctic islands, both land and sea, is not fully accepted by the U.S., and during the late 1960s and early 1970s this was of great concern to the federal government.[5] As one of the partners in the NORAD defence alliance, Canada has obligations to maintain adequate defence forces in the North, and particularly to allow, and co-operate in, the use of Arctic locations for the installation of early-warning radar and other military communications systems intended to defend North America against any surprise attacks from the Soviet Union. Reconnaissance aircraft, DEW-line stations and, more recently, satellite-tracking stations are the most visible parts of this defence system to non-military persons.

Perceiving northern Canada as either an economic larder or as a defence bulwark is primarily an outsider's view of the region. Most people living in the North, especially native people (who are not interested in living elsewhere in Canada), tend to see it differently. This is not to suggest that the people in the North agree on their vision of northern Canada or on what should be the priorities for development there. Many differences of opinion exist both among various native organizations and between native people in different parts of the North. Furthermore, non-native people are not unanimous, the greatest difference probably being between people born and raised in the North and those who have taken a job there, most likely only for a few years.

Such diversity of views has become more apparent to southern Canadians through such events as the Berger Inquiry hearings, held all along the Mackenzie Valley in 1975 and 1976. While this expression of public opinion could be regarded as a sign of a healthy democratic society, the lack of a clear consensus unfortunately weakens the political power which northern Canadians can exert within Canadian society as a whole. (This power in an electoral sense is already

---

4. Department of Indian Affairs and Northern Development, Mackenzie Valley Pipeline Inquiry (Commissioner: Thomas R. Berger), *Northern Frontier: Northern Homeland—The Report of the Mackenzie Valley Pipeline Inquiry: Volume One* (Ottawa: Minister of Supply and Services Canada, 1977).

5. See, for example, E. J. Dosman, editor, *The Arctic in Question* (Toronto: Oxford University Press, 1976).

very weak indeed because of the sparse population in the northern areas, especially in the Territories, which have only three M.P.s altogether in the House of Commons.)

Differences in cultural perspective on such issues as native land claims (and the related issues of economic development and control) between native people and non-natives in northern Canada also make it difficult for northerners' opinions and preferences to carry weight in southern Canada. Despite the extensive period of contact between aboriginal people and Europeans (later southern Canadians), there remains an enormous gap in understanding between them about what the North is like and how people can best live there.[6]

Even on such important matters as the definition of a society, little common ground has been reached. For instance, southern Canadians can talk glibly of the Canadian "nation" and the special place in it held by the native peoples. Northerners, native and non-native alike, are more likely to see themselves as a separate community or society different from that in the south. Within the northern society, further sub-divisions are seen between natives and non-natives, between Inuit and Indians, between status Indians and Métis, and so on. What is the "mainstream" of Canadian society into which we in southern Canada believe we would like to draw the northerners? All of these difficulties of definition appear in statements about the Canadian North and the place which northerners have in the Canadian nation or society.[7]

Given this brief discussion of northern Canada, its economic status and social character, let us move on to some comments about the communications systems in the North and their significance to northerners and southerners. Basically, the systems of interest here are the telecommunications/telephone systems and broadcasting. Land-based telecommunications networks usually depend on microwave links for long-distance connections between cities. However, where population is low and communities are separated, often by hundreds of miles, microwave is too expensive a technology to install. Alternatives have been high-frequency (HF) radio and, more recently, satellites. The former has been difficult to use on a regular, reliable basis in the North because of the weather and electromagnetic disturbances in the ionosphere which are associated with the polar regions of the earth. The latter technology can provide for the transmission

---

6. See, for example, Hugh Brody, *The People's Land: Eskimos and Whites in the Eastern Arctic* (London: Penguin Books Ltd., 1975).

7. For a full discussion of the problems in cultural differentiation and definitions of society, see Raymond Breton *et al.*, *op. cit.*, especially Part Two.

and reception of electronic signals that are virtually unaffected by the ionospheric disturbances.

Similarly for broadcasting networks (radio and television), the northern areas of Canada present large problems of signal distribution. Broadcasting being a technology which is most economical in metropolitan areas (where millions of households can be reached by one transmitter), the low population and its scattered distribution in the North make broadcasting coverage extremely expensive per household. A significant part of that cost is incurred in carrying radio and TV signals from the network centre to each local re-broadcasting transmitter. As with telecommunications networks, microwave and high-frequency radio face economic and technical difficulties in northern Canada. In a technical sense, satellite systems have "solved" the problem of providing long-distance communications links in the North, both for telecommunications/telephone systems and broadcasting. Reliable networks based on the use of satellite channels can be set up, and electronic signals can be sent and received in almost any location in the Canadian North.

When it is said that these things "can be done", however, one must remember that this refers to *technical* possibility and not necessarily to economic feasibility. In order to explore this aspect of satellites in Canada, it is essential to review the history behind their development, and the institutional structures which have been established to own and operate them. The discussion of Canadian satellite development has to be placed in the broader context of space research before the institutional framework and economic relationships established for the satellite "system" now and in the future can be examined.

The Canadian Space Program

Involvement in space activities by private industry and government laboratories in Canada goes back at least to the late 1950s (even earlier for research work on the earth's upper atmosphere). By 1963, the Canadian Ionospheric Research program was approved for funding by the federal government, with the implicit assumption that related research and development would be performed in Canadian industry. Ionospheric research via satellite began in 1959 with the Canada–United States project which eventually produced the Alouette and ISIS series of satellites. When Alouette I was launched in September 1962, Canada became the third country in the world (after the U.S. and the U.S.S.R.) engaged in space activities. This highly successful series of scientific satellites was followed by research and development on communications satellites.

In 1964, Canada was a founding member of Intelsat, the operator of the global communications satellite system which now serves most countries outside the Soviet Bloc. In early 1967, a study published under the auspices of the Science Secretariat of the Canadian government gave strong support to the development of space technology in Canada as a central theme in Canada's space program, in the following terms:

> Application of space technology to specific Canadian needs should be the central theme of the program. Canada needs satellites for TV and telephone services to the north, for augmenting communications east and west, for surveying natural resources, for surveillance of weather, spotting forest fires and ice in shipping lanes and for many other purposes. The prime objective for space technology in Canada is its application to telecommunications and survey problems of a large sparsely settled country.[8]

This "Special Study No. 1" of the Science Secretariat, which became known as the Chapman Report (after its principal author), influenced the direction of the federal government's thinking. In July 1967, a report was issued by the Science Council of Canada which endorsed, as Chapman did, the competence of Canadian industry to undertake the design and manufacture of the hardware for a domestic satellite system. By the end of 1967, the Pearson government had decided to use satellites to expand the domestic communications networks. Then, in March 1968, the Minister of Industry, the Honourable C. M. (Bud) Drury, issued a White Paper on "A Domestic Satellite Communications System for Canada", and this was used as the basis for the Telesat Canada Act, approved by Parliament in 1969.

By 1969, the federal government indicated that government space efforts would be shifting from ionospheric studies to satellite technology programs, and the Interdepartmental Committee on Space (ICS) was set up to review Canadian space activities.[9] It should be

---

8. J. H. Chapman, P. A. Forsyth, P. A. Lapp, and G. N. Patterson, *Upper Atmosphere and Space Programs in Canada*, Science Secretariat Special Study No. 1 (Ottawa: Queen's Printer, 1967), p. 109.

9. Membership in the ICS has changed slightly over the years. According to the 1979 Annual Report, it contains representation from the following departments and agencies: Communications; Energy, Mines and Resources; Environment; External Affairs; Fisheries and Oceans; Industry, Trade and Commerce; National Defence; National Research Council; Ministry of State for Science & Technology; Transport. It is interesting that neither Indian Affairs & Northern Development nor Secretary of State are represented, although the former has particular responsibilities for native people and the northern Territories while the latter has responsibilities for supporting social and cultural development among social groups, including native people.

noted that, in dealing with space activities, the ICS was given responsibility for reviewing three main areas: (a) ionospheric research; (b) surveillance or remote-sensing technology including the design of satellites for that purpose; (c) communications satellites, including research and development. While much of the public attention in the late 1960s and early 1970s in Canada was on communications satellites, the space research community continued to work on space systems for the other two areas as well.

In 1969, the Telesat Canada Act established the Corporation given responsibility to own and operate the Canadian satellite communications system.[10] Under Section Five of its statute, the corporate objects of Telesat are to "establish satellite communications systems providing, on a commercial basis, telecommunications services between locations in Canada". Also, Telesat is directed to "utilize, to the extent practicable and consistent with its commercial nature, Canadian research, design, and industrial personnel, technology and facilities in research and development connected with its satellite telecommunications systems and in the design and construction of the systems."

It was expected that the Government of Canada, the major telephone companies, and private shareholders would each have one-third ownership of Telesat.[11] However, the one-third of shares for general issue have never been put on the market; by 1972, the federal government and major telephone companies had each provided fifteen million dollars as the share capital of the Corporation. Despite the fact that Telesat was established by statute and given a monopoly position, it is not a Crown corporation—as its officials have pointed out on many occasions. They often describe the Corporation as "the carriers' carrier"; it can also be described as a mixed public-private enterprise.

Telesat's first satellite (Anik A-1) was launched in 1972. The Anik A series of satellites was designed and built under contract from

---

10. Statutes of Canada, *Telesat Canada Act* (R.S. 1970, c. T-4).

11. The Telesat Canada Act, section 27, authorizes the three categories of shareholders; although the proportions are not specified, it was understood from government statements and in Parliamentary debate on the Bill that there would be an approximately equal division of shares among the three types of shareholders. Schedule I of the Act lists the "approved telecommunications common carriers" which may own Telesat shares as: Alberta Government Telephones, Bell Canada, British Columbia Telephone Company, Canadian National Railway Company, Canadian Pacific Railway Company, The Island Telephone Company Limited, The Manitoba Telephone System, Maritime Telegraph and Telephone Company Limited, the New Brunswick Telephone Company Limited, Newfoundland Telephone Company Limited, Québec-Téléphone, Saskatchewan Telecommunications, and Ontario Northland Transportation Commission.

Telesat by an American company, Hughes Aircraft; the implicit government policy at that time was to achieve "subsystem expertise rather than trying to compete with Europe or the U.S. in full systems".[12] However, some space industry officials believed that national policy objectives for Canada might be better served if Canada itself developed capacity to build full space systems, not just subsystems for a foreign main contractor.

In April 1974, the first official statement of government space policy was issued by the Minister of State for Science and Technology. The main points of the policy were:

> The government endorses the principle that a Canadian industrial capability for the design and construction of space systems must be maintained and improved through a deliberate policy of moving government space research and development out into industry.
>
> Government purchasing policies should encourage the establishment of a viable research, development and manufacturing capability in Canadian industry.
>
> Canada will continue to rely on other nations for launch vehicles and services and we should enhance access to such services by participating in the supplying nation's space program.
>
> Departments involved should submit plans to ensure that, to the fullest extent possible, Canada's satellite systems are designed, developed and constructed in Canada, by Canadians, using Canadian components.
>
> Canada's primary interest in space should be to use it for applications that contribute directly to the achievement of national goals.
>
> Utilization of space systems for the achievement of specific goals should be through activities proposed and budgeted by departments and agencies within their established mandates.
>
> At the international level, Canada's ability to use space should be furthered by participating in international activities for the use and regulation of activities in space, negotiating agreements for the continuing access to science technology and required facilities, and maintaining knowledge of foreign space activities in order to respond quickly to potential opportunities and threats to national sovereignty, and at the national level, Canada's ability to use space should be furthered by the support of research appropriate to the need to understand the properties of space, the potentialities of space systems, and the search for potential applications, and technology programs to develop the industrial capacity essential to meeting future requirements for operational space systems.[13]

It is evident from this policy that heavy emphasis was to be placed on private-industry participation in research and development

---

12. Charles Dalfen, Department of Communications, quoted by Jocelyn M. Ghent, *Canadian Government Participation in International Science and Technology*, Science Council of Canada Background Study 44 (Ottawa: Minister of Supply and Services Canada, 1979), p. 41.

13. As summarized in Department of Communications, *The Canadian Space Program: Five-Year Plan (80/81–84/85)* (Ottawa: Minister of Supply and Services Canada, 1980), p. 17.

for satellite technology systems. Since 1974, even greater emphasis has been placed on the use of the Canadian space industry to produce advanced satellite technology systems for Canada and, optimistically, for sale to other countries. In 1975, the federal government indicated it would explore the setting-up of a prime contractor for Canadian spacecraft of all kinds, not just communications satellites. In 1977, the government said a primary objective of Canada's space programme should be "to demonstrate, as soon as feasible, the capability of SPAR Aerospace Ltd. to compete as a prime contractor for communications satellites".[14] This objective was reached on May 15, 1979, when Telesat Canada signed a contract with SPAR to act as prime contractor on the production of two satellites in the Anik-D series.

Communications Satellite Systems

Communications satellite systems, as with ionospheric research and remote-sensing technology, are continually becoming more sophisticated as each satellite series is launched. Satellite technology is rapidly evolving, and the manufacturing of spacecraft is not a mass-production phenomenon. This has two implications: (a) it is essential to spend large sums of money on research and development before any new satellite or satellite series is assembled; (b) a satellite may be unique or, at best, one of a handful of identical productions, so that mass-production economics cannot be applied either to the components or to the assembly techniques used. Therefore, companies engaged in spacecraft production do not design and build craft or components without contracts already in hand from customers. Also, the contracts normally have a part of the costs assigned for needed research prior to manufacture; indeed, many contracts in Canada and elsewhere are simply to conduct the research and development needed for future space technology and technical-support systems.

Canada has been in the forefront of civilian communications-satellite applications since the early 1970s, even if the satellites used were not completely designed and built by Canadian companies. The possibility of improving trans-Canada communications links through the use of satellites has appealed to the policy-makers for at least the past fifteen years and, in order to ensure that satellites would be used to meet Canadian priorities, it was decided by the federal government to set up a statutory corporation to own and operate all domestic communications satellites. As already mentioned, this corpora-

---

14. *Ibid.*, p. 18.

tion was named Telesat Canada and established in 1969. In the 1968 White Paper on satellite policy, the following statements were made:

> A domestic satellite system should be a national undertaking stretching across Canada from coast to coast, north to Ellesmere Island and operating under the jurisdiction of the Government of Canada.
>
> The satellites and earth stations together would form a single system under the control of a single management. This would provide the operational and technical control which is essential to facilitate the progressive incorporation of new technology, and so fulfil the minimum conditions for financial success.
>
> The organization should have a corporate form in order that it may sell its services efficiently to the common carriers and television systems; in order that it may compete effectively in those areas where competition is appropriate; and in order that it may finance its activities through a suitable combination of equity and debt capital.[15]

Essentially, in order to have a communications-satellite system, five different elements are needed:
1. the satellite itself (there may be several);
2. launching facilities to send the satellite into orbit;
3. the up-link earth stations (for transmission to the satellite);
4. the down-link earth stations (to receive signals);
5. connections with the terrestrial telecommunications networks and/or with the broadcasting networks, stations and cable television systems.

The first four of these elements are technical facilities of high complexity and sophistication and, therefore, of high cost. In Canada, it was decided not to spend money on developing launch facilities but instead to use those of the United States. The fifth essential element of the satellite system is the connection between the earth stations and the terrestrial telecommunications and broadcasting networks. This element does not require new technology so much as it requires structural changes in the existing networks and in the way they interface with each other. Without such connecting links, however, the satellite corporation cannot provide communications services to business and household customers. The co-operation of the telephone companies, more than that of the broadcasters or cable television operators, is vital to the usefulness of the Canadian satellite system (and, of course, to its economic viability).

The Telesat satellite system was designed originally to have two different transmission capacities: (1) a "heavy route" linkage between Toronto and Vancouver via major earth stations at Allan Park and

---

15. Honourable C. M. Drury, Minister of Industry, *A Domestic Satellite Communication System for Canada* (Ottawa: Queen's Printer, 1968), pp. 44, 46.

Cowichan Bay respectively; (2) a "thin route" network which could provide at least telephone service via small earth stations in isolated communities in the North and mid-North.[16] Technical integration of the ground facilities of the satellite system with the terrestrial networks of the Canadian telephone system was arranged efficiently so that, from the start of satellite operation in 1972, the satellite system was interconnected with the major telecommunications networks already in existence.

While television is the more publicly conspicuous content carried on the Canadian satellite system, the primary use for the satellite channels in Canada is for telecommunications (i.e., telephone and data communications) traffic. The Canadian common carriers, therefore, are the major users of the satellites, and the large telephone companies have benefited from Telesat policies which require customers to contract for point-to-point service through their local telephone company.[17] In 1976, Telesat announced that it planned to become a member of the Trans-Canada Telephone System (TCTS), the co-operative association of the major telephone companies in Canada, which manages interprovincial telecommunications traffic for its members. By joining TCTS, Telesat hoped to be assured that TCTS members would use the satellite facilities on a continuing basis.

Telesat's membership in TCTS was reviewed by the Canadian Radio-television and Telecommunications Commission (CRTC), which refused to permit such a move.[18] The CRTC declared that the Telesat-TCTS arrangement would not be in the public interest, mainly because it would make regulation of Telesat's service rates more difficult, and also because Telesat's ability to serve all common carriers (not only those which belong to TCTS) might be impaired. The Commission's decision was overturned by the federal Cabinet and, although court appeals may still be going on, Telesat has been, effectively, a TCTS member since 1977. (In 1983, TCTS was renamed Telecom Canada.)

Broadcasting by Satellite in the North

Although the effects on telecommunications policy may not have been fully anticipated, some possible impact of satellite communications on Canadian broadcasting policy must have been expected from the start. The Drury White Paper noted that a domestic satellite system

---

16. Telesat Canada, *A Canadian Satellite Communications System*, June 1971.

17. Clyne Committee, *op. cit.*, p. 52.

18. CRTC, Telecom Decision 77-10, August 24, 1977, *Telesat Canada, Proposed Agreement with Trans-Canada Telephone System*.

could have significant benefits for the distribution of television service in Canada.[19] First, it could make television service available in both English and French across the country, as it had not been to date. Second, it could do this sooner and at a lower cost than would be possible through expansion of existing terrestrial distribution facilities. Third, it would allow the extension of television service to many areas of the country previously unserved because of their remoteness from the main population centres and from the U.S. border.

To take advantage of the existence of the Canadian satellite system, a few networks have been developed to provide radio and television coverage in northern Canada. Given the high cost of leasing a satellite channel (it has been about one million dollars a year since Telesat began service in 1972, and is still close to that price in 1983), the starting of a satellite-fed broadcasting network cannot be undertaken without substantial funds being available. Telesat internal policy has favoured the leasing of full channels only (and for solid blocks of time—for example, a month or year, twenty-four hours a day), so that limited use of a satellite for part of a day or for occasional use as needed is not usually possible. While television transmission requires a full satellite channel, radio transmission needs a much smaller bandwidth; but again Telesat policy is not designed to respond easily to this type of satellite use.

The high cost of using satellite channels did not deter the Canadian Broadcasting Corporation (CBC) which, with special funding encouragement from the federal government, has leased several satellite channels since 1972. No commercial radio or television network in southern Canada, however, has opted to abandon terrestrial linkages and use satellites instead. Since 1981, a broadcasting consortium known as CANCOM has leased satellite channels to distribute its "package" of Canadian television and radio signals to remote and under-served communities, mostly in the mid-North.[20] CANCOM has recently received permission from the CRTC to redistribute several American television signals as well;[21] this is an excellent illustration of the trend towards extension of southern networks to the North, which satellites facilitate.

Aside from CANCOM, however, the history of satellite broadcasting to the North is largely that of the CBC. Starting in 1972, when Anik A satellites first began commercial operation, the CBC has been

---

19. Drury, *op. cit.*, p. 32.

20. CRTC Decision 81-252, April 14, 1981.

21. CRTC Decision 83-126, March 8, 1983.

a leading customer for Telesat. In the early to mid-1970s, the CBC was encouraged by the federal government to extend radio and television service (English and French) to unserved communities of five hundred or more people all across the country. This was done under a special funding programme granted to the CBC and known as the Accelerated Coverage Plan (ACP). Also proposed was a Northern Broadcasting Plan which was designed to extend service to northern communities of two hundred or more people. However, it appears this was never separately funded by Parliament and much of the northern extension has been done with ACP funds.[22] Both these plans presupposed the availability of satellite reception in locations where ground linkages were uneconomic or technically impractical.

For northern Canada, extension of service as such was not regarded as enough by the CBC planners and by the CRTC. ''Relevant programming'' was also envisaged, and this was the area where the CBC had the greatest difficulties, especially in regard to television.

The Northern Service in CBC Radio has been developed on a sub-regional basis in the northern Territories, has recently become more available in the northern parts of many provinces, and has achieved a rather successful blend of local (sometimes community-access), sub-regional, northern and national (Canada-wide) programming mix for its listeners across the North. This has been possible through a combination of factors: principally the relatively low cost of installing and operating a local radio transmitter with studio attached; the narrower bandwidth required for radio transmission (as compared to television); the flexibility of networking arrangements to allow programme origination from different centres at different times of the day; the relative ease with which people can be trained to produce radio programmes; and the use of various native languages (in addition to English or French, as appropriate) in northern programming, so as to reach most of the northern audience with some programmes each day.

Television, however, has been another matter altogether. While the radio service has generally been praised by northern residents, the television service to the North has been strongly criticized from the start of satellite service.

The first major opportunity for the expression of public dissatisfaction from northern residents was the CRTC Hearing on

---

22. Canadian Broadcasting Corporation, *Annual Report 1974-75*, pp. 40-41, and Annual Reports for following years.

CBC Network Licence Renewals in 1974.[23] At that hearing, complaints were heard by the Commission about the television service to the North on two main grounds.

First, the service received was not specifically designed for northern reception but was actually an internal delivery system between English network headquarters in Toronto and the CBC's regional-distribution centres in southern Canada; consequently, programs were received by northern viewers in haphazard order, with the same programme run twice in the same evening, for example, or at totally different times in successive weeks. (This problem was reduced when a special Northern Service was transmitted, although not on its own channel.)

The second major complaint about the television service in 1974 was that few, if any, of the television programmes could be considered relevant to northerners in their everyday experience of life; this was especially a problem for native people—even if they could understand English well enough to follow what was said.[24] The CRTC expressed its concern about these problems to the CBC in its licence decision and said that it expected the Corporation to prepare plans to deal with the complaints made. It was noted by the Commission that the CBC had received an inadequate budget for programming in the Northern Service.

By 1979 (the next Network Licence Renewal Hearing for the CBC), the situation had not improved for Northern Television.[25] Under the ACP, a few northern communities entitled to CBC service had voted against receiving television, although they did usually accept the radio service. Again, criticisms by individuals and community representatives from the North were levelled at the television service. At special hearings held in northern communities, the CRTC heard eighty-seven representations, most of them concerned about the irrelevance and intrusiveness of southern programming beamed to their area. Even the CBC officials at the hearings were ready to agree that the television service was unsuitable but their problem was lack

---

23. CRTC Decision 74-70, March 31, 1974, *Radio Frequencies are Public Property: Public Announcement and Decision of the Commission on the Applications for Renewal of the Canadian Broadcasting Corporation's Television and Radio Licences*, pp. 62-63.

24. Various interpretations have been put on the possible cultural effects of southern television programmes on the indigenous people of the North. Researchers from the social sciences have studied the effects and drawn different conclusions on the basis of the evidence gathered. For a selection of these differing views, see the *Journal of Communication*, Fall 1977 issue, which gives ten short articles on "Communication in the Far North".

25. CRTC Decision 79-320, April 30, 1979, *Renewal of the Canadian Broadcasting Corporation's Television and Radio Network Licences*, pp. 25-29.

of funds to produce, preferably in the North, appropriate content for northern viewers.

While native people have objected to the television service as irrelevant or culturally threatening, their hope is for a more relevant service using northern programme producers. However, most northern residents who are not native people tend to have criticisms which are slightly different, and their preferred solution is definitely different. For non-natives, the CBC Northern Television Service is unacceptable when it is the only channel available; they want more channels, and preferably the same choice as the Canadians in southern cities receive. Cultural threats are less a problem for them than the isolation from services they know other Canadians get.

Given these differences between native and non-native preferences in satellite television, and given the enormous costs attached to creating special services for the small northern population, as well as the complexities of language and culture which should be reflected in the programme content, the use of satellites for broadcasting television in the North is fraught with difficulties if one tries to respond to viewer demands. The CBC has tried to respond but has consistently pointed out, to the CRTC and others, that the necessary funds to produce a fully northern television service have not been provided by Parliament.

The prospects for future improvement of television in the North may not be totally bleak, however. One encouraging development has been the beginning of a network operated by the Inuit Broadcasting Corporation (IBC). The Corporation was set up in 1981 by five Inuit organizations in the Eastern Arctic, and its network went on the air in early 1982 via a satellite channel leased from Telesat by the CBC (to which the IBC was given access for a few hours each week). Programming is produced by Inuit people in the Inuktitut language and the programmes are received in about thirty-two communities, thus reaching approximately 20,000 Inuit in the Eastern Arctic (no such service is available yet in the Western Arctic).[26]

This sort of informal and part-time network, which allows for time to develop production expertise and to seek community response to programme content, is probably the ideal one for native people in the North. Much of the credit for the success of the IBC organization so far is probably due to the length of time in which Inuit organizations (such as the Inuit Tapirisat of Canada) have been discussing communications issues and problems in the Arctic communities. It

---

26. Information in this paragraph is from a leaflet issued by the Inuit Broadcasting Corporation in 1983.

may seem paradoxical that the Inuit, who are far fewer in number than the native Indians, should be much better served by satellite broadcasting. However, being fewer in number, and having fewer social divisions of language, culture, and treaty status, have helped the Inuit to organize themselves and to express clearly their priorities and preferences to government bodies such as the CRTC. Indian people have been much less fortunate in this respect. Finally, it must be noted that the IBC network depends entirely on federal funds of various kinds in order to exist and function effectively. Such a network is not self-supporting and can never be so.

Conclusion

In summary, the following points seem to be significant factors influencing the development of the satellite system in Canada. First, space research has been spurred by the interests of the scientific and technical research community and the federal government's response to funding requests in this field. Second, technical and economic development of satellite technology has been urged upon the government by the space "industry", which is evolving from the small aeronautics/aircraft-manufacturing sector in Canada. Third, the economic structures set up around the ownership and management of communications satellites have reflected the key role played by the major telephone companies and their preference for an integrated (noncompetitive) satellite-telecommunications system. Fourth, the high cost of research and development for satellite systems has required federal government involvement in legislation, corporate financing, and contract funding. Fifth, considerations of social benefit from these systems have had to give way before the crucial economic and technical concerns.

To these five points, another three could be added; they concern the use of satellites for broadcasting in particular. First, dependence on telecommunications traffic for economic survival has caused the satellite system to be less adaptable for broadcasting uses. Second, in providing service to the North, the satellite system has been used to extend the coverage areas of broadcasting networks based in southern Canada; it has not encouraged the establishment of new networks for the North. Third, despite the ability of satellite technology to ignore great land distances in extending signal coverage, the sparse population of the North is still an economic drawback in developing special broadcasting services.

The federal government appears to have given the highest priority to the value of the domestic satellite system as a part of a much larger space programme; space policy has a broader scope than does satellite policy alone. A great deal of money has been spent, and more will be spent, by the federal government to maintain facilities for space research within government departments and agencies, to support space research projects in universities, and to encourage space research and development in private industry.[27] This support for space research is in the cause of maintaining scientific leadership in the field, providing Canadian scientists and engineers with opportunities to work in Canada, and providing support to the research community generally.

However, funds spent on research (even on research and development) do not necessarily have economic benefits for Canada if no commercial production of satellite technology ensues. Domestic and foreign markets for Canadian technology have to be explored and encouraged. As a major step in this direction, the federal government set up Telesat with a special responsibility to buy Canadian technology and to provide satellite service throughout Canada on a commercial profit-making basis.

The primary reason for government participation in ownership of the satellite system has always been given as "national sovereignty" concerns. These concerns exist in two spheres: technological sovereignty and cultural or political sovereignty. Regarding the latter type of sovereignty, the Clyne Committee observed in 1979 that "satellite communications have greater significance for Canadian sovereignty than for that of any other country in the world."[28] Canadian ownership of communications systems has been guarded by the federal government through legislation and regulatory actions.

As already noted at the beginning of this paper, the Committee also said that the domestic satellite system is "one of the most potent instruments available for the social and cultural benefit" of many Canadians. Such statements sound optimistic but are rather vague as to how such benefit can be achieved. Also, they ignore the enormous gulfs between different social classes and different cultures in a society such as Canada.

Which culture or cultures will benefit from the use of satellites to extend their reach and their power within the whole society? Which segments of society and which regions of the country will bene-

---

27. DOC, *The Canadian Space Program*, pp. 12-13.

28. Clyne Committee, *op. cit.*, p. 54.

fit, and will they do so at the expense of others in the society? These are the crucial questions which we must answer in Canada if we are to plan the development of broadcasting services for the people of *all* regions of Canada.

15.   Advent of a New Era

The Conserver Society

Ray Jackson
Science Council of Canada

Concern about limits to the Earth's carrying capacity, and about the ecological interrelationship of living systems, has received repeated flurries of public attention for at least two hundred years, stirred by the writings of Malthus at the beginning of the nineteenth century and of Reginald Marsh at mid-century, John Muir around the beginning of the twentieth, Fairfield Osborn, William Vogt, Rachel Carson during the 1950s and 1960s, and many others. The latest flurry of attention, very probably, is here to stay.

In the early seventies a group of concerned individuals from the international managerial class, led by Aurelio Peccei of Italy, formed the Club of Rome and commissioned the report *Limits to Growth*, published in 1972.[1] In Canada, the Science Council sensed the same currents and in its 1973 report on *Natural Resource Policy Issues in Canada*[2] recommended "that Canadians as individuals, and their governments, institutions, and industries, begin the transition from a consumer society preoccupied with resource exploitation to a conserver society engaged in more constructive endeavours. Ideally, Canada could provide the leadership necessary to work toward more equitable distribution of the benefits of natural resources to all mankind". Later that year the Science Council decided to undertake a special study on the concept of a conserver society, which resulted in the report *Canada as a Conserver Society: Resource Uncertainties and the Need for New Technologies*, published in 1977.[3]

---

1. Donella H. Meadows, Dennis L. Meadows, Jorgen Randers, W. W. Behrens III, *The Limits to Growth* (New York: Universe, 1972).

2. *Natural Resource Policy Issues in Canada*, Science Council of Canada Report No. 19, Ottawa, January 1973.

3. *Canada as a Conserver Society: Resource Uncertainties and the Need for New Technologies*, Science Council of Canada Report No. 27, Ottawa, September 1977.

In the meantime the Science Council and several other federal government agencies, acting through the Department of Supply and Services, responded to a proposal from GAMMA, a consulting group centred around McGill University and the University of Montreal, to investigate the concept. GAMMA, under the leadership of Dr. Kimon Valaskakis, produced in 1976 a four-volume report, under the label *The Conserver Society Project*.[4] The report consisted of fifteen academic papers from various disciplines, ranging from philosophy and physics through anthropology and psychology to economics and politics, along with an integrating essay and review. The latter formed the basis for a popular book.[5] Among the assembled studies was one by Irene Spry, on "Non-Renewable Resources". Obviously Professor Spry was alive to this new concept and sympathetic with its meaning.

The concept or, rather, group of concepts took shape in Canada principally around the term "conserver society". However, these ideas were certainly not unique to Canada. They appeared virtually world-wide, under various names, though predominantly in the industrialized countries, which were more advanced in pollution, resource depletion, and other malaises of high consumption.

There was, after all, more to the perception than simply concern about impending limits to material resources—even when the concept of resources is expanded to include formerly "free" resources such as clean air, clean water, and living biosphere. High consumption, it turns out, is not an unalloyed good. There were questions, for example, regarding the eventual effects on human beings and social relations of an unending growth of consumption, and there were questions regarding the deliberate stimulation of consumption and waste as a "policy" for achieving economic "health" and for the indefinite postponement of problems of injustice, maldistribution, and misallocation.

Some observers, however, thought the concerns were greatly exaggerated. There were no real resource shortages, at least none that would not be solved by rising prices, substitution, and new extraction technologies,[6] and the urge to conserve was no more than an historical fluctuation, reacting to some of the obvious waste of the

---

4. Kimon Valaskakis, *et al.*, *The Conserver Society Project*: Vol. 1, The Selective Conserver Society; Vol. 2, The Physical and Technological Constraints; Vol. 3, The Institutional Dimension; Vol. 4, Values and the Conserver Society (Montreal: GAMMA, 1976).

5. K. Valaskakis, P. Sindell, G. Smith, I. Fitzpatrick-Martin, *The Conserver Society: A Workable Alternative for the Future* (Toronto: Fitzhenry & Whiteside; New York: Harper & Row, 1979). See also Lawrence Solomon, *The Conserver Solution* (New York: Doubleday, 1978).

6. Julian L. Simon, *The Ultimate Resource* (Princeton University Press, 1981).

"consumer society" which, in turn, may have been occasioned by an excess of enthusiasm in government for economic stimulation via consumer spending. The Malthusians, after all, have always been with us, even though before Malthus they were known by other names. Thus, it was argued, the import of the "conserver society" concept was superficial and transitory.

However, even the proponents of that view must have felt sometimes a vague sense of insecurity, that perhaps some features of the world have changed, and perhaps some principles of nineteenth-century economics are not as valid as they were. What this paper will attempt to do is to review some of the changes in the world and in thinking about it, that have taken place in recent decades—not *all* changes that have taken place, to be sure, but some of those that have been influencing, in one way or another, new ways of thinking about the world and its economic processes. The review will range over a number of disciplines, from physical sciences and technology, through psychology, economics, social relations, politics, values and perceptions, to morality. If this accomplishes nothing else, it may reduce the tenacity or the confidence with which some of the conventional ideas are held.

The Emerging Concepts

1. *Physical Sciences and Technology*

Earth's limits. The finitude of resources has been pointed out in such reports as *Limits to Growth*,[7] *Global 2000*,[8] and the *Worldwatch* papers.[9] The world population has become so large and technologies so powerful that it is now obvious that the Earth's material resources can be depleted. ("Depletion" does not mean absolute exhaustion, but entrance into a régime of steeply rising costs; metals can always be recovered from very dilute ores, given sufficient energy and technique, but the energy will eventually be sufficient to heat the Earth's atmosphere, either directly or through the greenhouse effect; and the

---

7. Meadows *et al.*, *op. cit.*

8. Gerald O. Barney, ed., *The Global 2000 Report to the President*, U.S. Superintendant of Documents, Washington, 1980.

9. The Worldwatch Papers: beginning with no. 1, *The Other Energy Crisis—Firewood*, in 1975, and now up to no. 55, *Whole Earth Security: A Geopolitics of Peace*. The Worldwatch Institute has maintained a constant concern with the sustainable use of the world's resources.

wastes must be put somewhere.) Thus policy begins to work towards a *sustainable* use of resources.[10]

Environmental carrying capacity. Similarly, there are observable or foreseeable limits to the absorptive capacity of the environment for wastes and contaminants. Production of fluorocarbons has become large enough to have a measurable effect on the ozone layer; combustion of fossil fuels is generating sufficient carbon dioxide to begin changing the climate; river basins, lakes, and whole water tables have become measurably contaminated with toxic chemicals. Governments are having to develop policies and controls against fouling our own nest.

Ecology. The science of ecology, though its roots can be traced back a century or more, has only relatively recently gained attention, but has been growing rapidly in size and in respect. It has clarified how systems of the biosphere, living creatures, are interrelated and interdependent—and how total efficiency and resiliency in use of resources is obtained in nature by filling every diverse niche.[11]

Thermodynamics. The alarm over energy as a scarce resource, triggered by the OPEC crisis of 1973, has drawn attention to the concept of entropy, as providing better guidance as to *what* and *how* to economize.[12] Carried further, entropy defined in terms of *information* (non-randomness) suggests principles for the conservation or valuing of negentropy in the form of differentiated materials, living systems, knowledge, and culture. Against the entropic tendency (third law of thermodynamics) of closed systems to run down to an ultimate state of "heat death" or uniform temperature (the jumbled uniformity of a garbage dump), the input of solar energy, the existing stores of energy and order, and the use of intelligence make it possible for living systems to build more and more complex forms, and ultimately for humans to build civilizations. Advances in the theory of non-equilibrium open "dissipative systems"[13] have clarified the principles of how such evolution may come about, and incidentally emphasize the importance of variety in the systems, the role of deviation-amplifying processes, positive feedback, and negentropy.

---

10. Lester R. Brown, *Building a Sustainable Society* (New York: Horton, 1981).

11. Paul R. Ehrlich, Anne H. Ehrlich, and John P. Holdren, *Ecoscience: Population, Resource, Environment* (San Francisco: Freeman, 1977).

12. Nicholas Georgescu-Roegen, *The Entropy Law and the Economic Process* (Harvard University Press, 1971).

13. Ilya Prigogine, *From Being to Becoming: Time and Complexity in the Physical Sciences* (San Francisco: Freeman, 1980).

World-shrinking technologies. Atomic weapons have made obvious enough the possibility of global annihilation, extinction of the human species by a few ideological fanatics. But there are also the space and satellite technologies, which have made it easy to appreciate the world as a small place and have given us the view of our small globe from the moon. Medical advances have speeded population growth; chemical instrumentation has revealed man-made environmental poisons that have even turned up in the polar ice caps. Computer technology has made possible the modelling of global systems to reveal some of the problems we face, and so on. Science and technology have changed our relationships to the physical world.

Bioengineering. Advances in the understanding of living matter (the structure of DNA, etc.) and medical technique, with increasing control over the beginning and end of life, have been bringing about profound changes in attitudes. Life, in the view of many, has been losing its sacredness and mystery. Control means that humans now have to accept the burden of moral responsibility for intervention in matters that were formerly assumed to be determined by fate, or God's will. Similarly, but at a deeper level, scientists are now beginning to take a conscious role in the shaping of genetic evolution. Thus a subtle change is taking place, from a view of humans as mechanistic (though rational) automatons in a deterministic (or fatalistic) universe, to a view of humans as "responsible" beings taking charge of their own development.

Limits of science itself—a new humility? Science, as a body of knowledge, is itself a living system, subject to evolution, revision, and self-correction. As we find out more about such matters as pollution of the environment, biology, and nutrition, we realize that some confident actions of the past (based on what was thought to be scientific knowledge) were mistakes. Often, learning more—for example, about causes of cancer—impresses us with how much we do *not* know. Research into the ultimate structure of matter finds the supposedly hard indestructible atoms dissolving into mere local states or appearances of a fundamental interconnected field,[14] raising questions of epistemology (why should we have thought that explanations in terms of ultimate irreducible marbles would have been more intellectually satisfying anyway?). Thus arrogance or over-confidence is coming to be tempered by modesty, and the critical attitude is seen as essential

---

14. David Bohm, *Wholeness and the Implicate Order,* (Boston: Routledge and Kegan Paul, 1982).

to science.[15] The general public, too, have become more critical of science, and suspicious of engineers. The possibility of scientific uncertainty, controversy, and error is evident to all. No one should any longer assume that a new/old technology will always be able to solve any problem.

Paradigm changes. Other branches of science—economics, psychology, even philosophy—have been known to model themselves on theories in the physical sciences. Thus changes in paradigms in physical sciences may be important, either as providing useful new models for thought in other spheres, or as revealing other patterns of thought to have been drawn from older paradigms and therefore to be potentially obsolete, unsound, or at least open to replacement by better models. The Copernican revolution, relativity, and now ecology, could be said to have helped displace conceptual frameworks from a man-centred view of the world. Quantum mechanics presented epistemological problems of experimental indeterminacy and, by emphasizing the role of the observer as disturber of the world by his experiments, drew attention to the fact that even in the physical sciences there is a dialectical interaction between man and nature—a feature of the world that was being excessively glossed over in the psychological and social sciences, in their desire to emulate the supposed rigour of physics. Quantum mechanics also posed problems for the interpretation of the fundamental structure of the world. The finding that, in some sense, fundamental particles often had to be thought of as being in two places at once was a puzzle only now being resolved in terms of a holographic interpretation of reality, still being debated among physicists. What we observe in experiments are "explicate" manifestations of an underlying "implicate" order, in which every local part in some sense contains every other part of the universe.[16] This conceptual model, inspired from the discovery of holography,[17] has been picked up also to explain the working of the human brain[18] and is transferring

---

15. Karl R. Popper, *Objective Knowledge: An Evolutionary Approach* (Oxford University Press, 1972).

16. Bohm, *op. cit.*

17. Attributed to Dennis Gabor, in 1948, becoming practical with the development of light-emitting *lasers* in 1960. By using wave-coherent light from a laser, rather than chaotic light from an ordinary heat-excited source, the information from a scene can be photographically captured in a different form. In place of a recognizable photograph, the holograph appears to be a mess of smudges. Yet, when illuminated by wave-coherent light similar to the original, the original scene is re-created. Moreover, this happens from illuminating any *part* of the holograph. Illuminating a larger area simply improves the definition.

18. Karl Pribram, in *Consciousness and the Brain*, ed. Gordon Globus *et al.* (New York: Plenum Press, 1976).

rapidly into other fields, including even application to new theories of political organization. The epistemological turmoil in physics stirred advances in the philosophy of science, revealing scientific theories as essentially provisional and corrigible. Science as open-minded and self-critical has replaced science as dogmatic and certain (though unfortunately the message seems not yet to have gotten through to all working scientists, nor to all teachers of science). Ecology, cybernetics, and systems theory have all helped to encourage modes of thought involving multiple interacting systems, often with multiple networks and circuits of causality rather than simple linear chains. Thus holistic world-views begin to displace or complement the linear-causal-reductionistic.[19] In principle, every technology or application of science involves action in the world and therefore involves questions of ethics and moral responsibility; but recent advances in medical sciences and bioengineering have presented ethical issues so starkly that the old convenient dichotomy between science and values, or science and religion for that matter, no longer seems to hold. These paradigm shifts have arisen, and are arising, out of modern science and therefore they are *new*, and the implications they have for other disciplines are also new. Even when it can be said that they merely draw attention to perennial philosophical issues, those issues must now be seen from new perspectives.

2. *Psychology*

Brain and mind. Neurophysiology, biochemistry, psychology, physical-electronic instrumentation, and computer sciences have combined to cast new light on the nature of thinking—the brain understanding itself—questions that were once thought to be the permanent preserve of epistemology, a branch of philosophy. We now have a holographic theory of thinking and memory; we have identified and can to some extent measure the specialized functioning of left and right cerebral hemispheres (very roughly, the left concerned with language and linear reasoning, the right with holistic perception and pattern recognition); and we find strong evidence for the simultaneous presence of other *levels* of thinking, for example, the mammalian and the reptilian brain.[20] The other levels, while subjectively inseparable from mental

---

19. Fritjof Capra, *The Turning Point* (New York: Simon & Schuster, 1982).

20. Paul D. Maclean, ''On the Evolution of Three Mentalities'', *Man–Environment Systems*, 5 (1975), pp. 213-24.

process, are often felt as affective, emotional, irrational. All levels, but particularly the latter, which are presumably those most closely interrelated with moods, values, emotions, and desires, are interlinked with the internal biochemical environment which in turn is modulated by behaviour, nutrition, hormone systems, medications, and thinking.

Needs and values. Hierarchies of human needs, and levels of self-expression reached by the healthy evolving person[21] show that not everyone, perhaps not even the "normal" person, is primarily concerned with or driven by the urge for material acquisition and/or self-interest. Altruism, co-operation rather than competition, concern for environment and the future, can be strong and "normal" motivations.

3. Economics

Externalities. The cross-impacts and distributed impacts of human activities, for example, pollution (such as acid rain), have raised awareness of the "costs of economic growth".[22] Economists now recognize the importance of total social costing and seek better economic accounting systems and better social indicators.[23]

Consumer Society. High consumption as the key to prosperity was touted through the 1950s and 1960s, but the excessive waste of the throw-away society became conspicuous, and inflation became an incurable disease.[24] Some economists have been seeking solutions in no-growth or steady-state concepts.[25] Others explore the implications of a "conserver society".

Finite world. The recognition of a finite world with resource limits changes the paradigm from one of unending expansion, open fron-

21. A. H. Maslow, *Toward a Psychology of Being* (New York: Van Nostrand, 1968); Clare W. Graves, "Human Nature Prepares for a Momentous Leap", *The Futurist*, April 1974.

22. Ezra Mishan, *The Costs of Economic Growth* (London: Staples Press, 1967); and *Technology and Growth* (New York: Praeger, 1970).

23. Bertram M. Gross, and J. D. Straussman, "The Social Indicators Movement", *Social Policy*, Sept.-Oct., 1974. See also David Brusegard, "Social Indicators and Public Policy", *The Human Context for Science and Technology*, Social Sciences and Humanities Research Council of Canada, Ottawa, 1980, in mimeo.

24. Bertrand de Jouvenel, « La société inflationniste », *Analyse et prévision 17* (March 1974).

25. Herman Daly, *Steady-State Economics*, (New York: Freeman, 1977).

tiers, a "cowboy economics",[26] to one of closing cycles, and optimizing within fixed stocks. Some economists (such as Georgescu-Roegen) emphasize the need to pay attention to real physical variables, for example, entropy, and not to assume that prices take care of everything.

Economic cycles. The current recession suggests to some economists that we are on the downward slope of the long fifty-year Kondratiev cycle, the upturn of which (in the late eighties) will be due to investment in a new set of technologies, probably replacing the previous cycle's characteristic energy- and materials-intensive high-waste technologies.[27]

Breakdown of theory. Economic theory is fragmented and in disarray. There is widespread loss of confidence in the "Neoclassical Synthesis" as having the answers to inflation, unemployment, or regional and world development. Such disarray or confusion is characteristic of a period of paradigm transition, in Kuhn's sense.[28]

Changing nature of work. Automation, robotics, computers, are displacing workers, possibly creating a bi-modal economy of the skilled and the non-skilled, and with it new problems of fair distribution of work and income. The classic problem of sharing in the means of production may come back in another form. Another result is that an increasing proportion of production is shifting into a mixed "informal" sector of self-help, part-time, bartered, familial, and voluntary work.

4. Social Relations

Stress. The high-consumption affluent lifestyle has its costs in stress, breakdown of family relationships, urban alienation, and crime. The reaction is expressed in various movements that try to rediscover or re-create a sense of community.

---

26. Kenneth E. Boulding, *Beyond Economics* (University of Michigan Press, 1968).

27. Christopher Freeman, ed., "Technical Innovation and Long Waves in World Economic Development", Special issue of *Futures*, August 1981; see also articles in October 1981.

28. Wassily Leontiev (letter), *Science*, July 9, 1982; and his essay "What Hope for the Economy?", in *N.Y. Review of Books*, August 12, 1982. Thomas S. Kuhn, *Structure of Scientific Revolutions*, 2nd ed. (University of Chicago Press, 1970).

Social limits to growth. In some respects all the "busy-ness" leaves people no better off than before—working harder but not in possession of more "positional" goods.[29]

Labour/Management. The complexity of products, such as automobiles, televisions, micro-electronics, means that greater delegation of responsibility is needed for efficiency and quality. New forms of worker self-management and participation in management are evolving.

Tolerance and egalitarianism. Electronic communications and rising educational levels are among the reasons for some decreases in discrimination on the basis of race, colour, sex, or religion. The balance, however, is difficult to assess, because some of the media, for example, films and television, have been exploiting violence, dulling sensitivities, and blurring the distinctions between reality and fantasy.

5. Politics

Small scale. Reactions are being expressed against the impersonality, bureaucracy, and insensitivity of big systems and big governments, which are seen as causes of inefficiency, waste, and a sense of loss of control by the individual.[30] The movement for "small is beautiful" in technology, economics, and political organization finds allies even in the politics of the "right".

Decentralization. A dispersion of economic and political power is sought for itself, and also because a smaller, local scale is better for closing ecological loops. There is growing interest in community-scale decentralist politics,[31] local initiatives for economic development, and even new versions of anarchism.

Participation. The feeling of loss of personal control, of big interests and big systems running away with things, leads to movements for "participatory" democracy, and the rise of public-interest groups.

---

29. Fred Hirsch, *Social Limits to Growth* (Harvard University Press, 1976).

30. Kirkpatrick Sale, *Human Scale* (London: Secker & Warburg, 1980). See also Leopold Kohr, *The Overdeveloped Nations: the Diseconomies of Scale* (New York: Schocken, 1978).

31. David Morris, *Self-Reliant Cities: Energy and the Transformation of Urban America* (San Francisco: Sierra Club Books, 1982).

New political parties. The feeling that old left-right polarities are becoming irrelevant inspires new alignments, and the formation of "green" or "ecology" political parties.[32]

6. Values and Perceptions

One small planet. The view of Earth from space has changed the worldview of many, from a cowboy, empty-frontier mentality to a conserving space-ship mentality.

Voluntary simplicity. The reaction to materialistic preoccupations and artificialities of the consumer society, as well as a sense of scarcity of time, inspires a search for simple alternative lifestyles, symbolized by back-to-nature movements, home gardening, and greenhouses.[33] Public opinion polls show that many people feel they have enough material goods; to acquire more has low priority.

Personal development. The perception that non-material needs are more important than material needs (at least past a certain point) has been expressed in a trend to new spiritual movements and new psychological and physical therapies. "Humangrowth" replaces economic growth.[34]

Appropriate technology. The impression that science and technology have been devastating the world with their massive interventions has resulted in anti-technology attitudes in some quarters. It has also stimulated a search for alternative, simpler, ecologically harmonious, and benign technologies.[35]

7. Morality

Universal morality. Every new movement, philosophy, or paradigm, if it is to endure, must be grounded in, or at least not incompatible

---

32. Shirley Williams, "The Challenge of the New Romantics", *The Guardian*, April 28, 1981, p. 19. Note also that the Green Party of Canada held its founding convention in Ottawa, November 4-6, 1983.

33. Duane Elgin, *Voluntary Simplicity: Toward a Way of Life that is Outwardly Simple, Inwardly Rich* (New York: Morrow, 1981).

34. Harlan Cleveland and T. Wilson Jr., *Humangrowth: An Essay on Growth, Values, and the Quality of Life* (Aspen Institute of Humanistic Studies, 1978).

35. Franklin Long and Sandy Oleson, *Appropriate Technology and Social Values: A Critical Appraisal* (Cambridge, Mass.: Ballinger, 1980).

with, fundamental morality; that is, respect for the feelings, rationality, and autonomy of other human beings.

Altruism. The perception of One Earth tends to bring forth the ethics of sharing, co-operation, helping others, as against the simple pursuit of self-interest (which had been encouraged by conventional economic theory and by market forces). Thus many are exploring "altruistic economics",[36] and increasingly using co-operative forms of economic and social organization.[37]

Justice. An awareness of limited resources means greater concern for an ethic of sharing, or for distributive justice, as against the open-ended ethic which assumes that the richer the rich become, the better for everyone, because they will pull the poor up behind them. This also means a concern for sustainability well into the future, and that our descendants be considered when decisions are made to share resources.

Diversity. The right of other humans to be different must be respected, as a simple moral obligation. To maintain diversity is also a simple practical policy for evolution, to guard against the mistakes of over-confident genetic engineers.

Creativity. The obligation to evolve, if that may be assumed to be a purpose of the human race, means that creativity, innovation, and diversity should be nurtured and valued (cf. Prigogine). This means keeping options open, and has other implications for policy.

Review

We have tried to track a cluster of new paradigms across the disciplines, beginning with the most solid and material, the physical sciences, and ending with the most tenuous, values and morality. Interestingly enough, as we do so, we seem to meet people coming the other way, people like Hazel Henderson, working from a base in economics,[38]

---

36. David Collard, *Altruism and Economy* (London: Martin Robertson, 1978).

37. Henk Thomas and Chris Logan, *Mondragon: An Economic Analysis* (London: George Allen & Unwin, 1982).

38. Hazel Henderson, *Creating Alternative Futures: The End of Economics* (New York: Anchor Press/Doubleday, 1978). Also, *The Politics of the Solar Age: Alternatives to Economics* (New York: Anchor Press/Doubleday, 1981).

Mark Satin from a base in "new age" politics,[39] Marilyn Ferguson from a basic position of spiritual transformation.[40] All of us probably suffer from a biased selectivity, a tendency to pick up evidence or interpret it in ways that suit our purpose. Thus some physicists may take exception to the interpretations that others of their number, such as Capra, Zukav, or Hofstadter,[41] have placed on theoretical developments in this or that corner of quantum mechanics, cosmology, or thermodynamics, and especially to the use or misuse of these concepts by interlopers from other disciplines—such as economists and (other?) theologians. Equally, social scientists have a right to be suspicious of the highly selective interpretations of what is "significant" coming out of their areas, arrived at, say, by a wandering physical scientist.

However, rather than being intimidated and driven off by these territorial claims, one would better regard these cross-disciplinary ventures, with their risk of distortions, as being all of a part. What we are doing is useful. It belongs in the category of Prigogine's mutually reinforcing deviation-amplifying processes, which are at the root of innovation, evolution, and creative change. We are helping evolution in the field of ideas by noticing the new, and amplifying it. There will be corrections later. Let us first form new hypotheses.

The starting point of our journey was the question, essentially, of whether the concept of a "conserver society" is new, or significant, or perhaps simply the recurrence of an old Malthusian nightmare about resources running out, brought on by the recession, or the energy crisis.

The review should have established that there is much that is new, and permanently so, not merely cyclical. To what extent does it all coalesce? At one time one might have imagined that there should be some kind of unitary logical structure defining the idea of a "conserver society", some consistent theoretical foundation, to be developed or uncovered as one would discover the structure of a building. The structure would be built logically from one or more primary causes which, in turn, might be causally linked one to another.

The exercise, however, may have helped to make it clear that such a paradigm would have been mistaken. Why indeed should one think that all-important developments in the patterns of thought must

---

39. Mark Satin, *New Age Politics* (New York: Delta, 1979).

40. Marilyn Ferguson, *The Aquarian Conspiracy: Personal and Social Transformation in the 1980's* (Los Angeles; Tarcher, 1980).

41. Capra, *op. cit.*; Gary Zukav, *The Dancing Wu-Li Masters: An Overview of the New Physics* (New York: Bantam, 1980); Douglas Hofstadter, *Godel, Escher, Bach: An Eternal Golden Braid* (New York: Basic, 1979).

conform to that simple model? Why should we assume that such models would best represent the real world?

It seems more fruitful to take our cue from the philosopher Alfred North Whitehead.[42] Then we might think of life or history as a process, the present being shaped as a nexus of converging world-lines that may or may not be related by anything more than their simultaneity. What we may then have is converging themes that to some extent resonate and reinforce one another, like vibrating strings on a harp.

The "conserver society" may be accepted as a suitable label for those new paradigms that cluster and bundle together towards the physical-sciences end of the spectrum of human interests. But the bundles overlap and their boundaries are arbitrary. The bundle with its centre of gravity towards psychology and spiritual transformation could well be labelled by Marilyn Ferguson's term "the Aquarian Conspiracy". The two are related, in a complex but inevitable way, because they co-exist in time and context.

Psychological Depths

A feature of the "conserver society" concept is that at times it seems to have excited a lively, even violent controversy among economists. The community has tended to split into two camps, the Cornucopians or growth-maniacs, and the neo-Malthusians, or doom-and-glooms, as they have characterized each other. The debate was hot and heavy at the 1982 and 1983 Annual Meetings of the American Association for the Advancement of Science, among such exponents as Julian Simon,[43] noted "conservative" futurist Herman Kahn, and Garrett Hardin ("The Tragedy of the Commons").[44]

It is characteristic of people, when their paradigms are threatened, to react in a very visceral and irrational way. Often they feel they are arguing purely intellectually and rationally, and cannot understand why their opponents seem so obtuse. In terms of the current theory of the triune brain, referred to below, the difficulty is easier to understand, if not to overcome. When territory is threatened, as

---

42. Alfred North Whitehead, *Process and Reality* (New York: Free Press, 1978).

43. Simon, *op. cit.*

44. Global 2000 Revised. Symposium organized by Herman Kahn and Julian Simon at the AAAS National Annual Meeting, Detroit, May 26-31, 1983. See also Hardin's review of Simon's book, *The Ultimate Resource*, in *The New Republic*, October 28, 1981, reprinted in *The Ecologist* 12, (Jan./Feb. 1982).

when non-professional economists try to talk about economics, the mammalian brain responds to alert all systems to a defence reaction. When a conceptual paradigm is threatened, it is felt deep down as a threat to personal integrity or identity, and a primitive defence reaction at the reptilian level is stirred up. The individual is often unaware of why he or she is getting so emotional about what should be an intellectual discussion.

However, some of the roots of these differences go even deeper than a reluctance to change, or a vested interest in present ideas or present affiliations. Two basic styles of behaviour seem to run throughout human history: one, that of sensate abandon, ranging from tranquil enjoyment to wild orgies; the other characterized by rational control, awareness of rules, and common sense, as in the cold light of dawn. These behaviour patterns are so typical that they were embodied in the personae of the Greek gods Dionysus and Apollo, and have persisted in one form or another throughout the work of philosophers, from Aristotle to Nietzsche, sometimes as a simple emotional/rational polarity, sometimes in more complicated forms. A present-day neuro-psychologist such as Paul Maclean, responsible for the concept of the triune brain,[45] might identify one with the limbic system of the brain, inherited from our mammalian ancestors, and the other with the cerebral cortex. Presumably the simple animal, dog or chimpanzee, lives entirely for the joys of the moment, carefree of the morrow, and heedless of what effects he might have on the resource base. With the cerebral cortex, man understands implications, makes rules, imposes controls on his own behaviour. The struggle for supremacy of cerebral control has inspired religion, philosophy, and drama. Even if the rational mind is regarded as only an instrument for achieving fundamental "felt" drives, it is still up to the rational mind to *select* the "higher" appetites or motives over the "lower". When the burden gets too heavy, humans revert to the carefree animal emotional state by wiping out the cerebral cortex with alcohol, drugs, or ceremony.

One might speculate, then, that behind the Cornucopian and Malthusian positions, there are unnoticed elements of the Dionysian and Apollonian—the Cornucopian incorporates a kind of wishful thinking that we can enjoy ourselves without limit and let the market, technology, and prices take care of all those concerns about resources; while the Malthusian harbours a kind of Calvinist suspicion that you can't enjoy yourself without paying for it somehow. The Malthusian

---

45. Maclean, *op. cit.*.

(Apollonian) cannot help thinking about the implications. The conclusion of this paper must be that the direction of evolution, and the fact of evolution, now leave us no choice. We have to put the Apollonian in charge.

The reason is that we have used the cerebral cortex to develop science and technology and change the world—to the point that we can no longer relax and trust the environment automatically to limit and contain the impacts of our activities. Having taken over control from Nature, we must now accept the responsibility for internalizing that control. Humanity has lost its childhood. We can no longer afford to be Dionysian, except in a limited sense.

The implications of having a cerebral cortex are several. Even some of the things we argue about, such as whether or not people are acting from self-interest, enlightened self-interest, or altruism, may come down to a matter of whether they are using their cerebral cortex properly, with adequate *span*.

The span of rational thinking does not have to be very great to appreciate the existence of other persons, and to appreciate that they, too, have feelings, cerebral cortexes, and self-identity. Kant's moral imperative follows logically—the right of others to pursue their self-interest, but also their right to be considered as fellow human beings, and also the recognition that the family, the group, or the species may be better off if the game-playing is raised to a higher level than narrow competitive self-interest. Co-operation pays. The higher the level of intelligence, the greater the span of thinking (usually the two go together), and the broader and more "enlightened" is the concept of self-interest.

In the resource sphere, too, a similar argument applies. Science has an urge to completeness. The more complete the data, the more inclusive the understanding or the explanation, the more scientific is the grasp. One could digress at this point into a discussion of whether the appreciation of the whole, in a given situation, is achieved by a high ability of the left-brain hemisphere to handle simultaneously a large number of parameters, or whether the appreciation of the whole is supplied by a well-functioning right hemisphere, but the choice does not matter greatly for the point to be made here. The point is that to use the cerebral cortex is to be rational; to be rational is to be scientific; to be scientific is to try to understand *completely*, and this means to understand the ecological consequences of what we do.

There are two principal new facts that have emerged in recent decades, or during the Spry lifetime: one is the growth of the ecological sciences; the second is the development of powerful technologies—

so powerful that we can no longer relax in the Dionysian mode, indulging our appetites unthinkingly, on the assumption that the environment will automatically absorb and limit our mistakes. We have made our bargain, and now we have no choice. The cerebral cortex has to accept responsibility. We need now an Apollonian economics.

To sum up, the fundamental objective of a "conserver" economics must be: to accept the responsibilities of owning a cerebral cortex, and *bring the (new) understanding of the physical and ecological context into the socio-economic design.*

Irene M. Spry

A Biographical Note

Gerald Friesen
University of Manitoba

Students of the North American fur trade do not often encounter political economists who specialize in natural resources, conservation, and rent. The reverse is no doubt equally true. Neither group contributes much, one suspects, to the functioning of that arm of the international women's movement known as the Associated Country Women of the World. But in these three areas, among others, Irene Spry is an important figure. She has won respect in each community and she has generated fruitful debates upon important issues in each field. She is a sounding-board and a critic, a confidante, and inspiration and friend for many students. One wonders how many early efforts in scholarship she has guided in her gentle way, and how many tyros flattered themselves that she took a special interest in their work, only to learn later that there were scores of other admirers, all of whom looked upon her as their own guardian angel.

Irene Spry is a child of the British Empire. She was born in 1907 in the Transvaal, South Africa, where her father, Evan E. Biss, ran a teachers' training college and was later an inspector of schools. Before she was three, the family moved to Bengal, where again her father was in the education service. As she recounted in an interview:

> We lived there for three years and then my mother took us back to England and left us with relatives while she went back to India—the awful problem of Imperial families. Then the war had broken out . . . and she couldn't get back, so my unfortunate aunt was stuck with the three of us and two cousins.[1]

Irene's childhood experience with the Empire/Commonwealth prefigured her career as a scholar and community leader. She recalls vividly and with enchanting effect her own adventures and her family's century-long associations with India and Africa:

---

1. The author conducted two long interviews with Irene Spry at her Ottawa home in the autumn of 1981. The transcripts will be placed in the Provincial Archives of Manitoba.

My mother's father was in the palm oil trade in West Africa where he died in 1884. He was a great friend of King Jaja, one of the African rulers in that area. . . . My mother's grandfather worked in Fort Hare in South Africa at the Mission School . . . my sister went to Kenya as a teacher when she graduated and married . . . [and] then moved to Nigeria . . . my father's father, grandfather and great-grandfather had all been in India. . . . His mother had been a child in the Indian mutiny and so had his father [who], at the age of twelve, had been stationed with a pile of bricks beside him to lash the hands of any mutineers who might try to climb onto the roof where great-grannie and her family had taken refuge. . . .

A friend of mine at Cambridge said, rather acidly, 'You remember nothing of any social significance.' Actually, I do remember a few things of social significance, such as the beggars in India. I'll never forget our bearer, who was the sort of head servant in the house, being married while we were there. We all went to the wedding and the bride couldn't have been more than seven, all dressed up like a Christmas tree and looking absolutely terrified . . . . And the enormous pressure of people: one *felt* the population pressure . . . .

I have very beautiful memories of the Hoogli, which is the mouth of the Ganges. I used to adore going on river steamers and seeing the phosphorescent light at the prow of the ship as it broke through the river going upstream . . . . In the hot weather, the rainy weather, when the monsoon was playing havoc with the climate of Dacca, we used to go up to a little place called Ghoon, near Darjeeling in the Himalayas. We couldn't see Mt. Everest but we could see Kujenjunga and, every evening, before I went to bed, I used to go out and look at it. Here was this magnificently beautiful mountain, apparently floating in the sky and being turned to all the colours of the rainbow as the sun set, shining on it.

In addition to this extraordinary range of experience, Irene's childhood was distinguished by the assimilation of her mother's strong views on the process of education. Her mother had an inquiring and fearless mind, it is evident, and believed that children should be encouraged to test their abilities and perceptions whenever opportunity arose. One of Irene's earliest memories of her mother concerns an episode in which her brother was discovered half-way up a conifer which looked, Irene says, "enormously tall: 'Go on Evan', his mother called, 'Go right to the top!' And he did." Irene says further:

She was an absolutely brilliant teacher. Nothing was ever taken for granted. Nothing was ever learned by heart. We learned the tables by setting out beans, seven beans three times over, and then counting them so you knew it was real . . . . Everything we studied, we illustrated. We made little paper dioramas of each historical episode she told us about or that we read about. When we were talking about the development of handicrafts she made us a little loom—and we actually did some weaving, so that everything had a concrete reality which supported the mental inquiry and learning that went with it. . . .

Irene managed her advanced education with a skill that must have been born in these early training sessions. At the London School of Economics (LSE), which she entered when she was seventeen, she was a student of Eileen Power, the great medieval historian, whom she recalls as "the most beautiful and wonderful person you could possibly imagine . . . the greatest thing she contributed to my mental development was to say, 'I will not read a single essay in which you use jargon. You have got to write so that any intelligent person could understand what you have to say.'" After a year at LSE she went to Cambridge for three years, taking the Economics Tripos, Parts 1 and 2:

> I was very fortunate in being there in what still seems to me to have been the great days of economics in Cambridge, when Keynes was formulating his startling new ideas; when A.C. Pigou was still working on the economics of welfare; when Dennis Robertson was a moderating influence on the Keynesian ideas (slightly more conventional in his monetary analysis but still extremely stimulating and interesting); when Maurice Dobb, with his left-wing leanings—a very pink-and-white young gentleman at the time— was developing what you might call updated marxism, I think; and when Gerald Shove . . . was throwing out all kinds of novel ideas which are now embodied in the structure of environmental thinking. He was the first person I ever heard, other than Pigou, talking about what would now be called 'externalities'—problems of noise created by certain types of industrial activities, certain kinds of transportation technology, which had effects on people but which were not taken into account in the pricing mechanism of the market and which therefore were ignored in economic decision-making . . . . He was really just at the threshold of important innovations in economic thinking but, alas, he died.
>
> Perhaps it wasn't so much lectures that were important at Cambridge. It was talk. The endless, exciting talk, the challenging of other people's ideas and having one's own ideas challenged, that was so important. I can't remember any evening when a group of us didn't meet to argue about something—not just economic problems, not just the things we were working on, but political problems, social problems, aesthetic problems.

Irene spent the summer of 1928 in Germany as an *au pair* and student of the language and then crossed the Atlantic to take a Master's degree in Social Research and Social Work at Bryn Mawr. The programme required factory experience and she was soon immersed in a safety study in an automobile parts plant and then in a project about married working women: "We were sent with questionnaires into the slummiest slums of Philadelphia to interview women about whether or not they used birth control methods. Poles, Italians, you name it. I didn't even know what birth control was. Why we weren't lynched, I'll never know." She also worked in a factory outside Boston and became the forelady in charge of a conveyor-belt section.

I had no idea what we were making. Bits of rubber came whizzing past on the conveyor belt and we stuck other bits of rubber onto them. I had to see that the bits were stuck in the right places and that the belt whizzed properly fast. It was only just as I was leaving that, by dint of most persistent questioning, I discovered that we were making rubber boots!

But the University of Toronto, where she was appointed lecturer in 1929 and became a don-in-residence and doctoral candidate, was to take her research interests in a different direction. Irene arrived in an Economics Department which took seriously its discussion during morning coffee and afternoon tea and which was adjusting rapidly to the great changes that were sweeping the discipline. She joined Vincent Bladen and Wynne Plumptre in writing a booklet for students on recent theories concerning monopolistic competition, especially those of Joan Robinson and Edward Chamberlin, which Bladen informally entitled "Mrs. Robinson's Curves". On Sundays, she was a painter in a lively circle of artists which included Barker Fairley and Norah McCullough. Throughout the decade, she was also a social crusader, as she termed it:

> I had in Cambridge been a member of the Labour Club and I had, from my father, largely, become interested in left-wing movements and certainly had a sort of missionary impulse to feel that one should do anything one could to help other people. As the Depression got worse and unemployment increased and the whole economy was simply breaking down as far as one could see, it seemed quite clear to a very young and very optimistic person that there were things that should be done. (I may say that Harold Innis didn't at all approve of such ideas.) But a group of people—Frank Underhill, Frank Scott, Harry Cassidy, King Gordon, Joe Parkinson, Wynne Plumptre and others—began to think that we had a responsibility to try to do something. Even the greenest and youngest lecturers at the university were constantly being asked to make speeches . . . which was really very bad indeed for a young academic. It gave one delusions of grandeur which were entirely unjustified and, I think, did divert one from getting on with finding out about the economy, which, having been exposed to Innis, I came to see was really what one was engaged in trying to do . . . . But, of course, the Depression was horrifying . . . . Out of that sort of feeling, the League for Social Reconstruction came into being . . . . We used to meet, not very often but periodically. A smaller group met more often to plan what was to go into the book we decided to write . . . . I did a couple of chapters in the book—I can't remember which ones now.

In this smaller group was Graham Spry, then the National Secretary of the Canadian Clubs and, later, editor of the *Farmers' Sun*. Irene met Graham at a League skating party:

> When he was living in Toronto, we met each other quite often because we were involved in similar things. I wouldn't say that he took me out because he didn't have any money at all but we did manage to go to movies sometimes . . . and I had a Model A Ford [which] he used to borrow.

Graham and Irene were married in 1938, at Chelsea Old Church, London, England. Gilbert Ryle, an Oxford philosopher, was best man, and Irene's brother understudied for her father, who was in Kenya.

The decade of the 1930s was a decade of scholarship for Irene. The Biss family perspective upon education fitted well with the Innisian University of Toronto tradition of field work in economics:

> There was a very strong feeling that it wasn't enough just to consider the theoretical analysis. One had to go and look at what really was happening. . . . because of course Toronto was . . . a centre of *political* economic studies rather than just abstract economics. This was largely due to the influence of Innis who was working on his seminal (I don't think there is any other word one can use) studies of . . . the elements in the economy that created disequilibrium situations, the "rigidities" as he called them, overhead costs and so on . . . .
>
> [At Toronto] instead of drawing curves to analyze hypothetical pricing situations, one went out and looked at the factories . . . talked to the engineers and entrepreneurs who made the decisions . . . and tried to get a picture of what actually went on in the industry with a view to describing it, so that one could try to think about the significance of what went on, instead of thinking in hypothetical and abstract terms. It was essentially an inductive approach to economic problems, instead of a deductive approach.
>
> When Professor Urwick was retiring, Innis edited a book in his honour called *Essays in Political Economy*. I did a piece for that in which I tried to disentangle the various ideas that were inherent in Innis' notion of rigidities and overhead costs. That was the first thing of any substance that I wrote and Innis, I think, was generously quite interested in it. From that time I began to work quite closely with him and eventually took over the first year course in Canadian economic history on "fish and fur".
>
> I was working on the development of hydro-electric power, basically. I started thinking about the Ontario Hydro-Electric Commission. Why was there public enterprise in Ontario and private enterprise in Quebec? What were the technical characteristics of the industry and the features of its cost structure? How were prices determined? It became quite clear to me that none of this was intelligible unless one went back into the history of the development of water power as a major source of energy. . . .
>
> It was in that connection that I came to know Innis very well and did some work with him on his book on the cod fisheries, for example, and also on the book that he never completed on the pulp and paper industry. He was enormously helpful as well as enormously stimulating. Really, my education in what I would now consider as realistic economic thinking I got from Innis rather than Cambridge.

Irene's first academic career ended with her marriage to Graham and their move to England, where Graham worked with an oil company (ARAMCO) and then with Sir Stafford Cripps. She had begun her dissertation on hydro but never got past the third chapter because, as she put it, "(a) Robin [their first child] was pending, (b) the war broke out, and (c) I found myself on a ship going back to Canada.''[2] She spent a year as an economic consultant for the National YMCA of Canada (in Toronto, Liz and Walter Gordon gave her and Robin shelter), and then went to Ottawa with the Wartime Prices and Trade Board and, later, the Commodity Prices Stabilization Corporation, experiences which taught her about government bureaucracy but also about public relations: ''Wartime controls were, effectively, the beginning of the consumer movement. The ordinary homemakers of Canada were mobilized to play their part as consumers in containing threatened price rises. Their work was a remarkable achievement.''

After the war, Graham was appointed by the new CCF Government of Saskatchewan as its Agent-General in the United Kingdom and Europe. Irene became the co-founder of Saskatchewan House, an institution still fondly recalled by a generation of students and travellers. So generous was Saskatchewan/Spry hospitality, it might be noted in passing, that upon their departure no fewer than 167 latchkeys were found to be missing! In addition to the formal entertaining, including a famous annual party on New Year's Eve, Irene became an ally of the Saskatchewan archives. This originated in a request by Lewis H. Thomas, the archivist, for material which might become part of a collection commemorating the hundredth anniversary of Captain John Palliser's expedition to western North America in 1857. And that, in turn, carried Irene to British archival repositories, Irish country houses, and to archival and other sources in New Zealand and what was then Ceylon. This initiated another phase in her academic career.

The search for Palliser resulted in two valuable books. One, which Irene described as the popular version of Palliser's official report, appeared in 1963 and has enjoyed a steady reputation ever since. It is the kind of narrative one takes upon a prairie journey, real or imagined, in order to retrace the steps and rediscover the perspective of travellers who preceded the railway and large-scale settlement. The second book, an edition of Palliser's official report and related papers, is a model of scholarly editing. In it are addressed not just the issues associated with Palliser but also the innumerable debates concerning landscape, fertility, climate, and natural history which have intrigued students of the region from that day to the present. Taken together with her articles on gentleman travellers and visitors' perceptions of North America, these studies represent a valuable introduc-

---

2. Robin Graham Michael Spry was born on October 25, 1939. Their second child, Richard Daniel Evan, was born on February 27, 1944, and their third child, Elizabeth Ann de Gaspé, on May 20, 1946.

tion to the world of Victorian politics, adventure, and scientific exploration.

Once launched on this new career as student of the Prairies, Irene found another community of scholars in the process of formation. The growth of the Canadian historical community had affected many fields of study in the 1960s, including the fur trade and Indian-white relations, and Irene became a central figure in the group of specialists in nineteenth-century western Canadian history. She has continued in this role to the present: inspiration and advisor, critic, and debater. She has set high standards for scholarship but also an ideal for scholarly behaviour. Her selfless contributions to the writing of others, her generous sharing of new information and her cheerful hospitality have gone far to set a standard and, indeed, to bypass the spitefulness that occasionally arises in any community and even in academe. Her scholarly contributions in this field of western Canadian history include two valuable articles on the transition from a native-dominated, non-industrial society to a European-controlled capitalist economic system in the last half of the nineteenth century. In these papers and in several more recent publications she emphasized the resiliency of the Métis in the face of the new order. Her discussion of their intermediary occupations, indeed, opened new avenues in the study of the Métis communities. And Irene's careful delineation of the changes in attitudes to property-holding in the prairie West, a perspective which suggested more clearly than ever before the economic implications of the industrial capitalist system, was an important original contribution. Perhaps her Commonwealth experience and economics training had led her to place the region in an international context; prairie experience in the last half of the nineteenth century, she implied, could best be understood within a comparative perspective and by reference to recent developments in the social history of other communities. Her writing has clarified the process of cultural change in the region and redefined the duration and problems of what she has called, using Polanyi's term, "the great transformation".

Irene renewed her association with economists, first at Saskatchewan and then at the University of Ottawa, in the years after she and Graham returned from London in 1967. She again became the pillar of a lunch-time conversation group, and soon established yet another circle of intellectual debate. Her contributions to scholarship in this field were a striking amalgam of the economic theory concerning rent and resources, on the one hand, and on the other, the historical analysis of property and social change which she had been developing in her western Canadian studies. The interests of the community, the obligation to distribute equitably the income from common property resources, and attention to the principles of conservation informed her work. Here, too, her generous and critical approach produced interesting scholarship.

Irene has also devoted a great deal of time and effort to an important international organization, the Associated Country Women of the World, and for more than twenty years was a mainstay of its executive committee:

> I went into it very reluctantly and with a haughty sort of academic view of these poor amateur volunteers. They were in fact doing development work on a splendid scale right at the village level . . . . I can give you an example of the movement's international importance. At the time of the Freedom from Hunger Campaign (FFHC) (we have consultative status with FAO, ECOSOC, and UNESCO) we were sent a draft statement about the aims of FFHC . . . about breeding better cattle and growing better crops and using more fertilizers and so forth—not a single word about using the food better, about better nutrition . . . so we sent in an amended statement . . . which was accepted by the FFHC . . . . Our international president was appointed—the only woman to serve on the committee set up to co-ordinate the Non-Governmental Organizations' work for the FFHC. What we do basically is to remind the international authorities that there are women and that the women are essential to the achievement of progress.
>
> And it isn't just the elite women . . . that are essential. It's the ordinary women who devote their lives to bringing up their families and running their homes who are absolutely essential if there is ever going to be progress throughout society, not just among a handful of people with special educational privileges. The thing about this movement which is to me so amazing is that it isn't the result of do-gooders imposing progress from the top. . . . It's the people in the villages and the people in the towns winning progress for themselves, winning for themselves educational opportunities in spite of extraordinary difficulties, winning for themselves a chance to take part in the development of their communities. By sharing experience, knowledge and other resources, internationally, we help each other in the struggle for development.

This optimism and determination is evident throughout Irene's career. She took the opportunities which arose, worked very hard to make sense of the intellectual issues which came her way, and never forgot the human qualities of decency and kindness that have won her a legion of friends and admirers. When asked if her career took a distinctive course because she was a woman, she responded in characteristic fashion: "Personally, I was never made to feel any different from my male colleagues. Oh, there were problems. I wasn't admitted to Hart House. I wasn't admitted to Keynes' economic club. But this was just like the weather. It was just something that existed. Individually and personally I always felt I was completely one of the group of scholars who were trying to understand what was going on in the world."

Irene M. Spry (née Biss)
Bibliography

Books

The Palliser Expedition: An account of John Palliser's British North
American Exploring Expedition 1857-1860. Toronto:
Macmillan, 1963, 310 pages (paperback edition, 1973).

The Papers of the Palliser Expedition 1857-60. Edited with Introduction and
notes for the Champlain Society. Toronto, 1968, 694 pages.

Natural Resource Development in Canada. Co-edited with Philippe Crabbé.
University of Ottawa Press, 1973, 344 pages. Includes Spry
article "Historical Perspective", pp. 23-47.

Buffalo Days and Nights. Reminiscences of Peter Erasmus as Told to
Henry Thompson. Edited with Introduction and notes for the
Glenbow-Alberta Institute. Calgary, 1976, 343 pages.

Chapters in Books

"Overhead Costs, Time Problems, and Prices". In *Essays in Political
Economy in Honour of E. J. Urwick.* Ed. H. A. Innis. University
of Toronto Press, 1938, pp. 11-26.

"Canada". In *The Living Commonwealth.* Ed. Kenneth Bradley. London:
Hutchinson & Co., 1961, pp. 137-61.

"Early Visitors to the Canadian Prairies". In *Images of the Plains.* Ed.
Brian W. Blouet and Merlin P. Lawson. Lincoln: University
of Nebraska Press, 1975, pp. 165-80.

"A Comment on Decentralized Resources Control". In *Natural Resource
Revenues: A Test of Federalism.* Ed. Anthony Scott. Vancouver:
University of British Columbia Press, 1976, pp. 250-56.

"Non-Renewable Resources". In *The Physical and Technological
Constraints,* Vol. 2 of *The Conserver Society Project.* Ed. Kimon
Valaskakis, *et al.* Montreal: GAMMA, 1976.

"The Great Transformation: The Disappearance of the Commons in
Western Canada". In *Man and Nature on the Prairies.* Ed.
Richard Allen. Regina: Canadian Plains Research Centre,
University of Regina, 1976, pp. 21-45. Revised version
published as "The Tragedy of the Loss of the Commons in
Western Canada". In *As Long as the Sun Shines and Water Flows.*
Ed. Ian A.L. Getty and Antoine S. Lussier. Vancouver:
University of British Columbia Press, 1983, pp. 203-28.

"The Prospects for Leisure in a Conserver Society". In *Recreation and
Leisure: Issues in an Era of Change.* Ed. Thomas L. Goodale and
Peter A. Witt. Pennsylvania: Venture Publishing, 1980,
pp. 141-53.

"Innis, the Fur Trade, and Modern Economic Problems". In *Old
    Trails and New Directions: Papers of the Third North American Fur
    Trade Conference*. Ed. Carol M. Judd and Arthur J. Ray.
    Toronto: University of Toronto Press, 1980, pp. 291-307
"Overhead Costs, Rigidities in Productive Capacity and the Price
    System". In *Culture, Communication and Dependency: The Tradition
    of H. A. Innis*. Ed. William H. Melody, Liora Salter and Paul
    Meyer. Norwood, N.J.: Ablex Publishing, 1981, pp. 155-166.
"The 'Private Adventurers' of Rupert's Land". In *The Developing West*.
    Ed. John E. Foster. Edmonton: University of Alberta Press,
    1983, pp. 49-70.

Articles and Published Papers
"Memorandum on Electric Power". For the Royal Commission,
    Provincial Economic Inquiry, Nova Scotia, *Appendices*. Halifax,
    N.S.: King's Printer, 1934, pp. 75-118.
"The Contracts of the Hydro-Electric Power Commission of Ontario".
    The Economic Journal, XLVI, no. 183 (September 1936), 549-54.
"Recent Power Legislation in Quebec". *CJEPS*, III, no. 4 (November
    1937), 550-58.
"Economic Aspects of National Unity". *Annual Review, The Commerce
    Journal*, University of Toronto, March 1938, pp. 36-40.
"The Royal Commission on Prices". *CJEPS*, XVII, no. 1 (February
    1951), 76-84.
"Energy Sources in Canada: A Further Comment". *CJEPS*, XXIV,
    no. 2 (May 1958), 272-80.
"Captain John Palliser and the Exploration of Western Canada". *The
    Geographical Journal*, CXXV, Part 2 (June 1959), 149-84.
"On the Trail of the Palliser Papers". *Saskatchewan History*, XII, no. 2
    (Spring 1959), 61-71.
"Did Palliser Visit Saskatchewan in 1848?". *Saskatchewan History*, XVI,
    no. 1 (Winter 1963), 22-26.
"Routes Through the Rockies", *The Beaver*, Autumn 1963, pp. 26-39.
"Prairies and Passes: Retracing the Route of Palliser's British North
    American Exploring Expedition, 1857-1860". *The Journal of the
    Royal Society of Arts*, CXIII, no. 5110 (September 1965), 807-26.
"The Transition from a Nomadic to a Settled Economy in Western
    Canada, 1856-1896". *Transactions of the Royal Society of Canada*,
    Vol. VI, Series IV (June 1968), Section II, pp. 187-201.
"Opportunities and Responsibilities, The Work of Member Societies of
    the Associated Country Women of the World". London,
    England: ACWW, 1971.
"Finite Resources, Growth and World Peace". In *Limits to Growth: The
    Canadian Challenge*. Mimeo. The Economics Society of Alberta,
    1973. Part IV, pp. 1-24.

"A Visit to the Red River and the Saskatchewan, 1861, by Dr. John
     Rae, FRGS". *The Geographical Journal*, 140, Part 1 (February
     1974), pp. 1-17.
"Consumer Interest and the Future of the Economy". *Conserver Society
     Notes* (Science Council of Canada), Vol. II, no. 3 (Summer
     1977), pp. 19-22.
"Lewis Cecil Gray, Pioneer of the Economics of Exhaustible
     Resources". Université Laval: Cahier de Recherche 7803
     (Groupe de Recherche en Économie de l'Énergie) 1978 (with
     Philippe Crabbé).
"The Pallisers' Voyage to the Kara Sea, 1869". *The Musk-Ox*,
     26 (1980), pp. 13-20.
"A County Waterford Explorer". *DECIES, Old Waterford Society*,
     Vol. XVII, May 1981.
"A Journey 'Down North' to Great Bear Lake and the Yukon in
     1935". *The Musk-Ox*, 31 (1982), pp. 73-78.
"The Cost of Making a Farm on the Prairies". *Prairie Forum*, VII,
     Spring 1982, no. 1, 95-99.
"The Mixed-Bloods and Métis of Rupert's Land before 1870", in *The
     New Peoples: Being and Becoming Métis in North America*, eds.
     Jacqueline Peterson and Jennifer Brown (Winnipeg: University
     of Manitoba Press, forthcoming).
"The 'Memories' of George William Sanderson, 1846-1936", Irene M.
     Spry, ed., with Introduction and notes, forthcoming in a
     special "Métis" issue of *Canadian Ethnic Studies*.
Encyclopedia Canadiana. Grolier Society of Canada, 1958. "Hydro-
     Electric Power", Vol. V, pp. 211-22; "Power Commissions,
     Provincial", Vol. VIII, pp. 288-92; "Water Power", Vol. X,
     pp. 273-90. Revision of earlier articles in *The Encyclopedia of
     Canada* (University Associates of Canada, 1937).
The Discoverers: An Encyclopedia of Explorers and Exploration. Ed. Helen
     Delpar, New York: McGraw-Hill, 1980. Biographies of
     Dr. W. B. Cheadle, Viscount Milton, Matthew Cocking,
     Henry Youle Hind, John Palliser, James Sinclair, H. J. (later
     General Sir Henry) Warre and Mervin Vavasour, R.E.
Dictionary of Canadian Biography. General Editors: G. W. Brown,
     D. M. Hayne, and F. G. Halpenny. University of Toronto
     Press. Also being published in French by Les Presses de
     l'Université Laval.
     "Cocking, Matthew". Vol. IV (1979).
     "Inkster, John". Vol. X (1972).
     "Sinclair, William, II". Vol. IX (1976).
     "Anderson, Samuel". Vol. XI (1982).
     "Palliser, John". Vol. XI (1982).
     "William Joseph Christie". Vol. XII (forthcoming).
     "Sinclair, James". Vol. VIII (forthcoming).

Papers

"Some Further Thoughts on the Economics of Open Access
          Resources", paper read before the Centre for the Study of
          Natural Resources, Queen's University, 1972.
"Natural Resources as an Engine of Growth in Canadian Economic
          History", paper read before a seminar of senior civil servants,
          Quebec City, 1976.
"The Development of Mining in the Province of Quebec", paper read
          before the Annual Meeting of the Quebec Metal Mining
          Association, 1976.
"The Role of Staple Exports in Canada's Economic Development",
          a paper presented to the Society of Graduate Students in
          History, Dalhousie University, 1979.
"Why We Need a New Theory of Demand", mimeo, 1980.
"Rent, Royalties and Taxes", mimeo, 1981.